A History of Post Keynesian Economics Since 1936

In loving memory of Jessie Everett King, 1914–2000

A History of Post Keynesian Economics Since 1936

J.E. King

Professor of Economics, Department of Economics and Finance, La Trobe University, Australia

Edward Elgar

Cheltenham, UK • Northampton, MA, USA

Published by
Edward Elgar Publishing Limited
Glensanda House
Montpellier Parade
Cheltenham
Glos GL50 1UA
UK

Edward Elgar Publishing, Inc.
136 West Street
Suite 202
Northampton
Massachusetts 01060
USA

A catalogue record for this book
is available from the British Library

Library of Congress Cataloguing in Publication Data
King, J. E. (John Edward)
A history of post Keynesian economics since 1936 / J. E. King.
p. cm.
Includes bibliographical references and index.
1. Keynesian economics—History. 2. Economics—History—20th century. I. Title.

HB99.7.K38 K56 202
330.15'6—dc21

2001053222

ISBN 1 84064 420 6

Typeset by Manton Typesetters, Louth, Lincolnshire, UK.
Printed and bound in Great Britain by Bookcraft (Bath) Ltd.

Contents

Introduction

> The Post Keynesian project represents both a recovery and an extension of the economic paradigm developed by Keynes. (Palley, 1996, p. 9)

This is a history of a dissident school of thought in macroeconomics, from its origins in the mid-1930s down to the end of the twentieth century. I agree with Thomas Palley. It is a recovery, because if Post Keynesians agree on anything – which is sometimes open to doubt – it is that the Grand Neoclassical Synthesis (Arestis, 1992) is a travesty of Keynes. It is an extension, because Post Keynesians deal with questions ignored or very largely neglected by Keynes, including economic growth, social conflict, income distribution and inflation. This book, then, is the story of how Post Keynesian economics emerged, extended its scope beyond the issues that Keynes had concentrated upon, posed a challenge to orthodox macroeconomics but ultimately failed to supplant it.

Some very important questions have already been raised in these first few sentences. What is the essence of Post Keynesian economics, its analytical core? Can it be defined only in a negative way, in terms of its opposition to neoclassical macroeconomics? Or is there a coherent positive Post Keynesian alternative to the mainstream? What, in any case, do we mean by a 'school of thought' in economics? What factors determine the progress, or lack of progress, of one school by comparison with other schools? Can we legitimately speak of progress in science at all? Has there been progress of any sort in economics? My answers to some of these questions will emerge as the story unfolds.

Philosophers and historians of science have managed to shed some light on the life and death of schools of thought. Thus Joseph Schumpeter recognized the existence in economics of 'groups of disciples' who 'gather round some teacher or some institution. By being interested in similar problems, by being taught similar ways of handling them, by exchanging and assimilating their views and results, they acquire a sort of mental family likeness'. The Physiocrats, Ricardians, Marxists and Keynesians were examples of such schools, each with 'its inner circle, its propagandists, its watchwords, its esoteric and its popular doctrine', together with 'a broad fringe of sympathizers'. For Schumpeter the leader was all-important, in intellectual life no less than in business (Shionoya, 1996, pp. 287–9).

Terence Hutchison, in contrast, emphasizes geography rather than leadership or intellectual coherence when writing of the 'Cambridge School', which has always been characterized by internal controversies and feuds:

> On the other hand, a remarkable feature of Cambridge economists in, roughly, the first half of the century, which could be said to justify the use of the term 'school', was that they tended to spend their whole, or almost their whole, careers as economists, from Freshman to Emeritus, in Cambridge, except for wartime breaks, or the odd session in foreign parts. These locational limits were reinforced by rather concentrated reading habits, and they tended to impart, in some cases, a considerable degree of what Dr. Gunnar Myrdal once called that 'attractive Anglo-Saxon kind of unnecessary originality'...which comes from confining reading largely – though not entirely – to the works of one's immediate colleagues. Thus, outside influences, in so far as they penetrated at all significantly – even the later influence of Marx – had to pass through a filter of Cambridge preconceptions. (Hutchison, 1981, p. 47)

There is an important element of truth in this, not least as it applies to the Cambridge Post Keynesians. And much the same could be said, for example, of the Chicago School of economics (Reder, 1982).

Schumpeter maintained that in the twentieth century the differences between competing schools of thought in economics were very much less than their adherents chose to believe, since economists had in fact reached agreement on the foundations of their science. Qualified support for this contention comes from Richard Whitley's detailed account of the intellectual and social organization of scientific activity, which hinges on the role of 'task uncertainty', that is to say, continuing disagreement on what is to be done by the practitioners of any particular scientific discipline. In the social sciences, in particular, 'separate schools may well form around opposed conceptions of the central issues and preferred ways of tackling them so that coordination and integration of their research becomes very difficult' (Whitley, 1984, p. 139). Task uncertainty is increased by the plurality and diversity of the audience to which scientific work is directed. Where lay approval is sought, where interest groups have a stake in the outcome and where funding comes from a variety of sources, the conditions are ripe for a proliferation of schools. Sociology comes at one end of Whitley's spectrum and theoretical physics at the other. Economics is somewhere in the middle, since in this discipline both theoretical uniformity and technical uncertainty prevail. The common (neoclassical) theoretical core cannot be applied to empirical problems in any simple or straightforward way, so that there is 'some scope for some theoretical deviance' and still more room for controversy over real-world applications (ibid., p. 186). But rival schools of thought are less prominent in the 'partitioned bureaucracy' that is economics than in the 'polycentric oligarchies' of the other social sciences.

According to Edward Tiryakian, three distinct schools of thought played a central role in the development of sociology between 1890 and 1945. The Durkheimian, Parsonian and Chicago Schools each constituted 'a small community of persons whose origin and formative period can be localized in time and place'. Every school requires a 'founder–leader', since typically 'the innovation in style, technique, and conceptualization which gives the school its primary identity is organized around a "master" and his pupils working together in an *atelier*, or workshop, or, in the case of literary schools, the workshop is one or more group journals or reviews' (Tiryakian, 1977, p. 216). There are strong similarities between schools of thought and dissenting religious sects. Both claim to be exposing error and bringing salvation, and both face at least initial hostility from the guardians of the temple. Generally the leader of the school will be surrounded by 'a small number of important "converts" who may be of the same generation as the leader, and therefore share his same historical situation (including what he finds disturbing about the present state of the discipline)'. Equally significant are the

> students, younger than the leader, who become his trusted lieutenants as they imprint his paradigm early in their career. Later on, when the leader–founder is gone, they will have the task of training a new generation, and, in part, their authority will stem from having been associates of the charismatic founder.

The leader may also require an interpreter because 'he has such an intense, innovative way of conceptualizing the reality of the world [that he] has trouble expressing himself in ordinary language'. Finally there are the 'auxiliaries' or foot-soldiers, who edit journals, write textbooks and occupy prominent positions in outside organizations, and the occasional 'patron' who provides material assistance to the school. If it is to succeed, a school thus requires a founder–leader, an institutional affiliation, a journal and a manifesto, that is, 'a document in the nature of a professional proclamation of its basic mode of perceiving and relating to the world' (ibid., pp. 219–23).

These ideas seem readily applicable to Schumpeter's 'Keynesian School' in its first decade (1936–46), which also happens to have been the last decade of Keynes's life. Keynes himself is evidently the charismatic founder–leader, and the *General Theory* his manifesto; the *Economic Journal*, which he edited until his death, propagated the new ideas. Alvin Hansen is the most important convert, James Meade and Joan Robinson the archetypal students, Roy Harrod and J.R. Hicks among the earliest interpreters. Tiryakian's account of the fate of a school that rapidly wins general acceptance is also highly instructive:

> As the school becomes more institutionally visible (analogous to the evolution of the religious community from sect to denomination), its membership size keeps

> increasing. Its core ideas (theories, methods, techniques) become popularized and no longer depend upon the founder directly teaching new recruits in face-to-face interaction. The charisma of the school becomes 'routinized'; its ideas become part of the standard conceptions of the discipline....
>
> ...Over time, and with an increased and perforce more heterogeneous membership, the presuppositions of the school become blunted, diluted, trivialized, or compromised. But since presuppositions are never fully articulated, it is always possible that the school may revitalize itself by a return to pristine presuppositions when investigations following a more articulate or explicit track of the paradigm seem fruitless, redundant, or, simply, from a scientific point of view, 'uninteresting'. (Ibid., p. 218)

Although it is derived from the history of sociology, this passage tells a story that is uncannily reminiscent of the emergence of the Grand Neoclassical Synthesis and its Post Keynesian challenger.

So much for the sociologists (and even Schumpeter referred to himself as a 'sociologist of science' when he wrote on these questions). The philosophers also have something to contribute, although, as I shall make much greater use of their ideas in Chapter 12, I shall deal with them very briefly here. One relevant notion (as the quotation from Palley suggests) is Thomas Kuhn's concept of a paradigm, variously defined but usually taken to mean both a broad frame of reference that defines a subject area and specifies the appropriate way of approaching it, and a detailed set of protocols for posing and solving narrower, specific scientific problems (Kuhn, 1970). Tiryakian's account of schools of thought in sociology is quite explicit in defining a school as a 'scientific community' (another Kuhnian term) that shares a common paradigm. Adherents to a particular school of thought operate within their own paradigm and are sometimes called upon to defend it against its rivals. Kuhn maintains that different paradigms are normally incommensurable; that is to say, their underlying preconceptions are so different that communication between scientists working in separate paradigms is extremely difficult, if not quite impossible. This is why he describes as a 'scientific revolution' the process whereby a scientific community shifts its allegiance from one paradigm to another.

A kindred notion is Imre Lakatos's 'scientific research programme', which consists of a core of unchallengeable truths, a set of instructions governing the conduct of research and a 'protective belt' of questionable, and testable, empirical propositions (Lakatos, 1978). As I shall suggest in Chapter 12, there are important differences between Lakatos and Kuhn on how to assess the merits of rival programmes, and indeed on whether such an assessment is possible in the first place. But there is also enough common ground for us to consider defining a school of thought as the ensemble of researchers who work within a specific research programme (or adhere to a particular paradigm) and often in some sense compete with the practitioners of rival paradigms (rival research programmes). The Ptolemaic and Copernican schools represent a classical instance from the history of natural science; Newton's and Einstein's physics constitute another.

Unfortunately things are not always as clear-cut at these examples suggest. Not, at least, in economics, where the boundaries between paradigms are often themselves contested or ill-defined, and where research programmes overlap in complex and often contested ways. This makes the definition of Post Keynesian economics no simple matter. For the moment I will evade this problem. The Israeli writer Amos Oz was once asked in a radio interview what he thought the necessary conditions were for someone to count as Jewish. Anyone stupid enough to claim to be a Jew, Oz replied, was *ipso facto* Jewish. I shall define my subject-matter in much the same way: all those who call themselves Post Keynesians automatically qualify. This is a sufficient condition for inclusion in my story, but it is not necessary. The term 'Post Keynesian' came into widespread use relatively late in the day (see below), and in any case many thinkers dislike labelling themselves, or others. It would be absurd to exclude major figures like Michal Kalecki and Piero Sraffa on the grounds that they never adopted the Post Keynesian title. For this reason I shall deal with a very broad church.

The story is even more complicated than this, since several of the founding fathers of Post Keynesianism (and Joan Robinson, the one important founding mother) had the same 'struggle of escape from habitual modes of thought and expression' that Keynes described in his own case in the Preface to the *General Theory* (Keynes, 1936, p. viii). For Robinson, these were the literally pre-Keynesian notions that she had acquired in the course of her education as a Cambridge economist. Sidney Weintraub and Hyman Minsky, on the other hand, had to fight for liberation from the neoclassical synthesis – 'pre-Keynesian economics after Keynes', to cite the title of an article by Robinson (1964). Arguably none of them entirely succeeded. Indeed, given the fuzzy borders between Post Keynesian and other economic ideas, the very idea of a clean break with the past is of questionable validity. The history of Post Keynesian macroeconomics is thus inevitably nuanced.

All this said, there is still a coherent story to be told. Early in the 1990s A.P. Thirlwall, who always described himself as a 'Keynesian' (without any qualifying adjective), summarized the 'six central messages of Keynes's vision'. These were the propositions that output and employment are determined in the product market, not the labour market; involuntary unemployment exists; an increase in savings does not generate an equivalent increase in investment; a money economy is fundamentally different from a barter economy; the Quantity Theory holds only under full employment, with a constant velocity of circulation, while cost-push forces cause inflation well before this point is reached; and capitalist economies are driven by the animal spirits of entrepreneurs, which determine the decision to invest (Thirlwall, 1993, pp. 335–7). I suspect that many avowed Post Keynesians would regard this as a reasonable minimum platform.

In addition, the Grand Neoclassical Synthesis, at least, offers a clearly-defined target. It has four components: the IS–LM model of national income and the rate of interest, a labour market analysis of employment and wages, a theory of economic growth and a Phillips Curve analysis of wage and price inflation. The IS–LM model came first, in the classic formulation of J.R. Hicks (1937). Then Franco Modigliani (1944) added an aggregate production function and a labour supply function to Hicks's equations, demonstrating that involuntary unemployment required either a perfectly elastic money demand curve (the so-called liquidity trap) or downward rigidity in money wages. Twelve years later Robert Solow (1956) extended the neoclassical synthesis to the long period, with a model of economic growth in which full employment is maintained by means of continuous substitution between capital and labour along the aggregate production function. Finally the rate of wage and price inflation was determined by the unemployment rate via the Phillips relationship which, in the canonical version of Samuelson and Solow (1960), was interpreted as a budget constraint or 'menu' for policy choice.

Keynes, as we shall see in Chapter 1, was favourably disposed to IS–LM and accepted much of orthodox labour market analysis (if not the conclusions that Modigliani and the other neoclassical economists drew from it). He had very little to say about the theory of economic growth and was not primarily concerned in the *General Theory* with the problem of inflation. Precisely because the *General Theory* was both ambivalent and incomplete, the Post Keynesians sought to recover and extend it. Their quest began in 1936, or even a little earlier where Joan Robinson and Michal Kalecki were concerned. It was still continuing, 66 years later. I have tried to write its history without losing sight of the most important themes, and for this reason the structure of the book is partly chronological and partly thematic. There is a price to be paid for this, in terms of the inevitable repetition and back-tracking that is required, but I think it is a price worth paying.

To the extent that such a distinction makes sense, my perspective is that of an intellectual historian, not a social historian. That is to say, I have focused on ideas rather than institutions – necessarily so, given my time-frame, since there was no large, well-developed network of self-proclaimed Post Keynesians until the 1970s (see Lee, 2000a, for a different approach). This is of course a matter of emphasis, not a dogmatic principle. Similarly I have concentrated on macroeconomic issues, and have relatively little to say about micro-economics. This is emphatically *not* because I believe that the two can be clearly separated, but in order to keep the book to a manageable length and avoid unnecessary duplication with the work of others (see Lee, 1998).

In Chapter 1, 'First reactions to *The General Theory*', I discuss two types of early responses to Keynes's book, those that established the neoclassical synthesis and those which can fairly be described as (proto-) Post Keynesian. The first category includes the reviews by David Champernowne, Harrod, Hicks, Meade and Brian Reddaway, together with related work by Hicks, Oskar Lange and the book-length teaching versions of Keynes's work by Meade and Joan Robinson. In the second category come some of Robinson's '1935 essays', brief but suggestive passages in early papers by Nicholas Kaldor, and a remarkable 1937 article by Hugh Townshend. I conclude this opening chapter by assessing Keynes's reactions to these interpretations of his ideas; like the *General Theory* itself, his responses displayed considerable ambivalence.

Chapter 2, 'An economist from Poland', introduces Michal Kalecki, who had arrived at many of Keynes's most important conclusions prior to 1936 and had on some issues already gone well beyond him. I outline the ways in which Kalecki criticized the *General Theory*, modified his own analysis in the light of Keynes's work and applied it to the important policy debates surrounding prewar reconstruction. Kalecki provided the foundations for a 'left Keynesian' approach to macroeconomic thought, and the chapter ends with a brief examination of the subsequent theories of monopoly capital that were set out by Paul Baran and Paul Sweezy, Josef Steindl and other economists strongly influenced by Kalecki.

Keynes had confined himself to the short period, assuming the capital stock to be given. The extension of his work to the long-period question of capital accumulation was begun by Joan Robinson as early as 1935. In Chapter 3, 'Generalizing *The General Theory*', I take this part of the Post Keynesian story down to the end of the 1950s, setting out the ways in which Richard Kahn, Kaldor and Robinson reacted to Harrod's model of economic growth. A distinctive Cambridge approach to income distribution also emerged from their critique, and this formed an integral part of the attack on neoclassical capital theory that I discuss in Chapter 4, 'Those Cambridge controversies'. The chronology gets a little messy at this point, since the Cambridge Post Keynesians never stopped thinking about growth, and their ideas on capital and distribution theory certainly did not commence with the publication of Sraffa's *Production of Commodities by Means of Commodities* (Sraffa, 1960). But Sraffa's book did mark an important watershed, and for this reason I have taken 1960 as the dividing line between the two chapters. Thus in Chapter 4 the emphasis shifts to the post-1960 capital controversies and the first, highly abrasive, large-scale and open confrontation between Post Keynesian and neoclassical ideas.

A quite different strand of Post Keynesianism was unfolding in the United States, and this forms the subject of Chapter 5, 'Outside Cambridge: the first

US Post Keynesians'. Here I examine the work of Sidney Weintraub and Hyman Minsky, two pioneers of Post Keynesian thought in North America whose escape from what by 1959 Weintraub was dismissing as 'Classical Keynesianism' was hard-won and protracted. I also discuss the early writings of Weintraub's most eminent student, Paul Davidson, who by the beginning of the 1970s had achieved both a penetrating critique of the neoclasssical synthesis and a comprehensive recovery of Keynes's theory of money. The 1970s were a crucial decade for the Post Keynesians. These were the years in which they came to define themselves as a distinct school of thought with its own research programme or paradigm, and to marshal their forces for a head-on clash with orthodox theory. In Chapter 6, 'Against the mainstream: Post Keynesian economics in the 1970s', I describe how they fought this battle and attempt to explain how they lost it. Among the old guard a crucial role was played by Robinson, who had at first high hopes of winning over the younger generation of economists, especially in the United States. Some did indeed rise to the challenge, most notably Alfred Eichner and Jan Kregel, but by the end of the decade it was clear that mainstream economics had survived what Robinson described as its 'second crisis'.

Developments outside the USA and the UK are the subject of Chapter 7, 'Economic heresy around the world'. Post Keynesian ideas proved much more influential in some countries than in others. In this chapter I describe the evolution of Post Keynesianism in Australia, Austria, Canada, France and Italy, paying some attention to national idiosyncrasies like the emergence of monetary circuit theory in France and the dominant intellectual authority exercised by Sraffa in Italy. The next two chapters are also thematical rather than chronological, although both deal primarily with developments after 1970, and in each I have tried to retain some sense of the sequence in which ideas emerged and events unfolded. Chapter 8, 'Money and the monetarists', is devoted to the history of Post Keynesian monetary theory, beginning with early criticisms of the Quantity Theory and moving through the campaign waged by Kaldor and others against monetarist thinking to the appearance of a fully-fledged Post Keynesian theory of endogenous money in the 1980s. In Chapter 9, 'Uncertainty, expectations and method', I focus on the connection between philosophy and economics. This chapter deals with the (re)discovery of Keynes's philosophical writings, the course taken by Post Keynesian thinking on questions of knowledge, uncertainty and the formation of expectations, and the implications of these developments for Post Keynesian views on the methodology of economics.

This leads back inexorably to the questions of how the Post Keynesian school might be defined – including the ways in which it has tried to define itself – and the related issue of its intellectual coherence. In Chapter 10, 'Keynes, Kalecki, Sraffa: coherence?', I outline Post Keynesian views on these matters, beginning with Geoff Harcourt's reflections on the aftermath of the capital controversies and his subsequent distinction between three streams of Post Keynesianism: Fundamentalist Keynesian, Kaleckian and Sraffian. I summarize the mutual criticisms levelled by each faction against the others, and assess the prospects for peaceful coexistence between them. Then, in Chapter 11, 'Post Keynesians and other deviants', I move to another, closely connected subject: the relationship between the Post Keynesian and other heterodox schools of economic thought. There are considerable areas of common ground between Post Keynesians and radical-Marxians, institutionalists, Austrians and New Keynesians, I suggest, but also important differences.

In Chapter 12, 'A promise that bounced?', I come back to some of the issues that I raised at the start. What might be understood by 'progress' in scientific research, and more specifically in economics? To what extent, and on what criteria, has Post Keynesian theory made progress since 1936? This requires a detailed investigation of the notion of scientific progress in the writings of Karl Popper, Thomas Kuhn and Imre Lakatos. I close with some (inevitably speculative) predictions as to the future prospects of Post Keynesian macroeconomic theory.

As I have already noted, the label 'Post Keynesian' was not in widespread or consistent use for several decades. It was occasionally employed in the 1950s with a chronological rather than a doctrinal meaning, describing rather loosely a wide range of developments in macroeconomics after the publication of the *General Theory*. Thus when Robinson wrote of 'post-Keynesian economics' (Robinson, 1960a, p. xiii), she was referring to her own theoretical work and that of Cambridge colleagues like Kahn and Kaldor, work which was in part a running commentary on the pioneering growth analysis of the Oxford economist Roy Harrod. Kaldor (1956, p. 98, n2) had already used 'post-Keynesian' in a similar way. In the United States the term also embraced the neoclassical synthesis. Several of the papers in Kenneth Kurihara's *Post-Keynesian Economics*, for example, represented the neoclassical version of Keynes, and Paul Samuelson later used the term in the title of an eclectic survey article discussing the work of Kahn and Kaldor in addition to that of A.C. Pigou, Milton Friedman and Robert Solow (Kurihara, 1954; Samuelson, 1964).

Rather surprisingly the tension, not to say inconsistency, between these uses of 'post-Keynesian' seems not to have been apparent at the time. From the mid-1950s, however, Sidney Weintraub of the University of Pennsylvania had been plugging away at 'Classical Keynesianism' and proposing a different reading of Keynes that emphasized the problem of inflation and gave pride of place to the aggregate supply and demand analysis sketched out in Chapter 3 of the *General Theory* (Weintraub, 1961). The Cambridge economists had instead concentrated on the deficiencies of neoclassical capital theory and their implications for the analysis of growth and income distribution. These concerns were by no means incompatible, but they were different, and there was at first enough mutual incomprehension to generate some ill-feeling on both sides of the Atlantic. A common front against the neoclassical synthesis emerged only in 1962, when Robinson, with characteristic rudeness, dismissed this majority interpretation as 'the bastard-Keynesian model' (Robinson, 1962c, p. 691).

Even then it took some years before the title 'post-Keynesian' was universally adopted. The term 'neo-Keynesian' enjoyed a certain vogue in the 1960s and remained in use to describe post Keynesian models until the end of the following decade (see, for example, Howard, 1979). At the same time Robinson flirted with the notion of an 'Anglo-Italian school', recognizing the contributions of Sraffa and of younger Italian theorists with close Cambridge connections such as Pierangelo Garegnani and Luigi Pasinetti. Not until the publication in the *Journal of Economic Literature* of the widely-read and influential survey article by Eichner and Kregel (1975) were the ideas with which this book is concerned finally and irrevocably known as 'Post-Keynesian', a usage cemented by the appearance in 1978 of the first issue of the *Journal of Post Keynesian Economics*. The terminology will in all probability never be entirely standardized. 'Post Keynesian' is still sometimes employed chronologically, as for example by the journalist Larry Elliott (1998) and the philosopher John Gray (1998), both of whom ought to have known better. Just to add to the confusion, Thomas Palley (1996) recently described as 'neo-Keynesian' the work of Modigliani, Tobin and other advocates of the neoclassical synthesis.

There are four different ways of writing 'Post Keynesian', depending on whether or not the term is hyphenated and on the capitalization (or not) of the prefix; I used all four in the previous paragraph. The founders of the *Journal of Post Keynesian Economics* chose to capitalize but to omit the hyphen. I shall follow this convention except where – as in the previous page or so – it would be clearly anachronistic to do so. To avoid unnecessary pedantry I shall use 'Post Keynesian' throughout the book to refer to all those economists who pass the Amos Oz test and to many who do not. The only exception is in direct quotations, where I shall follow the original text. All emphasis in quotations is that of the original author, unless otherwise stated.

Earlier versions of some chapters were presented at conferences: Chapter 1 at the Twelfth Conference of the History of Economic Thought Society of Australia, Canberra, July 1999 and at the Post Keynesian Study Group's Microeconomic Day-School, Bristol, October 1999; Chapter 10 at the Michal Kalecki Centenary Conference, Leeds, November 1999; and Chapter 12 at the Graz Conference of the European Society for the History of Economic Thought, February 2000. An earlier version of Chapter 1 was also presented at a seminar at the University of Lancaster in November 1999. An earlier version of Chapter 12 was published as 'Has there been progress in Post Keynesian economics?' in *Studi Economici*, 70, 2000/1, pp. 5–29. Much of the research on which this book is based was carried out during periods of study leave at Melbourne University, the University of Lancaster, the University of Bologna and the University of Leeds. It was assisted by a grant from the Australian Research Council.

I must also gratefully acknowledge the assistance of the following, none of whom is implicated in errors of fact or opinion: Philip Arestis, Simon Chapple, Victoria Chick, Bob Coats, Paul Davidson, Robert Dixon, Gilles Dostaler, Jamie Doughney, Gary Dymski, Peter Earl, Walter Eltis, Grant Fleming, the late Keith Frearson, Craufurd Goodwin, Peter Groenewegen, Geoff Harcourt, John Henry, John Hillard, the late John Hotson, Mike Howard, Peter Kenyon, Prue Kerr, Jan Kregel, Peter Kriesler, Marc Lavoie, Fred Lee, John McCombie, Bruce McFarlane, Brian MacLean, Julie Marshall, Egon Matzner, Christine Meagher, Will Milberg, Alex Millmow, the late Hyman Minsky, Basil Moore, Rosemary Moore, Anitra Nelson, Luigi Pasinetti, John Pheby, Bob Pollin, John Pullen, Riccardo Realfonzo, Peter Reynolds, Peter Riach, Russell Rimmer, Alessandro Roncaglia, Peter Rosner, Roy Rotheim, Kurt Rothschild, Julie Rowe, Claudio Sardoni, Malcolm Sawyer, Michael Schneider, Mario Seccareccia, Howard Sherman, John Singleton, John Smithin, David Spencer, Jim Stanford, Ian Steedman, Paul Sweezy, Tony Thirlwall, Jan Toporowski, Roy Weintraub and Mike White.

I am especially grateful to Roger Backhouse and Sheila Dow for comprehensive and constructive criticism; I have acted on some, but by no means all, of their suggestions.

1. First reactions to *The General Theory*

The *General Theory*, I would say, is a harp of many strings, not all of them well-tuned and some mutually most discordant. (Shackle, 1982, p. 435)

ONE, TWO, MANY *GENERAL THEORIES*

The struggle between the Walrasian and non-Walrasian interpretations of Keynes's macroeconomics had begun in 1936, or perhaps even earlier. As we shall see in Chapter 7, some modern Post Keynesians regard the 1930 *Treatise on Money* as in many ways a more advanced and more radical text than the *General Theory*. In any case, Keynes was notorious both for changing his mind and for rewriting his books in proof. The final version of the *General Theory* that went to the publishers in January 1936 – miraculously, it appeared in the bookshops within a month – differed substantially from earlier drafts and was itself less than entirely coherent. Reviewers and critics reacted to it in a variety of ways (Backhouse, 1999) and Keynes himself soon proved to be profoundly ambivalent on crucial theoretical issues. The seeds of the future Post Keynesian school were already sprouting. But the plant would not grow to maturity for another quarter of a century, and the seedling was not readily identifiable as such.

Keynes was not an especially modest man, and about the *General Theory* he was distinctly immodest. His new theory was *general*, he claimed, in a number of ways. Most importantly, it demonstrated that full employment was a special case. The principle of effective demand asserted that the level of employment was determined by the volume of aggregate demand, independently of the supply decisions of individual workers. If demand was inadequate, workers would be unemployed even if they valued the prevailing real wage more highly than the marginal disutility of working. The 'second classical postulate,' as Keynes termed it (Keynes, 1936, p. 5), was therefore in general false. (He retained the 'first classical postulate', equating the real wage to the marginal product of labour). 'Classical economics' – that is, the theory of employment accepted by Keynes's predecessors and by most of his contemporaries – represented only a special case. This was why he believed, as he told George Bernard Shaw in a famous letter in January 1935, that his new book 'will largely revolutionise – not, I suppose, at once, but in the course of the next ten years – the way the world thinks about economic problems' (Keynes, 1982a, p. 42).

There has been a great deal of controversy over what, precisely, constitutes the analytical core of the *General Theory*. By the end of the 1990s the great majority of Post Keynesians agreed that it is the principle of effective demand, as set out in the previous paragraph: output and employment are normally constrained by the level of aggregate demand, not by the supply considerations that predominate in neoclassical theory (see, for example, Arestis and Sawyer, 1998). Now there are two – more accurately, at least two – ways in which the principle of effective demand can be substantiated. Both require a theory of investment, and both can be found in the *General Theory*. The first rests on the propositions that the future is uncertain; that the returns to an investment project cannot be known in advance, even probabilistically; and that the decision to invest is thus non-rational in the rather peculiar sense in which economists understand the notion of rationality. That is to say, investment expenditure is not determined by a precise calculation of prospective costs and returns; in the nature of things, it cannot be so determined. This argument originated in Keynes's early philosophical thought, and can be regarded as an extension of the ideas expressed in his *Treatise on Probability* (Keynes, 1921; O'Donnell, 1989). It was set out, with great clarity, in Chapter 12 of the *General Theory*, where Keynes argued that instability arises 'due to the characteristic of human nature that a large proportion of our positive activities depend on spontaneous optimism rather than on a mathematical expectation, whether moral or hedonistic or economic'. Thus investment decisions depend upon the 'animal spirits' of entrepreneurs (Keynes, 1936, p. 161). Since decisions to save are determined by the psychological propensities of individuals (above all, of rentiers), there is no reason to expect the volume of investment expenditure planned by entrepreneurs to be exactly equal to the volume of saving that would be undertaken at the full employment level of aggregate income. Why, then, should full employment be regarded as anything other than a special case?

The 'classical' reply to this question invoked the rate of interest as the mechanism that brings saving and investment together at the level of income corresponding to full employment. (Remember that Keynes used 'classical' to denote the body of economic theory that is now much more commonly known as 'neoclassical'.) His own general theory of interest and money represented his attempt to refute this counter-argument. In the *General Theory* the rate of interest is a monetary variable, not the outcome of the 'real' classical factors of capital productivity and thrift. It depends instead on liquidity preference, and this is a speculative phenomenon reflecting the uncertainty of future bond prices in a world in which interest rates vary and capital gains and losses are unpredictable. This was all set out very clearly in Chapter 15.

If a monetary theory of the rate of interest was an essential part of Keynes's attack on the second classical postulate, it was also a source of great danger to his entire theoretical project, for it held out a huge temptation, which Keynes was unable entirely to resist. In Chapter 18 he succumbed to it, summarizing his theory in a way that invited its reformulation as a general equilibrium model linking saving, investment, income and the rate of interest in a system of simultaneous equations. That he did not do this particularly well is beside the point; others would very soon make a much better job of it. What Keynes had done, in Chapter 18, was to play down the radical uncertainty that dominates Chapter 12 and which, taken seriously, would have ruled out any stable functional relationship between investment and the interest rate. He had opened the door to the neoclassical synthesis and severely (perhaps fatally) undermined his claim to have provided a *general* rather than a special theory of employment. Keynes ought not, perhaps, to be criticized too harshly for this. The temptation to formulate macroeconomic theory as a general equilibrium system in which the rate of interest played a pivotal role was a very strong one: so strong, indeed, that even the young Michal Kalecki had succumbed to it (Kalecki, 1934; see also Chapple, 1995, Togati, 1998, and Chapter 2). And Keynes was under some pressure to set out his ideas in a manner that would render them palatable to his contemporaries, both from his own desire to win them over and from his close friend and adviser Roy Harrod (Keynes, 1973a, pp. 526–65).

There was a third version of Keynes's argument, contained in an early draft of his book but not included in the published version. Here Keynes made a fundamental distinction between the analysis of an 'entrepreneurial' and a 'cooperative' economy:

> It is easy to conceive of a community in which the factors of production are rewarded by dividing up in agreed proportions the actual output of their co-operative efforts. This is the simplest case of a society in which the presuppositions of the classical theory are fulfilled. But they would also be fulfilled in a society of the type in which we actually live, where the starting up of productive processes largely depends on a class of entrepreneurs who hire the factors of production for money and look to their recoupment from selling the output for money, provided that the whole of the current incomes of the factors of production are necessarily spent, directly or indirectly on purchasing their own current output from the entrepreneurs.
>
> The first type of society we will call a *real-wage* or *co-operative economy*. The second type, in which the factors are hired by entrepreneurs for money but where there is a mechanism of some kind to ensure that the exchange value of the money incomes of the factors is always equal in aggregate to the proportion of current output which would have been the factor's share in a co-operative economy, we will call a *neutral entrepreneur economy*, or a *neutral economy* for short. The third type, of which the second is a limiting case, in which the entrepreneurs hire the factors for money but without such a mechanism as the above, we will call a *money-wage* or *entrepreneur economy*.

> It is obvious on these definitions that it is in an entrepreneur economy that we actually live today. (Keynes, 1982b, pp. 77–8)

This is so evocative of Marx's analysis of the circulation process in capitalist and non-capitalist societies that it is difficult to believe that it could have been written by the same man who, in another letter to Shaw in the following year, denounced *Das Kapital* as 'dreary, out-of-date' academic controversializing (Keynes 1982a, p. 38). In the 1933 draft Keynes himself, citing the US author H.L. McCracken, noted the resemblance to Marx. In a cooperative economy the circulation process takes the form C–M–C′, the exchange of a commodity for money in order to obtain another commodity (this was what Marx had termed 'simple' or 'petty' commodity production). Under capitalism it is M–C–M′, or production for profit, which Keynes described as 'parting with money for commodity (or effort) in order to obtain more money' (Keynes, 1982b, p. 81). It is unlikely that Keynes had fallen briefly under the spell of his young Communist protégé Maurice Dobb. Probably he was influenced by another younger economist, the eminently non-Marxian Dennis Robertson, who had drawn a very similar distinction in his *Banking Policy and the Price Level* (Robertson, 1926, p. 19). Had he followed this path, Keynes might have been spared the temptation to formulate his theory in general equilibrium terms. It would have led him towards Marx and Kalecki and in the direction of the monetary circuit theorists, whose precursors included Schumpeter as well as Marx, but away from the neoclassical synthesis (see Chapter 7). Instead the 1933 manuscript was abandoned, to be rediscovered only in 1976 in a laundry basket in Tilton, Keynes's house in the Sussex countryside (Rotheim, 1981; Realfonzo, 1998).

KEYNES IN GENERAL EQUILIBRIUM

There is only one diagram in the *General Theory*. Provided by Roy Harrod, it is used to illustrate the important point that the rate of interest is indeterminate in classical analysis, rather than to encapsulate the argument of the book as a whole (Keynes, 1936, p. 180; cf. O'Donnell, 1999a). J.R. Hicks (1937) has received most of the credit – and more recently, in some quarters, the blame – for devising the first diagrammatic representation of Keynes's ideas. But the general equilibrium interpretation of the *General Theory*, on which the (in)famous diagram relies, occurred more or less simultaneously to a number of writers, just before and immediately after the book appeared. In addition to Hicks, the co-discoverers of IS–LM include David Champernowne (1936), Roy Harrod (1937a), James Meade (1936–7) and Brian Reddaway (1936). Meade had been a member of the original 'Cambridge Circus' in

1930–31, and Harrod was a respected and tireless critic of Keynes's successive drafts. Reddaway, by contrast, was just 23 years old (and en route to Australia) when he reviewed the *General Theory* for the *Economic Record*, and Champernowne (1912–2000) was no older than Reddaway when he wrote down his equation system (Darity and Young, 1995; Young, 1987). Clearly something of this sort was 'in the air'.

In the canonical version of this line of thought, Keynes's model consists of three equations in three unknowns (Hicks 1937, p. 153). The demand for money is a function of the level of income (via the transactions motive) and the rate of interest (through the speculative motive). This yields a relation between income and the interest rate that Hicks plotted as the upward-sloping LL (later, LM) curve. Investment is a function of the rate of interest (via the marginal efficiency of capital schedule, which 'determines the value of investment at any given rate of interest'), and income depends on investment through the propensity to consume and the multiplier. From these two relations Hicks derived his downward-sloping IS curve, which shows the combinations of income and the interest rate that are consistent with equality between saving and investment. Intersection of IS and LL gives equilibrium values of income and the rate of interest:

> They are determined together; just as price and output are determined together in the modern theory of demand and supply. Indeed, Mr. Keynes' innovation is closely parallel, in this respect, to the innovation of the marginalists. The quantity theory tries to determine income without interest, just as the labour theory of value tried to determine price without output; each has to give place to a theory recognising a higher degree of interdependence. (Hicks, 1937, pp. 153–4)

Where did this leave Keynes's claim to have 'revolutionized' economics? The youthful Champernowne and Reddaway did not presume to answer this question; nor did Meade, whose review is austerely mathematical. Hicks and Harrod were less diffident. In his original review article, Hicks had begun by disclaiming any interest in doctrinal history, but he could not resist drawing parallels between Keynes and 'the methods which have been common in Swedish economics for several years', along with the earlier work of Knut Wicksell and, above all, Alfred Marshall:

> The technique of this work is, on the whole, conservative; more conservative than in the *Treatise*. It is the technique of Marshall, but it is applied to problems never tackled by Marshall and his contemporaries.... Thus we have to change, not so much our methods of analysis, as some important elements in the outlook which we have inherited from the classics. (Hicks, 1936, pp. 238, 240, 253)

In the 'IS–LM' paper Hicks again stressed the Marshallian and Wicksellian roots of the *General Theory*, and attributed the original analysis of liquidity preference not to Keynes but to his much less well-known Cambridge colleague, Frederick Lavington. Keynes's '*special theory*' has the demand for money as a function of the interest rate alone. What Hicks terms the 'General Theory' has a transactions as well as a speculative motive for holding money. 'With this revision, Mr. Keynes takes a big step back to Marshallian orthodoxy, and his theory becomes hard to distinguish from the revised and qualified Marshallian theories, which, as we have seen, are not new.' Keynes's analysis was distinctive only if the LL curve were horizontal over the relevant range, so that a shift in the marginal efficiency of capital schedule affected only income, leaving the rate of interest unchanged. 'So,' Hicks concluded, 'the General Theory of Employment is the Economics of Depression.' It followed that 'The *General Theory of Employment* is a useful book; but it is neither the beginning nor the end of Dynamic Economics' (Hicks, 1937, pp. 152, 153, 155, 159; see Hicks, 1980–81 for his second thoughts).

Harrod agreed with this conclusion. He distinguished 'general economic theory' both from 'its specialist branches' and from the 'short-cuts' (that is, simplifying assumptions) that are useful to 'ordinary working economists':

> in my opinion Mr. Keynes's conclusions need not be deemed to make a vast difference to the general theory, but … they do make a vast difference to a number of short-cut conclusions of leading importance. Thus to those whom I may perhaps call without offence the ordinary working economists they ought, if accepted, to appear to constitute quite a revolution. (Harrod, 1937a, p. 75)

Little in Keynes's book was really new, Harrod continued, not even the theory of liquidity preference: 'In fact in Mr. Keynes's system all the old pieces reappear, but they appear in different places.' Thus the *General Theory* had achieved not 'a revolution in fundamental economic theory,' but rather a 'readjustment and a shift of emphasis' (ibid., pp. 82, 85).

Similar judgments soon began to appear from writers outside Keynes's immediate circle. One of the first was the Polish economist Oskar Lange, then working at the University of Chicago, who managed to combine a commitment to Marxian socialism with a strong interest in general equilibrium analysis. Lange acknowledged the influence of Reddaway and Hicks and, like the latter, distinguished two special cases. The demand for money could be written as a function only of the rate of interest ('Mr. Keynes's theory') or as a simple function of the level of income ('the traditional theory'). From this Lange inferred that 'both the Keynesian and the traditional theory of interest are but two limiting cases of what may be regarded to be the general theory of interest', in which both income and the rate of interest were important. 'It is a feature of great historical interest,' Lange continued, 'that the essentials of this general theory are contained already in the work of Walras', of which Keynes's analysis represents 'a considerable simplification' (Lange, 1938, p. 20).

Lange's objective was the mildly subversive one of providing a rigorous reformulation of underconsumption theory. More orthodox in every way was Franco Modigliani, whose 'Liquidity Preference and the Theory of Money and Interest' became a cornerstone of the neoclassical synthesis (De Vroey, 2000). Modigliani set out three 'alternative macrostatic systems' that included, in addition to the familiar IS–LM equations, an aggregate production function and a labour supply function. One was a 'Keynesian model', the other two being 'crude' and 'generalised' versions of the 'classical model' (the inverted commas are Modigliani's). His analysis led him to conclude that involuntary unemployment is consistent with economic equilibrium only in two special cases. The first requires downward rigidity of money wages, that is, a labour supply curve that is infinitely elastic below full employment. The second is the so-called 'liquidity trap', where the demand for money is infinitely elastic with respect to the rate of interest (Modigliani, 1944, pp. 65, 74). These arguments were illustrated by a series of IS–LM diagrams. Outside the liquidity trap, Modigliani maintained, 'It is the fact that money wages are too high relative to the quantity of money that explains why it is unprofitable to expand employment to the "full employment" level' (ibid., p. 77). Thus Keynes's theory was not in any sense general. On the contrary, it rested on 'very special assumptions about the supply of labor' (ibid., p. 45).

THE FIRST POST KEYNESIANS

Already in the mid- to late-1930s there were alternative voices, which insisted on the revolutionary nature of the *General Theory* and at least implicitly denied that Keynes's thinking could be assimilated as a special case of mainstream thought. In so doing, Joan Robinson, Hugh Townshend and Nicholas Kaldor all pointed in the direction of what would later become Post Keynesian economics.

Joan Robinson (1903–83) came from an upper middle-class English family; her father was a general. She studied at Girton College, Cambridge, graduating in 1925 and marrying the economist Austin Robinson in the following year. After two years in India she returned to Cambridge in 1929. A member of the 'Cambridge circus' of young economists who debated with Keynes the problems arising out of his *Treatise on Money*, Robinson soon earned a reputation as an original and creative theorist and as a vigorous critic and controversialist. She was (belatedly) appointed to a professorial fellowship at Cambridge in 1965, and after her retirement in 1971 continued to write and argue on economic themes until the end of her life.

Even before the publication of the *General Theory*, Robinson had begun to write a series of papers extending Keynes's analysis to areas that he had ignored, or passed lightly over. Not surprisingly, there are significant neoclassical elements in these '1935 essays', as she later described them (although the proofs arrived from the publisher in the autumn of 1936). But they also reveal a distinctive and unorthodox approach to the labour market, inflation, macroeconomic policy and the methodology of economics that make it legitimate to consider Robinson's *Essays in the Theory of Employment* as the very first Post Keynesian text. King (1996a) contains a fuller discussion; note that I deal with Robinson's attitude towards Marx in Chapter 2, and her long-period analysis in Chapter 3.

In her treatment of the labour market, Robinson set out a very explicit wage-push theory of inflation. Money wages depend on the relative bargaining power of unions and employers: 'a constant upward pressure upon money wages is exercised by the workers (the more strongly the better they are organised) and a constant downward pressure by employers, the level of wages moving up or down as one or the other party gains an advantage' (Robinson, 1937a, p. 2). If union organization was held constant, changes in money wages would depend largely on movements in effective demand. Workers who fear for their jobs are less likely to demand wage increases. And there are two further reasons:

> Second, the existence of unemployment weakens the position of the Trade Unions by reducing their financial resources and awakening the fear of competition from non-union labour. Thus even a Union which at the moment represents only employed workers will be more restrained in its action the greater the amount of unemployment outside. Third, the strategic and moral position of Trade Unions is strengthened when profits are rising and real wages falling. (Ibid., p. 4)

This allowed Robinson to redefine full employment. She rejected Keynes's definition as unnecessarily convoluted. 'The point of full employment,' she wrote, is simply 'the point at which every impediment on the side of labour to a rise in money wages finally gives way' (ibid., p. 9; cf. Keynes, 1936, pp. 15–16, 303).

This has important policy implications. For Robinson, unions determine the level of money wages; money wages determine the price level; given the money supply, the price level determines the rate of interest (via the transactions demand for money) and hence the levels of investment, effective demand and employment. Trade unions thus have considerable economic power:

> The control of policy is, in a certain sense, divided between the Trade Unions and the monetary authorities, for, with given monetary conditions the level of the rate of interest is largely determined by the level of money wages. A sufficient rise in money wages will always lead to a rise in the rate of interest and so check an increase in employment. (Ibid., p. 27)

The Quantity Theory, she maintained, could not provide an adequate account of the inflationary process. A year after the publication of her *Essays*, Robinson reviewed an analysis of the German hyperinflation of 1922–3 by the Italian monetarist C. Bresciani-Turroni. She criticized his emphasis on budget deficits and the consequent increase in the quantity and velocity of circulation of money. 'The missing item,' she claimed, was the increase in money wages obtained by the German unions at a time of low unemployment and increasing profits. Growth in the quantity of money was a necessary condition for the inflation, but it was not the cause: 'the essence of inflation is a rapid and continuous rise of money wages. Without rising money wages, inflation cannot occur, and whatever starts a violent rise in money wages starts inflation' (Robinson, 1938b, pp. 510–11).

This posed an acute dilemma for policy makers. High levels of employment and stable prices were incompatible, since 'even if full employment were attainable, it would create … acute instability of prices, a slight miscalculation in the forward direction leading to a rapid and accelerating rise in money wages' (Robinson, 1937a, p. 21). A rule for non-inflationary growth of incomes could, however, be established, since price stability 'requires that the level of employment shall be held sufficiently high to induce just that rate of rise in money wages which will offset the effects [on labour productivity] of increasing efficiency'. But Robinson feared that centralized control over money wage movements may be impossible, given the sectionalism of the trade unions and the lack of coordination of their wages policies (ibid., pp. 24, 28). Thus as early as 1935 she showed herself to be acutely aware of the inflationary dangers that would be posed by high levels of employment.

So much for money wages. In her treatment of real wages Robinson was equally unorthodox:

> The connection between movements in money wages and movements in real wages is largely accidental. There is a certain level of employment, determined by the general strategical position of the Trade Unions, at which money wages rise, and at that level of employment there is a certain level of real wages, determined by the technical conditions of production and the degree of monopoly. (Robinson, 1937a, p. 5)

She continued to accept the neoclassical principle of diminishing returns, and thus drew short-period curves relating real wages and employment that sloped downwards from left to right in the conventional manner (ibid., pp. 128–30). In the long period, Robinson argued, this need not be the case, and she drew a variety of long-period curves, some of them upward-sloping or backward-bending (see ibid., Figures 5 and 7, p. 127, and Figure 2, p. 125). It was entirely possible that the long-period curve might fail to intersect the labour supply curve altogether, so that 'there may be circumstances in which full employment cannot be reached by manipulation of the rate of interest' (ibid., pp. 127–8). And the comparative statics could also be perverse. A decline in labour demand, for example, might lead to both a fall in real wages and a *decline* in unemployment (see ibid., Figure 14, p. 133).

Robinson's interpretation of her labour market diagrams was even more striking than their geometry. The curve relating the level of employment to the real wage

> has some affinities with the conception of a demand curve...But it is fundamentally different in nature from an ordinary curve. The rate of wages is not an independent, and the amount of employment the dependent variable. Both are dependent upon variations in the rate of interest or the level of thriftiness. If circumstances are such that the level of employment is x, then the same circumstances produce a real wage rate y. For lack of a better term the curve will be described as a demand curve for labour, but it is important to bear in mind the distinction between this curve and an ordinary demand curve. (Ibid., pp. 123–4; cf. Davidson, 1983)

Robinson was, in effect, denying that the law of demand applied to labour. Employment was determined in the product market by the forces of effective demand. Given the level of employment, marginal productivity and the degree of monopoly in the product market then established the real wage rate. Causation was unidirectional: *from* employment *to* the real wage. It was therefore not possible for workers, unions or governments to increase employment by reducing real wages.

This, in turn, raised serious methodological questions. Twice in her *Essays* Robinson stated very clearly the crucial distinction between history and equilibrium that would come to dominate her later onslaught on the 'bastard Keynesians'. Her long-period 'labour demand curve', she acknowledged, was path-dependent and, for this reason, the very notion of long-period equilibrium must be questioned (Robinson, 1937a, p. 123). Her own characteristic analytical method, the comparison of different economies called Alpha and Beta, tracing the consequences of their different characteristics without pretending to tell a story of changes in historical time, was already being used in the *Essays* (ibid., pp. 116–18; see also Chapters 3 and 9).

The second proto-Post Keynesian was the British civil servant Hugh Townshend (1890–1974), who 'owes his reputation almost entirely to one brilliant article' (Chick, 1987, p. 662), published in the 'Notes and Memoranda' section of the *Economic Journal* in March 1937. Townshend had a mathematics degree from Cambridge, where he had prepared for the civil service examinations under Keynes's supervision. He was the co-author of a popular text on money (Curtis and Townshend, 1937) but, apart from a handful of book reviews, his brief article was his only contribution to the academic literature. In it he took issue with Hicks (1936), whose continued adherence to a modified version of the loanable funds theory of interest was not consistent with the *General Theory*. For Keynes the rate of interest was a function of the *stock* of monetary assets, and was not directly related to the *flow* of new loans. Accordingly, Keynes's theory was not a special case of the traditional theory but, as he himself insisted, more general:

> it would seem that Mr. Keynes's doctrine of liquidity-preference really involves a generalisation of the classical (marginal) theory of value. For, as usually stated, the marginal theory of value does not seem to distinguish clearly between exchange of existing assets (at the margin of exchange) and production of new assets (at the margin of production). (Townshend, 1937, p. 160)

Keynes's focus on stocks rather than flows had profound implications, Townshend suggested, for the theory of investment, the determination of the general price level, the relevance of barter models and the legitimacy of the method of long-period equilibrium in a monetary economy.

On the first question, Townshend emphasized the speculative element in all investment decisions. This was inevitable, since all durable assets

> have, as Mr. Keynes puts it, 'monetary attributes' in a varying degree. A kind of liquidity-premium attaches to them also. They, as well as money and monetary assets, have a value to hold for future exchange (i.e. for security or for speculation), causally independent of their value in present exchange, and determined by, and varying with, expectations; so that, since the prices of existing (held or exchanged) assets and of newly produced assets of the same kind must be equal, both must be influenced by these expectations. (Ibid., p. 159)

Although Townshend was writing before the publication of Hicks (1937), his approach to the problem of investment demand was clearly inconsistent with the existence of the stable IS function that is required for the IS–LM interpretation of the *General Theory*.

Nor is it compatible with a Quantity Theory approach to the general level of money prices. In a world where speculative influences predominate, the velocity of circulation can vary without limit:

> Any quantity of money, however small, will in theory support any prices, however high, provided it circulates fast enough. And any quantity of money, however large, is consistent with zero prices, provided it does not circulate at all, or with indefinitely low prices if it circulates slowly enough. (Townshend, 1937, p. 161)

But in practice money prices do not fluctuate 'wildly', at least in the short period. They must therefore be underpinned by conventions that cause price expectations to be stable. Townshend argued, following Keynes, that 'the best convention of price-stability in the short term may perhaps be the assumption that the level of money-wages (the money-price of labour) is approximately constant' (ibid., p. 165; cf. Keynes, 1936, pp. 265, 269–71). Wage rigidity, on this view, was not a 'friction' or 'market imperfection'; *pace* Modigliani, it did not require 'special assumptions' about the supply of labour. It was instead a necessary condition for the stability of a monetary economy.

And it was a *monetary* economy with which Townshend was concerned. In language very similar to that of Keynes's 1933 draft (which he cannot have seen), he defined a 'capitalist community' as 'one in which some people employ hired labour for future profit'. In such an economy 'people will also hold durable assets for future security'. Even without legal tender money, some asset or other will come to command a liquidity premium: 'We then have, in *all* essentials for the purpose of a theory of value, a monetary economy … Thus the text-book conception of a barter or non-monetary economy has no place in a discussion of value. The theory of value in a capitalist economy is the theory of money-prices' (Townshend, 1937, p. 166–7).

The roles played by asset prices, expectations, speculative behaviour and conventions also cast doubt on the relevance of any form of long-run equilibrium analysis: 'it would seem to follow that there can be no such thing as long-period dynamic economic theory, failing the (most unlikely) discovery of a plausible long-term convention of price-stability'. In the past, Townshend noted, 'prices have in fact moved all over the place'. It follows further that 'the search for laws to enable us to predict economic events far ahead, like eclipses, must be given up … The subject is just one in which, if Mr. Keynes is right, *theoretical* forecasts cannot be made'. More than this: 'there is in the real world no "long run" in which, e.g., perfect competition, where it may be supposed to exist in production, actually equates cost and supply-price at the margin: for the forces of competition are perpetually chasing the shifting relevant price-levels' (ibid., pp. 166, 169). As Robinson might have put it, history always overwhelms any tendency towards equilibrium.

Our third early Post Keynesian, Nicholas Kaldor (1908–86), was a writer as prolific as Keynes and scarcely more concerned with what he regarded as pettyfogging questions of intellectual consistency. Born in Budapest, Kaldor became a student at the London School of Economics in 1927, and joined the teaching staff there five years later. He remained at the LSE until 1947, when he went to work for the United Nations in Geneva. In 1950 he was appointed to a fellowship at King's College, and spent the rest of his life as a Cambridge economist. Kaldor's close and sometimes stormy relationship with Richard Kahn, Joan Robinson and Piero Sraffa represents an important part of the early history of Post Keynesian economics in England.

Initially, however, he was strongly influenced by the Austrian theory expounded by Friedrich von Hayek. After the publication of the *General Theory* he rapidly became a Keynesian (Thirlwall, 1987, pp. 24–31). The neoclassical component of Kaldor's thinking remained important; thus he used Hicks's IS–LM diagram to criticize Pigou (Kaldor, 1937a, p. 752, n2), and as late as 1960 he could write approvingly of 'Keynes's general equilibrium model' (Kaldor, 1960, p. 3). But there were also strong hints of heresy in his early work, in particular concerning the theories of money, capital and income distribution.

On the first of these questions, Kaldor cast doubt on the conventional treatment of the money stock as exogenously determined by the central bank, with a zero elasticity of supply. His 1939 article on speculation included a money market diagram with a highly elastic money supply curve, which he explained as follows:

> The elasticity of the supply of money in a modern banking system is ensured partly by the open market operations of the central bank, partly by the commercial banks not holding to a strict reserve ratio in the face of fluctuations in the demand for loans, and partly it is a consequence of the fact that under present banking practices a switch-over from current deposits to savings deposits automatically reduces the amount of deposit money in existence, and vice versa. (Kaldor, 1939b, p. 14, n1)

This claim points in the direction of much later Post Keynesian theories of endogenous money. The entire passage not only comes in a footnote, but it is also in parentheses, as if Kaldor felt it almost too obvious to be stated. There was even a suggestion that the money supply curve might be horizontal. The short-term interest rate, he maintained, 'can be treated simply as a datum, determined by the policy of the central bank' (ibid., p. 14; see also Chapter 8). Not too much should be made of this; Rochon (2000) argues convincingly that Kaldor was not a consistent endogenous money man until 1970. But at least the seeds of his later heterodoxy had been planted in the late 1930s.

Kaldor's attack on Austrian capital theory played a major role in his break with Hayek. He devoted several articles to criticizing the central Austrian concept of the 'period of production', drawing heavily on the work of the Chicago theorist Frank Knight and concluding that 'the quantity of capital employed by a firm, or the economic system as a whole, can be measured, or expressed, in terms of an investment period only under certain assumptions … which are so restrictive as to deprive the concept of any practical value' (Kaldor, 1939a, p. 42; cf. Kaldor, 1937b, p. 65). Since 'capital – real capital' consists of heterogeneous objects, there can be 'no absolute, or unique, measure' of the capital–labour ratio (Kaldor, 1939a, p. 42). But Kaldor was at best halfway to Piero Sraffa's subsequent 'Cambridge critique' of orthodox capital theory (see Chapter 4). He proposed a capital-intensity index of his own, the ratio between the 'initial cost' and the 'annual cost' of producing a particular stream of output. Kaldor also sidestepped the problem of aggregation over firms through the time-honoured device of the Marshallian 'representative firm', and concluded confidently that (contrary to Hayek's assertion) the capital–labour ratio declined in cyclical upswings because of the fall in the cost of labour relative to that of capital (ibid., pp. 112–13, 124, 133–7). Equally, there was no suggestion of reswitching in Kaldor's analysis.

There are, however, three places in Kaldor's published work between 1938 and 1941 which point towards the macroeconomic theory of distribution for which he would later become famous (Kaldor, 1956, which is discussed in Chapter 3). Two of them were in his discussion of the trade cycle. In 'Stability and Full Employment', Kaldor noted that there was a danger of hyperinflation when planned investment exceeded planned saving. It could, however, be eliminated if money wages were held constant, 'by Government decree or by a combination of entrepreneurs', since 'the rise in prices will imply a shift to profits (in the distribution of income), and since such a shift increases savings (because capitalists save a higher proportion of their income than wage-earners) the cumulative process will come to an end when profits have risen sufficiently to provide the [necessary] savings'. Similarly, the government could 'increase savings by altering the distribution of income in favour of profits, and vice versa', for example by changing social security contributions, wage subsidies or regressive taxes on consumption expenditure (Kaldor, 1938, pp. 649, 650). Thus changes in the relative shares of wages and profits played an important role in maintaining macroeconomic stability. Kaldor repeated this argument in his well-known 'Model of the Trade Cycle', where he justified the steep slope of his savings function at high levels of employment by arguing that 'when activity is at a high level, prices will tend to rise relatively to wages, there will be a shift in the distribution of incomes in favour of profits, and thus an increase in the aggregate propensity to save'. He made much the same point in the following year, in the course of another attack on the hapless Pigou (Kaldor, 1940, p. 82; 1941, p. 462).

TEACHING VERSIONS OF *THE GENERAL THEORY*

Kaldor never published a textbook, but Robinson wrote at least three (Robinson, 1937b, 1960b; Robinson and Eatwell, 1973). When, a few years ago, I was promoting her *Essays* as possibly the first Post Keynesian book, someone suggested to me that her *Introduction to the Theory of Employment* (Robinson, 1937b) should instead be regarded as the original bastard Keynesian text. He had a point. There are no diagrams in Robinson's *Introduction*, no references to production functions or to neoclassical microeconomic analysis, and no explicit use of the IS–LM apparatus, but the underlying ideas are certainly there. Nor is there any great theoretical or policy gulf between her teaching version of the *General Theory* and that found in Part I of James Meade's *Introduction to Economic Analysis and Policy* (Meade, 1936), which had appeared in the previous year. And Meade, as we have seen, was one of the inventors of IS–LM.

Robinson began uncontroversially by attributing unemployment to deficiency of demand, itself the result of an imbalance between entrepreneurial investment decisions and individuals' desire to save (Robinson, 1937b, p. 40). New capital goods will be produced only if their cost of production is less than the price of existing capital goods, which in turn depends on their expected earnings and on the rate of interest. 'The rate of interest is thus an extremely important influence upon investment.' It is determined by the interaction of an interest-elastic demand curve and an exogenously given (and by implication vertical) supply curve, since 'The custom of preserving a strict cash ratio gives the Bank of England power to control the total amount of bank deposits.' The rate of interest has no unambiguous effect on the desire to save, which varies with the level and distribution of income and with the wealth effects of changes in share prices (ibid., pp. 24, 58, 32–7, 64–5).

But, while the rate of interest was a monetary phenomenon, and 'it is clearly absurd to say that [it] is determined by the supply and demand of capital', it was also true that 'the conception of the rate of interest as the regulator of the economic system contains an important element of truth'. Severe unemployment would drive down money wages, reducing the demand for money and lowering the rate of interest; this would raise both investment and employment. Robinson went even further. At or near full employment, she argued, an increase in thriftiness would reduce the rate of interest, and this 'must lead to a more or less commensurate increase in investment'. For this reason the conventional analysis of 'an ideal self-regulating system … [does] apply in a broad general way to the actual world' (ibid., pp. 66, 68).

Her treatment of wages was no less orthodox, so much so that it was soon denounced as reactionary anti-working class propaganda by the Marxist Jürgen Kuczynski (1937). Real wages varied inversely with the level of employment, Robinson maintained, while the general level of money wages depended crucially on the unemployment rate. In the upswing of the cycle, falling unemployment enables unions to push up money wage rates. Since this does not produce any increase in real wages, the ensuing increase in money wages 'is neutral from the point of view of workers taken as a whole'. It may even be unfavourable, since 'When unemployment has fallen very low, a rapid rise in money wage sets in, the demand for money in the active circulation increases, the rate of interest is driven up, investment falls off and unemployment increases again.' Thus it is that 'in normal times full employment can never be attained,' unless the rate of interest is constantly falling (Robinson, 1937b, pp. 47–8, 51, 62–3).

There is evidently some tension between Robinson's pessimism in this passage and her residual faith in the 'ideal self-regulating system'. Taking the *Introduction* as a whole, the pessimism won out. Already under the influence of Michal Kalecki, and clearly echoing a theme that was beginning to preoccupy Roy Harrod, she hinted at a long-run problem that Keynes had set aside:

> Now, the tragedy of investment is that (unless stimulants are applied) it can never remain at a constant level. For if the rate of investment one year is the same as the last, then, generally speaking, the level of employment and incomes and therefore the level of demand for goods will be the same in the second year as in the first. But all the time capital is accumulating, and in the second year there is a larger amount of equipment available to meet the same demand for commodities. The rate of profit consequently falls off, future prospects are dimmed by the decline in present receipts, and in the third year new investment appears less attractive to entrepreneurs than in the second. (Ibid., p. 92)

The result was a downward spiral in investment, income and employment. In this passage Robinson neglected the effect of capital accumulation on productivity growth. But she also drew on the stagnationist ideas of Alvin Hansen. Since population growth was slowing, she argued, the pace of innovation was falling, and the opening up of new territories had come to an end, the inducement to invest was now too weak, relatively to thriftiness, for full employment to be maintained (ibid., pp. 25–6, 98).

Her conclusion was, however, cautious rather than apocalyptic, and her policy recommendations were quite moderate by the standards of the time. Robinson advocated higher spending on public works, a more egalitarian fiscal policy to reduce thriftiness, expansionary monetary policy to reduce the rate of interest, and the payment of a Social Dividend to every citizen, financed by creating money (ibid., pp. 26–30, 36–7, 70–72, 73–4). She immediately qualified this last suggestion by pointing to 'the violent rise of prices, collapse of the exchange and general confusion associated with galloping inflation' that might be expected if payments were to continue after full employment had been attained (ibid., p. 74). Neither in theory nor in policy terms was Robinson's *Introduction* an especially radical text.

James Meade's *Introduction to Economic Analysis and Policy* was not in any sense more conservative than this, though his book was much longer and more comprehensive than Robinson's. The first of the five parts offered a 94–page discussion of macroeconomic issues, entitled simply 'Unemployment'; this was, in effect, Meade's beginners' guide to the *General Theory.* Three microeconomic sections followed, dealing respectively with 'Competition and Monopoly', 'The Distribution of Income' and 'The Supply of the Primary Factors of Production'. In his preface Meade thanked Joan Robinson for commenting on these first four sections (Meade, 1936 [1937], p. vii). The book concluded with 100 pages on 'International Problems'. Here he called for international monetary cooperation and expressed some sympathy for the argument that protection might legitimately be used to defend employment if international agreement were not forthcoming. The final chapter was an almost Leninist account of 'The Economic Causes of War'.

In what follows I shall deal exclusively with the first part of Meade's *Introduction*. The theme of the opening chapter, 'Can the Economic System Work?', is that mass unemployment *can* be eliminated without recourse either to socialism or to a revolutionary change in the monetary system. The supporters of Major Douglas were thus mistaken. But this is not to say that purchasing power *must* be sufficient when people save part of their income: 'indeed, in face of the recent depression such a contention would be nonsense' (ibid., pp. 5, 8). To solve the problem of unemployment, Meade argued, it was necessary to increase investment expenditure, as outlined in Chapters 2–5; or to induce greater consumption expenditure (Chapter 6); or perhaps to reduce unit costs of production without simultaneously reducing total demand (Chapter 7, where this possibility offered Meade an opportunity to analyse the relationship between wages and employment).

He explained in Chapter 2 how investment depends on the expected rate of profit and on the rate of interest. Not just private capital formation but also public investment and private housing expenditure were sensitive to variations in the interest rate, which was therefore 'a very important instrument in controlling the total demand for commodities'. Meade then demonstrated how 'the Bank of England can control the amount of money in existence' through open market operations, and how this in turn determined the rate of interest. He presented this as a radical form of analysis, which 'involves a revision of many popular and orthodox ideas about monetary policy. Much greater and more sudden variations in the rate of interest may be necessary than have been usual in the past, if economic policy is to maintain a high level of employment'. However, as he argued in Chapter 4, 'The Control of Banking Policy', government control over the rate of interest could be achieved within the existing, privately-owned banking system. Nationalization of the banks was not necessary, though it might be desirable for other (that is, microeconomic) reasons (ibid., pp. 17, 22, 28, 35–6).

Nevertheless, Meade continued, monetary policy might prove insufficient to prevent a slump. Difficulties were posed by the time-lags between expansionary open-market operations and the resulting fall in the rate of interest, and between this and the consequent increase in investment expenditure. If, moreover, the price level did begin to fall, deflationary expectations might discourage investment so much that monetary expansion proved ineffective. This indicated a need for public works expenditure to prevent a fall in the price of capital goods as the economy began to turn down. Public works should be financed by borrowing, not by taxation, but in the context of a budget balanced over the cycle as a whole. A National Investment Board should require the public authorities to plan their capital development three to five years in advance and 'invite' private industry to follow suit, offering financial incentives to encourage compliance. In fact, Meade concluded, 'an important argument in favour of the socialization of industries is that it would help to cure unemployment by giving the state this extra power of control over expenditure on capital development' (ibid., pp. 38, 44, 48). Joan Robinson almost certainly agreed with this, but her own *Introduction* took a much more cautious approach.

A 'third and less orthodox method of controlling the total volume of expenditure' was proposed in Chapter 6. If state control of investment proved inadequate, attention must also be paid to consumption expenditure. Meade suggested that 'consumers' credits' might be granted (especially to the unemployed) as soon as a slump began, financed by printing money that would be redeemed from the proceeds of the increased tax rates that should be levied once unemployment fell below the 'standard' level. This would operate without any appreciable time-lag, it would provide income to those who needed it most, and it would supply 'an automatic guide to determine when consumers' credits should be paid'. Similar measures might be taken to stimulate consumption out of property income, but they could not function automatically and would be subject to significant time-lags in their effects. There was in any case, Meade argued, a strong argument in favour of 'a more equal distribution of income in order to stimulate expenditure on consumption goods' (ibid., pp. 50, 55, 59–60).

His third 'cure' for unemployment was to cut money costs of production (in effect, wages), so long as this could be done without thereby reducing aggregate money expenditure. In Chapter 7, then, he turned to the relationship between 'Wages and Unemployment'. Meade distinguished very clearly between real and money wage rates. Diminishing returns to labour apply, so that higher employment requires a reduction in real wages; on this question, Meade was uncompromisingly neoclassical. Lower money wages would raise employment only if they led to a fall in the price level, when the resulting decline in the demand for money for transactions purposes would reduce the rate of interest and therefore stimulate investment. But in practice Meade, like Keynes, was opposed to money wage cuts, which were difficult to obtain, carried significant dangers (of debt deflation and the depression of expectations), and were an unnecessarily indirect route to a goal that could be achieved directly by increasing the quantity of money. Meade did conclude, however, by warning unions not to try to increase employment by demanding higher money wage rates, and to be prepared to accept a fall in real wages for their members as employment expanded (ibid., pp. 61–73).

The macroeconomic section of Meade's *Introduction* ended on an equally cautionary note. In Chapter 8, 'The Proper Criterion for Policy', he dealt at length with the inflationary perils of demand expansion. The rate at which money wages increase, he argued, is inversely related to unemployment: 'the smaller the volume of unemployment, the smaller will be the pressure of unemployed workers seeking jobs in the trade, and so the greater will be the ability of those already employed in the trade to insist successfully upon a higher wage-rate'. A policy for incomes was implied in this. Money wages can grow at a rate equal to the rate of increase in labour productivity 'without any rise in the money price of commodities becoming necessary to prevent the growth of unemployment'; that is, with zero inflation. In the previous chapter Meade had already identified the 'standard' volume of unemployment as a policy target. 'This volume we have now defined precisely. Unemployment is of the "standard" size when it has been just sufficiently reduced for money wage-rates to start rising at the same rate as the marginal product of labour' (ibid., pp. 75–7).

The 'standard' level of unemployment could be reduced by improving the organization of the labour market, and also by the exercise of restraint on the part of trade union wage negotiators. But, given this level of unemployment, there were grounds for the exercise of caution in the application of expansionary monetary policy, lest unemployment should fall too fast and inflation result. Meade suggested that policy should be designed to reduce unemployment only 'by a certain percentage (e.g. 10 per cent)' of its excess about the 'standard' each year (ibid., pp. 78–9, 83). There are clear intimations here of the Meade of the 1970s, preoccupied with wage inflation and union power (Meade, 1982). As already noted, however, the Joan Robinson of the 1935 essays and the 1937 *Introduction* would have concurred, with this and with many other aspects of his book. In the late 1930s, at least, the battle lines between the neoclassicals and the Post Keynesians were far from clearly drawn.

KEYNES HAS SECOND THOUGHTS

Although he lived for another ten years after the publication of the *General Theory*, Keynes was unable to respond to the controversy his work aroused in any systematic way. He suffered the first of a series of heart attacks early in 1937, and after his recovery the outbreak of war in September 1939 meant that his energies were fully occupied until his death with problems of war finance and postwar reconstruction. There was no revised edition of his book – clearing the way for the subsequent efforts of Harcourt and Riach (1997) - and no comprehensive, point-by-point reply to his critics. What Keynes thought about the various interpretations of his ideas can, however, be inferred from a handful of published articles and a quite substantial volume of correspondence. The picture that emerges is one of the same ambivalence that had characterized the *General Theory*.

The first and most obvious point is that Keynes never once repudiated the IS–LM interpretation of the *General Theory*. On the contrary, he endorsed it warmly. 'I like your paper,' he wrote to Harrod in August 1936, 'more than I can say. I have found it instructive and illuminating and I really have no criticisms. I think that you have re-orientated the argument beautifully' (Keynes, 1973b, p. 84). A few days earlier he had congratulated Reddaway: 'I enjoyed your review of my book in the *Economic Record*, and thought it very well done' (ibid., p. 70). In March 1937 he wrote to Hicks in a similar vein: 'At long last I have caught up with my reading and have been through the enclosed [Hicks, 1937]. I found it very interesting and really have next to nothing to say by way of criticism' (ibid., p. 79). This was more than an ill-considered first reaction, or the normal courtesy extended to friends and colleagues. Oskar Lange was neither a colleague nor a personal friend, and yet Keynes noted in 1938 that 'Mr. Robertson refers with approval to an article by Dr. Lange [Lange, 1938] which follows very closely and accurately my line of thought. The analysis which I gave in my *General Theory of Employment* is the same as the 'general theory' explained by Dr. Lange on p. 18 of this article, except that my analysis is not based (as I think his is in that passage) on the assumption that the quantity of money is constant' (Keynes, 1938, p. 321, n1).

Nevertheless, when Keynes came to 're-express' the central message of the *General Theory* in an important article in the *Quarterly Journal of Economics*, he emphasized radical uncertainty and the consequent volatility of investment. Classical economics, he claimed, had assumed that uncertainty could be reduced to 'the same calculable status as that of certainty itself' (Keynes, 1937a, p. 213). This was a crucial mistake:

> Actually, however, we have, as a rule, only the vaguest idea of any but the most direct consequences of our acts … the fact that our knowledge of the future is fluctuating, vague and uncertain, renders wealth a peculiarly unsuitable subject for the methods of the classical economic theory. This theory might work very well in a world in which economic goods were necessarily consumed within a short interval of their being produced. But it requires, I suggest, considerable amendment if it is to be applied to a world in which the accumulation of wealth for an indefinitely postponed future is an important factor; and the greater the proportionate part played by such wealth accumulation the more essential does such amendment become. (Ibid., p. 213)

By 'uncertainty' Keynes did not 'mean merely to distinguish what is known for certain from what is only probable'. Rather,

> The sense in which I am using the term [uncertainty] is that in which the prospect of a European war is uncertain, or the price of copper and the rate of interest twenty years hence, or the obsolescence of a new invention, or the position of private wealth holders in the social system in 1970. About these matters there is no scientific basis on which to form any calculable probability whatever. We simply do not know. (Ibid., p. 214)

People deal with uncertainty by forming conventional judgments, in which the views of others play an important role. But such a view of the future, 'being based on so flimsy a foundation', is 'subject to sudden and violent changes'. Thus, since it depends on unstable and insecurely based expectations of future profits, 'It is not surprising that the volume of investment ... should fluctuate widely from time to time' (ibid., pp. 214–15, 218). All this had been ignored by classical economics, Keynes concluded: 'In a system in which the level of money income is capable of fluctuating, *the orthodox theory is one equation short* of what is required to give a solution' (ibid., p. 222; emphasis added). It is surely revealing that, even in this most unWalrasian of papers, Keynes was unable to resist an allusion to general equilibrium analysis.

But he was also complementary to the authors of non-Walrasian expositions of his theory. 'I consider the book as a whole a bit uneven', he wrote to Joan Robinson just before the publication of her *Essays*, 'as my comments will have told you already'. He had indeed been severely critical of technical errors in an early draft of her chapter on the foreign exchanges. 'But the general effect is splendid, full of originality and interest' (Keynes, 1973b, p. 147). He corresponded at some length with Hugh Townshend in 1936–8, accepting many of his detailed criticisms of particular points in the *General Theory* and (of course) accepted Townshend's paper for the *Economic Journal*. Unfortunately the correspondence between Keynes and Townshend on the article has not survived, but there is no reason to suppose that Keynes had any strong criticisms of it (Keynes, 1982b, pp. 236–47, 255–9, 288–94). And we know that he endorsed Nicholas Kaldor's critique of Pigou, IS–LM and all (Keynes, 1973b, pp. 266–7; cf. Young, 1987, pp. 112–13).

In August 1938 he received a two-volume work by the future Nobel laureate Jan Tinbergen, which contained the first serious econometric analysis of the determinants of investment (Louçã, 1999). Keynes was profoundly unimpressed, describing Tinbergen's work as 'charlatanism' and as 'a mess of unintelligible figurings' (Keynes, 1973b, pp. 305, 289). This was in private correspondence with Roy Harrod and Richard Kahn, but he was almost as harsh in his published review (Keynes, 1938), his rejoinder (Keynes, 1940) and in earlier letters to Tinbergen and to a League of Nations colleague, R. Tyler. Terms like 'black magic' and 'statistical alchemy' (Keynes, 1940,

p. 156) convey the strength of his feelings. Writing to Tyler, he spelled out his objections in considerable detail:

> If we were dealing with the action of numerically measurable, independent forces, adequately analysed so that we knew we were dealing with independent atomic factors and between them completely comprehensive, acting with fluctuating relative strength on material constant and homogeneous through time, we might be able to use the method of multiple correlation with some confidence for disentangling the laws of their action; though, even so, our results might be only very approximate so long as we were limited by our technique to linear relations.
>
> In fact we know that every one of these conditions is far from being satisfied by the economic material under investigation. (Keynes, 1973b, p. 286)

The determinants of investment, he wrote to Tinbergen, offered '*prima facie* extremely unpromising material' for econometric research, and there were good theoretical reasons for this. 'Is it assumed' in Tinbergen's work, he asked Tyler, 'that the future is a determinate function of *past statistics*? What place is left for expectation and the state of confidence relating to the future?' (ibid., pp. 295, 287).

Keynes had already reacted unfavourably to the pioneering econometric analysis of Henry Schultz in Chicago, taking the opportunity to articulate his own thinking on economic methodology. As he told Harrod in July 1938:

> It seems to me that economics is a branch of logic, a way of thinking; and that you do not repel sufficiently firmly attempts à la Schultz to turn it into a pseudo-natural-science …
>
> … it is of the essence of a model that one does *not* fill in real values for the variable functions. To do so would make it useless as a model …
>
> Economics is a science of thinking in terms of models joined to the art of choosing models which are relevant to the contemporary world. It is compelled to be this, because, unlike the typical natural science, the material to which it is applied is, in too many respects, not homogeneous through time.
>
> … as against Robbins, economics is essentially a moral science and not a natural science. That is to say, it employs introspection and judgements of value. (Keynes, 1973b, pp. 296–7; original emphasis)

Keynes's distaste for the econometricians' 'pseudo-analogy with the physical sciences' (ibid., p. 300) cannot be doubted, but its exact implications remain controversial. 'The notion of testing the quantitative influence of factors suggested by a theory as being important is very useful and to the point,' he admitted to Tyler. The problem with Tinbergen's approach was the 'false precision' to which it pretended: 'It may be that a more rough and ready method which preserves the original data in a more recognisable form may be safer' (ibid., p. 289). Keynes even offered Tinbergen some practical suggestions, including breaking down his data into several sub-periods and estimating an equation for each of them separately, and focusing on other, more tractable, problems. The inherent difficulty in estimating the determinants of investment 'does not mean, I agree, that there may not be problems within the general field of the trade cycle which would provide suitable material'. The relationship between investment and income, Keynes continued, 'having regard to the time lags involved, I should regard … as *prima facie* a promising case' (ibid., p. 295). One quite reasonable interpretation of his worries is that they were concerned with the practical problems of econometric work rather than reflecting a root-and-branch, in-principle objection to rigorous statistical work on economic data (Bateman, 1990). But the opposite view also has some merit, since it can plausibly be argued that fundamental uncertainty entails a non-ergodic universe in which standard econometric techniques are simply inapplicable (Lawson, 1989; see also Chapter 9).

Evidently it was not just the harp of the *General Theory* that Keynes had failed to tune. His book had provoked two different and essentially incompatible interpretations, and he had proved incapable of choosing between them. Many of Keynes's disciples were no less ambivalent. But the principle of effective demand could be approached from a quite different direction, largely avoiding Marshall and Walras and coming much closer to Marx. This was the route taken by the Polish socialist Michal Kalecki, whose work forms the subject of the next chapter.

2. An economist from Poland

> But I do not think that it is necessary, if one would advance Keynes's claims to greatness, to argue that we might not have reached the same destination by other routes or at a later date; to name only one other, Michal Kalecki was independently approaching the same goal. (A. Robinson, 1946, p. 42)

KALECKI BEFORE KEYNES

In March 1939 the readers of the *Daily Worker* were introduced to the ideas of 'a Polish economist now in this country'. This review of Michal Kalecki's *Essays in the Theory of Economic Fluctuations* (Kalecki, 1939) was written by Maurice Dobb, himself a Cambridge economist and one of the Communist Party of Great Britain's leading theoreticians. Kalecki's book, Dobb admitted, was not easy reading. But 'the mind behind the pen is one of unusual distinction and originality', and his work was directly relevant to the real problems of contemporary capitalism. Kalecki had broken with traditional economic theory in two important areas. 'First, he starts by assuming that capitalists are always monopolists (in some degree)', and this led him to treat the capitalist share in national income as determined by the degree of monopoly power that they enjoy rather than by conventional marginal productivity considerations. 'Secondly, he devotes special attention to what Marx called the problem of "realisation of surplus value". Here his ideas have some affinity with those of Rosa Luxemburg, as he himself points out.' Kalecki's account of economic crises, Dobb continued, was similar to that of Keynes, 'but handled in such a way as to place the main emphasis on "the falling rate of profit" as the inevitable cause of crises under capitalism' (Dobb, 1939, p. 8).

Born in Łódź in 1899, Kalecki studied engineering at Warsaw Polytechnic without graduating, and was forced by his father's financial difficulties to earn his living as a commercial journalist. Much of his early theoretical work was published in trade papers and in the socialist press, and has only recently become available in English. He worked for seven years at the Institute for Business Cycle and Price Research in Warsaw, before moving briefly to Sweden and then to England, where he spent the period 1936–45. After the war he was employed first by the International Labour Organisation in Montreal and then by the United Nations in New York, before returning to Poland in 1955 to escape McCarthyism in the United States. He served as a government adviser, and was also a professor in Warsaw. A very independently-minded non-party socialist, Kalecki was often in trouble with the authorities; shortly before his death in 1970 he resigned his official positions in protest against officially inspired anti-Semitism and the persecution of his younger colleagues. Kalecki is a major figure in the history of Post Keynesian economics. In addition to the considerable intrinsic merit of his ideas and the power of his theoretical system, he formed a crucial bridge between Keynesian and Marxian thinking, which was crossed from both directions by dissident economists of the calibre of Joan Robinson, Paul Sweezy and Josef Steindl.

Very little is known of the influences on the young Kalecki. Almost entirely self-taught as an economist, he seems, on the evidence of his early writings, to have absorbed a certain amount of 'classical' economics in addition to the Marxism of Luxemburg and of Mikhail Tugan-Baranovsky. Some of his initial work, for example, is very clearly pre-Keynesian, since it presupposes a world in which saving drives investment rather than the other way round (Osiatynski, 1990, pp. 423–4). Prior to 1935, at least, Kalecki's ideas must have been in a state of perpetual flux. He can, for example, claim the dubious distinction of having devised an IS–LM model of his very own, four years before the publication of the *General Theory*. In his article 'Three Systems', Kalecki constructed a 'quasi-equilibrium' model with three simultaneous equations in three endogenous variables: investment expenditure, the real interest rate and the level of employment. In terms of its assumptions, most of its behavioural relations and its conclusions, this was an IS–LM model (Kalecki, 1934; cf. Chapple, 1995).

By 1933, however, Kalecki was already approaching intellectual maturity. The evidence is contained in his remarkable model of the business cycle, repeatedly reworked and revised but already substantially complete in its original Polish version. The model was presented to the academic world at the 1935 Leyden conference of the Econometric Society and published both in French and in English in the same year before appearing, in yet another guise, in his 1939 *Essays*; full details, together with a comparison of the various versions, are provided by Jerzy Osiatynski, the editor of Kalecki's *Collected Works* (Osiatynski, 1990, pp. 436–46). In most references to Kalecki in this chapter, the first date is that of original publication and the second is that of the relevant volume of his *Collected Works*; page citations are from the latter.

The summary of his trade cycle model that follows is based upon the version published in 1935 in *Econometrica*. This article was the first exposition of Kalecki's model available to readers of English, and aroused considerable interest. He began by writing an equation for real gross profit

(B), which is the sum of capitalist consumption (C) and accumulation (A). Consumption by capitalists consists of a constant part (C_1) and a variable part that is proportional to real gross profits (λB). Kalecki did not use the term, but λ is the marginal propensity to consume out of profits. He now made the 'classical' assumption that both workers' savings and their incomes from property are negligible. Thus all saving is performed by capitalists, and A is equal to gross investment. Since

$$B = C + A \tag{2.1}$$

and

$$C = C_1 + \lambda B, \tag{2.2}$$

it follows that

$$B = C_1 + \lambda B + A \tag{2.3}$$

and

$$B = \frac{C_1 + A}{1 - \lambda}. \tag{2.4}$$

Equation (2.4) tells us that real gross profit is proportional to the aggregate expenditure of capitalists on consumption and on accumulation, the factor of proportionality being λ, the capitalists' marginal propensity to consume. As Joan Robinson later observed, in the limiting case where $\lambda = 0$, Kalecki's argument can be summarized very simply: 'the workers spend what they get, and the capitalists get what they spend' (Robinson, 1966, p. 341).

Since capitalist consumption is 'not very elastic' (Kalecki, 1935 [1990], p. 120), it follows that the principal factor causing fluctuations in aggregate profits is changes in investment activity. Kalecki maintained that investment decisions depend on the expected net yield, which is equal to the gross profit expected from a project, minus depreciation and interest payments. In aggregate terms, he wrote investment orders (I) as a positive function of capitalists' expenditure ($C_1 + A$) and a negative function of the existing capital stock (K):

$$I = m(C_1 + A) - nK. \tag{2.5}$$

This is Kalecki's equation (11) (ibid., p. 124); the reason for the negative effect of K on I was not very clearly explained in the 1935 article, but emerged more clearly in the 1939 *Essays* version, as we shall see shortly.

With the addition of a time-lag between the placing of investment orders and the delivery of the new capital goods, and some extensive and tedious mathematical manipulations, Kalecki's cycle model was complete. Drawing on US, German and British data, Kalecki introduced realistic values for the parameters of his model and simulated a cycle in investment activity of eight to 12 years, plotted in the figure in his article (ibid., p. 135). He concluded by discussing the monetary implications of his analysis. 'The question may still arise of where capitalists find the means to increase at the same time the production of capital goods and their own consumption.' In principle, he suggested, 'we may say that these outlays are "financing themselves"', as one capitalist's expenditure creates income for others. In practice, though, 'credit inflation' would be necessary during the upswing of the business cycle, partly due to the likely increase in the price level and the consequent rise in the volume of transactions, and partly in order to provide an 'investment reserve' when the timing of investment orders was out of step with the production of new capital goods (ibid., pp. 137–8).

The mathematical foundations of Kalecki's model were soon assessed by Ragnar Frisch and Jan Tinbergen, who were to share the first Nobel prize in economics for their work on econometrics (Frisch and Holme, 1935; Tinbergen, 1935); Frisch confirmed the integrity of the analysis. Kalecki's vision of the cyclical instability of the capitalist economy continues to exert a considerable intellectual attraction (Sawyer, 1996). It was, quite explicitly, a *capitalist* economy that Kalecki was attempting to analyse. It is capitalist entrepreneurs, not workers, or consumers, or households, who make all the running. Fluctuations in investment expenditure determine the path that is taken by total output, and they have a multiplier effect. While investment decisions are based on capitalists' expectations of future profitability, profits in aggregate depend on investment expenditure through Kalecki's 'realization' mechanism. As he wrote in a later article about the behaviour of capitalists: 'it is clear that they may decide to consume and to invest more in a certain short period than in the preceding period, but they cannot decide to earn more. It is therefore their investment and consumption decisions which determine profits, and not the other way round' (Kalecki, 1942, p. 259). There are echoes here of the 'widow's cruse' and 'banana' parables of Keynes's *Treatise on Money* (Keynes, 1930, vol. I, pp. 129, 176–8), though there is no evidence that Kalecki was aware of them, at least in 1935; significantly, neither parable was repeated in the *General Theory*. In the same year as the first (Polish) version of his trade cycle appeared, Kalecki published an obscure and difficult article, again in Polish, entitled 'On Foreign Trade and "Domestic Exports"', in which he set out a model of the export multiplier and pointed very clearly in the direction of much later Post Keynesian models of balance of payments-constrained growth (Kalecki, 1933; King, 1998b).

THE IMPACT OF *THE GENERAL THEORY*

In 1935 Kalecki was awarded a Rockefeller scholarship. In February of the following year he left for Sweden, where he intended to write a book 'which (one can surmise) would be a synthesis of his theory of the business cycle with elements of a general theory of capitalist reproduction and the mechanism of the business upswing, which he had been developing since the end of 1932' (Osiatynski, 1990, p. 498). The *General Theory* was published in the very same month, and Kalecki soon obtained a copy. It induced him to give up his plans for a book of his own, at least temporarily. The blow to his morale did not affect his work for very long. Kalecki soon wrote an incisive and critical review of the *General Theory* for the Polish journal *Ekonomista*, which became available in English only after his death (Kalecki, 1936 [1990]; Targetti and Kinda-Hass, 1982). Keynes's book, Kalecki wrote, 'is, without any doubt, a turning point in the history of economics'. He emphasized two aspects of Keynes's analysis: 'the determination of short period equilibrium with a given production apparatus, once the level of investment (per unit of time) is given', and the determination of the level of investment itself. The first problem, at least, 'has been solved in Keynes's theory very satisfactorily' (Kalecki, 1936 [1990], p. 223). Rather than summarizing Keynes's own exposition, however, Kalecki offered his own formulation, encapsulated in a diagram.

Figure 2.1 illustrates the equilibrium of a representative firm. Abstracting from raw material costs and depreciation, profit-maximizing output (*OC*) is given by the condition that marginal value added equals marginal labour cost. The area *OABC* is equal to total value added, and the shaded area is capitalist income, while the non-shaded part of *OABC* represents the income of the workers. Aggregating over all firms, *OABC* is national income, expressed in Keynes's wage units. On the Kaleckian assumption that workers do not save, the shaded area (total profits) is equal to the sum of capitalist consumption and investment:

> We are already able to show the crucial role of the expenditure of capitalists on consumption and investment in the determination of the short-term equilibrium … A spontaneous change in worker expenditure cannot happen because (as we have assumed) they spend exactly as much as they have earned. But when capitalists are considered, a spontaneous change in expenditure is highly probable either by means of spending reserves or by contracting new debts. Let us suppose that they raise their expenditure by a certain amount in a unit of time. Then the marginal value added curves will shift up to the point where the sum of the shaded areas matches the higher value of capitalist expenditure for consumption and investment….
>
> … the sum of capitalist expenditure determines the position of the value added curves in such a way that the sum of the shaded areas, that is, of capitalist income,

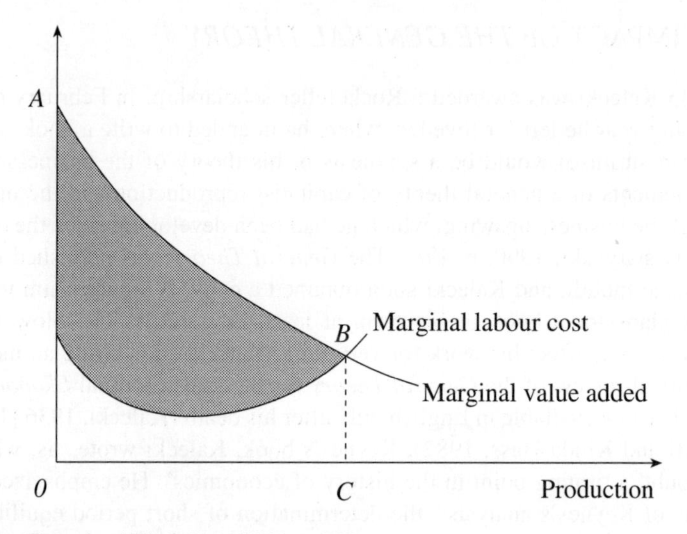

Source: Targetti and Kinda-Hass (1982, p. 247).

Figure 2.1

> is equal to their expenditure. Thus the level of expenditure (expressed in wage units) is the crucial factor in determining the short-term equilibrium. (Kalecki, 1936 [1990], pp. 225–6, 227)

This implied, Kalecki continued, that causation runs from investment to saving, not vice versa. In fact 'we can say also that investment forces savings whose value is equal to the value of this investment' (ibid., p. 227).

This led Kalecki to his fundamental criticism of the *General Theory* (Asimakopulos, 1971). Keynes argued that investment is a negative function of the rate of interest because the increase in the price of investment goods that results from higher investment reduces the expected profitability of subsequent projects. But this, Kalecki objected,

> does not say anything about the sphere of investment *decisions* of the entrepreneur, who makes his calculations in 'disequilibrium' on the basis of *existing* market prices of investment goods. It shows only that if the expected profitability, calculated on the basis of this price level, is not equal to the rate of interest, a change in the level of investment will occur.... Using the terminology of Swedish economists, one can say that Keynes's theory determines only the *ex post* level of investment, but that it does not say anything about *ex ante* investment. (Kalecki, 1936 [1990], p. 230)

There was a further problem. Since a rise in investment will stimulate a general economic recovery, it is also likely to cause an upward revision of profit expectations, and this in turn will induce a further increase in investment. 'Therefore,' Kalecki concluded, 'it is difficult to consider Keynes's solution of the investment problem to be satisfactory. The reason for this failure lies in an approach which is basically static to a matter which is by its nature dynamic' (ibid., p. 231).

The remarkable diagram with which Kalecki illustrated his version of the principle of effective demand also appeared, slightly redrawn, in later writings (Kalecki, 1938 [1991], p. 11; 1939 [1990], p. 243). It indicates that he was taking a strong interest in neoclassical theory, as suggested by his reference in the review article to 'a cumulative Wicksellian process' (Kalecki, 1936 [1990], p. 231). This is confirmed by his use of marginalist analysis in the earlier variants of his distribution model. A 1938 *Econometrica* article was his first attempt to explain the profit share in national income by reference to product market conditions, and here he used an explicitly neoclassical formulation, drawing on Abba Lerner's (1934) definition of the 'degree of monopoly' as the ratio of the difference between price and marginal cost to price:

$$\mu = \frac{p - m}{m}. \qquad (2.6)$$

In perfect competition, where price equals marginal cost, there is no monopoly power, and $\mu = 0$; profits are also zero. The greater the degree of monopoly, the higher the gap between price and marginal cost and the greater the share of profits in the total revenue of the firm. Kalecki now applied the profit-maximizing principle. When marginal revenue equals marginal cost, μ is equal to the inverse of the elasticity of the firm's product demand. Some rather clumsy algebra led Kalecki to the conclusion that, for the economy as a whole, 'The relative share of gross capitalist income and salaries in the aggregate turnover is with great approximation equal to the average degree of monopoly', that is, to the inverse of the average elasticity of product demand (Kalecki, 1939 [1990], pp. 240–41).

Kalecki's use of neoclassical theory must, to some extent, have emanated from a conscious tactical decision to employ conventional analytical methods so that his own innovations might be more readily understood by the profession as a whole. In one or two articles it was carried to excessive lengths, most apparent in the dreadful 'Supply Curve of an Industry Under Imperfect Competition' (Kalecki, 1940). None of Kalecki's central ideas, however, require a neoclassical framework, and he abandoned it in later reformulations of his pricing and distribution model (Kriesler, 1987).

THE 1939 *ESSAYS*

Neither in immediate response to Keynes nor subsequently did Kalecki write a comprehensive treatise of his own, still less a popular textbook. His books all consist of self-contained essays on related themes, with the connections rarely made explicit, even though he was in general more consistent than many theorists in linking his micro and macroeconomic analysis (Kriesler, 1987). Together with Kalecki's characteristic terseness and inelegant style, this must have restricted his influence relatively to that of Keynes, whose best writing is of very high literary quality and is still read for pleasure (though admittedly neither statement is true of the bulk of the *General Theory*). Kalecki's *Essays in the Theory of Economic Fluctuations* are a prime example of his shortcomings as a writer. Even the painstaking editorial revisions of his young research assistant, Brian Tew, cannot hide the fact that it is the work of an engineer, not an essayist.

There were six chapters, three of them revised versions of previously published papers (Tew, 1999). The first was an embellishment of his *Econometrica* article on income distribution, revealing the capitalist share in national income to be inversely related to the degree of monopoly and the price of raw materials. Apart from the neoclassical algebra, it had a number of noteworthy features. One was the reassertion of Kalecki's lifelong belief that average variable cost is constant over a very wide range of output, rising steeply only in those (rare) cases when full capacity working is approached (Kalecki, 1939 [1990], p. 239). A second important point was his rejection of technical change and the elasticity of substitution as factors relevant to a theory of distribution. In effect, this was a repudiation of marginal productivity theory, despite Kalecki's continuing use of the marginalist theory of the firm. Empirical evidence led him to conclude that the share of wages was roughly stable over the cycle, since offsetting changes occurred in the degree of monopoly and the price of raw materials relative to manufactured goods. In the long run he expected the wage share to decline, owing to a secular increase in the degree of monopoly in '*Spaetkapitalismus*' (late capitalism), unless raw material prices continued to fall (ibid., pp. 242, 247). This was a common theme in contemporary Marxism, which linked the decline in competition to an increasing profit share in net output, from which (it was argued) there resulted a chronic deficiency in aggregate demand and a strong tendency towards stagnation (Howard and King, 1992, ch. 1). Kalecki ended the first essay with a rare rhetorical flourish: 'Monopoly appears to be deeply rooted in the nature of the capitalist system: free competition, as an assumption, may be useful in the first stage of certain investigations, but as a description of the normal state of capitalist economy it is merely a myth' (ibid., p. 252).

The second essay, not previously published, had the title 'Investment and Income'. It can best be interpreted as an effort to insert class relations into the Keynesian multiplier. A multiplier relation is, of course, implicit in the 1933 cycle model via the 'factor of proportionality' in equation (2.4) above. But this determined aggregate profits, not aggregate income. Kalecki's 1939 version of this relationship, however, was explicitly formulated as an income multiplier. First he showed how an increase in investment expenditure raised both capitalists' saving and consumption expenditure by capitalists and workers; the latter led to an increase in income in the consumer goods sector, creating a further increase in saving by the capitalists in that branch of the economy. Taking both sectors, it can be seen that 'additional expenditure on investment ΔI creates an equal addition to saving ΔS'. This analysis, Kalecki maintained, is 'contained in the famous Marxian scheme of "extended reproduction"', even if Marx himself had not been able to 'approach the idea of the key position of investment in the determination of the level of total output and employment'. Rosa Luxemburg's treatment of the problem was not only superior to Marx's, but also set out the issues 'perhaps more clearly than anywhere else before the publication of Mr. Keynes's *General Theory*' (ibid., pp. 254–5).

Next Kalecki extended the analysis to the case of an open economy with a government, using elementary national income accounting identities to show that 'investment' must be redefined to include the export surplus and the budget deficit (ibid., pp. 255–7). Kalecki's algebra was rather confusing, and he carefully avoided the use of familiar Keynesian terminology, but the argument was simple enough (ibid., pp. 258–61). The wage share in national income (α) is constant, for the reasons given in the first essay; thus the share of non-wage income is also constant, and equal to $(1 - \alpha)$. Kalecki assumed that workers do not save, and that consumption out of non-wage income is positive but constant. Thus the marginal propensity to save out of non-wage income is unity, and the marginal propensity to save out of income as a whole is $(1 - \alpha)$. The multiplier is then the reciprocal of the non-wage share:

$$\frac{\Delta Y}{\Delta I} = \frac{1}{1-\alpha}. \tag{2.7}$$

The principle can be illustrated using Kalecki's own numbers. If in the United States $\alpha = 0.32$, then when national income rose by one dollar wages increased by 68 cents, all of which were spent; and non-wage incomes increased by 32 cents, all of which were saved. The marginal propensity to save was 0.32, and the multiplier was 1/0.32 = 3.125 (ibid., p. 258, n).

In simplified expositions of Kalecki's model, like that of Joan Robinson cited above, non-wage incomes are often described as 'profits' and their recipients as 'capitalists'. Kalecki himself was careful to make it clear that the class of non-wage earners included rentiers, salaried workers and dole claimants in addition to entrepreneurs. Indeed, he discussed at some length the implications of distributive shifts between these categories, and also modified the analysis to allow for time-lags between changes in incomes and the corresponding changes in consumption spending (ibid., pp. 261–9). But these were relatively minor qualifications. While he attempted to improve the presentation of his model in subsequent work (see, for example, Kalecki, 1943a), he always defended the underlying principles. Unlike the Keynesian multiplier, the Kaleckian multiplier depends on the share of wages in national income and on the propensity to save out of non-wage incomes.

The third essay dealt with money wages and real wages in a very simple model of a two-class closed economy with perfect competition in all industries. Profits, in aggregate, are equal to investment plus capitalist consumption. A reduction in money wages will therefore raise employment, Kalecki maintained, only if it induces capitalists to increase their expenditure on investment or luxury consumer goods. 'Such a state of affairs is, however, extremely unlikely.' In all probability capitalists would place new investment orders only when their expectations of higher profits, stimulated by the wage reduction, had been realized. 'Even should they give new orders at once, the technical time-lag between investment orders and the actual production of investment goods would prevent the latter from increasing immediately' (Kalecki, 1939 [1990], p. 276). Similar time-lags would apply to capitalist consumption. But, if neither investment nor capitalist consumption has risen, employment will also remain constant; prices will fall in the same proportion as money wages, leaving real wages unchanged (ibid., p. 277). The same conclusion can be drawn in the case of imperfect competition, unless the existence of 'sticky' prices leads to an increase in profit margins in wage goods industries. In this case the demand for wage goods will decline, and employment in this sector will fall. 'Thus, paradoxically, both employment and real wages are here reduced by the wage cut. And when this has occurred, there will still be no incentive for capitalists to increase their consumption and investment' (ibid., p. 279).

Minor modifications are necessary to allow for different savings propensities on the part of entrepreneurs, rentiers, clerks and managers. On balance, Kalecki concluded, money wage reductions may cause employment to rise or to fall, but not by very much; and, while they may reduce real wages and cut the wage share in national income, these effects will also tend to be rather small (ibid., pp. 282–3). He concluded by assessing the political implications of this 'Keynesian theory of wages' (ibid., p. 284). Contrary to the protestations of 'certain "workers' friends"', union wage struggles and strikes should be supported: 'For a rise in wages tends to reduce the degree of monopoly, and thus to bring our imperfect system nearer to the ideal of free competition.' And resistance to wage cuts 'prevents the degree of monopoly from rising in the slump to the extent it would if "free competition" prevailed on the labour market. Although, in fact the relative share of manual labour is more or less stable, this would not obtain if wages were very elastic' (ibid., pp. 284–5). Kalecki did not believe, however, that 'the fight for wages' could drastically improve the distribution of income. Higher taxes on profits and on capital would be necessary for this to be achieved, and it was unlikely that a capitalist government would have either the will or the power to introduce such measures.

Kalecki's fourth essay, on 'The Principle of Increasing Risk', brought him back to the theory of investment. As we have seen, in his review of the *General Theory* he had been severely critical of Keynes's treatment of this vital question. His starting-point in the essay was, however, very similar: the individual entrepreneur continues to invest up to 'that level at which the marginal rate of profit is equal to the sum of the rate of interest p and the rate of risk o' (ibid., p. 286). Why, Kalecki asked, was the optimum amount of investment finite? He rejected two conventional answers, diseconomies of scale and imperfect competition. Instead he suggested that marginal risk increased with the quantity of investment. This was true for both borrowers and lenders:

> For the greater the investment, the greater is the reduction of the entrepreneur's income from his own capital when the average rate of profit falls short of the rate of interest …
>
> If, however, the entrepreneur is not cautious enough in his investment activity, it is the creditor who imposes on his calculation the burden of increasing risk, charging the successive portions of credits above a certain amount with a rising rate of interest. (Ibid., pp. 287–8)

Thus neither diseconomies of scale, nor imperfect product markets, nor Keynes's mistaken emphasis on increasing marginal costs in investment goods industries, were necessary for there to be a limit to profitable investment; the principle of increasing risk provided a sufficient explanation. In the fifth essay Kalecki dealt with the long-term rate of interest. Its 'remarkable stability' (ibid., p. 293) over the trade cycle showed that booms would normally come to an end before full employment was reached, and also reinforced the argument of the third essay concerning the impact of money wage cuts on employment. A lower price level would indeed reduce the transactions demand for money and reduce short-time interest rates. But this was 'without practical importance', since it is the long rate that is significant for investment decisions (ibid., p. 283).

The *Essays* concluded with yet another reformulation of Kalecki's model of the trade cycle. This one was notable for his attack on the IS–LM analyses of Meade, Hicks and Lange who, he argued, greatly exaggerated the stability of the 'conditional equilibrium' that they identified. Failing to distinguish between investment decisions and investment, and ignoring the influence of investment on the size of the capital stock, they did not realize that their supposedly stable equilibrium level of income 'is attained only at the top of the boom and at the bottom of the slump' (ibid., p. 313). Kalecki's argument here was quite informal, and it was illustrated by a set of diagrams rather than the mathematical underpinnings found in earlier expositions of his model. The diagrams seem, however, to have inspired Nicholas Kaldor's first cycle model, and Hicks himself later rose to the challenge (Kaldor, 1940; Hicks, 1950). Kalecki ended by summarizing his theory of the cycle, which relied on 'the fact that investment is not only produced but also producing'. Investment expenditure increases aggregate demand, which improves business conditions and stimulates further increases in investment. At the same time it adds to the capital stock, competing with older equipment and depressing profit expectations: 'The tragedy of investment is that it causes crisis because it is useful. Doubtless many people will consider this theory paradoxical. But it is not the theory which is paradoxical, but its subject – the capitalist economy' (Kalecki, 1939 [1990], p. 318).

KALECKI'S WAR

Kalecki continued to worry away at the questions he had raised in the 1939 *Essays*. Among his many wartime publications were brief articles on the theory of distribution and the theory of profits (Kalecki, 1941, 1942). The latter was included, along with papers on costs and prices, interest rates, and another reworking of his trade cycle model, in the short book, *Studies in Economic Dynamics* (Kalecki, 1943a). He found time, too, for a brief but devastating attack on the Pigou effect. A.C. Pigou had claimed, in the spirit of the emerging neoclassical synthesis, that a full employment equilibrium could always be established if there were sufficient downward flexibility in money wages. This was true, Kalecki pointed out, only if the stock of money was backed by gold. Since it was in fact largely backed by 'credits to persons and firms', the gains to money holders from a fall in the price level would be offset by losses to bank debtors:

> If in the initial position the stock of gold is small as compared with the national wealth, it will take an enormous fall in wage rates and prices to reach the point when saving out of the full employment income is zero. The adjustment required would increase catastrophically the real value of debts, and would consequently lead to wholesale bankruptcy and a confidence crisis. The adjustment would probably never be carried out to the end: if the workers persisted in their game of

> unrestricted competition, the Government would introduce a wage stop under pressure from employers. (Kalecki, 1944a [1990], p. 132)

There are echoes here of Irving Fisher's debt-deflation theory of economic crisis, which was to have a profound influence on the Post Keynesian thinking of Hyman Minsky (see Chapter 5).

Most of Kalecki's energies, however, were now devoted to policy questions. Working at the Oxford Institute of Statistics with a talented group of economists that included Thomas Balogh, Frank Burchardt, E.F. Schumacher, Josef Steindl and David Worswick, Kalecki wrote dozens of short papers on many aspects of war finance. His critical confrontation with Keynes continued with an attack on *How To Pay For The War* as being excessively generous to the wealthy. Kalecki proposed instead that total expenditure be rationed in order to share the burden of the war more equitably, and provoked a considerable controversy in which his alternative did not fare especially well (King, 1998a).

Easily his most important wartime article, however, was a brief and entirely non-technical paper that he contributed to the journal, *Political Quarterly*. Here Kalecki took it as proven that there were no economic reasons why a government spending programme could not secure full employment, and instead discussed the political difficulties that would arise. There were three reasons why big business was opposed to such a programme: '(i) dislike of government interference in the problem of employment as such; (ii) dislike of the direction of government spending (public investment and subsidizing consumption; (iii) dislike of the social and political changes resulting from the *maintenance* of full employment' (Kalecki, 1943b [1990], pp. 349–50). The first objection implied that the level of employment depended primarily on the state of business confidence, which was thus the principal constraint on economic policy. The second was used to require that government spending be confined to areas like roads, schools and hospitals where it did not compete with private investment. Subsidies to mass consumption would pass this test, Kalecki acknowledged, but would nonetheless be rejected by big business on ideological grounds: 'For here a "moral" principle of the highest importance is at stake. The fundamentals of capitalist ethics require that "You shall earn your bread in sweat" – unless you happen to have private means' (ibid., p. 351).

Most important was the third reason for objecting to full employment maintained by state expenditure. Capitalists knew full well that, 'under a regime of permanent full employment, "the sack" would cease to play its role as a disciplinary measure. The social position of the boss would be undermined and the self-assurance and class-consciousness of the working class would grow'. Profits would be higher under full employment, and any rises in wage rates would come at the expense of the rentiers: 'But "discipline in the factories" and "political stability" are more appreciated than profits by business leaders. Their class instinct tells them that lasting full employment is unsound from their point of view and that unemployment is an integral part of the "normal" capitalist system'. Electoral considerations, however, would make it impossible for governments to renounce all responsibility for employment. A 'political business cycle' could therefore be expected. Counter-cyclical government spending would come under pressure from capitalist and rentier interests, which would force a return to more orthodox policies. A nineteenth-century cycle would be restored artificially: 'Full employment would be reached only at the top of the boom, but slumps would be relatively mild and short lived' (ibid., pp. 351, 355).

In his contribution to the Oxford Institute of Statistics's volume, *The Economics of Full Employment*, Kalecki confined himself to more narrowly economic questions. He distinguished 'Three Ways to Full Employment'. One of them – stimulating private investment by reducing interest rates or cutting taxes on profits – would probably require the accumulation of capital far in excess of the quantity needed to produce consumer goods, and it might in any case founder on the pessimistic expectations of entrepreneurs. The alternative methods – government expenditure in the form of public investment and subsidies to mass consumption, and redistribution of income from the rich to the poor – offered much greater prospects of success (Kalecki, 1944b). A more formal version of this argument was presented in a later paper, 'Full Employment by Stimulating Private Investment?' The full employment level of national income would increase over time, Kalecki noted, owing to growth in population and in the productivity of labour. Thus the quantity of private investment required to attain this level of income must continually increase, most likely at an increasing rate since saving would rise faster than income. But if capital were to accumulate faster than the growth rate of income, the rate of profit would fall, and this would require 'a continuous (and rather rapid) reduction of the rate of interest' if full employment were to be preserved (Kalecki, 1945a [1990], p. 381). To avoid this problem the budget deficit should be allowed to grow in order to finance public investment 'at the rate actually required for satisfying the needs of the community, while all government spending above this level is devoted to subsidizing mass consumption' (ibid., p. 383).

Here Kalecki touched on the theory of economic growth, which will be considered in the following chapter. Political problems aside, he saw no reason why in the United Kingdom full employment should not be achieved by suitable government policies after the war. This was not true, however, of the United States, where unemployment had been much higher before 1939, productivity growth was faster, and a more unequal distribution of income and the resulting higher propensity to save meant that a much larger budget deficit would be needed (Kalecki, 1945b). Kalecki's pessimistic predictions concerning the prospects for the postwar United States were savaged by another émigré economist, W.S. Woytinsky (1946), to whom he replied, repeating his earlier arguments (Kalecki, 1947). When he returned to this question, in the mid-1950s, Kalecki argued that the precarious postwar prosperity of the capitalist world was due entirely to massive armaments expenditures (Kalecki, 1955). It was a position shared by many radicals in the West.

KALECKI AND THE 'LEFT KEYNESIANS'

As a poor foreigner in Cambridge, with limited, highly-accented English and uncertain prospects, Kalecki was befriended by Joan Robinson. She referred to him affectionately as 'my Pole', helped to find work for him and interceded on his behalf with Keynes in the latter's capacity as editor of the *Economic Journal* (Osiatynski, 1991, pp. 530–35). In return he taught her a great deal, as she often admitted in print. Above all, Kalecki made her take Marx seriously. He was not himself an orthodox Marxist: he had no time for the labour theory of value, and took his historical materialism from diverse and mainly heretical sources, not from Kautsky or Lenin. But there was an undeniable and powerful strand of Marxism in Kalecki's thought, and by the early 1940s he had convinced Robinson that the *General Theory* was best interpreted from a Marxian perspective.

This was evident in her *Essay on Marxian Economics*, where Robinson acknowledged Kalecki's influence and set out to reconstruct both Marx and Keynes along Kaleckian lines. She did not mince her words, describing the labour theory of value as very largely irrelevant, repudiating the Hegelian elements in Marx's thought and criticizing him for not clearly recognizing the significance of effective demand (Robinson, 1942, pp. 22, 44, 50–51). Nonetheless, Robinson concluded, Marx could be rescued from himself and his ideas revitalized as if he were a sort of premature Keynesian. Thus repackaged, his macroeconomics offered distinct advantages over that of Keynes: 'Marx, however imperfectly he worked out the details, set himself the task of discovering the law of motion of capitalism, and if there is to be any hope of progress in economics at all, it must be in using academic methods to solve the problems posed by Marx (ibid., p. 95).

At this stage in her life Robinson was still a 'liberal socialist' (Thompson, 1997); her Maoism was a product of the 1960s (Robinson, 1969). Both Robinson and Kaldor were involved in the writing of the Beveridge Report on full employment, on which Kaldor was a major influence. Robinson had been an active member of the Fabian Society since the beginning of the 1930s, and in 1942–3 wrote a series of articles and pamphlets in which she advocated the radical reconstruction of British society after the war. Kaldor, too, moved significantly to the left in the early 1940s (King, 2001). However, Kaldor wrote nothing on Marx until the mid-1950s, when he revealed himself to be a severe critic of the Marxian theory of economic development (Kaldor, 1957a). Robinson always gave at least as good as she got in arguments with orthodox Marxists, as can be seen in her polemical 'Open Letter from a Keynesian to a Marxist', which was directed (without naming him) at the then Stalinist Ronald Meek (Robinson, 1953, pp. 19–23). But already, with the publication of her little book on Marx, Robinson was well on the way to becoming the most influential British representative of the so-called 'Left Keynesians', who wanted to put class analysis, imperialism and military expenditure into the *General Theory*.

In the United States a similar position was occupied by another unorthodox Marxist, Paul Sweezy. Briefly a Hayekian, then a liberal Keynesian, Sweezy moved rapidly to the left in the late 1930s. He also taught Marxian economics at Harvard under the benign supervision of Joseph Schumpeter, and acquired an unparalleled knowledge of the German literature on the theory of economic crises. The first 12 chapters of his *Theory of Capitalist Development* contained a masterly survey of nineteenth- and early twentieth-century Marxian economic theory, while the final seven chapters offered an original view of the monopoly phase of capitalism that brought together the principal strands of Marxian and Keynesian thinking. Following Hilferding and Lenin, Sweezy argued that the growth of monopoly represented a new stage of capitalism with distinct laws of motion. The decline of competition had important macroeconomic consequences: investment would be lower than in competitive capitalism, and the wasteful costs of circulation would be higher. Unlike competitive capitalists, monopolists must take into account when making investment decisions the depressing effect of the new capacity on the price of their product. They would therefore tend to invest less, reducing effective demand and creating a strong tendency to stagnation. The growth of commercial and distributive costs worked against this by increasing demand for the individual monopolist and expanding consumption expenditure for the entire economy. But these expenses were unproductive, and Sweezy concluded that monopoly capitalism was characterized by increasing waste (Sweezy, 1942, pp. 278–85; Howard and King, 1992, chs 1, 6).

Sweezy's ideas were very largely formed before he encountered Kalecki's work, but he soon recognized the similarities. The two men established a firm personal friendship during Kalecki's nine years in New York and when, with Paul Baran, Sweezy wrote his best-known book, *Monopoly Capital*, he included a generous tribute to the Polish economist (Baran and Sweezy, 1966

[1970], p. 66). The book was an elaboration on themes first developed in Sweezy's *Theory of Capitalist Development*. The 'giant corporation' was as ruthless a profit maximizer as the individual entrepreneur who dominated the earlier phase of US capitalism. Competition still occurred, but price wars had been replaced by increased product differentiation, faster product innovation and a more intense sales effort. Costs of production continued to fall, widening profit margins for the individual corporation and increasing the economic surplus at the macroeconomic level. This 'law of the rising surplus' was at the core of *Monopoly Capital*. The surplus could not be absorbed, Baran and Sweezy maintained, by growth in capitalist consumption or investment. Only increasing selling costs and massive military expenditure had prevented a recurrence of the Great Depression, and stagnation was the normal condition for monopoly capital (ibid., chs 5–7).

There was a third contributor to Left Keynesianism. Josef Steindl was an Austrian socialist refugee who, after being briefly interned as an enemy alien, worked for most of the war with Kalecki at the Oxford Institute, where he made important theoretical and empirical contributions to the analysis of the firm (Steindl, 1945). His masterpiece, though, was completed only after his return to Austria. In *Maturity and Stagnation in American Capitalism*, Steindl argued that the displacement of free competition by oligopoly, which had become apparent in many US manufacturing industries by the 1890s, had increased profit margins and reduced the degree of capacity utilization. High and increasing levels of excess capacity had discouraged investment expenditure, reducing the rate of growth of aggregate demand and further depressing capacity utilization (Steindl, 1952 [1976], pp. 131–7, 191–2; cf. Scitovsky, 1993). Significantly, Steindl concluded his book by linking his own theory to that of Karl Marx. Both emphasized 'the idea of a production of surplus value which is not realised'. Marx's 'underconsumption approach,' Steindl concluded, needed only to be supplemented by allowing for the effects of excess capacity on the rate of capital accumulation, so that Steindl's own analysis had deep Marxian roots (ibid., p. 246). When a second edition of *Maturity and Stagnation* appeared, in 1976, it was published, appropriately enough, by Sweezy's Monthly Review Press in New York. Steindl now claimed (like Baran and Sweezy) that prosperity had been maintained after 1945, and capacity utilization had remained high, only 'as a result of the heavy increase in public expenditure (mainly on arms)'. By 1976, however, it was clear that the postwar boom had ended. Unemployment was increasingly being used as a weapon against inflation, and 'thus we witness stagnation not as an incomprehensible fate, as in the 1930s, but stagnation as a policy' (ibid., pp. xii, xvii; cf. Steindl, 1990, pp. 107–26, 166–79).

It is most unlikely that Keynes would have agreed with the Left Keynesians. His dismissive attitude to Marx was noted in the previous chapter, and while some scholars regard him as some sort of socialist this is hotly contested (compare O'Donnell, 1999b, with Fitzgibbons, 1988, p. 188) There is evidence, too, that he became more rather than less conservative in the final years of his life (Skidelsky, 1998). The political implications of the *General Theory* had been contentious from the start. In the United States the book was regarded by many as a dangerous attack on the capitalist system, and a textbook as mild as Lorie Tarshis's *Elements of Economics* became the target of a ferocious campaign of proto-McCarthyist dimensions (see Chapter 5). Many Marxists, on the other hand, viewed Keynes with great suspicion. His avowed intention, after all, was to save capitalism from itself, and his continued endorsement of the 'first classical postulate' had led him to conclude that the restoration of full employment required cuts in real wages for those already in work. Keynes gave further hostages to fortune when he wrote, in the preface to the German edition of the *General Theory*, that the theory of output as a whole was more easily adapted to the conditions of a totalitarian economy than the traditional theory of price and distribution under free competition (see Schefold, 1980).

Thus some orthodox Marxists dismissed Keynes as an apologist for Fascism, while the future as it appeared to many others was also bleak. In *Nineteen Eighty-Four* George Orwell described the Left Keynesian vision with chilling clarity. Emmanuel Goldstein's political manifesto, 'The Theory and Practice of Oligarchical Collectivism', contains a chapter entitled 'War and Peace', in which the shadowy dissident leader argues:

> The primary aim of modern warfare … is to use up the products of the machine without raising the general standard of living. Ever since the end of the nineteenth century, the problem of what to do with the surplus of consumption goods has been latent in industrial society….
>
> The problem was how to keep the wheels of industry turning without increasing the real wealth of the world. Goods must be produced, but they must not be distributed. And in practice the only way of achieving this was by continuous warfare.
>
> The essential act of war is destruction, not necessarily of human lives, but of the products of human labour….
>
> War, it will be seen, not only accomplishes the necessary destruction, but accomplishes it in a psychologically acceptable way. In principle it would be quite simple to waste the surplus labour of the world by building temples and pyramids, by digging holes and filling them up again, or even by producing vast quantities of goods and then setting fire to them. But this would provide only the economic and not the emotional basis for a hierarchical society. (Orwell, 1949 [1980], pp. 855–6)

Orwell, it seemed, knew his Keynes.

A KALECKIAN SYNTHESIS?

In 1955 Kalecki returned to Poland, where possession of *Nineteen Eighty-Four* would have been a serious crime. His explanation of the continuing postwar prosperity, however, was in some ways similar to that of Emmanuel Goldstein. Continually increasing armaments expenditure, financed by budget deficits, offered the only effective means of overcoming the basic contradictions of capitalism. The obstacle – and here Kalecki parted company with Orwell's hero – was not economic but political. Dogmatic ideological opposition to government spending, even on weapons, had been responsible for the 1954 US recession. Even if a catastrophic crisis like that of 1929–35 was unlikely, Kalecki concluded, very slow growth and low rates of capacity utilization were inevitable (Kalecki, 1955). He never wavered in his bleak assessment of the prospects for contemporary capitalism (see Kalecki, 1962, and the conversation reported by Worswick, 1999, p. 285).

Kalecki had spent the previous eight years working for the Economic Department of the United Nations. Here he had employed much of his time analysing the problems of the Third World, and had begun to develop a distinctive approach to the economics of development that would profoundly influence Post Keynesian development theory in later decades (McFarlane, 1996). Back in Poland, his attention inevitably turned to the economics of socialism. Kalecki tried to steer a middle course between the grotesque excesses of the Stalinist super-industrializers and the equally excessive faith in the market mechanism exhibited by some economic reformers (Toporowski, 1996a). He continued to work, and publish, on the economic theory of advanced capitalism, without ever producing the treatise that might have represented a Kaleckian *General Theory*.

Already in 1954 he had published a third volume of essays, 'in lieu', as he explained in the Foreword, of a second edition of the 1939 *Essays* and the 1943 *Studies*. Kalecki set out his distribution theory in non-marginalist terms, with the algebra simplified; the 1954 version is the canonical exposition of his model. Subsequent chapters covered profits, investment, the rate of interest and the theory of the business cycle, and at the end of the book Kalecki introduced new material on erratic shocks in the cycle and on the analysis of economic growth. But *Theory of Economic Dynamics* 'covers the same ground as the previous two books and the basic ideas are not much changed,' though 'the presentation and even the argument have been substantially altered' (Kalecki, 1954 [1991], p. 207). Later papers dealt with growth theory and inflation, and he made yet another attempt to improve his analysis of investment and revise his business cycle model accordingly (Steindl, 1981; Sawyer, 1996). Kalecki's last article included trade union power in his distribution theory, via the impact of wage bargaining on mark-ups and hence on the degree of monopoly (Kalecki, 1971).

If there is no single source book for Kaleckian economics, a synthetic account could certainly be assembled from his many essays. Joan Robinson made several such attempts, formal and informal (Robinson, 1966, 1971b, 1977a; Bhaduri and Robinson, 1980). Soon after his death in 1970 book-length appraisals began to appear (Feiwel, 1975; Sawyer, 1985) and models of monopoly capitalism emerged that owed a great deal to his thinking (for example, Cowling, 1982). There is some controversy over the theoretical connection between Kalecki and the Left Keynesians. Thus Andrew Trigg argues that stagnationist models rest on an accelerator approach to investment, and a supposedly inexorable upward tendency in the non-wage share in aggregate income, that Kalecki himself had repudiated. The so-called 'Kaleckian' model, he maintains, 'is simply a hybrid of parts of Marshallian and Keynesian economics … it contradicts the fundamental tents of Kalecki's system' and thereby represents a 'bastardization' of his ideas (Trigg, 1994, p. 107).

It would be generally agreed, however, that, broadly speaking, the following properties must characterize any authentic Kaleckian model:

1. Economic theory must be realistic, in the sense that it must be directed towards the analysis of a capitalist economy in which the ownership of capital brings power in addition to income, and where the decisions of workers, consumers and households are of very limited significance.
2. Class conflict is a fundamental characteristic of capitalism, and capitalists especially display a highly developed sense of class consciousness. Any threat to their power provokes an immediate response. Political considerations may therefore be more important in explaining the dynamics of the business cycle than economic variables, narrowly defined.
3. There is no such thing as the long run, defined independently of the set of short periods which constitute it. The notion that neoclassical equilibrium analysis applies in such a long run is profoundly mistaken.
4. If there are 'microfoundations' for macroeconomics, there are also 'macrofoundations' for microeconomics. Pricing, distribution and investment will be determined quite differently in conditions of full employment and substantial excess capacity.
5. Free competition is a very special case, relevant only to agriculture. Industrial product markets are oligopolistic, and here prices are formed by the application of a mark-up to the variable costs of production, the size of this mark-up varying with the degree of monopoly.
6. The profit *share* in national income depends on the degree of monopoly, but the *level* of profits is determined in aggregate by capitalist investment

decisions, along with the size of the trade surplus (deficit) and the budget deficit (surplus).

7. Full employment is also a special case, and is most unlikely in peacetime unless the volume of military expenditure remains very high. In other words it is probable that private investment will be too low, and the profit share too high, for stagnation to be avoided without recourse to the 'military Keynesian' solution.

These propositions do not amount to a complete macroeconomic system, unlike the neoclassical synthesis. Methodologically, it can be argued, Kalecki's commitment to 'open-system thinking' prevented him from formulating a comprehensive, fully integrated and therefore closed model (see Chapter 9). It is certainly true that he himself remained dissatisfied until the end of his life with his investment equation and thus also with the formulation of his trade cycle model. And there are other lacunae. Discussion continues, for example, on the role of money in Kalecki's analysis, on his treatment of uncertainty, and on the even more fundamental question whether someone accustomed to writing down an equation whenever he tried to solve a problem could ever really escape the stultifying effects of orthodox economic methodology. We shall return to these questions in later chapters. First, though, we must explore the very Kaleckian theme of the 'tragedy of investment': that is, the long-term consequences of the accumulation of capital, which form the subject of the next chapter.

3. Generalizing *The General Theory*

> Keynes's *General Theory* smashed up the glass house of static theory in order to be able to discuss a real problem – the causes of unemployment. But his analysis was framed in terms of a short period in which the stock of capital and the technique of production are given. It left a huge area of long-run problems covered with fragments of broken glass from the static theory and gave only vague hints as to how the shattered structure could be rebuilt. (Robinson, 1956, p. v)

MR HARROD'S EQUATION

In this chapter I discuss the efforts of Keynes's Cambridge followers to extend his economics to the long period, and to create a Keynesian theory of distribution and growth. As far as possible I shall ignore questions of capital theory, which are the subject of the following chapter. There is inevitably some awkwardness in this, as the analysis of accumulation is inextricably linked with those arguments about the choice of techniques, the productivity of capital and the significance of aggregate production functions that came to the fore in the so-called 'Cambridge capital controversies' (Harcourt, 1969, 1972). The latter, however, really took shape only after the publication in 1960 of Piero Sraffa's *Production of Commodities by Means of Commodities*, while Cambridge growth theory was very largely a product of the 1950s. Indeed, concern with the issues dates back to 1936.

By its author's own admission, the *General Theory* dealt only with the short period (Keynes, 1936, p. 245; but see Milgate, 1983; Rogers, 1997). Two eminent reviewers soon took Keynes to task for his lack of concern with long-period analysis. A.C. Pigou criticized the glaring inconsistency (as he saw it) of assuming both positive net investment and an unchanging capital stock (Pigou, 1936, p. 122), while Joseph Schumpeter objected even more forcefully that Keynes's was 'the theory of another world'. Its static nature, Schumpeter complained, made a convincing treatment of investment quite impossible. By ignoring the innovative behaviour of entrepreneurs, Keynes 'eliminates the most powerful propeller of investment, the financing of changes in production functions', so that his account of investment decisions 'has hardly anything to do with the investment process in the actual world' (Schumpeter, 1936, pp. 693–4).

Criticisms similar to those of Pigou were also made, in private correspondence, by a much less orthodox economist. The veteran underconsumptionist J.A. Hobson had always argued that depression was the result of oversaving. In the final years of his life he revised his analysis to bring it closer to that of Keynes. The sequence of events, he wrote to Keynes shortly after the publication of the *General Theory*, was as follows. The rich obtained too large a share of national income, of which they saved an excessive proportion; this induced excessive investment, which gave rise to a capital stock that was too large, relative to the demand for consumption goods; the effect of this was a collapse in investment and a consequent decline in output and employment. In his reply, Keynes simply refused to consider the possibility of excessive investment (their 1936 correspondence is discussed by King, 1994c).

In effect Hobson's argument rests on the same accelerator principle, linking the level of investment to the rate of change in output, that underpins most underconsumption theories (Schneider, 1996, pp. 87–8). By arranging what he himself termed a 'marriage' of the accelerator and the multiplier, Roy Harrod took the first steps towards a generalization of the *General Theory* to the long period (Harrod, 1939, p. 16). His justly famous 1939 *Economic Journal* article was not, however, Harrod's first attempt to construct a dynamic macroeconomic model. Three years earlier, in his book *The Trade Cycle*, he had introduced the accelerator as 'The Relation', and his interests always centred on economic fluctuations rather than on growth theory *per se* (Harrod, 1936, pp. 53–65; Besomi, 1999).

Harrod began the 1939 article by asserting the need for the theorist to 'think dynamically', by which he meant 'the derivation of propositions in which a rate of growth appears as an unknown variable' (Harrod, 1939, pp. 15, 17). His 'Fundamental Equation' set the equilibrium or 'warranted' rate of growth of output in a one-commodity economy (G_w) equal to the average propensity to save (s) divided by 'the value of the capital goods required for the production of a unit increment of output', that is, the desired incremental capital–output ratio (C):

$$G_w = \frac{s}{C}. \tag{3.1}$$

In this equation 'The value of C depends on the state of technology and the nature of the goods constituting the increment of output. It may be expected to vary as income grows and in different phases of the trade cycle; it may be somewhat dependent on the rate of interest' (ibid., p. 17). Assume provisionally that C is constant. Then, in Harrod's own example, where 10 per cent of income is saved and the 'capital coefficient' per annum is equal to 4, the capital stock will grow at 2.5 per cent per annum and the warranted rate of growth of output will also equal 2.5 per cent. 'The warranted rate of growth,' he explained, 'is taken to be that rate of growth which, if it occurs, will leave all parties satisfied that they have produced neither more nor less than the right amount.' It is thus the equilibrium rate of growth, but Harrod preferred 'the unprofessional term warranted' to emphasize the 'highly unstable' nature of the moving equilibrium that he had established (ibid., pp. 16–17).

Consider the implications of a difference between the actual rate of growth (G) and the warranted rate. If output is excessive ($G > G_w$), the actual increase in the capital stock per unit of output (C_p) will fall below that which is desired (C). Entrepreneurs will therefore increase investment, and the resulting multiplier process will increase the rate of growth of actual output, further widening the gap between G and G_w:

> Similarly, if G falls below G_w, there will be a redundance of capital goods, and a depressing influence will be exerted; this will cause a further divergence and a still stronger depressing influence; and so on. Thus in the dynamic field we have a condition opposite to that which holds in the static field. A departure from equilibrium, instead of being self-righting, will be self-aggravating. G_w represents a moving equilibrium, but a highly unstable one. Of interest this for trade-cycle analysis! (Ibid., p. 22)

Now suppose that $G = G_w$, and there is an increase in the propensity to save. This will raise G_w, so that (with G now less than G_w) investment will fall and a cumulative decline in output will commence. Harrod's economy is precariously balanced on a knife-edge (though he himself disliked the term).

A further complication results from recognizing the existence of a maximum or 'natural' rate of growth, subsequently denoted as G_n, which is equal to the growth rate of the labour supply plus the rate of (neutral) technical progress. There is no reason, Harrod argued, why the natural and warranted rates of growth should coincide, and even fewer grounds for expecting full employment of labour to be maintained:

> Consideration may be given to that warranted rate which would obtain in conditions of full employment; this may be regarded as the warranted rate 'proper' to the economy. *Prima facie* it might be supposed healthier to have the 'proper' warranted rate above than below the natural rate. But this is very doubtful.
>
> The system cannot advance more quickly than the natural rate allows. If the proper warranted rate is above this, there will be a chronic tendency to depression; the depressions drag down the warranted rate below its proper level, and so keep its average value over a term of years down to the natural rate. But this reduction of the warranted rate is only achieved by having chronic unemployment. (Ibid., p. 30)

Conversely, if $G_w < G_n$, the warranted rate may be 'twisted upwards by an inflation of prices and profit', since entrepreneurs will be attempting to raise output faster than the capacity of the economy is able to grow.

So much for the theory. What were the prospects for stability in an actual capitalist economy? The accelerator mechanism may be somewhat weakened, Harrod noted, by the existence of a substantial level of autonomous investment, not related to the current level or rate of change of income. Monetary policy might help, since a low rate of interest would increase C and might also reduce s. 'It is not suggested, however, that a low rate of interest has sufficient power of its own to keep down the warranted rate without the assistance of a programme of public works to be kept permanently in operation.' Even this might not be adequate to offset the effects of the 'relatively high' warranted rate and the resulting tendency for the system 'to relapse into depression before full employment is reached in a boom' (ibid., pp. 26–7, 32, 33). Stagnation might therefore be the normal state for mature capitalism.

EARLY REACTIONS TO HARROD

Joan Robinson had already begun to worry about these questions before Harrod published his seminal article (Eatwell, 1983; Kregel, 1991). One of her 1935 essays dealt with the theory of employment in the long period, where the equilibrium level of output is that corresponding to zero net saving and a constant capital stock. A reduction in the rate of interest will increase investment and raise effective demand. 'As soon as we overstep the narrowest boundary of the short period,' however, there is also a negative effect. Investment adds to the stock of capital, reducing its marginal efficiency and lowering the inducement to invest in subsequent periods. The net effect on equilibrium output in the long run is unclear (Robinson, 1937a, p. 80). There is a further complication affecting the level of employment, since the lower interest rate will induce an increase in the capital–labour ratio. Robinson dealt with this in an essentially neoclassical way; the use of more 'roundabout' methods of production increases the marginal product of labour, raises real wages and alters the relative income shares of workers and capitalists. Then she introduced a classical savings function: 'the capitalists, in short, are much richer individuals than the workers, and are consequently more addicted to saving. It follows that any change in distribution which increases the share of labour in a given total income will reduce the amount of saving corresponding to that level of income' (ibid., p. 82; cf. ibid., p. 15). Thus the impact of a decline in the rate of interest on saving, and hence on income, depends on the technical conditions of production. If (plausibly) the elasticity of substitution between capital and labour is close to unity, so that the relative shares of capital and labour are approximately constant, a cut in the interest rate will tend to reduce employment because of the resulting increase in the capital–labour ratio (ibid., p. 86).

This part of Robinson's essay was a tantalizing mixture of neoclassical orthodoxy and macrodistributional heresy, the latter resembling the contemporary views of Michal Kalecki and anticipating the much later work of Nicholas Kaldor. Heterodoxy won, with her forceful denial that unemployment was inconsistent with long-period equilibrium. Any resulting fall in money wages, Robinson argued, could increase employment only through the reduced transactions demand for money, which would lower the rate of interest. But this, as we have seen, may *reduce* employment, setting off a downward spiral in output and the price level:

> In a community with perfectly plastic money wages the level of prices may be always moving toward zero without setting up any tendency permanently to reverse the situation which is causing prices to fall. It is thus impossible to argue that there is any self-righting mechanism in the economic system which makes the existence of unemployment impossible, even in the longest of runs. (Ibid., p. 87)

Robinson did not attempt any formal modelling to support these conclusions, offering instead a handful of discursive footnotes indicating how the analysis might be represented diagramatically (but she did not provide the diagrams). One described a backward-bending curve 'connecting the rate of interest with the equilibrium level of employment', which I have drawn as Figure 3.1. Robinson noted that the maximum level of employment might fall well short

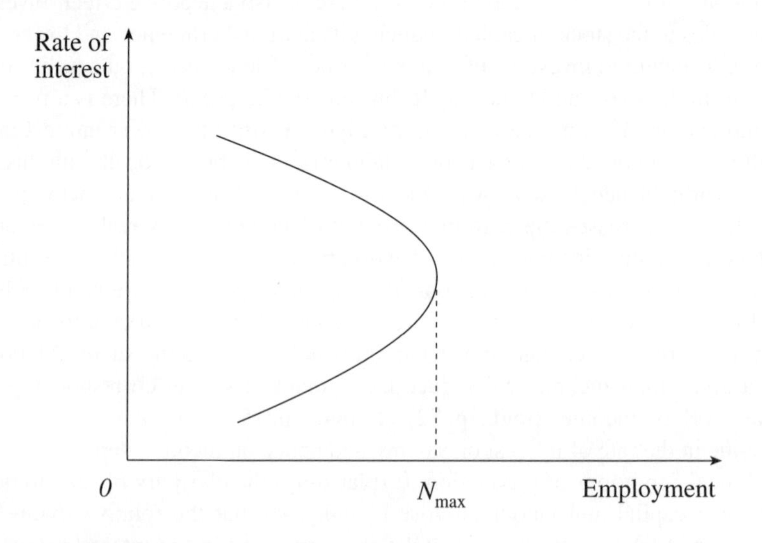

Source: Derived from Robinson (1937a, p. 91 n1).

Figure 3.1

of full employment, and that considerably more bizarre cases than that shown in the figure were entirely possible (ibid., p. 91, nn1 and 2; cf. King, 1996b, pp. 174–5).

Robinson and Harrod were not personally close, and they seem not to have corresponded on issues of economic dynamics. They reviewed each other's books with courtesy but without enthusiasm (Robinson, 1936; Harrod, 1937b). Robinson herself made little progress in the area for more than a decade. Soon after the essay on the long period appeared she published a brief article on the classification of technical change (Robinson, 1938a). Later, in her *Essay on Marxian Economics*, she contrasted Keynes's pathbreaking work on the theory of short-period fluctuations with the continuing neglect of the long period:

> Marx was mainly concerned with long-run dynamic analysis, and this field is still largely untilled. Orthodox academic analysis, bound up with the concept of equilibrium, makes little contribution to it, and the modern theory has not yet gone much beyond the confines of the short period. Changes over the long run in real wages and in the rate of profit, the progress of capital accumulation, the growth and decay of monopoly and the large-scale reactions of changes in technique upon the class structure of society all belong to this field. (Robinson, 1942, p. 95)

Almost a calculated slight to Harrod, this was the penultimate paragraph of the book. It was a statement of intent, not a summary of achievement.

The Cambridge oral tradition has it that Robinson turned her attention to economic dynamics during the wet summer of 1948, when the intended climbs on Alpine peaks were replaced by long discussions in damp valleys with her companions Richard Kahn and Piero Sraffa (Harcourt, 1995a, p. 41). At all events, the occasion for her first systematic foray into growth theory was an extended review of Harrod's lectures, *Towards a Dynamic Economics*, which were published in that year (Harrod, 1948). Her exposition of his analysis was broadly favourable. Harrod quite rightly denied that 'there is any natural tendency for thriftiness to adjust itself to capital requirements' (Robinson, 1949, p. 72) and gave short shrift to orthodox arguments involving interest rate movements and reductions in money wages. When Robinson examined the implications of a natural rate of growth that exceeds the warranted rate, a strong Marxian influence was evident in her thinking. It created a situation, she explained, in which

> the amount of employment associated with a given stock of capital is continually falling as technical progress takes place, so that there will be a progressive increase in unemployment...This is a kind of unemployment which is not contemplated in the General Theory. It may be appropriately called Marxian unemployment (as opposed to Keynesian unemployment, which is due to deficiency of effective demand). For though nothing is farther from his thoughts, Mr. Harrod has led us

> to Marx's theory of the reserve army of labour, which expands and contracts as the growth of population runs faster or slower than the rate of capital accumulation. (Ibid., p. 81)

This case of inadequate productive capacity reflected 'the situation of overpopulated, backward countries'. In advanced economies the problem was one of excess capacity, which 'may emerge if investment is maintained for a time above the rate required for steady progress with full employment'. Harrod had exposed 'the Hobsonesque limit upon accumulation' (ibid., p. 82), which generated chronic unemployment and secular stagnation: 'The analysis seems to bear a close resemblance to Hobson's thesis that saving causes crisis because there is no outlet in consumer demand for the goods which the new capital equipment produces. Mr. Harrod's analysis provides the missing link between Keynes and Hobson' (ibid., p. 80). Harrod took the point, contributing a sympathetic introduction to the (posthumous) fourth edition of Hobson's *Science of Wealth* (Harrod, 1950).

Robinson complained, however, that Harrod's 'ingenious and instructive manipulation of his three *G*'s' (Robinson, 1949, p. 83) was far removed from reality. She raised four objections, three of which would become recurrent themes in her own writings on growth. Her first criticism was that Harrod neglected the influence on the propensity to save of the distribution of income and wealth:

> It can be plausibly argued that the phenomenon of excessive thriftiness is a product of excessive inequality, and that measures to correct inequality, which may be advocated on their own political or humanitarian merits, would, as a by-product, permanently reverse the position, and make deficient thriftiness the normal rule. There seems very little point in discussing artificial measures for absorbing excessive savings until this great question has been argued out. (Ibid., pp. 83–4)

Second, although Harrod's perspective was a dynamic one, his 'is a world without history. Every change that took place in the past was digested, so to speak, as it occurred. Time rolls on in a homogeneous stream, and it makes no difference at what point we dip into it' (ibid., p. 69). It was thus a world with no war damage to be repaired (in 1948!), no Marxian unemployment to be countered, no dustbowls to be rehabilitated or scientific discoveries to be embodied in new capital equipment. 'In short, Mr. Harrod's world must not be confused with Europe, Asia or America.' Third, Harrod assumed that all 'worthy enterprises' could obtain the necessary finance, whereas in fact 'There is no knowing how much potential investment, which would provide a genuinely useful outlet for saving, is now held up by the imperfections of the capital market' (ibid., p. 84). Finally Robinson took issue with Harrod's treatment of technical change, which in his model 'falls like the gentle dew from heaven'. But new techniques must be embodied in new equipment;

productivity growth is constrained by the existence of great numbers of 'relatively backward' producers; and scientific knowledge is 'not just like the weather, but is susceptible to being directed and speeded up'. 'In short,' she concluded, 'Mr. Harrod's G_n is not a natural datum, but an object for policy and organisation', and therefore likely to vary with the actual rate of growth (ibid., p. 85). Many of these insights were developed further in Robinson's *Accumulation of Capital*, as we shall see in the next section.

Nicholas Kaldor had already made significant contributions to the theory of the trade cycle (Kaldor, 1938, 1939b, 1940). He did not, however, confront Harrod's analysis of economic growth. In 1940 the activities of the London School of Economics were transferred to Cambridge for the duration of the war, so that Kaldor and Robinson became neighbours. Very soon they were close friends. They were both active participants in the wartime debate over postwar reconstruction, during which Kaldor was an important influence on the Beveridge report on full employment. He developed a taste for involvement as a policy adviser, which he indulged first as an international civil servant and then, after his return to Cambridge in 1950 as Fellow of King's College, as a member of the Royal Commission on the Taxation of Profits and Income (Thirlwall, 1987, pp. 90–95, 113–29).

Not until 1954 did he return to the theory of economic dynamics with a major, if rather speculative, article on the relationship between economic growth and the trade cycle. Kaldor noted that the cycle theories developed after the publication of the *General Theory* – and here he included his own 1940 effort – had severed any connection between cycles and growth by modelling 'a perpetual oscillation around a stationary equilibrium position' (Kaldor, 1954, p. 54). These early, 'purely "static"' models, he continued, had been improved by the insertion in later variants of a long-term growth rate, but this merely involved 'the superimposition of a linear trend introduced from the outside on an otherwise trendless model without altering, in any way, its basic character' (ibid., pp. 56, 63). The central reason, Kaldor maintained, why 'some human societies progress so much faster than others' can be traced back to 'human attitudes to risk-taking and money-making' (ibid., p. 67). Thus the Schumpeterian entrepreneur was the crucial missing link between cycle and trend:

> The same forces therefore which produce violent booms and slumps will also tend to produce a high trend-rate of progress ... And Schumpeter's hero, the 'innovating entrepreneur', whom we dismissed so summarily and rather contemptuously at the beginning, is found, after all, to have an honourable place, or even a key role, in the drama – even though we prefer to endow him with a rather more variegated character. He is a promoter, a speculator, a gambler, the purveyor of economic expansion generally, and not just of the 'new' techniques of production. (Ibid., pp. 70–71)

Kaldor was careful to acknowledge that the precise relationship between cyclical fluctuations and long-term growth 'is far too complex to be reducible (at present) to a simple mechanical model'. This, too, was a declaration of intent.

THE ACCUMULATION OF CAPITAL

Unlike Kaldor, Robinson had remained in academic life throughout the post-war period, and was less involved in public debate than she had been previously. She was working away at what she intended to be her masterpiece, a systematic treatise on Keynesian theory in the long run. Her book was published in 1956, 20 years after the *General Theory*; its author was 53, the same age as Keynes had been in 1936. Five years earlier she had written an introduction to the English translation of Rosa Luxemburg's *Accumulation of Capital* (Robinson, 1951a), and now she took over Luxemburg's title. Robinson's own *Accumulation of Capital* ran to 435 pages; there was no mathematics, and the 14 diagrams were safely quarantined in an appendix. It was elegantly written, without the staccato brusqueness that disfigured much of her later work. It was also very tightly argued and rather austerely presented. After making generous acknowledgments in the preface, Robinson offered the reader very few signposts to the literature in the body of her text; doctrinal questions were largely confined to a series of 'Notes' at the end.

The core of the argument was set out in Chapters 7–9, where Robinson developed a model of a two-class, two-sector economy with no choice of technique. For profits to exist, it was necessary that workers produce a surplus of output over the consumption requirements of their families. On the assumption that workers do not save, and entrepreneurs do not consume, the rate of profit was then equal to the rate of growth of output. There was a strong Marxian flavour to this, and Robinson's discussion of the relationship between the investment-goods and consumption-goods sectors also came from volume II of *Capital*, via Kalecki and her own reading of Rosa Luxemburg. The possibility of growth was partly a technical matter and partly a question of social institutions and political power. A surplus would be produced only if real wages were held down, for example by the existence of a reserve army of labour in an adjacent peasant farming sector (Robinson, 1956, p. 73). Otherwise growth would run into an 'inflation barrier' resulting from the 'head-on conflict between the desire of entrepreneurs to invest and the refusal of the system to accept the level of real wages which the investment entails; something must give way. Either the system explodes in a hyper-inflation, or some check operates to curtail investment' (ibid., p. 48). The height of this inflation barrier depended on 'the level of real wages that the workers are willing to accept and able to enforce' (ibid., pp. 83–4). Normally, however, it operated 'only in conditions of full employment' (ibid., p. 49). More generally, in the absence of technical progress the rate of growth of the labour force sets a maximum to the possible rate of accumulation. 'When accumulation fails to reach this rate there is growth of long-period unemployment' (ibid., p. 84).

In Chapter 9 Robinson allowed for technical progress, but on the very restrictive assumptions that there was at any time a single dominant technique of production in each sector, and that labour productivity grew at the same rate in both branches. The outcome was steady-state growth (she termed it 'stability' or 'smooth development'), in which productive capacity increased at the same rate as output per head, the employment rate was constant, and the relative size of the two sectors was unchanged. This state of affairs, Robinson argued, was extremely precarious. She identified four reasons why the conditions for stable growth might break down. First, the rate of technical progress might alter unexpectedly. Although in this case 'there is a path which it is possible for the economy to follow to a new line of smooth development ... there is no mechanism provided by the capitalist rules of the game that can be relied upon to steer the economy on to the appropriate course' (ibid., pp. 91–2). A prolonged slump or an inflationary boom were more likely. The second problem was posed by 'under-consumption': if real wages remained constant while labour productivity grew, consumption demand would stagnate, excess capacity would emerge and employment would decline. 'The main defence against the tendency to stagnation comes from pressure by trade unions to raise money-wage rates', so that (ironically) 'the most progressive entrepreneurs become the allies of the trade unions' (ibid., p. 94). Third, there was no guarantee that the accumulation of capital would take place at exactly the required rate. In the case of 'weak accumulation', where the capital stock grew less rapidly than output per head, employment would fall and 'technological unemployment' would ensue. In the converse situation, 'strong accumulation' would force the economy out towards its inflation barrier. This was to be preferred, Robinson suggested, since the pressure on profitability of rising real wages was likely to induce more rapid technical progress (ibid., pp. 94–6). But – and this was the fourth source of difficulty – any bias in technical change would create problems of its own (ibid., pp. 97–8).

If all these problems were overcome there would be 'no internal contradiction in the system'. In the resulting 'golden age', technical progress is neutral and proceeding steadily; accumulation is just fast enough to provide productive capacity for all the available labour; real wages rise at the same speed as productivity; and the rate of profit on capital is constant. Robinson did not wish this to be taken as a description of capitalist reality. On the contrary, she used the term 'golden age' to indicate that 'it represents a mythical state of affairs not likely to obtain in any actual economy'. If technical progress and population growth are exogenously determined, the golden age does, however, correspond to 'a state of economic bliss, since consumption is then increasing at the maximum technically feasible rate' (ibid., p. 99). In Harrod's terminology, the natural, warranted and actual growth rates are all equal (ibid., p. 99, n1); significantly, this is the only reference to Harrod in the first 207 pages of the book. But 'technical progress is not a natural phenomenon, and there is no limit to human ingenuity'. Hence there is nothing 'natural' about a golden age. Productivity growth is endogenous, and 'The limit to the rate of growth of wealth, over the long run, is set not by technical boundaries but by the lethargy which develops when the goad of competition and rising wage rates is blunted' (ibid., pp. 99–100).

All this was set out in a mere 38 pages, on the provisional assumption that entrepreneurs faced no choice of technique. The next 72 pages of the *Accumulation of Capital* (Chapters 10–17) dealt with the 'technical frontier', which was at first unchanging and then allowed to shift as a result of innovation. Discussion of this part of the book is deferred to Chapter 4 below, since important questions of capital theory are involved and Robinson soon came to change her mind under the profound influence of Piero Sraffa's *Production of Commodities by Means of Commodities* (Sraffa, 1960). Her rejection of Harrod's knife-edge was largely, though not entirely, independent of the choice of technique. She stated it explicitly not in Chapter 9 but in one of the 'Notes on various topics' that were collected together at the end of the book. 'Our analysis of accumulation in the long run,' Robinson writes, 'is largely an elaboration of R.F. Harrod's model, yet we have nowhere come across his central problem. It is interesting to enquire why this should be so' (1956, p. 404). The difference between her model and Harrod's, she suggested, was to be found in their treatment of the savings ratio. For Robinson the ratio of saving to income depended on the distribution of income between profits and wages. Given that the propensity to save out of profits is (much) greater than that out of wages, 'a higher share of wages, which entails a lower share of profit, in total income means a higher proportion of total consumption to total income'. Thus, she concluded, 'there is a possible golden age corresponding to any combination of propensities to save with technical conditions'. In Harrodian language, 'we have had no trouble from a warranted rate independently determined', since 'In a golden age the actual rate of growth and the natural rate of growth are equal to each other, and the warranted rate of growth has accommodated itself to them'. In fact the 'important distinction is that between the *actual* and the *natural* rate of growth' (ibid., pp. 405–6).

This was not, perhaps, always as clearly expressed as it might have been; it should certainly have come in the body of the text and not have been hidden away at the back of the book. Robinson further muddied the waters by alluding to another way in which Harrod's instability problem might be overcome. 'A higher real-wage rate entails a higher degree of mechanisation,' she claimed, so that the Harrodian capital coefficient ('the ratio of income to capital') was also variable (ibid., p. 406). Capital–labour substitution was of course to form the theoretical basis for the neoclassical solution to Harrod's problem; unknown to Robinson, Robert Solow was already working on a seminal article in this vein (Solow, 1956). Within a few years it was apparent that there were two ways of overcoming the knife-edge: the Cambridge (England) principle of variable relative shares and a flexible average savings ratio, and the Cambridge (Mass.) analysis of a variable capital–output ratio with continuous substitution along a smooth neoclassical production function (see, for example, Hahn and Matthews, 1964, pp. 783–801). In 1956, however, these battle lines had yet to be drawn.

ALTERNATIVE THEORIES OF DISTRIBUTION

Late in October 1955, when *The Accumulation of Capital* was already in press, Nicholas Kaldor presented a paper on 'Alternative Theories of Distribution' to the famous 'secret seminar' in Cambridge. (In fact there was nothing particularly secret about the seminar, which was organized by Robinson and Kahn on a 'by invitation only' basis.) Kaldor's paper had been written in a very great hurry while he was preparing to depart (on a year's sabbatical leave) for a world tour that would take him to India, China, Latin America and the United States. As Robinson reported somewhat sardonically to Richard Kahn, himself exiled to Switzerland for a year:

> We had Nicky at [*sic*] Tuesday. His aim was to get his own theory clear before reading mine. It was quite a good evening but he was a bit disappointed that he has not got any further. He set out to find a theory of the constant relative shares and after going after Ricardo, Walras, etc. (this was quite fun) came down for the Widow's Cruse theory that given p-to-consume out of wages and profits each separately the shares are determined by the rate of investment. But when about 11.15 I asked him how he got the share of investment constant he did not seem to have any views. I fear it will be a long time yet before he has 'figured out' enough for it to be possible to argue about the fine points. Meanwhile I amuse myself explaining it to the research students...The general view seems to be that Nicky hadn't much to say that wasn't obvious.[1]

Nevertheless, the published version was to become one of the most frequently cited articles in the entire Post Keynesian literature (Kaldor, 1956; cf. Targetti, 1992, pp. 143–59). It began with a lucid critical exposition of classical and neoclassical distribution theory and culminated in Kaldor's own, justly celebrated, macroeconomic model of relative income shares. He rejected Kalecki's 'degree of monopoly' theory of distribution as tautological or, if reformulated to avoid this charge, as too vague to be helpful. His own, 'Keynesian', theory began with the surprisingly unKeynesian assumption of full employment. Kaldor distinguished two broad categories of income, wages and profits, which accrued to two classes of income recipients with different (but constant) savings propensities. Thus

$$Y = W + P, \tag{3.2}$$

and

$$S = S_w + S_p = s_w W + s_p P, \tag{3.3}$$

where $s_w < s_p$. The fundamental condition for macroeconomic equilibrium, that planned investment equals planned savings, can then be written as

$$I = s_p P + s_w W. \tag{3.4}$$

Dividing both sides by the full employment level of income, Y, and rearranging terms, we have:

$$\frac{P}{Y} = \frac{1}{s_p - s_w} \cdot \frac{I}{Y} - \frac{s_w}{(s_w - s_p)}. \tag{3.5}$$

Equation (3.5) reveals the profit share to be a function of s_p and s_w and of the ratio of investment to income, which Kaldor treated as 'an independent variable, invariant with respect to changes in the two savings propensities'. If s_w and s_p are constants, the profit share is thus a direct function of the investment ratio: 'a rise in investment, and thus in total demand, will raise prices and profit margins, and thus reduce real consumption, whilst a fall in investment, and thus in total demand, causes a fall in prices (relatively to the wage level) and thereby generates a compensating rise in real consumption' (Kaldor, 1956, p. 95). In the special case where workers do not save, so that $s_w = 0$, equation (3.5) can be simplified to

$$\frac{P}{Y} = \frac{1}{s_p} \cdot \frac{I}{Y}, \tag{3.6}$$

which corresponds in general terms to the Kaleckian proposition that 'capitalists earn what they spend, and workers spend what they earn' (ibid., p. 96; see Chapter 2 of the present volume).

Kaldor continued by relating his analysis to the Harrod growth model. His argument was rather obscure, but the basic message was very simple. The Harrodian knife-edge was a chimera. Since the aggregate savings ratio was a variable, not a constant, 'the "warranted" and the "natural" rates of growth are not independent of one another; if profit margins are flexible, the former will adjust itself to the latter through a consequential change in P/Y' (ibid., p. 97). This, it will be recalled, is precisely the conclusion that Robinson had reached in her *Accumulation of Capital*. Kaldor diverged sharply from Robinson's analysis, however, in his discussion of the likelihood of full employment. She regarded the 'golden age' as at best a useful pedagogic device, while he believed that it was actually attainable, provided only that the profit share was sufficiently flexible. The profit share might be constrained from above, for example, by the subsistence wage needs of the workers, or from below by the minimum profit requirements of the capitalists. If these constraints are not binding, Kaldor concluded, 'there will be an inherent tendency to growth and an inherent tendency to full employment'. Indeed, ' a tendency to continued economic growth will only exist when the system is only stable at full employment equilibrium', as appeared actually to be the case, in the long run, in 'the "successful" capitalist economies of Western Europe and North America' (ibid., p. 99).

This macrodistribution model was not original to Kaldor. As he acknowledged, it can be traced back to the 'widow's cruse' analogy in Keynes's *Treatise on Money* and to passages in Michal Kalecki's work (Kaldor, 1956, p. 94, n3; cf. Keynes, 1930, I, p. 129; Kalecki, 1942). Other forerunners include Maurice Dobb (1929) and – arguably – the early nineteenth-century classical analysts of 'forced saving' (Hayek, 1932). Kaldor himself had already published a popular version of the model in an entry for *Chambers' Encyclopaedia* (Kaldor, 1950), and similar models were proposed by his contemporaries Kenneth Boulding (1950) and Frank Hahn (1951). What was new, in the 1956 version, was the clarity of the argument, the use of algebra, and the sheer effrontery of the exposition. 'I am not sure,' Kaldor wrote in what must have been a deliberately provocative conclusion, 'where "marginal productivity" comes in in all this' (Kaldor, 1956, p. 100). At least Robinson had shown some respect for her elders; evidently Kaldor had none.

There were some serious substantive problems, however. Kaldor's discussion of the Harrod growth equations left a lot to be desired, and his treatment of the necessary conditions for stable growth was much less methodical and systematic than Robinson's. This prompted sustained and sometimes vitriolic criticism from her and (even more so) from Richard Kahn (King, 1998c). Kaldor's profoundly unKeynesian argument for the necessity of full employment convinced almost no-one; it was soon satirized by his neoclassical opponents, who took to describing him as 'Jean-Baptiste Kaldor' (Samuelson,

1964, p. 345). Equation (3.5) poses another, very obvious, problem. If workers save, they acquire property; this must be presumed to yield them an income; but then their savings will exceed *swW*, so that equation (3.3) is incorrect.

This difficulty was soon resolved by Luigi Pasinetti, who had graduated from the Catholic University of Milan and done graduate work at Cambridge and Harvard before taking up appointments first at Nuffield College, Oxford and then, for 15 years from 1961, at King's College, Cambridge. In 1976 Pasinetti returned permanently to the Catholic University of Milan. In his article on macrodistribution theory he demonstrated that the workers' propensity to save was irrelevant to the Kaldorian model. Pasinetti's analysis revealed that the profit share was in all cases determined by the capitalists' propensity to save and the share of investment, so that Kalecki's aphorism applied even if $s_w > 0$. He began by replacing equation (3.3) with

$$S = S_w + S_c = s_{ww}W + s_{pw}P_w + s_cP_c. \tag{3.7}$$

Here Kaldor's *p*-subscript has also been replaced by *c*, P_w and P_c are workers' and capitalists' profits, respectively, and s_{ww} and s_{pw} are the *two* workers' savings propensities, reflecting their savings out of their wages and their property incomes. It is assumed that $0 < s_{ww} < s_{pw} < s_c < 1$. In steady-state growth, workers' and capitalists' capital (K_w and K_c, respectively) grow at the same rate (g), so that

$$s_{ww}W + s_{pw}P_w = gK_w \tag{3.8}$$

and

$$s_cP_c = gK_c. \tag{3.9}$$

Since

$$P_c = rK_c, \tag{3.10}$$

it follows from equation (3.9) that

$$r = \frac{g}{s_c}, \tag{3.11}$$

which Pasinetti referred to as the 'Cambridge equation': the rate of profit is equal to the growth rate, divided by the capitalists' propensity to save. Neither of the two workers' savings propensities features in equation (3.11). Its corollary is equation (3.6), with the previously noted change in subscript: this simple equation for the profit share applies generally, not merely to the special case where workers do not save (Pasinetti, 1962; Kurz and Salvadori, 1995, ch. 15).

The 'Pasinetti theorem' proved to be remarkably robust, surviving the introduction of government and overseas sectors and of a rate of interest below the rate of profit (Panico and Salvadori, 1993). Kaldor's subsequent 'neo-Pasinetti theorem' adapted the model to a corporate economy, with the distinction between firms and households replacing that between workers and capitalists (Kaldor, 1966b). This, in turn, inspired important work on the relationship between corporate investment plans and pricing behaviour, which is discussed in Chapter 6 below (Eichner, 1973; Harcourt and Kenyon, 1976; Wood, 1975). Amid all this apparent success, however, the limitations of the Kaldor–Pasinetti model should not be overlooked. It works only in a Robinsonian golden age, where steady-state growth occurs under conditions of sustained full employment. Its relevance to the real world of 'actually existing capitalism' is therefore somewhat doubtful.

AFTER 1956

Critical reaction to Robinson's *Accumulation of Capital* was muted. It was reviewed in the major British and US journals but seems to have been little read. In the *Economic Journal* the econometrician Tibor Barna praised the realism of Robinson's work: she 'manages to keep both feet on the ground', so that 'her simplifications are precisely those which emphasise the characteristics of our modern economy'. Her stress on technical progress was in marked and welcome contrast to the neoclassical focus on the static choice of techniques, and the entire analysis lent itself to empirical verification (Barna, 1957, pp. 490, 493). The (mainly) neoclassical theorist Abba Lerner, writing in the *American Economic Review*, was much less complimentary. The book was full of errors and confusions, Lerner complained, and did little to advance the subject. Possibly this was not entirely Robinson's fault: 'Reading this book does not alter one's previous feeling that there is not really very much that economics can tell us about the accumulation of capital' (Lerner, 1957, p. 694).

Robinson herself later identified two 'outright errors' in the *Accumulation of Capital*, neither of them disastrous. She admitted that the book had been found very difficult, owing largely to the terseness of the exposition of its principal arguments, especially in the crucial Chapter 8 (Robinson, 1962a, pp. v–vi). At Kaldor's suggestion her partner Richard Kahn attempted to summarize the core analysis in a short article (Kahn, 1959), but this, too, was very heavy going. Robinson's own *Essays in the Theory of Economic Growth* were intended as an accessible introduction to her ideas. Three of the papers, on 'normal prices', technical progress and optimal growth, were reprints of journal articles, the latter including a (very) little Kaldorian algebra (Robinson, 1962a, pp. 121, 124–5). The remaining essay, 'A Model of Accumulation', contained an illustration of the relation between actual and desired accumulation in the form of the so-called 'banana diagram' (Figure 3.2). Here the *A* curve shows the expected rate of profit as a function of the rate of accumulation that generates it; in effect it depicts the Kaleckian proposition that capitalists earn what they spend. The *I* line shows the rate of profit that is required to induce each rate of accumulation. Above *D* accumulation is too fast to satisfy firms' profit requirements, and they will tend to scale down their investment plans. Between *S* and *D* the rate of accumulation is too low, and firms will plan to increase it. Below *S*, 'the economy has fallen below its stalling speed and is heading toward even greater ruin and decay than it now suffers' (ibid., p. 49). Thus Harrod's warranted rate of growth is represented by point *D* in Figure 3.2.

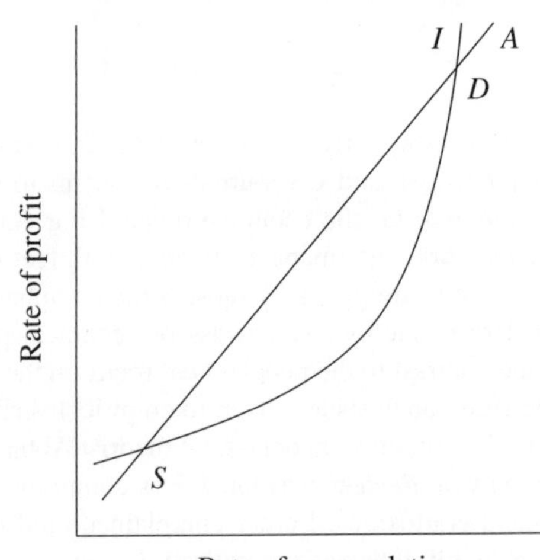

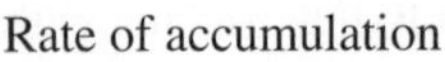

Source: Robinson (1962a, p. 48).

Figure 3.2

If this rate of accumulation is actually achieved, and if it has been operating for some time, so that the structure of the capital stock is completely adjusted to entrepreneurs' requirements, a state of 'tranquillity' will prevail. She had described it in the *Accumulation of Capital*:

> We may speak of an economy in a state of *tranquillity* when it develops in a smooth regular manner without internal contradictions or external shocks, so that expectations based on past experience are very confidently held, and are in fact constantly fulfilled and therefore renewed as time goes by. In a state of perfect tranquillity the prices ruling to-day, in every market, are those which were expected to rule to-day where any relevant decisions were taken in the past; the quantities of goods being sold, costs, profits and all relevant characteristics of the situation are turning out according to expectations; and the expectations being held to-day about the future are those that were expected in the past to be held to-day. A state of tranquillity corresponds to the position of a balance which has long since got over wobbling, and is not liable to have its weights changed for some time. (Robinson, 1956, p. 59)

Even then, full employment of labour is not guaranteed. The *Essays* contained a taxonomy of 'golden', 'platinum' and 'bastard' ages of growth, in effect providing a summary of the various logical possibilities in the relationship between the actual, warranted and natural rates of growth (though again Robinson stubbornly refused to use Harrod's terminology). In the various golden ages there is steady growth, but full employment is normally unattainable because of deficient animal spirits (the 'limping golden age'), a maximum growth rate that is too low ('the restrained golden age') or the inflation barrier (the 'bastard golden age'). In the various platinum ages steady growth itself is precluded by unsuitable initial conditions: the capital stock is either above or below that desired by entrepreneurs, so that the actual growth rate is either increasing or decreasing rather than steady over time. Full employment may, or may not, eventuate (Robinson, 1962a, pp. 51–9).

The *Essays* made no more impact than the *Accumulation of Capital* had done. Robinson soon lost patience with abstract growth theory and turned her attention to more practical questions of economic development, above all in the context of Maoist China (see, for example, Robinson, 1969). Contrary to Barna's expectations, her theoretical work did not lend itself to empirical investigation, and it had no obvious policy applications. Her analysis of growth was entirely non-mathematical, and this alone was probably enough to isolate her in an economics profession more and more dominated by mathematical modelling. Robinson may well have had logic on her side, but increasingly it was technique that counted.

Nicholas Kaldor was also no formalist (he had actually failed mathematics as a student at the London School of Economics). Unlike Robinson, however, he never attempted to make a virtue out of necessity and was prepared to accept technical assistance on occasion (Kaldor and Mirrlees, 1962). Also unlike Robinson, Kaldor made his principal contributions to the analysis of economic growth after 1956, not before. Beginning in 1957, in fact, a stream of papers flowed from his pen, with a series of loosely-related growth models, more or less rigorously formulated. Kaldor was less single-minded than

Robinson in his pursuit of a single, coherent and comprehensive model of economic growth. 'Kaldor's views have undergone a number of changes,' it was noted sardonically in 1964, 'and there is reason to believe that they have not yet attained their steady state' (Hahn and Matthews, 1964, p. 797). If he was much less meticulous than Robinson, it could be argued that he was also a more creative thinker.

In the 1957, 'Mark I', model (Kaldor, 1986a, p. 20), his starting-point was empirical, not analytical. Any satisfactory growth model, he argued, must be able to account for 'the remarkable historical constancies revealed by recent empirical investigations'. These included constant shares of wages and profits in national income, a constant capital–output ratio, and a constant rate of profit (Kaldor, 1957b, pp. 591–2). Kaldor's model differed from that of Harrod in two important respects. He assumed full employment, not as a 'stylized fact' but as a matter of theoretical necessity, and claimed that 'A state of Keynesian under-employment equilibrium, whilst it is perfectly consistent with a static short-period equilibrium, is therefore inconsistent (except by a fluke) with a dynamic equilibrium of steady growth' (ibid., p. 594). Kaldor's model also 'eschews any distinction between changes in techniques (and in productivity) which are induced by changes in the supply of capital relative to labour and those induced by technical invention or innovation' (ibid., p. 595). This is because technical progress tends to be embodied rather than disembodied in nature. That is, new capital equipment is normally required if new techniques are to be introduced, so that the rate of technical progress is limited by the rate of capital accumulation. For this reason Kaldor rejected as 'arbitrary and artificial' the conventional distinction between movements along a 'production function' and shifts in the 'production function' (ibid., p. 596; the inverted commas are Kaldor's).

He formalized this argument, to a degree, via his Technical Progress Function (Figure 3.3). Here the curve TT' shows the relationship between the rate of growth of output per head and the rate of growth of capital per head. Some (disembodied) technical progress is possible even with zero capital accumulation; thus the technical progress function cuts the y axis at T. The curve is convex to the origin because 'there is likely to be some maximum beyond which the rate of growth in productivity could not be raised, however fast capital is being accumulated' (ibid., p. 596). (A linear function could have been integrated to give the traditional neoclassical production function, as noted by Black, 1962). Steady-state growth occurs at P, where per capita output and capital are growing at the same rate. With full employment and constant relative shares, real wages grow as fast as labour productivity and the rate of profit is also constant.

In Harrodian terms, Kaldor concluded, 'the system tends towards an equilibrium rate of growth at which the "natural" and the "warranted" rates are

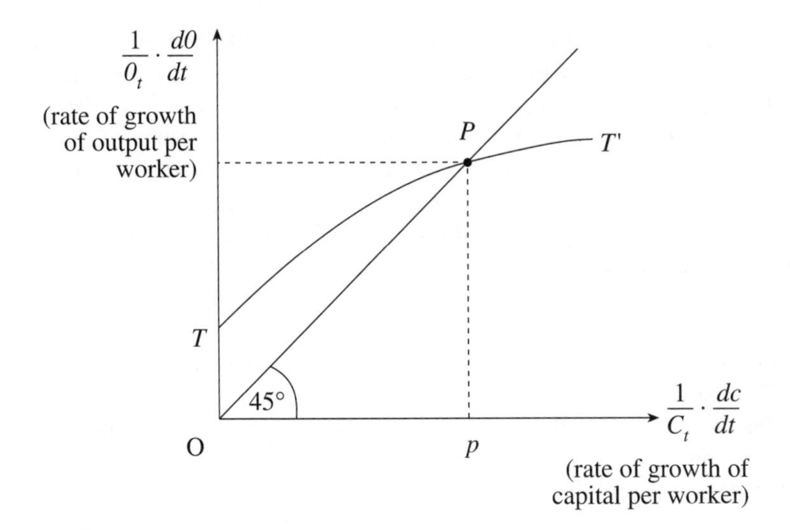

Source: Kaldor (1957b, p. 597).

Figure 3.3

equal, since any divergence between the two will set up forces tending to eliminate the difference; and these forces act partly through an adjustment of the "natural" rate, and partly through an adjustment of the "warranted" rate' (Kaldor, 1957b, p. 612). The first adjustment came through changes in the rate of (embodied) technical progress and the second via the Kaldorian distribution mechanism described in the previous section of this chapter. This was, however, true only in advanced capitalism. In the early stages of economic development, as Marx had recognized, technical progress was not powerful enough to offset the effects of rapid population growth, and a reserve army of labour had kept real wages at the subsistence level. Once technical change overtook population growth, Marx's analysis was in need of fundamental revision since real wages began to rise at the same rate as labour productivity; a new era had commenced in which steady-state growth was possible (ibid., pp. 618–21). It was not, however, inevitable, since smooth growth might be upset both by the irregular clustering of innovations over time and by disequilibrating movements in income distribution due to rigidities in real wages and profit margins (see also Harcourt, 1963, 1965). Echoing the 'Left Keynesians' whose views were discussed in Chapter 2, Kaldor pointed to the prospect that 'over-saving' might 'bring about a major breakdown in the process of investment and economic growth, such as occurred during the great depressions of the 1880s or the 1930s'. Alternatively, growth might coexist with rapid inflation (Kaldor, 1957b, p. 623).

Five years later, in his 'Mark II' growth model, Kaldor allowed for the effects of replacement investment but avoided the concept of 'capital' altogether. He now respecified the technical progress function as a relationship between the rate of growth of labour productivity and the rate of growth of investment per head, defining equilibrium as a state in which these two growth rates were equal. Kaldor and his co-author James Mirrlees paid some attention to the policy implications of their model. To increase the rate of growth, they argued, governments must attempt to stimulate technical dynamism, for example by spending more on scientific education and research and by encouraging better management that was more receptive to technological change. These comments reflected Kaldor's continuing political involvement. The United Kingdom's relatively low growth rate was a major issue at the time, and Harold Wilson's invocation of the 'white heat of technology' played an important part in the rhetoric of his successful 1964 election campaign (Thompson, 1997, p. 185). Kaldor himself was a prominent, colourful and controversial policy adviser to Labour governments in 1964–70 and 1974–6 (Thirlwall, 1987, pp. 228–57).

Analytically, though, he soon moved on. By 1966, when he was appointed to a personal chair at Cambridge (a year later than Joan Robinson), he had already abandoned any commitment to steady-state growth theory in favour of something very different. In his inaugural lecture Kaldor explained the poor postwar growth record of the British economy in terms of its premature 'maturity'. Output per head was already almost the same in all sectors; above all, there were no more reserves of low-productivity agricultural labour to move into manufacturing, a process which had contributed significantly to the rapid overall growth in productivity in Western European countries after 1945. Kaldor drew on the statistical relationships established by the Dutch economist P.J. Verdoorn to argue that the growth rate of manufacturing output was the driving force in productivity growth in the entire economy. Manufacturing enjoyed economies of scale and generated externalities that did not apply either in agriculture or in services (Kaldor, 1966a). This argument formed the basis for the Selective Employment Tax that he subsequently proposed to encourage movement of labour out of the service sector and into manufacturing (Thirlwall, 1987, pp. 188–92, 241–6).

Verdoorn's Law proved to have problems of its own, both theoretically and empirically (Rowthorn, 1975; Thirlwall, 1983). Kaldor soon came to repent of his 1966 assumption that growth was supply-constrained, by a shortage of labour, and instead emphasized the role of demand, especially export demand. In a 1970 analysis of regional policy he rejected the neoclassical focus on resource endowments, on the grounds that in manufacturing the accumulation of capital must be regarded as an effect as well as a cause of growth. Drawing on Gunnar Myrdal's concept of 'circular and cumulative causation', Kaldor pointed to the way in which growth in demand caused higher output through the operation of a foreign trade 'supermultiplier'. Because of increasing returns, rapidly growing areas enjoyed above-average productivity growth rates and declining relative unit labour costs, and consequently obtained an increasing degree of competitive advantage (Kaldor, 1970b). Never one to shrink from analytical excess, Kaldor concluded that since investment is induced by growth it must be deemed to be endogenous, leaving exports as the *only* exogenous component of effective demand (Thirlwall, 1994, p. 76). The resulting Kaldorian theory of balance of payments constrained-growth has since been developed, in more moderate terms and with considerable empirical success, by others (McCombie and Thirlwall, 1994). As for Kaldor, he was a man of many growth theories, not one. It is doubtful whether this ever worried him.

HISTORY VERSUS EQUILIBRIUM

Perhaps the single most important difference between Post Keynesian and neoclassical economists is their treatment of equilibrium. For neoclassicals, equilibrium is the natural state of affairs, an almost inexorable consequence of the rational pursuit of individual self-interest. Disequilibrium implies that there are unexploited gains from trade, and is therefore only a transitory phenomenon. This helps to explain why neoclassical theorists find it so hard to make sense of involuntary unemployment (De Vroey, 1998).

Robinson and Kaldor began their careers as equilibrium economists. They ended up as severe critics of both the concept itself and of its relevance to any actual capitalist economy, and this position was powerfully reinforced by their experience as growth theorists. Robinson's definition of 'tranquillity' has already been quoted. It points to a radical notion of path-dependency that she was to stress, more and more, as her exasperation with mainstream analysis grew in her old age. Already in 1956 she was complaining that 'The metaphor of equilibrium can be applied to economic affairs only with great caution'. Equilibrium positions tend to contain within themselves the causes of disequilibrating change, 'as though the balance were to grow restless and begin to shift without any change in the weights' (Robinson, 1956, p. 57; cf. Robinson, 1953). Thus the course of economic development was very difficult to describe in mechanical terms:

> When a market reacts to a change in circumstances, we cannot liken it to the reaction of the balance to a once-for-all change in the weights. However the balance wobbles about, it will come to rest in exactly the same position; but in most economic reactions the path the market follows, while it is adapting itself to a change, has a long-persisting effect upon the position that it reaches. (Robinson, 1956, p. 58)

An increase in demand for a particular commodity will raise profits and attract new capacity. The resultant 'overshooting' will eventually reverse this process, 'but the extent of the overshoot in the first place determines how much shrinkage will follow and so has an influence for a long time after it occurred (as if the balance were liable to get lodged on a nail if one of its wobbles is too violent)' (ibid., p. 58). Robinson's sceptical attitude towards the use of the equilibrium method was a constant theme in the final decades of her life (see, for example, Robinson, 1962a, pp. 22–3; 1971a, 1974).

Kaldor took an almost identical line in his criticism of neoclassical analysis:

> there is nothing in the theory to explain how the system gets into equilibrium and what happens when it is out of equilibrium. The 'production frontier' which is supposed to shift at some exogenous rate in time is meaningful only if the system is actually *on* the frontier and not *within* it. For any movement of the system *toward* the frontier increases capital as well as output, and therefore changes at least one of the parameters which define the 'frontier'. (Kaldor, 1973 [1979], p. 277; original emphasis)

He had reached this Robinsonian conclusion by a route of his own, beginning in the mid-1930s under the influence of Allyn Young (Kaldor, 1934; cf. Young, 1928) but increasingly mapped out for him by the role of technical progress and increasing returns in his analysis of economic growth. The firm's cost curves are irreversible, Kaldor argued in a critique of J.R. Hicks: 'the productivity of capital will depend not only on its quantity, but also on the rate at which it is changing, or has been changing in the past' (Kaldor, 1961, pp. 2–3). Since new technology must be embodied in new equipment there can be no question of a unique relationship between output and capital, and the very concept of its 'marginal productivity' was meaningless: 'Everything depends on past history, on how the collection of equipment goods … has been built up' (Kaldor and Mirrlees, 1962, p. 188). Evidently the vexing question of capital theory can no longer be avoided.

NOTE

1. Robinson to Kahn, 31 October 1955: Richard Kahn Papers, RKP 13/90/5/211–16.

4. Those Cambridge controversies

> One figure above all was revered. Piero Sraffa, an old Stalinist Fellow of Trinity College, had published virtually nothing for over thirty years, until his masterpiece appeared, the enigmatically entitled *Production of Commodities by Means of Commodities*. In one of Evelyn Waugh's novels, the hero is plagued by voices, which he imagines are being broadcast by fellow passengers on his ship. In a futile effort to distract them, he takes from the ship's library and reads aloud the most boring book he can imagine, Charles Kingsley's *Westward Ho!* Had Sraffa's book been available, he would certainly have succeeded in his task. (Ormerod, 1998, p. 157)

FIRST LIGHT

To neoclassical economists, marginal productivity theory served a number of purposes. First, it explained the existence of profit in terms of the twin forces of productivity and thrift, and also justified it in ethical terms. (Note that Post Keynesians tend to think of income from capital as 'profit', and neoclassicals as 'interest'.) Although this apologetic function was later energetically denied, it is quite transparent in the work of John Bates Clark (Henry, 1995). Second, marginal productivity provided an explanation for the shares of labour and capital in total output. In the simplest version, constant relative shares were entailed by the assumption of a Cobb–Douglas production function, on which considerable econometric evidence had accumulated (Douglas, 1948). More generally, given a wide range of values for the elasticity of substitution between capital and labour, it was easy to show that shares would normally vary only slightly as the capital–labour ratio changed (Bronfenbrenner, 1960). Third, capital–labour substitution in response to changes in relative factor prices could be invoked, as it had been by Austrian trade cycle theorists, to account for cyclical fluctuations in investment activity (Hayek, 1931). Finally, this same process of factor substitution was eventually employed in Solow's neoclassical model of economic growth in order to eliminate the Harrod instability problem, with the warranted rate of growth reconciled to the natural rate through changes in the capital–output ratio induced by variations in relative factor prices (Solow, 1956; Swan, 1956).

All of this rested on the crucial assumption that 'capital' was a commodity, with properties like those of any other commodity. In particular it was necessary to suppose, first that the 'quantity of capital' was an unambiguous notion and could therefore be measured without undue difficulty, and second that capital was a 'normal' good with a downward-sloping demand curve. The rate of profit (in neoclassical language, the rate of interest) could then be regarded as an index of capital scarcity, so that the standard neoclassical analysis of substitution could be applied. We saw in the previous chapter that the Cambridge growth theorists raised doubts on this score. In the early 1960s they launched a sustained attack on all aspects of the orthodox analysis of capital, which was defended by the neoclassical theorists Franco Modigliani, Paul Samuelson and Robert Solow from MIT, in Cambridge, Massachusetts, and by James Meade, Christopher Bliss and Frank Hahn in Cambridge, England. The resulting 'Cambridge controversies', engagingly described by Harcourt (1969, 1972), were very largely responsible for the emergence of Post Keynesian economics as a distinct school of thought.

It was evident well before 1960 that something was seriously wrong with the neoclassical theory of capital. One of its creators, the Swedish economist Knut Wicksell, expressed the first reservations. As he wrote to Alfred Marshall in 1905:

> the theory of capital and interest cannot be regarded as complete yet ... so long as capital is defined as a *sum of commodities* (or of value) the doctrine of the marginal productivity of capital as determining the rate of interest is never quite true and often not true at all – it is true individually but not in respect of the whole capital of society. (Cited by Harcourt, 1972, p. 16, n1)

The problem, as Wicksell realized, was that the measurement of capital was not independent of the rate of interest. Drawing on the work of earlier theorists like Eugen von Böhm-Bawerk, Friedrich von Hayek attempted to escape from this trap by deft use of the Austrian concept of the 'period of production', according to which productivity is enhanced by the use of more time-consuming, 'roundabout' or 'capitalistic' methods of production (Steele, 1997). But Hayek's efforts to establish an unambiguous index of the capital intensity of production proved unsuccessful, as Wicksell would have known and the young Nicholas Kaldor had demonstrated between 1937 and 1942, both in general terms and in the specific context of Hayek's model of the trade cycle (see Chapter 1).

This, as Kaldor later emphasized, was a London School of Economics controversy in which Cambridge theorists were not directly involved. Piero Sraffa was already criticizing neoclassical theory in private correspondence, but not yet in print. As he wrote to Joan Robinson in October 1936:

> If one measures labour and land by heads or acres the result has a definite meaning, subject to a margin of error: the margin is wide, but it is a question of

degree. On the other hand if you measure capital in tons the result is purely and simply nonsense. How many tons is, e.g., a railway tunnel?

If you are not convinced, try it on someone who has not been entirely debauched by economics. Tell your gardener that a farmer has 200 acres or employs 10 men – will he not have a pretty accurate idea of the quantities of land & labour? Now tell him that he employs 500 tons of capital, & he will think you are dotty – (not more so, however, than Sidgwick or Marshall).[1]

Certainly Keynes did not challenge the prevailing theory of capital, to which his own concept of 'marginal efficiency' was intimately related. He believed that the 'classical' (read, neoclassical) theory of value and distribution would come into its own once intelligent macroeconomic policies had established full employment (Keynes, 1936, p. 378). Although the *General Theory* had little more than this to say on questions of distribution, Keynes did endorse the 'first classical postulate', setting the real wage equal to the marginal product of labour and affirming the existence of a negative relationship between real wages and aggregate employment (ibid., p. 5). When John Dunlop (1938) and Lorie Tarshis (1938) convinced him that real wages did not in practice decline as employment increased, Keynes recanted graciously enough, but only at the empirical level (Keynes, 1939a). Analytically he remained a Marshallian, committed, in broad terms at least, to the traditional marginal productivity theory as applied to labour, if not (perhaps) to capital.

It was a commitment he shared, in the 1930s, with Richard Kahn and Joan Robinson. Robinson never accepted the apologetic use of the theory, and was always keen to stress the complications posed by imperfect competition, but in the 1930s her dissent went no further than this. And it was Kahn, after all, who had (co-)discovered the concept of marginal revenue, which Robinson had employed so profitably in her *Economics of Imperfect Competition*, her first analytical tour de force (Kahn, 1929 [1989]; Robinson, 1933). In private Kahn and Robinson delighted in describing themselves as 'the marginalists' and pouring scorn on an older generation who had failed to comprehend the new tools of analysis.[2] The attraction of the new apparatus was very strong; even Michal Kalecki had felt compelled to set out his 'degree of monopoly' model of relative shares in marginalist terms (see Chapter 2).

Two Cambridge economists did have other ideas. As early as 1929 the Marxist Maurice Dobb, whose thinking somewhat uneasily combined the ideas of Marx and Marshall, attacked the orthodox theory of wages on the grounds that the labour supply and demand curves were not independent of each other. This made the terms of exchange in the labour market indeterminate, Dobb suggested, and also had broader and more serious implications:

If one is to speak of a general equilibrium where utility and disutility equate at the margin, one must *assume* a certain relationship between the worker's loaf and his

> labour, which is itself the result of an indeterminate bargain. Had a different bargain, or a different scale of production, been arrived at previously, a different relation between utility and disutility and a different equilibrium might have been established. And it is in this sense that the solution of the problem of distribution is logically prior to the solution of the problem of value. (Dobb, 1929, p. 519)

Dobb took this no further, but his friend Piero Sraffa (1898–1983) was already working on a much more comprehensive critique of mainstream theory. Not, as Paul Ormerod claims, a Stalinist, Sraffa was a non-party socialist who had been a close friend of the Italian Communist leader Antonio Gramsci when they were both young activists in Turin, and was a constant source of support and assistance for Gramsci during his decade of imprisonment by the fascist regime. An early attack on the probity of the Italian banking system, published at Keynes's instigation in the *Manchester Guardian*, had caused Sraffa to fall foul of Mussolini, and after brief teaching appointments at the Universities of Perugia and Cagliari he moved in 1927 to Cambridge, where he spent the rest of his life. Sraffa's reputation was cemented by his devastating critique of Marshallian price theory (Sraffa, 1926; Sylos Labini, 1985). Since he disliked teaching, Keynes arranged for him to be in charge of the Marshall Library and to supervise research students. In 1930 Sraffa was appointed by the Royal Economic Society to prepare for publication the works and correspondence of David Ricardo, a project completed (with help from Dobb) only in 1973.

None of Sraffa's admittedly very sparse publications between 1926 and 1960 gave a great deal away, but a variety of unpublished drafts and handwritten notes preserved in his papers (now in the Wren Library at Trinity College) show that he was working, continuously if somewhat erratically, on a comprehensive critique of orthodox economic analysis. His powerful attack on Hayek's *Prices and Production* had condemned the Austrian theorist for failing consistently to distinguish a monetary from a non-monetary economy, and in particular for neglecting the role of money as a store of value. Hence money had been 'neutralized' from the start, and this vitiated Hayek's discussion of saving and interest (Sraffa, 1932; cf. Hayek, 1931). Sraffa's brilliant introduction to his new edition of Ricardo's *Principles* not only offered a new and distinctive interpretation of classical political economy, but also gave some indication of his own ideas on the surplus approach to economics (Sraffa, 1951). But there was barely a hint at the onslaught on neoclassical theory that would eventually appear.

This was partly a question of personality, as Nicholas Kaldor's memorial tribute suggests:

> I suppose that the clearest memory of Piero we share is of him riding along the avenue and over the Backs on his afternoon bicycle ride, with cap, scarf and

> gloves, a solitary, self-contained person, shy and distant in manner. Yet that appearance was deceptive. To those who knew him he revealed extraordinary warmth and strong emotions both towards friends and towards causes. (Kaldor, 1984, p. 150)

His (much younger) compatriot and friend Luigi Pasinetti remembers Sraffa as reserved, almost secretive, concerning his own thinking, capable of devastating criticism but rarely constructive in his comments on the work of others (Pasinetti, 1998). Pasinetti had arrived in Cambridge only in the mid-1950s, and it is possible that Sraffa had been more forthcoming in private conversation in earlier years. (The 1936 letter previously quoted is suggestive in this regard.) So far as I know Sraffa never accused Robinson of plagiarism, but Kaldor did in a furious letter to Richard Kahn in 1960:

> If there is a 'conspiracy of silence' about Joan's writings, I think it is due, as I told you before, to a widespread resentment at the way in which she absorbs other people's ideas, then put [*sic*] them out under her own trade mark, and then expects everyone to respect it.[3]

At all events it was Robinson who, in her 1952 article on Harrod's theory of growth, had first expressed her worries in print: 'how are the quantities concerned measured?', she asked, with particular reference to capital. Presumably in current prices, she replied briefly, before moving on (Robinson, 1952b, p. 43).

Two years later she returned to her question, devoting a major paper to 'The Production Function and the Theory of Capital'. In the short period there is no problem, since the quantity of capital is fixed. 'As soon as we leave the short period, however, a host of difficulties appear. Should capital be valued according to its future earning power or its past costs?' The former method was tempting, but unworkable:

> When we know the future expected rate of output associated with a certain capital good, and expected future prices and costs, then, if we are given a rate of interest, we can value the capital good as a discounted stream of future profit which it will earn. But to do so, we have to begin by taking the rate of interest as given, whereas the main purpose of the production function is to show how wages and the rate of interest (regarded as the wages of capital) are determined by technical conditions and the factor ratio. (Robinson, 1954, p. 81)

The cost of production approach was also problematical, and for the same reason: 'The cost of capital includes the cost of capital goods, and since they must be constructed before they can be used, part of the cost of capital is interest over the period of time between the moment when work was done in constructing capital goods and the time when they are producing a stream of output' (ibid., p. 82). Once again, the rate of interest must be known independently of the production function, and cannot, therefore, be determined by it.

One solution might be simply to abandon the concept of the production function. But Robinson was reluctant to do so, for it did express 'a genuine problem'. If a few men with bulldozers are employed to clear a road in Alpha, while in Gamma hundreds of men do the same job with shovels and ox-carts, 'it seems pretty clear that the main reason for this state of affairs is that capital in some sense is more plentiful in Alpha than in Gamma'. This does not mean, however, that there exists a strong tendency for the rate of profit to adjust so that capital is fully employed – let alone labour. Indeed, 'the very notion of accumulation proceeding under equilibrium conditions at changing factor ratios bristles with difficulties' (ibid., p. 99), since the speed of adjustment is no less important than its direction: if capital per man is rising rapidly some capitalists' plants appropriate to a variety of degrees of mechanisation will be operating side by side. The most serious question, however, arises because of uncertainty, which poses

> the formidable problem of how to treat expectations when the rate of profit is altering. An unforeseen fall in the rate of profit ruptures the conditions of equilibrium. Capitalists who are operating on borrowed funds can no longer earn the interest they have contracted to pay, and those operating their own capital find themselves in possession of a type of plant that they would not have built if they had known what the rate of profit was going to be....
>
> Thus, the assumptions of equilibrium become entangled in self-contradictions if they are applied to the problem of accumulation going on through time with a changing factor ratio. To discuss accumulation we must look through the eyes of the man of deeds, taking decisions about the future, while to account for what has been accumulated we must look back over the accidents of past history. The two points of view meet only in the who's who of goods in existence today, which is never in an equilibrium relationship with the situation that obtains today. (Ibid., p. 100)

The complex and contradictory relationship between history and equilibrium was to be the most important theme in Robinson's mature critique of orthodox economics (see Chapter 9). At this stage in her career, though, she was reluctant to repudiate neoclassical analysis in its entirety. The fact remained, returning to the road builders, that 'employment per unit of output is much higher in Gamma than in Alpha, and it seems obvious that this is connected with the fact that real wages there are much lower' (ibid., p. 96). Robinson continued to insist on a negative relationship between relative factor prices and factor proportions.

THE ACCUMULATION OF CAPITAL REVISITED

In the second volume of her *Collected Economic Papers* Robinson reprinted 'only the negative part of this article as the constructive parts are better done in my book, *The Accumulation of Capital*' (Robinson, 1960a, p. 130). She dealt with the relationship between the wage rate, the rate of profit and the choice of techniques in Chapters 10–18 of the book, with diagrams confined to an Appendix (Robinson, 1956, pp. 101–76, 411–25). Robinson seems to have regretted the latter decision: my copy, a 1966 reprint of the (very lightly revised) 1965 second edition, has a bookmark with a numerical example on one side and one of the relevant diagrams on the other, suggesting that she now attributed more importance to the diagrammatic exposition of her ideas. The example, summarized in Table 4.1, links output, capital and distribution for three different techniques. All magnitudes are expressed in physical units of a composite commodity; the real wage is set equal to one unit of this commodity; and it is assumed that 50 men are employed (ibid., p. 107).

Table 4.1

	Technique		
	Alpha	Beta	Gamma
Capital	100	50	25
Output	65	60	55
Capital per man	2	1	0.5
Output per man	1.3	1.2	1.1
Wage bill	50	50	50
Profits	15	10	5
Rate of profit (%)	15	20	20

Source: Adapted from Robinson (1956, p. 107).

It can be seen from the table that Gamma and Beta are equally profitable; with the wage set at unity, the rate of profit is 20 per cent in each, while for Alpha it is only 15 per cent. Robinson used these numbers to draw a 'productivity curve' relating output to inputs of capital. Note that such curves are *not* neoclassical production functions:

> Technical relations are shown by any one of our productivity curves. But the 'production function' also purports to show the relation between wages and profits which gives equilibrium in a given state of technical knowledge. This cannot be

> deduced from a productivity curve, for each curve is drawn for a particular rate of interest. Given the technical conditions, we have to know the real-wage rate (or the rate of profit) as a separate datum (dependent in a static state on the thriftiness of rentiers) in order to determine within what range of real-capital ratios the possible conditions of equilibrium lie. (Ibid., p. 414, n1)

As Piero Sraffa would soon put it, the system 'moves with one degree of freedom' (Sraffa, 1960, p. 11). Thus either the real wage or the rate of profit must be determined outside the model. Unlike the neoclassical production function, Robinson's productivity curve *cannot* be differentiated with respect to capital to give the rate of profit endogenously.

The productivity curve corresponding to the data in the table is drawn as Figure 4.1, which is derived from Robinson (1956, p. 412, Figure 1). I have slightly simplified her overelaborate exposition, which can however be formalized in a rigorous way (Salvadori, 1996). Output per worker is measured on the vertical axis; *OA*, *OB* and *OC* are the levels of output per worker in the three techniques. There is also a fourth technique, Delta, not included in the table, with output per worker of *OD*. Capital per worker is measured on the horizontal axis: for Gamma it is 25/50 = 0.5 (= *Oc*), and for Beta it is 50/50 = 1 (= *Ob*). The 'curve' $\alpha\beta\gamma\delta$ is the productivity curve, 'showing the relationship between output and the real capital-ratio *when capital is reckoned at the given notional interest rate*' (Robinson, 1956, p. 412; emphasis added). Since Beta and Gamma are equally profitable, entrepreneurs will use them indifferently. The linear segment $\gamma\beta$ is that over which a greater proportion of Beta equipment is used. The wage rate is given by *OW* (= 1), so that profit per worker is *WC* (= 0.1) when only Gamma equipment is in use and *WB* (= 0.2) when only Beta plant is in operation. The respective profit rates are given by *WC*/*Oc* and *WB*/*Ob*, which are both equal to 20 per cent. Simple geometry reveals that this is also equal to 1/*ON*, the rate of profit corresponding to the real wage rate *OW*.

In Figure 4.1 the productivity curve is upward-sloping and concave to the origin: given the rate of profit, output per head is higher, the greater is capital per head, but decreasingly so. A different productivity curve can be drawn – indeed, *must* be drawn – for each different rate of profit, as in Figure 4.2 (derived from ibid., p. 413, Figure 2; this is the diagram reproduced on my bookmark). Here the productivity curve $\alpha_2\ \beta_2\ \gamma_2\ \delta_2$ is that depicted in Figure 4.1; the curve $\alpha_3\ \beta_3\ \gamma_3\ \delta_3$ relates to a lower wage and higher rate of profit; and $\alpha_1\ \beta_1\ \gamma_1\ \delta_1$ represents a higher wage and a lower profit rate. 'The thick line,' Robinson explains, 'represents all the positions of static equilibrium which are possible in the given technical conditions with a range of wage rates from the Delta–Gamma wage rate to one somewhat above the Beta–Alpha wage rate. This may be called a real-capital-ratio curve' (ibid., pp. 413–14).

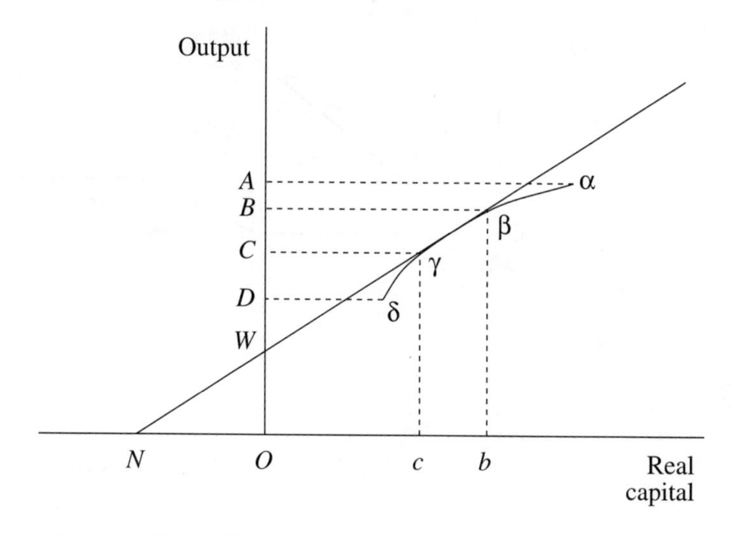

Source: Robinson (1956, p. 412).

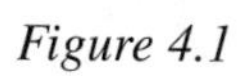
Figure 4.1

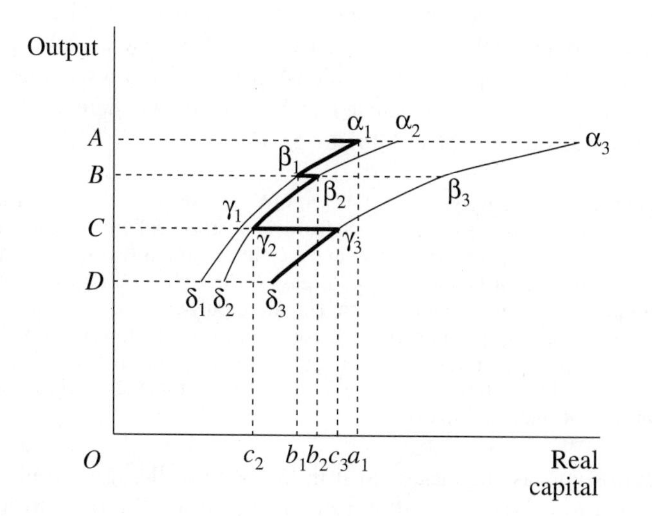

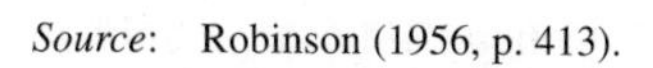
Source: Robinson (1956, p. 413).

Figure 4.2

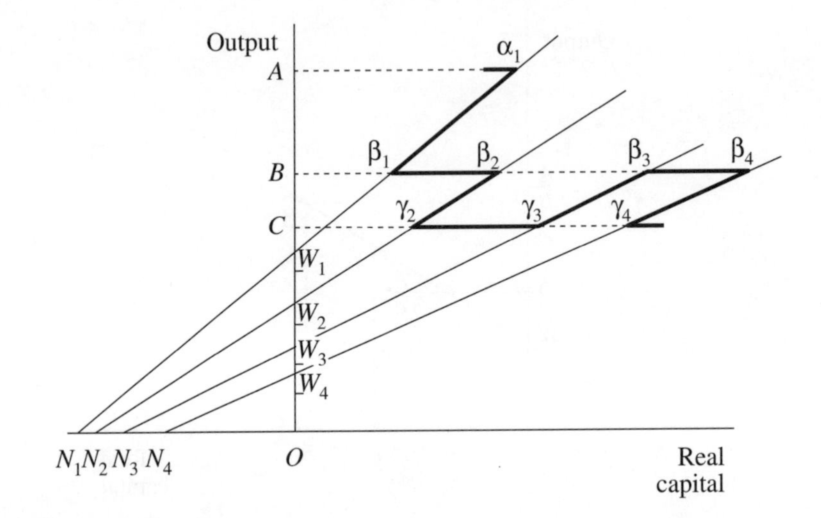

Source: Robinson (1956, p. 417).

Figure 4.3

Figure 4.2 illustrates what Robinson believed to be the normal shape of the curve, with lower profit rates corresponding to more mechanized techniques of production, and vice versa: Delta–Gamma in curve 3, Gamma–Beta in curve 2 and Beta–Alpha in curve 1. But she also drew a real-capital-ratio curve to illustrate 'a "perverse" relationship' in which a lower rate of profit corresponded to a less mechanized technique, drawn here as Figure 4.3 (which is based on ibid., p. 417, Figure 5). Here,

> As the real-wage rate rises from OW_4 to OW_1 and the rate of profit falls from $1/ON_4$ to $1/ON_1$, the system moves from a position where Gamma and Beta techniques are equally profitable and accumulation is raising the degree of mechanisation from Gamma to Beta, passes through a range over which Beta technique alone is used, and then comes into a range where once more Beta and Gamma are equally profitable, but the degree of mechanisation is falling from Beta to Gamma. For rates of wages higher than OW_3 (with rates of profit lower than $1/ON_3$) the relations are 'normal', and at OW_2 the degree of mechanisation begins to rise again. (Ibid., p. 418)

This 'curiosum', as she described it in the body of the text, would soon be taken much more seriously. Robinson attributed its discovery to her Cambridge friend, the agricultural economist Ruth Cohen (1906–91), only to dismiss it as 'a somewhat intricate piece of analysis which is not of great importance' (ibid., p. 109, n1). 'As a general rule,' she concluded, 'the degree of mechanisation of the technique brought over the frontier by a higher wage rate is higher than that corresponding to a lower wage rate' (ibid., p. 109).

Thus Robinson remained faithful to a (suitably reformulated) marginal productivity theory of distribution, since – as she put it in a 1957 article intended partly as a response to Nicholas Kaldor – 'the idea that the "elasticity of substitution" is trying to express is an important element in the theory of relative shares' (Robinson, 1957 [1960], p. 154; she wrote this paper for a French journal and for some reason waited three years before publishing it in English). The 'animal spirits' of the entrepreneurs may lead them to invest at an unsustainable rate (leading, in Harrod's terms, to a warranted rate higher than the natural rate). The effect of this will be to raise real wages faster than labour productivity and thus to reduce the rate of profit:

> Since a falling rate of profit is associated with rising capital per unit of output, relative shares once more may go either way. The greater the substitutability between factors in production and between commodities in demand the more accumulation can be absorbed with a given long-run fall in the level of the rates of profit on capital, and the greater the tendency for the relative share of profits to rise. (Ibid., p. 156)

Despite her probing questions on the neoclassical theory of capital and the meaning of the aggregate production function, Robinson's views on income distribution were thus essentially the same in 1957 as they had been 20 years previously (Robinson, 1937a, pp. 114–19; Harcourt, 1996a).

Kaldor's position had always been quite different. He returned to the subject in his 1956 article on 'Alternative Theories of Distribution', in which he criticized Wicksell's efforts to integrate Austrian capital theory with Walrasian general equilibrium analysis. The Wicksellian treatment of capital as the product of time and labour had foundered, Kaldor noted, on the impossibility of defining an average or aggregate 'period of production'. This failure, he continued, posed serious problems for any neoclassical theory of distribution, since

> the 'marginal rate of substitution' between Capital and Labour – as distinct from the marginal rate of substitution between labour and land – can only be determined once the rate of profit and the rate of wages are already known. The same technical alternatives might yield very different 'marginal rates of substitution' according as the ratio of profits to wages is one thing or another. (Kaldor, 1956, p. 91)

As he explained in his 1957 growth model paper, this difficulty is especially severe in a growing economy where continuous technical progress is taking place and the capital goods produced in one period are therefore qualitatively different from the capital goods produced in the next period. In such circumstances 'the measurement of the stock of *real* capital must therefore necessarily be based on some (more or less arbitrary) convention', for example the total weight of steel contained in the capital equipment concerned (Kaldor, 1957b, p. 599). In Kaldor's own model the rate of profit depends only – via the 'Cambridge equation' discussed in the previous chapter – on the rate of growth and the capitalists' savings propensity. There is no room for marginal productivity (ibid., p. 613).

MR SRAFFA'S *PRODUCTION OF COMMODITIES*

The result of more than 30 years of reflection, Piero Sraffa's *Production of Commodities by Means of Commodities* was a very thin volume: 95 pages of text, seven of which were blank or bore only chapter titles, and just over two pages of – very important – prefatory remarks. The book was almost unbearably terse. Sraffa cited just seven authors, of whom only Alfred Marshall (d.1922) and Philip Wicksteed (d.1927) survived into the twentieth century (the others are Quesnay, Smith, Ricardo, Torrens and Marx). He acknowledged the help of not a single living economist, but did thank three mathematicians; one of these, Frank Ramsey, the author of a celebrated paper on the theory of optimal saving, had died in 1930 (Sraffa, 1960, pp. vi–vii). Sraffa's prose is elegant but spare and uncompromising. It is an extremely difficult book to read but in my opinion not at all – *pace* Ormerod – a boring one.

As the most perceptive of the reviewers noted, one of Sraffa's aims was to rehabilitate classical economics, the term 'classical' being used here in a non-Keynesian sense to denote the school of thought that included Quesnay and Smith and culminated in the work of Ricardo and Marx (Meek, 1961). Sraffa focused on production rather than exchange, emphasized input–output relationships and highlighted the production and distribution of a physical surplus of outputs over the inputs that are needed to produce them. His perspective was Ricardian more than Marxian, since for the most part he treated labour as one input among many and made no use of the concepts of abstract labour, surplus labour or exploitation. At the time this led orthodox Marxists to reject his analysis as vulgarly 'neo-Ricardian' (Rowthorn, 1974). Other, more ecumenical, Marxists argued that Sraffa's method, if not his substantive theory, was essentially that of Marx (Meek, 1973; cf. Harcourt, 1980). Probably both Ricardo and Marx would have understood Sraffa's algebra, which in its simplest form set out the relations that must hold between commodity prices, the wage rate and the rate of profits in a competitive capitalist economy:

$$
\begin{aligned}
(A_a p_a + B_a p_b + \ldots + K_a p_k)(1+r) + l_a w &= A p_a \\
(A_b p_a + B_b p_b + \ldots + K_b p_k)(1+r) + l_b w &= B p_b \\
\ldots \\
(A_k p_a + B_k p_b + \ldots + K_k p_k)(1+r) + l_k w &= K p_k
\end{aligned} \tag{4.1}
$$

Here the constants $A_a \ldots K_a$ represent the quantities of the commodities $A \ldots . K$ used in the production of A; $A_b \ldots K_b$ are the amounts of B used in the same industries; and so on. The constants $L_a \ldots L_k$ are the corresponding inputs of homogeneous labour, while the unknowns $p_a \ldots p_k$ are the respective commodity prices; w is the (uniform) wage rate, and r the common rate of profits.

In the preface Sraffa warned the reader against supposing 'that the argument rests on a tacit assumption of constant returns in all industries'. Keynes had anticipated the likelihood that this mistake would be made (ibid., pp. v–vi), and as early as 1928, in a letter to Sraffa, Pigou had dismissed an early version of his analysis as being nothing more than Walras with constant returns.[4] 'In fact', Sraffa insisted,

> no such assumption is made. No changes in output and (at any rate in Parts I and II) no changes in the proportions in which different means of production are used by an industry are considered, so that no question arises as to the variation or constancy of returns. The investigation is concerned exclusively with such properties of an economic system as do not depend on changes in the scale of production or in the proportions of 'factors'.

This 'classical' standpoint, Sraffa continued,

> has been submerged and forgotten since the advent of the 'marginal method'. The reason is obvious. The marginal approach requires attention to be focused on change, for without change either in the scale of an industry or in the 'proportions of the factors of production' there can be neither marginal product nor marginal cost. In a system in which, day after day, production continued unchanged in those respects, the marginal product of a factor (or alternatively the marginal cost of a product) would not merely be hard to find – it just would not be there to be found. (Sraffa, 1960, p. v)

This hinted at one major aim of Sraffa's formal analysis, which was to demonstrate that a rigorous theory of value and distribution could be articulated without reference to marginal productivity or to the equilibrium of demand and supply. More than that: it was necessary to do so, given the non-existence in Sraffa's system of marginal products and marginal costs.

The system was assumed to be in a 'self-replacing state', which meant that the output of each commodity was at least equal to the inputs of it that are used to produce itself and all other commodities:

$$\begin{aligned} A_a + A_b + \ldots + A_k &\le A \\ B_a + B_b + \ldots + B_k &\le B \\ &\ldots \\ K_a + K_b + \ldots + K_k &\le K \end{aligned} \tag{4.2}$$

The 'national income' of the system was the sum of the surplus outputs of each commodity, multiplied by their prices; Sraffa set it equal to unity by definition, so that

$$\begin{aligned} &[A-(A_a + A_b + \ldots + A_k)]p_a + [B-(B_a + B_b + \ldots + B_k)]p_b \\ &+\ldots+[K-(K_a + K_b + \ldots + K_k)]p_k = 1. \end{aligned} \tag{4.3}$$

This gave him $k + 1$ equations and $k + 2$ variables (the k prices, w and r). Thus 'the system can move with one degree of freedom; and if one of the variables is fixed the others will be fixed too' (ibid., p. 11). One way of removing this 'degree of freedom' and thereby closing the system was to specify a subsistence wage, as the classical economists had done. Sraffa objected, however, that 'besides the ever-present element of subsistence, [wages] may include a share of the surplus product' (ibid., p. 9). Later he argued that the rate of profits rather than the wage should be treated as the independent variable: 'The rate of profits, as a ratio, has a significance which is independent of any prices, and can well be "given" before the prices are fixed. It is accordingly susceptible of being determined from outside the system of production, in particular by the level of the money rates of interest' (ibid., p. 33). Precisely what Sraffa intended by this unusually enigmatic statement has been the subject of considerable controversy (see Pivetti, 1996; Nell, 1999; and Chapter 10). For the present, we need note only that the distribution of income must be determined outside the model, and thus independently of the theory of value. Whether it is fixed by conditions in the money market, as Sraffa himself seemed to imply, by the Kaleckian degree of monopoly, by the outcome of the class struggle between capitalists and workers, or by the Cambridge growth equation, is in this context a secondary issue. The relative shares of wages and profits cannot, however – and this is the really important point – be determined by reference to the 'marginal products' of the 'factors of production'.

If Sraffa had little or nothing to say about the determinants of income distribution, his analysis did permit him to explore the consequences of changing the relative shares of workers and capitalists. When he traced the effects of varying the rate of profit, some strikingly counter-intuitive results were obtained. Consider the very simple example that Sraffa analysed on p. 37 of *Production of Commodities*, in which labour is the *only* input into two industries, one of which produces vintage wine and the other oak chests.

In the first industry, 20 units of labour in year 17 yield one barrel of wine fit for drinking in year 25; in the second, one unit of labour is used to plant a tree in year 1 and a further 19 units to chop it down and make the chest in year 25 (trees grow rapidly in Sraffaland!). The price equations for the two industries can be written, by analogy with equations (4.1), as

$$p_a = 20w(1+r)^8 \tag{4.4}$$

and

$$p_b = 19w(1+r)^{25}. \tag{4.5}$$

For the two activities to be equally profitable, the price of wine must return to the capitalist a sum equal to the wage costs plus interest at the prevailing rate of profits over the eight years required for the wine to mature. Similarly, the price of the chest is the sum of the wage costs of the tree-fellers and the coopers, incurred in the current period, plus that paid to the tree-planter 25 years earlier, suitably augmented. The difference in the price of the two commodities is therefore given by

$$p_a - p_b = 20w(1+r)^8 - 19w(1+r)^{25}, \tag{4.6}$$

and is plotted in Figure 4.4, where Sraffa has (arbitrarily) set $w = 1 - (r/25\%)$. It can be seen from the figure that the price of wine increases relatively to that of the chest as r rises from zero to 9 per cent, falls for values of r between 9 per cent and 22 per cent, and then rises again from 22 per cent to 25 per cent (which is the maximum rate of profits that can be paid in this example).

Sraffa modestly summarized the implications in a long bracketed paragraph:

> The reduction to dated labour terms has some bearing on the attempts that have been made to find in the 'period of production' an independent measure of the quantity of capital which could be used, without arguing in a circle, for the determination of prices and of the shares in distribution. But the case just considered seem conclusive in showing the impossibility of aggregating the 'periods' belonging to the several quantities of labour into a single magnitude which could be regarded as representing the quantity of capital. The reversals in the direction of the movement of relative prices, in the face of unchanged methods of production, cannot be reconciled with *any* notion of capital as a measurable quantity independent of distribution and prices. (Ibid., p. 38)

As we shall see in the next section, this conclusion was soon reformulated, with the associated phenomenon of 'capital reversal' proving fatal to the neoclassical conception of the rate of profits (rate of interest) as an index of capital scarcity.

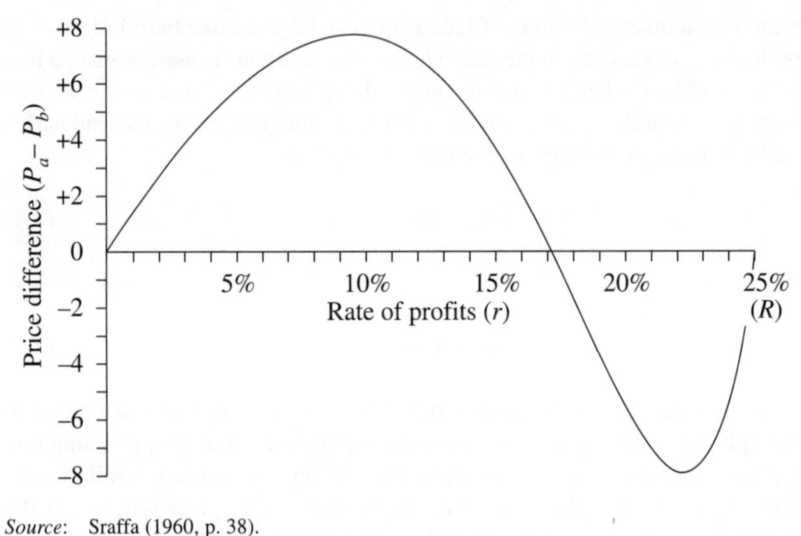

Source: Sraffa (1960, p. 38).

Figure 4.4

In his example Sraffa assumed that there was only one method of production for each of the two commodities. In just over six pages at the end of his book he turned to the problem that had so agitated Joan Robinson in her *Accumulation of Capital*: the choice between alternative methods of production, and the conditions under which capitalists will be induced to switch from one method to another. His exposition was even more terse than usual (ibid., pp. 81–7).The Sraffian analysis of reswitching would soon prove to have serious implications for mainstream theory, but its significance did not emerge at all clearly from his own discussion. The sub-title of his book was 'Prelude to a Critique of Economic Theory', and in the preface he prepared his readers for the worst:

> It is, however, a peculiar feature of the set of propositions now published that, although they do not enter into any discussion of the marginal theory of value and distribution, they have nevertheless been designed to serve as the basis for a critique of that theory. If the foundation holds, the critique may be attempted later, either by the writer or by someone younger and better equipped for the task. (Ibid., p. vi)

True to form, the only points in the book where he did try to explain the full implications of his criticisms were the paragraph previously cited and the following passage, some 30 pages earlier:

> It may be added that not only in this case but *in general* the use of the term 'cost of production' has been avoided in this work, as well as the term 'capital' in its quantitative connotation, at the cost of some tiresome circumlocution. This is because these terms have come to be inseparably linked with the supposition that they stand for quantities that can be measured independently of, and prior to, the determination of the prices of the products. (Witness the 'real costs' of Marshall and the 'quantity of capital' which is implied in the marginal productivity theory.) Since to achieve freedom from such presuppositions has been one of the aims of this work, avoidance of the terms seemed the only way of not prejudicing the issue. (Ibid., p. 9)

Sraffa must have been aware of, but chose not to mention, the fact that these criticisms had already been expressed in print by his friends Joan Robinson and Nicholas Kaldor.

THE CAMBRIDGE CONTROVERSIES

Perhaps not surprisingly, the reviewers did not know what to make of *Production of Commodities*. The long review by Harcourt and Massaro (1964) was beyond reproach, having been approved, line by line, by Sraffa himself. But the eminent Chicago economist Melvin Reder (1961) missed the point entirely. Even Roy Harrod floundered, prompting a brief reply from Sraffa that is notable both as his very last published work and as his clearest statement of the fundamental objection to orthodox capital theory: without a unit of measurement independent of distribution and prices, the neoclassical argument is inevitably circular (Harrod, 1961; Sraffa, 1962). The review by Ronald Meek (1961) was accurate and incisive on the relationship between Sraffa's ideas and those of the classical economists and Karl Marx, but barely mentioned the implications for mainstream economic theory. Even Joan Robinson, who wrote two reviews of *Production of Commodities*, seemed to Luigi Pasinetti not fully to have grasped the fundamental arguments at the time (Robinson, 1961, 1965b; Pasinetti, 1996). And Nicholas Kaldor simply ignored the book for two full decades until he was forced to confront Sraffa's work when commissioned to write his obituary (Kaldor, 1985b). Ironically the first to expose the depth of the Sraffian critique were defenders of neoclassical theory. Admittedly it was at the prompting of Pierangelo Garegnani, a former PhD student of Sraffa's who happened to be visiting Cambridge (Mass.) in 1961 and focused the attention of Paul Samuelson on the troublesome phenomena of reswitching and capital reversal (Birner, 1996; Samuelson, 1999). It was Samuelson's attempts to solve these two problems – repeated and tenacious attempts, but ultimately unsuccessful – that initiated the Cambridge controversies.

Reswitching and capital reversal undermined two fundamental propositions of neoclassical capital theory, relating the rate of profit to the capital intensity of production technology. The neoclassicals claimed, first, that successive reductions in the rate of profit would induce profit-maximizing firms to switch to new techniques with continually increasing capital–labour ratios. This claim was refuted by the possibility of reswitching, in which previously abandoned techniques with higher capital–labour ratios return to use at *lower* values of the rate of profit. The neoclassical economists claimed, secondly, that the relationship between the rate of profit and the capital–labour ratio was monotonically decreasing: lower profit rates are associated with increased use of capital relative to labour. This was refuted by the possibility of capital reversal, for which reswitching is a sufficient but not a necessary condition.

These conclusions can be illustrated by a two-sector example taken from Harcourt (1975, pp. 318–21), which is in effect derived by drastically simplifying Sraffa's equations (4.1). In an economy that produces a consumption good and a capital good, using inputs of homogeneous labour and the capital good, the price equations can be written as

$$\begin{aligned} wl_c + rp_k k_c &= 1 \\ wl_k + rp_k k_k &= p_k, \end{aligned} \tag{4.7}$$

where l_c, l_k, k_c and k_l are the relevant input coefficients (which collectively make up a 'technique') and p_k is the price of the capital good expressed in units of the consumption good. Manipulation of equations (4.7) yields an expression for the rate of profit in terms of the wage rate. This is the 'wage curve' or 'factor price frontier':

$$w = \frac{1 - rk_k}{r(k_c l_k - k_k l_c) + l_c}, \tag{4.8}$$

which is a straight line only if $k_c/l_c = k_k/l_k$, so that the bracketed term in the denominator disappears. Similarly, the (relative) price of the capital good can be written as

$$p_k = \frac{l_k}{r(k_c l_k - k_k l_c) + l_c}, \tag{4.9}$$

which is constant as the rate of profit changes only in the same special case, when

$$p_k = \frac{l_k}{l_c}. \tag{4.10}$$

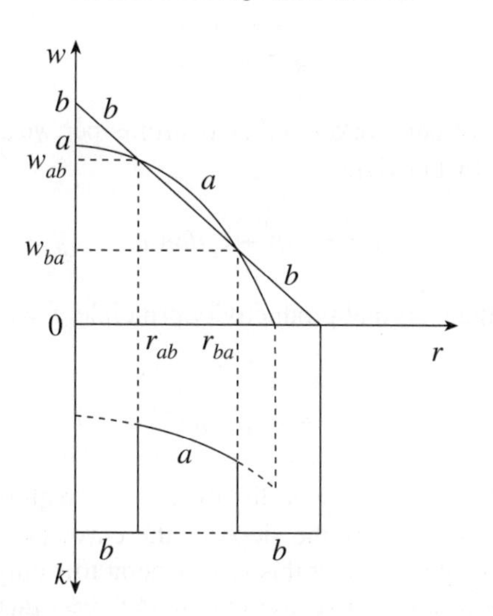

Source: Harcourt (1975, p. 321).

Figure 4.5

A separate set of equations like (4.8) can be obtained for each production technique. In the upper panel of Figure 4.5 wage curves are drawn for two techniques, *a* and *b* (Harcourt, 1975, p. 321, Figure 15.2). The lower panel plots the corresponding relationship between the rate of profit and the capital–labour ratio. Since the physical ratio of the capital good to labour is constant, this represents the effect of changes in p_k as r varies. Technique *b* has a linear wage curve, while that for technique *a* is concave to the origin. For $r < r_{ab}$, *b* will be used since, for any given wage rate, it offers a higher rate of profit. At $r = r_{ab}$ there is a switchpoint: over the range r_{ab} to r_{ba}, technique *a* is the more profitable one. Then, at $r = r_{ba}$, the system *switches back* to technique *b*. Thus the upper panel of the figure depicts an example of reswitching.

Capital reversal is shown in the lower panel. Between $r = 0$ and $r = r_{ab}$, the value of capital per man is constant and equal to *b*. At the first switchpoint it drops to that corresponding to the new profit-maximizing technique, that is, to *a*. As the rate of profit increases, up to r_{ba}, the value of capital per worker *rises* steadily; and it jumps again, discontinuously, at the second switchpoint, when the system moves back to the technique *b*.

One final, very important, implication concerns the distribution of income between wages and profits. Since the shares of workers and capitalists exhaust the total product, it follows that

$$q = rk + w, \tag{4.11}$$

where q is net output per worker and rk is profits per worker. Total differentiation of equation (4.11) yields

$$dq = r \cdot dk + k \cdot dr + dw. \tag{4.12}$$

But, according to the marginal productivity principle, $r = dq/dk$, so that, from (4.12),

$$k = -dw/dr. \tag{4.13}$$

The marginal productivity theory of distribution thus requires that the value of capital per worker is given by the slope of the envelope of the wage curve, $-dw/dr$. Now it is easy to see that this is in general true only for a *linear* wage curve. With a concave wage curve, as in Figure 4.5, $k > -dw/dr$, and the reverse is true for a convex wage curve. But equation (4.11) is true by definition, so that equation (4.13) is in general false. In other words, the marginal productivity theory of distribution holds only if the wage curve is linear, that is, only in the special case where $k_c/l_c = k_k/l_k$ (Bhaduri, 1966). And this is precisely the special case where capital reversal cannot occur and where (if there are several techniques of production) reswitching is impossible.

All this had been established by 1966, after a last-ditch attempt to salvage neoclassical capital theory had been destroyed by Luigi Pasinetti (Pasinetti, 1966; see also Garegnani, 1970; Harcourt, 1972, ch. 4). What it meant for the future of economic theory was a much harder question. Some of Sraffa's disciples decided that *Production of Commodities* should be treated as 'a brick rather than a broom', as one Australian economist put it to me, and set about building a comprehensive new theory on Sraffian foundations. The 'surplus approach' to economics involves a rehabilitation of the classical theory of value and distribution (Garegnani, 1984). It takes as data, not the preferences, resource endowments and technologies of neoclassical theory, but rather the size and composition of output, the technical conditions of production and one distributional variable: either the real wage or the rate of profit. Garegnani defines the 'analytical core' of classical value theory as

> the set of logically necessary and mathematically exact relationships that link relative prices, the real wage and the profit rate given the fundamental data.... In the present context, logical necessity should be understood to mean that, given the data, if we impose the condition that profit rates be equalized across sectors, then the profit rate and long-period normal prices *must* coincide with those established in the solution to that system. By contrast, the data themselves – the real wage, final outputs and the production coefficients – depend upon historical and institu-

tional factors and on the complex interplay of political and social forces. (Mongiovi, 1998, p. 258)

Thus all the really interesting and important questions concerning the level of output, the pace of accumulation and the distribution of income lie outside the core. If Garegnani had used Lakatosian language he might have described them as constituting the 'protective belt' of the Sraffian 'research programme' (see Chapter 12).

This is not the only way of interpreting Sraffa (Roncaglia, 1991), but it proved to be a very influential one. It inspired an entirely new approach to the history of economic thought, in which the great watershed was not the *General Theory*, or even the replacement of 'scientific' by 'vulgar' political economy, as the Marxists had always maintained, but rather the displacement of long-period equilibrium analysis by the method of 'temporary equilibrium' theorizing. On this view the real villain was the J.R. Hicks of *Value and Capital* (Hicks, 1939), while Ricardo, Marx, Marshall and Sraffa were all on the side of the angels (Garegnani, 1976). So, too, was Keynes, little though he knew it. Precisely because the determination of output is *not* in the core of the 'neo-Ricardian' analysis, surplus theorists advocated a Keynes–Sraffa synthesis in which the principle of effective demand would be grafted onto a rigorously non-neoclassical model of long-run value and distribution (see Garegnani, 1990). This was more than many Post Keynesians could stomach; the ensuing controversies are discussed in detail in Chapter 10.

For a time it seemed that Joan Robinson, at least, would join the neo-Ricardians. She became an enthusiastic propagandist for Sraffa's work and a strident critic of those who continued to cling to the wreckage of neoclassical theory (Robinson, 1970). Yet there proved to be a profound ambivalence in Robinson's reaction to the capital controversies. She had been the very first to refer in print to reswitching and capital reversal, which, as we have seen, featured in her *Accumulation of Capital* as a mere 'curiosum' (Robinson, 1956, pp. 108–9). Even after the publication of Sraffa's book, she continued to describe them dismissively as 'certain cranky cases' (Robinson, 1962a, pp. 31, 122). Later, after she had established herself as the world's leading scourge of neoclassical theory, she tended to minimize the importance of reswitching and capital reversal and to emphasize instead the distinction between history and equilibrium. There were good methodological reasons for this (see Chapter 9), but something else may have been involved: an element of guilty conscience, Luigi Pasinetti suggests, since she recognized an intellectual debt to Sraffa that he unaccountably refused to permit her to acknowledge in print (Pasinetti, 1996). Residual attachment to neoclassical analysis also played some part, combined with a fear of the destructive consequences of abandoning the principle of substitution altogether. There was some justification for Nicholas Kaldor's savage taunt:

> But the main point on which we differ is your thorough-going neoclassicism which, despite all your protests, permeates your thinking on this whole business.... On the matter of the rate of profit, the choice of techniques and the amount of capital per head, your position is thoroughly orthodox and entirely wrong.[5]

He himself, as we saw in Chapter 3, had simply given up the concept of capital as hopeless, and also quite unnecessary. Even Roy Harrod claimed, in a subsequent controversy with Robinson, that the notion of aggregate capital played no role in his growth theory (Harrod, 1970, p. 739).

THE END OF THE AFFAIR?

Mainstream theorists adopted a number of defensive strategies in order to cope with the capital débâcle. The most blatant was to press on regardless, either asserting 'faith' in the continued practical relevance of the neoclassical parables (Ferguson, 1969) or simply ignoring the Cambridge controversies altogether. The 'new growth theorists' of the 1990s followed this course, as – shamefully – Samuelson himself was to do in later editions of his introductory textbook (Samuelson and Nordhaus, 1992, pp. 273–6, 549–53). Economic methodologists have puzzled over the reasons for this obstinate, if not obscurantist, tenacity (Ahmad, 1991, has a full bibliography). One American Marxist made quite a reputation for himself with a brilliant short paper demonstrating that all the familiar neoclassical results could be obtained from a 'production function' which, when plotted diagrammatically, spelled out the word 'HUMBUG' (Shaikh, 1974). Ideology, it seemed, was never far from the surface in the capital controversies.

An alternative strategy was to concede defeat on the analytical issues but to deny their importance, on either practical or theoretical grounds. Thus Harcourt's discussant at the 1973 conference of the Association of University Teachers of Economics in the UK dismissed the question of income distribution as uninteresting:

> it appears that neoclassical economics no longer has an answer to the question of how aggregate income is distributed between wages and profits. Now it has always puzzled me somewhat as to why this should be thought such an important question. After all, the relative share of different classes has very little long-run significance from a social welfare point of view unless the relative size of the classes remains constant. There is absolutely no reason to suppose that this will be true in general. In any case, even if we were in a stationary state in which the

> numbers of capitalists and workers were constant.... the relative share of a social class provides a decidedly crude index of welfare; frequently we would be just as interested in what was happening to distribution *within* a class or social group. It therefore seems to me that despite its long tradition the issue of aggregate long-run distribution is simply not an area of much relevance to contemporary problems. (Vanags, 1975, p. 335)

Mark Blaug made the same point in a widely-read pamphlet published by the Institute of Economic Affairs, an influential right-wing think-tank (Blaug, 1974). But the Cambridge (UK) critics were correct in arguing that capital could not in general be aggregated, the econometrician Franklin Fisher conceded. Indeed, he had demonstrated as much in a series of articles in the late 1960s and early 1970s (for example, Fisher, 1969). 'I would have thought it a fair claim that this work settled the Cambridge versus Cambridge debate,' he claimed 30 years later. It had been puzzling, then, to learn that the question of aggregate capital was still being taught, 'with great fervour', at Cambridge (UK) in the 1990s, and that his own work seemed to be completely unknown there (Fisher, 1998, pp. 39–40).

This spilled over into a broader theoretical counter-attack. None of the Cambridge criticisms applied to disaggregated neoclassical theory of the general equilibrium variety, Frank Hahn maintained. Thus the Post Keynesian critics were tilting at windmills which had long been retired from everyday use:

> The neo-Ricardians, by means of the neoclassical theory of the choice of technique, have established that capital aggregation is theoretically unsound. Fine. Let us give them an alpha for this. The result has no bearing on the mainstream of neoclassical theory simply because it does not use aggregates. It has a bearing on the vulgar theories of textbooks. But textbooks are not the frontier of knowledge. (Hahn, 1975, p. 363)

And the Sraffa model, Hahn continued, was merely a special case of Walrasian general equilibrium with fixed coefficients of production; 'there is not a single formal proposition in Sraffa's book which is not also true in a General Equilibrium model constructed on his assumptions' (ibid., p. 362). It transpired, however, that the Walrasian defence was unsustainable since the model proved to have fatal flaws of its own (Lavoie, 1992a, pp. 36–41). Hahn himself later admitted ruefully that he and his colleagues had managed to write only the overture to a complete neoclassical model; the opera had eluded them. 'I am even more disappointed that so few realise that a start has yet to be made' (Hahn, 1994, p. 258). The musical metaphor is intriguing, given that the sub-title of Sraffa's book is 'Prelude to a Critique of Economic Theory'!

The capital debates were a very important episode in the history of Post Keynesian thought, if only because they boosted both the morale and the claims to methodological morality of the younger generation of dissident economists whose challenge to orthodox theory in the 1970s is discussed in Chapter 6. First, however, we need to take stock of developments outside Cambridge. By the early 1960s a quite different strand of Post Keynesianism was beginning to emerge in the United States, with the work of Sidney Weintraub, Hyman Minsky and Paul Davidson, none of whom took any great interest in capital theory.

NOTES

1. Piero Sraffa to Joan Robinson, 27 October 1936, Joan Robinson Papers, vii/Sraffa, King's College, Cambridge, cited in Bradford and Harcourt (1997, p. 131).
2. Kahn's letters to Robinson describing his tour of the United States in 1933 are replete with such references, and make extremely interesting and entertaining reading throughout: Richard Kahn Papers, 13/90/1, King's College, Cambridge. Rosselli (2001) provides a brief discussion.
3. Nicholas Kaldor to Richard Kahn, 22 April 1960, Kaldor Papers, NKP 3/30/176, King's College, Cambridge.
4. A.C. Pigou to Piero Sraffa, [?] January 1928, Piero Sraffa Papers, C239, Trinity College, Cambridge; reprinted in Naldi (1998, p. 514, Document 2).
5. Nicholas Kaldor to Joan Robinson, 22 April 1960, Kaldor Papers, NKP 3/30/176, King's College, Cambridge.

5. Outside Cambridge: the first US Post Keynesians

> This is the *cul-de-sac* of Classical Keynesianism, being driven to recommend measures designed to reduce employment or enlarge unemployment in the midst of levels of unemployment that are already too large.
>
> It is here that weeds have overrun the garden cultivated by Keynesians, and the spirit of Lord Keynes must somewhere be writhing in discomfort and disbelief at what has been done to the seeds he planted – and all in his name. (Weintraub, 1961, pp. 24–25)

IN THE BEGINNING

Almost without exception the critics of orthodox capital theory who featured in the previous chapter were English or Italian, the latter having strong affiliations with Cambridge. The first signs of Post Keynesianism in the United States can be detected by the early 1960s, but only with some difficulty. None of the theorists whose work is described in this chapter played any part in the capital controversies, and the precise nature of their relationship with the Cambridge economists remained unclear for some time.

Although the originators of the neoclassical synthesis were also British, the new ideas were quickly taken up in the USA and soon acquired a distinctive North American flavour. One important propagator of neoclassical Keynesianism was Oskar Lange, a Polish economist working at the University of Chicago, whose analysis of the 'optimum propensity to consume' was the first serious extension of the IS–LM model (Lange, 1938). Equally important was Alvin Hansen (1887–1975), an established academic economist whose conversion to Keynesian macroeconomics symbolized the triumph of the new ideas over the old. Both in his introductory *Guide to Keynes* (Hansen, 1953) and in more advanced theoretical and policy writings, Hansen proved to be an immensely influential popularizer of the neoclassical interpretation of Keynes's thought, which was often described as the 'Hicks–Hansen model'. At a more advanced level, Franco Modigliani (1944) added to the IS–LM model a neoclassical analysis of the labour market, demonstrating that downward rigidity in money wages was – in the absence of Keynes's 'liquidity trap' – the only factor that could prevent the achievement of full employment in the neoclassical synthesis (see Chapter 1). A more elaborate version of this argument was developed by Don Patinkin (1956), whose model hinged on the 'real balance effect'. Patinkin maintained that a falling wage and price level, which increased the real value of wealth, was sufficient to raise aggregate expenditure to the level needed for the maintenance of full employment.

Even more significant, perhaps, than these advanced contributions was the teaching version of the *General Theory* presented by Paul Samuelson in his best-selling textbook, *Economics*, first published in 1948. Samuelson was responsible for the now almost universally employed 'Keynesian cross' or income–expenditure diagram, in which equilibrium gross domestic product is determined by the intersection of an aggregate expenditure function and a 45-degree line. He also invented the term 'neoclassical synthesis' (in the third, 1955, edition) to summarize the combination of Keynesian macroeconomics and neoclassical microeconomics that he presented in a simplified and highly accessible form in his text. Samuelson's book spawned a large number of imitators, all very similar in structure, content and even size (Samuelson, 1948; see also Skousen, 1997; Samuelson, 1997).

Almost from the start there were alternative interpretations of Keynes's ideas, making use of the aggregate supply and demand model that he described, but did not graph, in Chapter 3 of the *General Theory*. This model played an important part in the early history of Post Keynesianism in the United States, as we shall see in subsequent sections, since the neglect of aggregate supply conditions in the neoclassical synthesis was central to the critiques of both Sidney Weintraub and Paul Davidson. One proto-Post Keynesian treatment was offered by Lorie Tarshis (1911–93), a former student of Keynes's, whose *Elements of Economics* was published in the year before Samuelson's text. Tarshis provided an idiosyncratic version of Keynes's aggregate supply curve, drawn in price/quantity (P,Q) space rather than the aggregate proceeds/employment (Z,N) space specified by Keynes himself. In fact Tarshis's aggregate supply curve is simply the conventional industry supply curve writ large, and there is no aggregate demand curve (Tarshis, 1947, pp. 448–50; cf. King, 1994a). This was almost certainly the first attempt in print to draw Keynes's missing diagram, but it cannot be said to have succeeded.

Tarshis's book as a whole was also a failure, but this was for strictly non-academic reasons. The broad tone of the *Elements* was (mildly) social democratic, and in the political environment of the time – the Cold War was just beginning – this was enough to unleash a vicious conservative campaign against Tarshis which destroyed any chance he might have had of competing effectively with Samuelson in the textbook market (Harcourt, 1982a; Colander and Landreth, 1996; Hamouda and Price, 1998). Political pressures also served to minimize the influence of Michal Kalecki in North America, even though he was living in New York (and working for the United Nations) between 1946 and 1954. McCarthyism made any serious consideration of Kaleckian economics impossible in the United States before the radical revival of the late 1960s and early 1970s that is discussed in Chapter 6 (see also King, 1996c).

Another North American author with incipient Post Keynesian leanings was Dudley Dillard (1913–91), whose *Economics of John Maynard Keynes* bore the sub-title, 'The Theory of a Monetary Economy' and paid more attention to monetary phenomena than most of its contemporaries. It also included the first aggregate supply and demand diagram drawn to meet Keynes's specifications, that is, drawn in *Z,N* space. The diagram was not, however, very clearly explained, and the entire apparatus was soon replaced by an income–expenditure model illustrated by means of a Samuelsonian 45-degree or 'Keynesian cross' diagram (Dillard, 1948, pp. 30–38). Dillard developed close affinities with institutional economics, and after his death tribute was paid to him in the *Journal of Economic Issues* (Wray, 1993). In later life he proved sympathetic to Post Keynesianism (Dillard, 1984), but he cannot be said to have exercised any great influence over its early theoretical evolution.

SIDNEY WEINTRAUB, JEVONIAN SEDITIONIST

In fact the founding father of Post Keynesian economics in the United States was neither Tarshis nor Dillard but Sidney Weintraub (1914–83), who was the first seriously to challenge what he later described (following Jevons) as 'the noxious influence of authority' in contemporary economic theory (Weintraub, 1983, p. 234). Born in Brooklyn, Weintraub graduated from New York University and spent 1938–9 at the London School of Economics before returning to the USA in the spring of 1939. After demobilization he taught for some years at St. John's University in New York, moving to the University of Pennsylvania in 1950. Apart from a brief Canadian interlude (at the University of Waterloo in 1969–71), Weintraub spent the rest of his life in Philadelphia. With his former student Paul Davidson he established the *Journal of Post Keynesian Economics* in 1978, and co-edited it until his death.

Although in later years he proudly proclaimed himself a heretic, there was little evidence of this in the first decade and a half of his professional life, in which he published regularly on both macroeconomic and microeconomic topics in all the leading journals. Weintraub's two textbooks, *Price Theory* and *Income and Employment Analysis*, were original, not to say quirky in places, but far from iconoclastic. Indeed the former was Marshallian to the core, and in the latter Weintraub offered enthusiastic endorsement of the

Walrasian interpretation of Keynes that had been provided by Lange, Hansen and Patinkin (Weintraub, 1949, 1951). As late as 1958, in his *Approach to the Theory of Income Distribution*, he used the IS–LM model without offering any explicit criticism of it, and reaffirmed his intention of remaining firmly within the mainstream of economic analysis (Weintraub, 1958, pp. vii–viii, 154–5).

Quite suddenly, at the end of the 1950s, all this changed. There were three components of Weintraub's heresy, loosely but clearly related to each other. The first involved his commitment to the aggregate supply and demand model of effective demand, now reinterpreted as a challenge to orthodox analysis. The second was his strong interest in the distribution of income between wages and profits, which had been evident in the *Approach* but (again) reinterpreted in a manner critical of the neoclassical synthesis. Finally, Weintraub came to focus on the causes of inflation and became a stern critic of what he termed the 'Classical Keynesian' inability to determine the price level simultaneously with the levels of real output and employment. His principal target here was the Keynesian cross diagram. Initially, at least, Weintraub was less critical of IS–LM, although he eventually came to realize that the Hicks–Hansen approach that he had once supported suffered from essentially the same defects as the income–expenditure model.

He claimed that Keynes's aggregate supply and demand model, drawn in *Z,N* space, overcame these difficulties. Weintraub had been one of the first

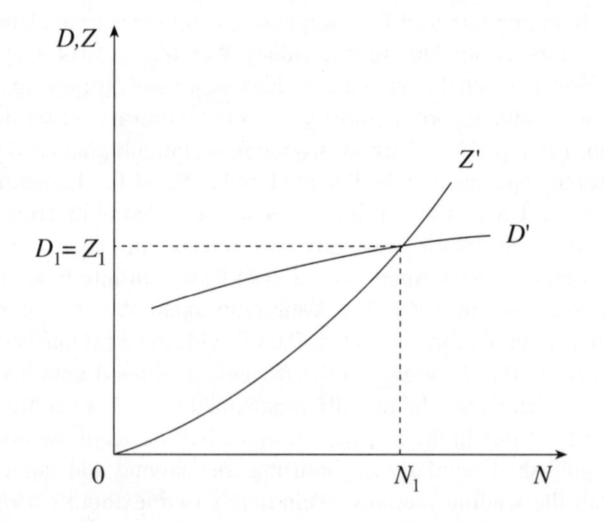

Source: Weintraub (1958, p. 39).

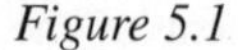
Figure 5.1

theorists clearly to identify a Keynesian agggregate supply function, with Marshallian microfoundations. In Figure 5.1, Z' is the aggregate supply function; it shows how each level of expected money proceeds generates a particular level of employment through the supply responses of firms. Weintraub assumed diminishing returns to labour, so that Z' is convex to the origin. D' is the corresponding aggregate demand curve, relating aggregate intended money expenditure to the level of employment. It is concave to the origin, effectively mimicking the shape of the standard consumption function. Equilibrium employment is N_1, with aggregate proceeds of Z_1 (Weintraub, 1956, 1957, 1958, ch. 2).

This became the basis for Weintraub's analysis of distribution, which was again derived from a Marshallian model of the individual firm (Weintraub, 1958, pp. 65–71). Aggregate supply and demand merged with distributional concerns to produce the theory of cost-push inflation, driven by money wage changes, that became the *leitmotif* of his mature work. A critical influence here was the brief stagflationary episode of 1957–8. The term is of course anachronistic, since the word 'stagflation' was not used before the 1970s, but the phenomenon provided a foretaste of the much more drastic deterioration in macroeconomic conditions that occurred in the early 1970s, with unemployment and the inflation rate increasing at the same time. This, Weintraub argued, could not be reconciled with the 'Classical Keynesian' approach to inflation, newly reformulated in terms of the Phillips relation, which made inflation a strictly decreasing function of the unemployment rate (Weintraub, 1961).

Weintraub drew on historical data to pose a theoretical alternative. In aggregate, he concluded from the empirical evidence, the *wage-cost mark-up* tended to be approximately constant over long periods of time. That is, for the economy as a whole,

$$P = kW/A, \tag{5.1}$$

where P is the price level, W is the average money wage, A is the average product of labour and k is the inverse of the wage share, or more precisely the ratio between business gross product and employee compensation. Roy Weintraub tells me that his father hoped that this equation would come to be known as 'Weintraub's constant mark-up equation', with k referred to as 'Weintraub's constant', and was disappointed when this did not come to pass.

Equation (5.1) applies, to repeat, only for the whole economy, and not necessarily to any individual company or sector. This qualification is important, for Weintraub went to great pains to deny that equation (5.1) had any inherent connection with mark-up pricing behaviour at the level of the firm. For many years he remained a loyal Marshallian, yielding ground to Kaleckian pricing models only towards the end of his life, and then only with some reluctance. As his friend Abba Lerner wrote, in 1968:

> During my stay in Cambridge what disturbed me most, and I could never get to the bottom of it, was the continuous fulmination against 'marginalism'. I understand you to say that we have to turn to marginalism to make any coherent and complete statement, including the explanation of what makes Keynesianism what it is, and I am in *vehement* agreement. I would like to see a diatribe against the fulmination rather than the gentle way in which you put it.[1]

The appropriate – that is, the macroeconomic – interpretation of equation (5.1) is evident if it is rewritten in terms of annual percentage rates of change, on the empirically justifiable assumption that k is constant. Thus

$$\dot{P} = \dot{W} - \dot{A}, \tag{5.2}$$

so that the rate of price inflation is equal to the rate of growth of money wages, minus the rate of growth of average labour productivity. This, Weintraub claimed, is '*probably the most important economic law, in the true sense, that economists have to work with*' (Weintraub, 1959, p. 33). His argument was as follows. In equation (5.2) causation runs from right to left. Thus, with k constant and $\dot{A}$ exogenously determined (and rather small), the rate of price inflation depends on the rate at which money wages increase. To control inflation, restraint in money wage growth is essential.

There were some rather obvious implications for monetary theory in this (see Chapter 8). Weintraub, however, devoted the final two decades of his life to beating the drum for incomes policy. In the early 1970s he achieved considerable fame for an article, co-authored with Henry Wallich, which argued for a tax-based incomes policy (or TIP), fighting inflation by means of market incentives in the form of a tax on excessive wage increases rather than the more fashionable resort to direct wage controls (Wallich and Weintraub, 1971). TIP, he argued relentlessly over the ensuing decade, was 'antiinflation, not antilabor' (Weintraub, 1978, p. 123). It was in fact an alternative to the destruction or emasculation of the unions that might otherwise be required to defeat inflation (and was, indeed, the policy adopted in the 1980s in Britain and the USA by the Thatcher and Reagan governments). The aim of TIP was 'to stiffen the backbone of industrialists' (ibid.) by increasing the cost to them of settling a dispute on the union's terms, and thereby encouraging them to pay no more than could be justified by the average annual increase in labour productivity in the economy as a whole. Allowing for modest price inflation of no more than 2 per cent per annum, this would allow money wages to grow at 4–5 per cent while preserving the existing wage and profit shares in total output. TIP was energetically promoted and vigorously debated in the 1970s and early 1980s, but never implemented. For some years, however, at least in the USA, Post Keynesian economics was associated in the public mind with support for incomes policy and with very little else.

There was nothing especially original in Weintraub's theoretical analysis. He himself claimed only to be disinterring Keynes's theory of the price level, which can be found in both the *Treatise* and the *General Theory* (Keynes, 1930, vol. I, ch. 10; Keynes, 1936, bk V). The constancy of relative shares had long been recognized as a problem deserving investigation, for example by Nicholas Kaldor in his celebrated 1956 article on alternative theories of distribution (see Chapter 3). Equation (5.2) had been stated explicitly, in words if not in symbols, by Joan Robinson in 1935 and James Meade in 1936 (see Chapter 1), and the Cambridge Post Keynesians had been consistent supporters of wages policy ever since; Joan Robinson once told Geoff Harcourt that 'incomes policy' had been her middle name from 1936 onwards. And by 1960 there was a substantial literature on cost-push inflation, much of it with only the loosest of connections to Post Keynesian thinking (Bronfenbrenner and Holzman, 1963).

Weintraub's main contribution was twofold. First there was his energetic, persistent and single-minded advocacy of a tax-based incomes policy, and second the skilful use of his inflation equation to attack the neoclassical synthesis. It was the latter that brought him much closer to the Cambridge Post Keynesians. The first contact was an unhappy one, with both Robinson and Kahn replying brusquely to his efforts to enlist their support, apparently in the belief that he was tilting at windmills long since demolished in the Fens. Once they realized that he was attacking a real target, albeit a North American one, they mellowed, and Weintraub received an apology from Robinson:

> I am sorry you should be so much offended with Kahn and myself. If I wrote discourteously it must be because I was in a frantic rush. Please accept my apologies. On the main question this is evidently a 'semantic misunderstanding'. To you 'Keynes's theory' means some latter-day nonsense, while to us, the old guard, it is a coherent system of analysis in which the wage–price relation is an essential part.[2]

Her own first onslaught on the 'bastard Keynesians' soon followed, directed at the 'latter-day nonsense' emanating from her former Cambridge colleague Harry Johnson (Robinson, 1962c). Weintraub and Robinson established a firm friendship that eventually took her to Canada, where she combined a visit to her young granddaughter in Ontario and collaboration with Weintraub at the University of Waterloo.

By this time Robinson had many North American contacts (Turner, 1989). She was too firmly set in her analytical ways to be significantly influenced by

Weintraub, but he shifted his position on several issues in response to her. Thus he extended his criticism of the 'Classical Keynesians' to encompass Walrasian interpretations of the *General Theory*. He also took a much greater interest in the Cambridge distribution model, paying repeated and fulsome tributes to the 'Kaldor–Kalecki–Robinson revolution' in economic theory, repudiating the neoclassical aggregate production function and even asserting the compatibility of Keynes and Sraffa. But Weintraub's break with the old ideas was never complete, as can be seen from his continuing efforts to weave together the macroeconomic and microeconomic strands in distribution analysis and, as late as 1982, to rehabilitate Hicks's original IS–LM model (Weintraub, 1982). His Post Keynesianism was a hard-won, almost a reluctant, achievement (King, 1995c; see also E.R. Weintraub, 2001).

HYMAN MINSKY, HEDGEHOG

Our second US Post Keynesian, Hyman Minsky (1919–1996) was a late developer. Whereas Weintraub, only five years his senior, had been publishing since the early 1940s, Minsky's first papers appeared only in 1957. He took even longer than Weintraub to free himself from the grip of the old ideas, and by his own admission became a Minskyian only very gradually, the process remaining incomplete until the mid-1970s (King, 1996a). Born into a socialist family in Chicago, Minsky studied in the economics department at the University of Chicago, which in the early 1940s was much more pluralist than it later became. After war service he returned to academic life, teaching at Brown University (1949–57) and Berkeley (1957–65) before moving to Washington University in St. Louis, where he spent the remainder of his career. Minsky obtained considerable first-hand experience of the working of financial institutions from his 20-year association with the Mark Twain banks in St. Louis, which he regarded as 'his laboratory' (Minsky, 1992, p. 355). He remained active as a fellow of the Jerome Levy Institute at Bard College, writing and lecturing, until his death.

In terms of Isaiah Berlin's celebrated fable, Minsky was most definitely a hedgehog rather than a fox: 'There is a line among the fragments of the Greek poet Archilocus which says: "The fox knows many things, but the hedgehog knows one big thing"'(Berlin, 1953, p. 1; cf. Dymski and Pollin, 1992). Minsky's big idea was the financial instability hypothesis: the proposition, in a nutshell, that capitalism is inherently unstable because of the way in which financial markets operate. For Minsky the Great Crash of 1929 was the most important event in modern economic history. His was a Wall Street vision of capitalism: the critical decisions are financial, and the crucial agents are bankers and their corporate clients, not millowners and factory hands or even human resource managers and union negotiators. The financial system is innately fragile, and this fact is responsible for the business cycle. Investment must be financed, and this requires loans from the banks. But bankers' lending criteria vary over the cycle, lurching from unnecessarily severe to excessively lax and back to unduly severe again. As the economy begins to recover from a downturn, and memories of the previous crisis fade, lenders become less and less nervous about their customers' ability to repay. In consequence there is a movement from 'hedge' to 'speculative' and then to 'Ponzi' finance.

The first involves borrowing against a stream of future revenues sufficient to repay both interest and principal. The second provides finance for projects that will cover interest obligations but not, or not without great difficulty, the repayment of the principal. Ponzi finance – the name came from a notorious Italo-American swindler of the early twentieth century – provides loans to pay the interest on previous borrowings. As an economic boom gathers speed, and speculative and Ponzi borrowers begin to default, lenders call in existing loans and refuse to make new ones, choking off real investment expenditure. 'Fire sales' of real assets cause a collapse in asset prices and further discourage the purchase of new capital goods. Financial fragility therefore has real economic consequences, sometimes (as in 1929) disastrous ones (Minsky, 1982).

In its fully developed form, the financial instability hypothesis made Minsky a trenchant critic of neoclassical Keynesianism, though he argued that Keynes himself had taken a quite different view (Minsky, 1975). Minsky's own presumption was always that capitalist economies were unstable, with no tendency to achieve stable growth at full employment. Economic models couched exclusively or chiefly in real terms, dealing with capitalism as if it were a barter economy, were worse than useless. The IS–LM model was at best irrelevant, since the changes in interest rates on which it relied were swamped by the effects of debt default and credit rationing. 'Imperfections' and 'rigidities' in the labour market had little or nothing to do with unemployment, and the labour market was not in any case where the real action occurred. (Downward) price flexibility was part of the problem, not the solution: Minsky drew on Irving Fisher's 'debt-deflation' theory to dismiss the Pigou effect, arguing that there was an inevitable and massive asymmetry between gainers and losers in a deflationary process, since the losers went bankrupt and their discretionary expenditure fell to zero (Minsky, 1986, ch. 6).

His approach to economic policy was equally unorthodox (King, 2000). Unlike Weintraub, Minsky's primary concern was with depression, not inflation. *Can 'It' Happen Again?* was the title he gave to a major collection of his essays (Minsky, 1982). The 'It' referred to the 1929 crash, and the answer to his question was 'Yes, unless …'. The myopic behaviour of agents in financial markets, he believed, made close regulation of their activities essential. It was unlikely, however, to be sufficient for the effects of financial instability to be avoided. Minsky argued that the 'lender of last resort' function of the central bank was crucial in preventing a repeat performance of the Great Depression, and he had little sympathy with the moral hazard objection to baling out the private sector. Financial fragility was not the product of an overindulgent Federal Reserve, and the consequences of a public failure to intervene in a financial crisis were potentially disastrous. Central banks could only contain financial fragility, and were unable to eliminate it; but this, Minsky maintained, was very much better than doing nothing.

As far as fiscal policy was concerned, Minsky advocated big government, with big deficits. In part this was a reflection of his relative lack of concern for inflation and his commitment to tight full employment; he was urging the benefits of a 3 per cent unemployment rate when most contemporary economists regarded 5 per cent as a laudable target (Minsky, 1965; cf. Samuelson and Solow, 1960). But there were also important financial arguments in favour of large budget deficits. Comparing the relative stability of the US financial system in 1962 with its fragility in 1929, Minsky concluded:

> the large increase in the relative size of the federal government has changed the financial characteristics of the system so that the development of financial instability will set off compensating financial stabilizing changes. That is, the federal government not only stabilizes income but the associated increase in the federal debt, by forcing changes in the mix of financial instruments owned by the public, makes the financial system more stable. (Minsky, 1963b, p. 103)

The big increase in risk-free federal debt, itself the product of successive budget deficits, served to supplement the effects of built-in fiscal stabilizers.

This point was greatly reinforced when, quite late in his career, Minsky stumbled onto the Kaleckian theory of aggregate profits (see Chapter 2). The financial instability hypothesis began life as a theory of corporate financial *commitments*. Kalecki allowed Minsky to complete it with a theory of financial *resources*. Total profits, in a Kaleckian model, are the sum of private investment expenditure, net exports and the budget deficit. Aggregate income is the sum of profits (P), wages (W), taxation (T) and imports (M); aggregate expenditure is equal to consumption by capitalists (C_c), consumption by workers (C_w), investment (I), government spending (G) and exports (X). Thus, since in equilibrium total income equals total expenditure,

$$P + W + T + M = C_C + C_W + I + G + X. \quad (5.3)$$

On the Kaleckian simplifying assumption that workers do not save, and capitalists do not consume, $C_c = 0$ and $C_w = W$, so that

$$P = I + (G - T) + (X - M). \tag{5.4}$$

This means that the financial position of the private sector is strengthened, *ceteris paribus*, the greater the gap between government spending and taxation revenues (Minsky, 1977, 1982, ch. 2). For this reason Minsky was vigorously opposed to the theory – if not always to the deficit-spending *practice* – of Reaganomics (Minsky, 1981–2).

Hyman Minsky's Post Keynesianism was highly individual, perhaps even more so than that of Sidney Weintraub and in quite different dimensions. Minsky had no particular objection to aggregate supply and demand analysis or to a tax-based incomes policy, but did not regard them as especially interesting or important. He took no interest in the analysis of production, in the operation of product markets or in pricing theory, and Sraffa's critique of neoclassical theory left him cold. Most of the issues that excited the Cambridge Post Keynesians, in fact, failed to arouse Minsky. Growth without cycles, he believed, was simply impossible; 'real' analysis without money was futile; paradoxes in capital theory and alternative models of income distribution were at best amusing academic games. He was critical even of Paul Davidson's monetary theory:

> I do have a serious substantive quarrel with his approach, which is the approach adopted by Joan Robinson and Kregel among others. They insist upon defining as a base for their argument a steady growth process and elucidating the circumstances under which this process can be maintained. They also conclude more or less in passing that the maintenance of steady growth is difficult if not impossible under capitalist processes.
>
> My perspective is that once you define the financial institutions of capitalism in any precise form then the normal path of the economy is intractably cyclical and the problems [*sic*] of macroeconomic theory is to spell out the properties of the cyclical process. Thus much of what is very valid in Paul's analysis is diminished in significance because of his basic approach.... within a cyclical perspective uncertainty becomes operational in the sense that myopic hindsight determines the current state of Keynesian/Robinsonian Animal Spirits: without a cyclical perspective uncertainty is more or less of an empty bag.[3]

Even more than Weintraub, Minsky was in intellectual terms a loner, who founded no school and attracted few disciples. His relations with Weintraub and with Paul Davidson were soured by his dismissive review of the latter's *Money and the Real World* (Minsky, 1974), and although Minsky was a patron of the *Journal of Post Keynesian Economics* he never published there. Indeed, his affinities were with the New Keynesians almost as much as the

Post Keynesians (see Chapter 11), while the institutionalist *Journal of Economic Issues* devoted much of its June 1997 issue to a series of tributes to him. But there was no Minsky school, and relatively few obvious Minsky disciples: Steven Fazzari, Randall Wray, perhaps Charles Kindleberger (as far as the historical significance of the financial instability hypothesis is concerned) and a few radical monetary theorists like Gary Dymski and Robert Pollin (Fazzari and Papadimitriou, 1992). Nevertheless, Minsky's impact on the development of Post Keynesian economics in the United States was considerable, if diffuse and not always immediately discernible. He contributed significantly to the 'structuralist' perspective on monetary endogeneity that will be discussed in Chapter 8, and was a major influence on his former student Victoria Chick, herself a major Post Keynesian monetary theorist in the United Kingdom.

PAUL DAVIDSON: MONEY AND THE REAL WORLD

Paul Davidson belonged to a later generation than Minsky, yet because he was an early starter his published work began only a couple of years after that of the older man. He graduated in science from Brooklyn College, and between 1950 and 1952 was a research student in biochemistry at the University of Pennsylvania before dropping out. After military service during the Korean War, Davidson returned to Pennsylvania to study economics. Here he came under the influence of Sidney Weintraub, who supervised his doctoral dissertation and significantly affected his views on economic theory and policy. In 1958 Davidson moved to Rutgers University, where he remained (except for a brief interlude as an oil company executive) until 1986. Since then he has taught at the University of Tennessee at Knoxville, from which base he continues to edit the *Journal of Post Keynesian Economics*. An excellent brief account of Davidson's contribution is given by Rotheim (1996).

Two of his distinguishing characteristics as an economic theorist were established very early in his career, both of them under the influence of Sidney Weintraub. The first relates to the distribution of income. Davidson wrote his doctoral dissertation (supervised by Weintraub) on the historical evolution of distribution theories, and it was good enough to be published as a book. His studies led Davidson to reject both the Kaleckian approach to the relative shares of wages and profits and the Kaldorian macrodistribution model based on differences in workers' and capitalists' savings propensities (Davidson, 1960). Unlike Weintraub he never relented on either question. Davidson was always profoundly unimpressed by Michal Kalecki, regarding it as a strong point in favour of Keynes that his analysis is more general than the Kaleckian model, since it extends to perfectly competitive markets as well as to any number of different degrees of monopolistic imperfection.

This point was made very clearly in Davidson's second book, a jointly authored text on *Aggregate Supply and Demand Analysis*. Dedicated to and obviously inspired by Weintraub, this was the first attempt to set out Keynesian macroeconomic theory at the introductory level entirely in terms of the aggregate supply and demand model. It was a commercial failure, selling only 3000 copies and soon disappearing from the market. Intellectually, though, it was more successful, providing a comprehensive and coherent teaching alternative to the neoclassical synthesis that Davidson would draw on repeatedly in subsequent decades (see, for example Davidson, 1994). As with Weintraub, the foundations of Davidson's aggregate supply function were strictly Marshallian, derived from a provisional assumption of perfect competition but capable of extension to imperfect competition by the simple device of varying the price elasticity of product demand (Davidson and Smolensky, 1964, pp. 128–31).

One area in which Davidson and Smolensky made a clear break with orthodoxy was the labour market. Their conclusions are important enough to be quoted at length:

> [The] neoclassical demand curve for labor absolutely requires the assumption of unchanging product demand schedules. The stability of these product demand functions depend [*sic*] on assumptions about (1) the constancy of consumer tastes, (2) the constancy of income and its distribution among consumers, and (3) the constancy of all other prices. These assumptions are obviously inapplicable for any analysis attempting to determine what the effect of changes in money-wages will have [*sic*] on effective demand. With any change in employment due to a change in the money-wage rate, there must be concomitant changes in aggregate real income (and its distribution) in the economy. Thus, at least, assumption (2) underlying the individual product demand curve is inapplicable. Accordingly, the neoclassical aggregate demand curve for labor must be rejected as being inapplicable to an analysis which involves changes in output and employment, and an aggregate demand curve for labor must be derived which is based on shifting rather than constant product demand curves. (Ibid., pp. 176–7)

Davidson continued to attack the neoclassical treatment of labour demand throughout his career. It formed a major element in his critique of New Classical Economics (see Chapter 9) and of New Keynesian theory (see Chapter 11).

There was relatively little on money in the Davidson and Smolensky text, but this omission was soon rectified in a series of articles published in the late 1960s that formed the basis for Davidson's masterpiece, *Money and the Real World* (Davidson, 1972a). This was a long and difficult book, but a short and accessible summary was provided in the *Economic Journal* article that bore the same title (Davidson, 1972b). Davidson's aim was to recover the core of Keynes's monetary theory, which he found as much in the *Treatise on Money* as in the *General Theory* and which he believed to have been lost in the errors and obfuscations of the neoclassical synthesis. His first and most important claim was that money was not neutral, even in the long run. Davidson defended this proposition as early as 1965 in an article rehabilitating the 'finance motive' for holding money, which Keynes had added to his analysis of liquidity preference in a post-*General Theory* restatement of his ideas (Keynes, 1937a). 'Considering that Keynes felt that the finance motive was the coping stone of his liquidity preference theory,' Davidson noted, 'it is surprising to see that the concept has practically disappeared from the literature.' In fact 'the finance motive provides the link to demonstrate that the aggregate demand for money function is *not* independent of events in the real sector', so that money is not neutral (Davidson, 1965, pp. 12–13). Since firms held money to assure themselves that they would be able to carry out their investment plans, there was no reason to suppose that the transactions demand for money would be a stable function of the level of output; rather it would depend on expected future investment expenditure, which was notoriously unstable. Thus, as Joan Robinson had recognized, the finance motive was 'one of the dynamic elements in the static Keynesian model' (ibid., p. 16; cf. Robinson, 1952a, pp. 80–87). It entailed both that the IS and LM functions were interdependent and – for Davidson this was the crucial point – that the demand for money was not a linear homogeneous function of real output.

Thus the so-called 'classical dichotomy' could not be sustained, and any attempt to partition the economy into separate 'real' and 'monetary' sectors was mistaken. Changes in monetary conditions would affect real output and employment levels, while changes in the price level might originate in the 'real' economy, especially in the labour market and the process of money wage determination. Since all neoclassical models of general equilibrium depended ultimately on the assumption that money was neutral, it followed that they were relevant only to barter economies, and had nothing to say about capitalism. This was true even of self-proclaimed 'Keynesian' models of portfolio balance like those of James Tobin, which made sense only if it were supposed that Say's Law held and involuntary unemployment was therefore assumed away at the outset (Davidson, 1968a).

Many neoclassical theorists paid lip-service to the role of time and uncertainty in determining the demand for money, recognizing that in a world of complete certainty where all transactions took place at the same time there would be no rational motive for holding an asset that yields no return. But, Davidson argued, this *was* only lip-service: 'Patinkin, Friedman, Tobin and others ... have ignored Keynes's insistence that certain propositions were so uncertain in principle as to be incapable of having any numerical value; and they have instead substituted the concept of quantifiable, predictable risk for uncertainty' (Davidson, 1972b, p. 102). In a world of certainty-equivalence, however, there would be no reason to make contracts in money terms, as Keynes knew very well:

> It is only in a world of uncertainty and disappointment that money comes into its own as a necessary mechanism for deferring decisions; money has its niche only when we feel queasy about undertaking any actions which will commit our claims on resources on to a path which can only be altered, if future events require this, at very high costs (if at all). (Ibid., p. 104)

Keynes also knew, Davidson continued, that money must have certain essential properties if it is to function effectively: a zero (or negligible) elasticity of production and a zero (or negligible) elasticity of substitution. The first property poses significant problems for Post Keynesian monetary theory (see Chapter 8), but the second is both uncontroversial and extremely important. It means that an increase in the desire for liquidity cannot spill over to any appreciable extent into the demand for other goods: 'the demand for a store of value, in an uncertain world, does not generate the demand to commit resources. Thus the virtuous interaction between supply of resources and the demand for resources which is succinctly expressed via Say's Law is broken' (Davidson, 1972a, p. 145).

There were substantial implications for economic policy. One was that (downward) money wage flexibility was neither a necessary nor a sufficient condition for full employment. On the contrary, since the money wage rate was 'the anchor upon which the price level of all producible goods is fastened' (ibid., p. 153), its approximate stability, in both directions, was essential to the stability of the entire monetary system of production. Michal Kalecki's rejection of downward flexibility in money wages rested on very similar arguments; it was used to good effect in his demolition of the Pigou effect (see Chapter 2). Writing in the inflationary 1960s, Davidson was understandably more concerned with upward movements in money wage rates. He distinguished three causes of inflation: diminishing returns, as firms' marginal costs rise with increases in output; higher profit margins, due to increases in the degree of monopoly power; and a tendency for money wages to grow more rapidly than labour productivity (Davidson and Smolensky, 1964, pp. 180–82). None of them could be overcome by the application of a simple rule governing the rate of monetary expansion. On the contrary:

> In an uncertain world … where expectations are volatile and unpredictable … the relationship between the required increase in the money supply and the increase in real wealth is much too complex to be handled by any simple rule. Money clearly matters in the process of economic growth in a monetary economy, but a simple

> rule can be no substitute for wise management of the money supply. (Davidson, 1968a, p. 318)

Thus monetary policy must be discretionary rather than rule-driven, and 'should be oriented solely toward achieving full employment and economic growth'. Inflation was best combated by means of an incomes policy (Davidson, 1968b, p. 95).

Davidson's critique was directed not just at Milton Friedman and the monetarists (see Chapter 8), but also at self-proclaimed Keynesians like Tobin. Indeed his major article on 'Money, Portfolio Balance, Capital Accumulation and Economic Growth' (Davidson, 1968a) was primarily a critique of Tobin, whose failure to respond still rankled with Davidson a quarter of a century later (King, 1994b, p. 365). Despite his increasing estrangement from the mainstream of the profession, Davidson remained a Marshallian rather than a Kaleckian in matters of microeconomic theory and method, and his relations with the Cambridge Post Keynesians were never tranquil. On sabbatical leave there in 1970–71, he aroused such hostility with his interpretation of the neo-Pasinetti theorem (see Chapter 3) that Robinson refused to speak to him for a while. Then they corresponded, Davidson leaving his replies to Robinson's written queries on her desk during the coffee break for her to respond to them. Finally, and against the advice of the seminar organizer, he invited Robinson and Richard Kahn to the presentation of his paper:

> So, I come in and Joan's not there, and I start talking. She walks in with Richard Kahn, three or four minutes late, sits down, and I say two or three more things. She suddenly gets up and she says – because she's already seen the draft of the paper, of course, which she had criticized – she gets up and says, 'I think you've got it all wrong.' I say 'Wait a second!', and she walks up to the blackboard and spends the next 15 minutes explaining what it's all about. And then – I'm sort of too much of a gentleman to interrupt her while she's doing all this – but I knew what I was going to say. And then when she's finished she says, 'All right, Richard, let's go', and she walks out before I can say anything. (King, 1994b, p. 367)

Three years later Davidson received an apology, of sorts, from Robinson (Turner, 1989, p. 198).

Political differences had helped to create this atmosphere of antagonism, as Davidson was quick to recognize. The opening chapter of his *Money and the Real World* contained 'A Table of Political Economy Schools of Thought' ranged from left to right, with the 'Monetarist–Neoclassical' school representing the 'extreme right' and the 'Neoclassical–Bastard Keynesian' school standing to the 'right of centre'. At the 'extreme left' was the 'Socialist–Radical' tendency, with the 'Neo-Keynesian' or Cambridge Post Keynesians (Joan Robinson, Kaldor and Pasinetti are named) occupying a position 'left of centre'. In the middle was the 'Keynes School', '[a]n exceedingly small group who have attempted to develop Keynes's original views on employment, growth, and money, e.g. Harrod, Lerner, and Weintraub' – and of course Davidson himself (Davidson, 1972a, pp. 3–4).

This should probably not be taken too seriously. Abba Lerner supported Davidson and Weintraub on the question of incomes policy, but he was never a Post Keynesian, any more than the increasingly conservative Harrod. By this time Robinson was well to the left of most of her colleagues at Cambridge, singing the praises of Mao's China and the (North) Korean economic miracle (Robinson, 1965a), while Kaldor and Kahn were on the way to earning life peerages for advising the Wilson Labour governments. They might all have taken issue with Davidson's description of their view of the government's role ('Laissez-faire except for macroeconomic controls over incomes') and the outside observer might have wondered how this placed them to the left of the 'Keynes School' ('Laissez-faire except for macroeconomic controls over money, investment decisions, and the earnings system'). But Davidson *was* correct in suggesting that there was a difference in the political attitudes of the 'Anglo-Italian' and North American Post Keynesians, and that this affected the positions they took on both theoretical and political questions.

Despite these frictions, by 1970 Post Keynesian economics was firmly established on both sides of the Atlantic, its advocates united in asserting the revolutionary significance of Keynes's ideas and in warning 'that what passes for "Keynesian" economics is nothing but pre-keynesian simplicities camouflaged with some Keynesian cosmetic terminology' (Davidson, 1972a, p. 1). They agreed not only in their criticism of the neoclassical synthesis but also on major policy issues and, to a somewhat lesser extent, on the analytical alternative that they had to offer. Rejection of Say's Law, reaffirmation of the principle of effective demand and the relevance of involuntary unemployment in both the short and long run, insistence on the importance of uncertainty and historical time: all this was common ground. There were certainly differences of emphasis, with the Cambridge Post Keynesians being much more concerned with growth and distribution theory while the Americans focused on money and (with the exception of Minsky) on aggregate supply and demand analysis. But the areas of agreement were broad enough, and the time appeared ripe, for the head-on confrontation with the neoclassical mainstream that forms the subject of the next chapter.

NOTES

1. Abba Lerner to Weintraub, 20 November 1968, Sidney Weintraub Papers, Special Collections Department, Duke University Library, Box 1, Folder 19.

2. Robinson to Weintraub, 4 January 1961, Sidney Weintraub Papers, Special Collections Department, Duke University Library, Box 1, Folder 12. (This correspondence appears to have been initiated by Richard Kahn, who wrote to Weintraub complaining about his neglect of Keynes – and Kahn – in a 1960 article on wage inflation (Weintraub, 1960); Kahn to Weintraub, 29 November 1960, and Weintraub to Kahn, 5 December 1960, Sidney Weintraub Papers, Special Collections Department, Duke University Library, Box 1, Folder 11.)
3. Hyman Minsky to Sidney Weintraub, 19 November 1974; Sidney Weintraub Papers, Special Collections Department, Duke University Library, Durham, North Carolina, Box 3, Folder 3.

6. Against the mainstream: Post Keynesian economics in the 1970s

> A new scientific truth does not triumph by convincing its opponents and making them see the light, but rather because its opponents eventually die, and a new generation grows up that is familiar with it. (Planck, 1949, pp. 33–4, cited in Kuhn, 1962 [1970], p. 151)

THE BATTLE OF THE PARADIGMS

The impact of the Cambridge capital controversies on the fledgling Post Keynesian movement was very substantial (see Chapter 4). It seemed for a while to many critics of neoclassical economics as though the enemy had been taken on and beaten, on its own ground: the mainstream theories of capital, distribution and growth had been shown to be incoherent, and their most authoritative defenders had admitted as much. There was a real prospect – or so it appeared to the enthusiasts for the new ideas – that 'Cambridge', 'Anglo-Italian', 'neo-Keynesian' or 'Post Keynesian' economics might constitute a potentially lethal threat to orthodox thinking. It was not just a question of a head-on confrontation. This was a battle that the dissidents were likely to win.

With the benefit of hindsight it can be seen that this febrile optimism had no basis in reality. In the early 1970s, however, the impregnability of the neoclassical citadel was by no means obvious. Three additional developments gave the besiegers real grounds for hope. First, there was a diffuse and ill-defined but very widespread feeling that mainstream economics had lost its way, retreating from the traditional concern with serious social problems into a formalistic fortress where resort to trivial mathematical puzzles and ever-more elaborate econometric techniques had severed any connection between the economic theorist and economic reality. Presidential addresses and high-profile guest lectures were increasingly devoted to 'the crisis in economics', and profound dissatisfaction with the state of the discipline was expressed by elder statesmen who had no discernible link to the Post Keynesian rebels (Phelps Brown, 1972; Ward, 1972; Worswick, 1972). Second, and clearly if rather loosely related to this, was the worldwide rise of political radicalism, especially among students. The student movement was stimulated by opposition to the Vietnam war and the role of the academy in supporting the US war machine. This soon spilled over into criticism of the curriculum, which in the case of economics necessarily absorbed the self-criticism of the elders but went very much further in search of an alternative analytical framework capable of accommodating radical concerns with imperialism, poverty, war and underdevelopment (Pateman, 1972; Hunt and Schwartz, 1972).

Finally, there was the important intellectual influence of contemporary developments in the history and philosophy of science which was touched on in the Introduction. Thomas S. Kuhn, whose book *The Structure of Scientific Revolutions* was widely read and enthusiastically discussed by dissident economists in the decade after its publication, was the central figure here (Kuhn, 1962 [1970]). Drawing extensively on the history of the natural sciences, Kuhn cast doubt on the dominant positivist view of the growth of scientific knowledge. For the most part, he argued, scientists were not the sceptical beings depicted by Karl Popper, constantly seeking to falsify hypotheses and always open to the possibility of overturning the bases of accepted truth. Most scientists, most of the time, operated within a firmly entrenched paradigm that established a framework of ideas and an agenda for research, and carried out modest but useful 'normal science' that posed no threat to the paradigm itself. Such challenges arose only in times of scientific crisis, when embarrassing theoretical or experimental anomalies could not be accounted for within the dominant paradigm. Under such circumstances, and only then, there arose the prospect of a scientific revolution in which the old paradigm might be rejected in favour of a new one, which would prove fundamentally incommensurable with the old one, prescribing new ways of doing research and new criteria for the assessment of scientific theories.

The language of scientific revolutions was especially appealing to Post Keynesians. The master himself had expected to 'revolutionize' economic theory (see Chapter 1), and shortly after his death the prominent econometrician Lawrence Klein had published an influential primer on the new macroeconomics with the title *The Keynesian Revolution* (Klein, 1947). In the later 1960s and early 1970s Kuhn's ideas resonated much more widely, with economic methodologists and historians of economic thought debating vigorously the status of the marginalist and Keynesian 'revolutions' in economic science (Hutchison, 1978). Radical and Post Keynesian theorists had more immediate concerns. The signs of a crisis in neoclassical economics were there for all to see; the rival paradigm was ready and waiting; surely a new and decisive revolution in economic theory was already under way?

This, at least, is how the Post Keynesians saw things in the early 1970s. They fervently believed that they were living in revolutionary times, with economics on the verge of a paradigm shift. This explains their optimism, which proved to be wildly excessive. It accounts, too, for the arrogance and condescension that they were often accused of, sometimes justly. They were, after all, dealing with antagonists whom they believed to be the modern equivalents of pre-Copernican astronomers. When Joan Robinson declared that the older generation of economists was a lost cause and the future lay with the young graduate students, there was a sense in which she could claim Kuhn's authority. In all previous scientific revolutions, as he had noted, established researchers tended to cling to the losing ideas. Thus paradigm shifts necessarily involved a process of generational change (Kuhn, 1962 [1970], ch. XII). As Robinson wrote of her 1973 textbook, *Introduction to Modern Economics*: 'The main purpose of the book ... was to get it into the hands of American students. There is a lot of prejudice among American professors of economics against our line, but once the students know about the book they will demand that their faculties allow them to use it.'[1] If only it had been that simple.

JOAN ROBINSON: NEW ORLEANS AND AFTER

Something of the flavour of these exchanges can be savoured in the text of the Richard T. Ely lecture that Joan Robinson gave at the New Orleans meeting of the American Economics Association in December 1971. For once the president of the AEA was a dissident. This was the veteran institutionalist and Keynesian John Kenneth Galbraith, a longtime friend of Robinson's and celebrated critic of US capitalism and its apologists in academic economics (Galbraith, 1958, 1967). Galbraith now offered her the most important platform she had ever occupied. Robinson took full advantage of it, delivering an abrasive, challenging, deliberately provocative indictment of neoclassical economics that was designed to polarize her audience between the old and conservative and the young and progressive. Even her title was Kuhnian: 'The Second Crisis of Economic Theory'. The first crisis, Robinson argued, had resulted from the failure of contemporary macroeconomics to account for the Great Depression. It had given rise to the Keynesian Revolution, but for neoclassical economists Keynes's *General Theory* 'was too great a shock. Orthodoxy managed to wind it up in a cocoon again'. By introducing Walrasian microfoundations, which abolished historical time and thereby eliminated uncertainty, mainstream theorists had put Keynes to sleep (Robinson, 1972, pp. 3, 4). This was an echo of Robinson's earlier critique of the neoclassical synthesis, which she had scathingly described as 'pre-Keynesian economics after Keynes' (Robinson, 1964).

The first crisis, she maintained, had not been fully resolved before the second crisis set in. The new crisis involved microeconomic questions of allocation and distribution: 'The first crisis arose from the breakdown of a theory which could not account for the *level* of employment. The new crisis arises from a theory that cannot account for the *content* of employment' (Robinson, 1972, p. 6). Neoclassical theory was unable to explain the increase in world poverty, which Robinson regarded as a necessary consequence of economic growth. It had failed to come to terms with 'the notorious problem of pollution', which was too large to be confined to 'a few minor points discussed under the heading of "externalities" that could easily be put right' (ibid., p. 7). Orthodoxy had simply closed its eyes to the massive wasteful expenditure on armaments, which had proved necessary to maintain full employment. And there was no coherent neoclassical theory of distribution, which meant that mainstream analysis could contribute nothing to an understanding of either the relative shares of wages and profits or the causes of inequality in employment incomes. At this point, Robinson concluded, the first and second crises came together. Inflation was both the cause and the effect of conflict over distribution. It was the effect, because the irreconcilable income claims of different classes and groups put great pressure on the price level. It was also the cause, since inflation itself 'has destroyed the conventions governing the acceptance of [the] existing distribution'. She concluded by denouncing the 'evident bankruptcy of economic theory which for the second time has nothing to say on the questions that, to everyone except economists, appear to be most in need of an answer' (ibid., pp. 9, 10).

The immediate impact of Robinson's lecture was remarkable. The speech itself 'was greeted by an overflow audience with enthusiasm rarely seen at academic gatherings' (Fels, 1972, p. ix). As she herself wrote, sardonically, to Richard Kahn, 'The young ones got the points and everyone clapped and cheered. I was looking round to see if anyone had the moral courage to remain seated at the end but I think no-one did.'[2] The informal meetings that took place at New Orleans played an important part in the early evolution of Post Keynesianism in the United States (Lee, 2000a; Turner, 1989, pp. 182–4). The Ely lecture was essentially a propagandistic summary of Robinson's new book, *Economic Heresies* (Robinson, 1971a). This was aimed at the professional economist and more particularly at the graduate students in whose openness to the new paradigm she placed such great faith. But the battle of ideas had also to be fought at the bottom, in the introductory principles course where young and impressionable new students made their first contact with economic theory. For 20 years the textbook market had been dominated by Paul Samuelson's *Economics* and its various clones, all preaching more or less sophisticated versions of the neoclassical synthesis. Samuelson himself was in no doubt as to the significance of his market dominance, subsequently stating in a newspaper interview: 'I don't care who writes a nation's laws – or crafts its advanced treaties – if I can write its economics textbooks' (Nasar, 1995, p. C1, cited by Skousen, 1997, p. 150). To force through the impending revolution in economics a rival text was required, which would do for the new paradigm what Samuelson's had done so successfully for the old one. On her return from New Orleans Robinson sat down to write it, in partnership with her young Cambridge colleague John Eatwell, a follower of Piero Sraffa who was already making a reputation for himself as a critic of general equilibrium theory.

The ambitious new text, *An Introduction to Modern Economics* (Robinson and Eatwell, 1973), was published with very high hopes. The aim of the authors was to break into the North American market in a very big way, winning endorsements by dint of pressure from radical students over the opposition of the conservative professors. But the text proved to have serious flaws in both execution and design. It was too difficult for newcomers to economics and too idiosyncratic in its selection of topics. The publishers refused to proceed with the anticipated American edition, and the expected challenge to Samuelson never materialized. The failure of the text epitomized – if it did not significantly contribute to – the successful resistance of the old paradigm to the challenge of the new (King and Millmow, 2002).

THE RECONSTRUCTION OF POLITICAL ECONOMY?

Energetic support for the new paradigm came from two young Americans, Jan Kregel and Alfred Eichner (1937–88). Kregel had studied in Cambridge and taught at Bristol and Southampton, in addition to the United States and the Netherlands, before settling in Italy. In the 1970s he was above all an enthusiastic campaigner for Joan Robinson's ideas. Eichner learned his economics at Columbia University in New York, where he came under the influence of the institutionalist Eli Ginsberg and acquired a penchant for economic history and for the unorthodox ideas of Gardiner C. Means. Eichner taught first at Columbia (1961–71), then at the State University of New York at Purchase (1971–80) and finally at Rutgers University. As a Post Keynesian he was very largely self-taught, but he was heavily influenced by his prolonged correspondence with Joan Robinson between 1969 and 1975, in the course of which she convinced him of the need to integrate a Kaleckian macroeconomic theory of profits into his initially microeconomic analysis of the giant corporation (Arestis, 1989; King, 1996c, pp. 153–6; the Robinson–Eichner correspondence is printed in its entirety in Lee, 2000b).

Between 1971 and 1973 Kregel published three books contrasting neoclassical and Post Keynesian theory, two of them full-length texts aimed at graduate students and the third a brief critical comparison of 'neo-Neoclassical' and 'neo-Keynesian' growth theory. *Rate of Profit, Distribution and*

Growth: Two Views was written in Cambridge in 1968–9 under the powerful influence of Joan Robinson. In it, Kregel summarized the orthodox and Post Keynesian approaches to capital theory. All neoclassical analyses of economic growth, he claimed, had been undermined by the Sraffian capital critique. Neither Samuelson, nor Solow, nor Tobin had been able to provide a convincing theory of the rate of profits, and this had proved fatal to their treatment of growth. Even Harrod, who was careful to avoid reliance on orthodox capital theory, had no explanation of the rate of profits and therefore no means of escape from the 'knife-edge' of instability. Kregel argued that Keynesian models were superior to neoclassical models of growth on two counts. They included a logically consistent theory of the profit rate, which was determined by the propensity to save out of non-wage income; and they specified investment rather than saving as the independent variable. 'The important difference' between the neoclassical and neo-Keynesian models, Kregel concluded, 'is in the assumption about investment' (Kregel, 1971, p. 197). This book enjoyed the (rare) privilege of a review in the *Journal of Political Economy*, where Geoff Harcourt – who had just completed his own book-length account of the capital controversies – criticized Kregel for relying excessively on equilibrium theory rather than discussing the actual processes of growth and distribution over time (Harcourt, 1973).

Kregel's *Theory of Economic Growth* was a 90 page introductory text. It began with a historical survey, contrasting the classical–Marxian or 'real cost' approach to growth theory with the purely subjective analysis of the neoclassical economists. Turning to modern theories of growth, Kregel traced a direct line of descent from Keynes through Kalecki to Harrod and thence to the Post Keynesian treatment of growth and distribution developed by Robinson, Kaldor and Pasinetti. He concluded by repeating his attack on the 'neo-Neoclassical' models of Samuelson and Solow, whose 'assumptions are chosen to illustrate the belief that free enterprise will produce full employment and steady growth with market prices reflecting scarcity values' (Kregel, 1972a, p. 85). The Post Keynesian model, Kregel maintained, was already being extended to the problems of underdevelopment, public finance, international trade, financial assets and technical change, and to allow for uncertainty, money and disequilibrium states. Increasingly it would benefit from the incorporation of Marxian insights. The underlying economic philosophy of the two paradigms, Kregel concluded, 'is obviously quite different.... The choice between the two approaches to economics and growth presented above is more than one of logical consistency. It concerns the basic method of thought and the future usefulness of economics itself' (ibid., pp. 87, 90).

The third of Kregel's texts, *The Reconstruction of Political Economy* (Kregel, 1973), went into a second English edition and was soon translated into Italian. Its focus was positive rather than critical and comparative. Kregel offered a synthesis of Keynes's short-period theory and its Post Keynesian long-period extension, in the spirit of classical political economy. For much of the book he drew heavily on Joan Robinson's *Accumulation of Capital*, augmented by Sraffa, with brief discussions of the work of Kaldor and Pasinetti at the end of the book. Kregel concluded with a call for a more intensive Post Keynesian analysis of government activity, economic history and non-equilibrium states. 'In terms of strengthening the theory', however, 'the largest gap remains on the micro level', in the theory of price formation in corporate capitalism (Kregel, 1973, p. 207).

This was where Eichner made his contribution. He began by presenting empirical evidence demonstrating that, in the United States, prices in oligopolistic industries were much less sensitive to aggregate demand conditions than prices in competitive industries. Eichner linked this to the long-standing literature on 'cost-plus' pricing behaviour under oligopoly (Hall and Hitch, 1939; Lee, 1998). The determinants of the 'plus factor' or mark-up, however, had yet to be satisfactorily explained. Eichner suggested that the mark-up 'depends on the demand for and supply of additional investment funds by the firm or group of firms with the price-setting power within the industry' (Eichner, 1973, pp. 1189–90). In other words, the price leader used its market power to obtain the level of internally generated funds required to finance its intended investment expenditures.

Eichner identified three constraints on the generation of 'cash flow' by means of manipulating the mark-up: the substitution effect, the entry factor and the threat of government intervention. The first referred to consumers' ability to switch to competing products when the relative price of a good increased. The second, which had already featured prominently in the oligopoly pricing models of P.W.S. Andrews (1949) and Paolo Sylos Labini (1962), derived from the firm's anxiety about the potential entry of new producers attracted by the higher profit levels in the market concerned. Taken together, Eichner suggested, these two constraints could be interpreted as attaching an implicit interest rate to the use of internally generated funds. The third constraint (to which he paid relatively little attention) depended on the vigour with which governments pursued antitrust or anti-monopoly policies.

Instead of using algebra, Eichner formalized his argument in a four-quadrant diagram. The R-curve in quadrant IV of Figure 6.1 shows how the implicit interest rate (R) rises, at an increasing rate, as the mark-up (n) increases. In quadrant II the $\Delta F/p$ curve illustrates the increase in internal funds per period ($\Delta F/p$) as the mark-up rises. From these two relationships Eichner derived a supply curve of additional internal funds ($S_{1'}$), which is drawn in quadrant I. The higher the mark-up, the greater the funds that are generated, but the higher also is the implicit interest cost. On the assumption that the supply to the firm of external investment finance is perfectly elastic at

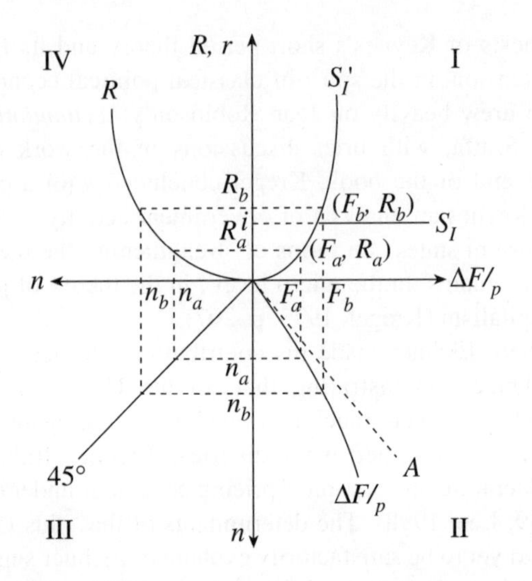

Source: Eichner (1973, p. 1192).

Figure 6.1

an interest rate of *i* per cent (as shown by S_1), the effective supply curve of investment funds from all sources is given by $S_{1'}$ up to *i* and by S_1 thereafter. Depending on its demand curve for additional investment funds (D_1), the firm will either rely entirely on internal finance or resort to external borrowing for a part of its needs.

The first case is illustrated in Figure 6.2a, where the firm generates F_1 internally by imposing a mark-up of n_1. In Figure 6.2b, which illustrates the second possibility, a mark-up of n_2 generates OF_2 internally, leaving F_2F_3 to be raised from the external capital market. An algebraic version of the model can be found in Eichner (1987), where the mark-up was described (by analogy with the turnover tax in the former Soviet Union) as 'the corporate levy'.

Eichner claimed that his model 'provides the micro-economic foundation for post-Keynesian macro-dynamic theory' (Eichner, 1973, p. 1196), making it possible to specify the precise mechanism by which the aggregate savings ratio increased in response to a higher ratio of investment to income in the Kaldor–Pasinetti models discussed in Chapter 3. Kaldor himself had attempted to extend his analysis to the corporate economy, an effort that was later carried on by his student Adrian Wood (Kaldor, 1966b; Wood, 1975). Something of the sort is implicit in the Kaleckian model of Josef Steindl (see Chapter 2), and another formalization of the same insight can be found in the influential paper of Harcourt and Kenyon (1976).

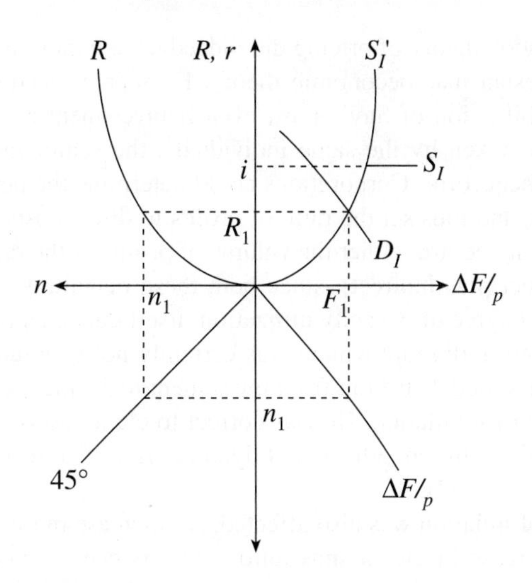

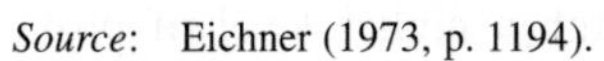
Source: Eichner (1973, p. 1194).

Figure 6.2(a)

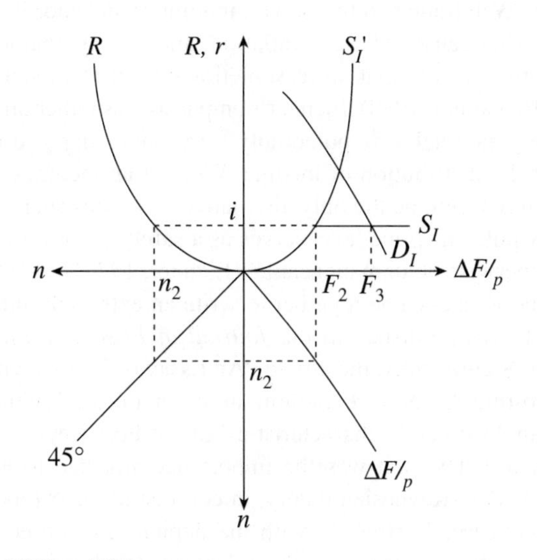

Source: Eichner (1973, p. 1194).

Figure 6.2(b)

This unorthodox theory of pricing did indeed have important repercussions for Post Keynesian macroeconomic theory. Eichner insisted that it did not entail the rehabilitation of Say's Law, even if investment and savings decisions were now taken by the same individuals, the senior managers of the oligopolistic 'megacorp'. Corporations could determine the percentage value of the mark-up, and thus set the ratio of profits to direct costs of production. But they could not control either the volume of profits or the ratio of profits to total costs (direct plus indirect), since both these magnitudes were strongly affected by the degree of capacity utilization, itself dependent on the level of effective demand. Full employment was certainly not guaranteed, and causality in Eichner's model still ran from investment to saving, as in the original Kaldor–Pasinetti formulation. He was correct to claim, however, that he had identified 'a quite different adjustment dynamic from that usually described' (Eichner, 1973, p. 1197).

The theory of inflation was also affected. An increase in the rate of growth required an increase in the savings ratio, and this necessitated a rise in the profit share in national income, achieved through a higher level of profit mark-ups. If unions now tried to defend the existing wage and salary share, 'the basis for a wage-price inflationary spiral will thus have been laid' (ibid., p. 1197). In effect, though Eichner did not use the term, he was arguing that 'profit-push' was just as likely a cause of cost inflation as the 'wage-push' forces identified by Weintraub and other Post Keynesian advocates of incomes policy. Weintraub had focused on ignorance and coordination problems as the underlying causes of wage inflation, and was sympathetic to the prisoner's dilemma models that were sometimes used to model these insights (Maital and Benjamini, 1980). Eichner's emphasis was rather different, pointing to the entirely rational – if potentially very damaging – origins of social conflict over the distribution of income. Without an incomes policy, he concluded, inflation might be the only alternative to serious sociopolitical unrest. Alternatively put, 'the price level serves as a safety valve for social pressures that might otherwise be unmanageable' (Eichner, 1973, p. 1198).

Eichner and Kregel came together to write an extremely influential survey article, which was published in the *Journal of Economic Literature* in December 1975. Significantly, the article, 'An Essay on Post-Keynesian Theory', bore the sub-title 'A New Paradigm in Economics'. Eichner and Kregel identified four 'distinctive characteristics' of the Post Keynesian approach to economic theory. The first was the importance attached to growth and dynamics, since 'Post-Keynesian theory, in contrast to other types of economic analysis, is concerned primarily with the depiction of an economic system expanding over *time* in the context of *history*' (Eichner and Kregel, 1975, p. 1294; original emphasis). The Post Keynesian method of analysis was much more important than any specific conclusions that might be drawn from it, its purpose being 'to replace what Mrs. Robinson refers to as "pseuso-causal" models predicated on "logical" time with historical models that are empirically testable predicated on real time' (ibid., p. 1295). Hence Post Keynesian theory was concerned, in the last resort, with disequilibrium analysis. Its second distinguishing feature, Eichner and Kregel maintained, was its emphasis on the distribution of income between wages and profits. Both Kregel and, more recently, Eichner had demonstrated that the underlying Cambridge model could be applied equally to a corporate economy in which 'the savings propensity of the capitalist class becomes the savings propensity of the corporate sector' (ibid., p. 1299).

The third important characteristic of the Post Keynesian paradigm was the 'monetized production economy' theory outlined by Keynes, in which financial institutions played a central role, money and real wages varied independently of each other and the distinction between 'discretionary' and 'non-discretionary' expenditure was crucial in determining the level of economic activity. The Post Keynesian analysis of macroeconomic disequilibrium required that careful attention be paid to the rate of growth of discretionary expenditure (corporate investment, government spending and household expenditure on consumer durables), along with the Harrodian warranted rate of growth and the 'potential' or natural rate of growth (ibid., pp. 1300–1304). Finally, the Post Keynesian paradigm had a distinctive 'microeconomic base', with exogenously determined money wages and administered prices which were set on a 'cost-plus' basis, the mark-up on direct costs of production being established (as in Eichner's 1973 model) by the corporation's demand for investment finance. This led to a distinctive Post Keynesian analysis of inflation, with conflict over the distribution of income between wages and profits at its core (ibid., pp. 1305–8).

Eichner and Kregel had relatively little to say about the methodological differences between the rival paradigms. In a summary table at the end of their article, however, they compared neoclassical and Post Keynesian economics in terms of the 'purpose of the theory'. The aim of neoclassical theory, they argued, was 'to demonstrate the social optimality if the real world were to resemble the model', while Post Keynesians instead attempted 'to explain the real world as observed empirically' (ibid., p. 1309). They concluded by alluding to the Kuhnian theme that competing paradigms were incommensurable. Neoclassical theory was intended as 'the basis for an optimal decision rule', while Post Keynesian analysis aimed at 'general statement[s] about the empirically observable world'. Small wonder, then, that proponents of the two paradigms 'often seem to be talking past' each other. 'The problem of communication is, of course, compounded when the neoclassical theory is used for a purpose for which it is not suited, that of explaining the real world' (ibid., p. 1310).

Precisely what is meant by 'realism' in economics remains controversial, even among Post Keynesians (see Chapter 9). But the claim that neoclassical theory was irrelevant to contemporary capitalist reality – that, in Joan Robinson's words, it is the theory of socialism, not capitalism – was at the core of the Post Keynesian critique of mainstream analysis. Eichner repeated it in his monumental posthumous treatise on Post Keynesian theory (Eichner, 1991), in his editorial contributions to *A Guide to Post Keynesian Economics* (Eichner, 1979) and in a 1983 attack on neoclassical methodology. The latter, pejoratively entitled 'Why economics is not yet a science', declared mainstream theory to have become 'intellectually bankrupt' (Eichner, 1983, p. 205). The scientific way of thinking, Eichner suggested, could be characterized by a distinctive epistemology, a 'set of rules for discerning what is false' (ibid., p. 207). Neoclasssical theory failed the four tests of coherence, correspondence with the empirically observed real world, comprehensiveness and parsimony, and its microfoundations 'represent a source of fundamental error', being totally lacking in empirical validity (ibid., p. 211). Post Keynesian economics offered a comprehensive and robust alternative. It relied upon income effects rather than substitution effects, fixed coefficient technology represented by the Leontief inverse matrix, and a macroeconomic theory of income distribution instead of the incoherent marginal productivity approach.

Why then, Eichner asked, had this new and superior paradigm failed to supplant the old one? His answer centred on the sociology of the economics profession or, in other words, on the nature of 'economics as a social system'. Faced with their evident lack of success in validating empirically the key elements of the neoclassical synthesis, the theorists had simply retreated into mathematical formalism. They were able to maintain the old discredited paradigm though their control over the system of rewards and incentives for academic economists. Conformity with the canons of neoclassical theory remained a necessary condition for an individual's career progress. 'At every stage in the development of an economist, beginning with the first introductory course, the neoclassical theory serves as a screening device to filter out the disbelieving' (ibid., p. 233). This, Eichner concluded, explained why economics had yet to become a science.

THE FAILURE OF THE NEW PARADIGM

I shall deal later in this chapter with the outcome of the purely intellectual battles between the Post Keynesian and neoclassical paradigms (see also Chapter 12). Eichner's conclusion, however, reflects his disillusion with the defeat of the Post Keynesians in the institutional warfare of the later 1970s. It had indeed been a comprehensive defeat, most apparent in the utter failure of Cambridge political economy to reproduce itself. Here the process of generational change had gone in entirely the wrong direction. Robinson and Kahn had vacated their chairs in 1971 and 1972, respectively, followed by Kaldor in 1975, on reaching the mandatory retirement age. They had not been replaced by Post Keynesian economists of comparable stature. Indeed, Kahn's successor was a distinguished and highly combative Walrasian: famously, 'K' was scratched out and 'H' inserted on the office door of the new Professor Frank Hahn. Attempts to obtain a chair for Kaldor's brilliant protégé Adrian Wood were unsuccessful, and by the end of the 1970s the big guns in the Cambridge faculty of economics were all neoclassical. On the other side of the Atlantic Sidney Weintraub and Hyman Minsky remained in splendid isolation in Philadelphia and St. Louis, while the Post Keynesians at Rutgers University were eventually routed after a long and bitter war of attrition that eventually drove Paul Davidson to Tennessee and probably contributed to the early death of Alfred Eichner. This was more than the usual academic infighting: it involved heresy hunting to protect the true (neoclassical) faith and, in all probability, more than a little political victimization as well. There were plenty of precedents for the latter in the history of twentieth-century American universities, not least in economics departments (Lifschultz, 1974).

No less striking was the creeping exclusion of Post Keynesian authors from all the leading mainstream journals. Weintraub, for example, was proud of the fact that he had published more or less simultaneously back in 1942 in the *American Economic Review*, *Journal of Political Economy* and *Quarterly Journal of Economics* – 'an uncommon feat, I suspect' (Weintraub, 1983, p. 224). After he came out as a heretic in the early 1960s he found it more and more difficult to have his papers accepted by referees and editors who were increasingly intolerant of dissent. Similar problems faced Minsky and Davidson, both of whom had published in the 'top journals' at the start of their careers but now were more and more forced to look elsewhere. In the crucial case of the *American Economic Review* the Post Keynesians waged a brief and acrimonious campaign against the managing editor, George Borts, whose hostility towards heterodoxy was unusually pronounced (Lee, 2000b, pp. 136–46). They did not succeed. Almost 30 years later John Harvey, the Executive Secretary of the International Confederation of Associations for the Reform of Economics (ICARE) and himself a Post Keynesian, was continuing the fight for much greater diversity in articles published in the journals of the American Economic Association (see *http://www.econ.tcu.edu/icare/main.html*).

Equally blatant discrimination began to be practised by foundations in the allocation of research grants, as Paul Davidson recalled:

> In 1980 I applied for a grant from the National Science Foundation to write *International Money and the Real World* [Davidson, 1982]. They have a set of peer evaluators, an inside group which is the traditional bit, and then they bring a few outside evaluators as well. Then they send you all the evaluators' reports anonymously, and then their decision. Well, their decision was to turn me down, and when you looked at it – you have to rate it from 1 to 5, good to bad, and then explain why. All the outside evaluators rated me 1, excellent and so on, 'Davidson has a great track record, *Money and the Real World* [Davidson, 1972a] was a very innovative new book, and so on and so forth, he ought to be trying to extend it to the open economy.' All the insiders, who were the established, orthodox people – because they're the people who always are in there, the Martin Feldsteins of the world, they are the ones who also get the grants because they wash each other's backs, you see – all the insiders said no, that it was either poor or only fair. One of the insiders had the most telling observation of them all. He said something like, 'It is true that Davidson has a very good track record and surprisingly good publications, but he marches to a different drummer. If he's marching to a different drummer, if his music is different, then he ought to get his own money and not use ours'. (King, 1995a, p. 33)

It was a story that many other dissident economists in the United States could sympathize with.

The British Post Keynesians were more fortunate, at least for a time, since the *Economic Journal* remained open to Robinson, Kaldor and their supporters throughout the 1970s. It was edited at Cambridge until the late 1970s, with some members of its editorial board sympathetic to Post Keynesian thinking and others no doubt favourably disposed to the work of eminent Cambridge economists of any persuasion. Even here, however, the shutters were beginning to come down. Thus Geoff Harcourt's paper on the relationship between mark-ups and investment decisions was rejected by the *Economic Journal* in very dubious circumstances, and it eventually appeared in the Swiss-based *Kyklos* (Harcourt and Kenyon, 1976; cf. Harcourt, 1995b). The *Journal of Economic Literature*, under the benign editorship of the quasi-institutionalist Mark Perlman, remained open to Post Keynesian work, as did *Australian Economic Papers*, where Harcourt's influence remained strong (see Chapter 7). Elsewhere, Post Keynesian articles were less and less in evidence.

The Post Keynesians reacted to their exclusion in the way that embattled minorities typically do respond to persecution: they huddled together, settled (or at least suspended temporarily) their internal differences and set about the creation of alternative institutions. In the United States, small pockets of Post Keynesian economics became established in radical departments at the New School for Social Research in New York, at the University of Massachussets (Amherst) and the University of California (Riverside) and, somewhat later, at the University of Notre Dame. A handful of Post Keynesians remained in Cambridge, where they were joined in 1982 by Harcourt. Elsewhere in the

United Kingdom, the then polytechnics offered a safer haven than the established universities, one of them giving its name to an influential series of polemical articles and research reports, the *Thames Papers in Political Economy*, edited by Philip Arestis at Thames Polytechnic between Autumn 1974 and Spring 1990. And this was by no means the only new outlet for Post Keynesian writing. The increasingly close links between Post Keynesians, institutionalists, radical political economists and (Catholic) social economists that grew up in the 1970s have been documented by Lee (2000a), who notes how important Post Keynesian articles began to appear in the institutionalist *Journal of Economic Issues* (founded in 1969), the *Review of Radical Political Economics* (also first published in 1969) and the *Review of Social Economy* (which dates from the 1940s but was revitalized in the early 1970s). In Britain a rather weaker connection developed with the Conference of Socialist Economists and its *Bulletin*, soon retitled *Capital and Class*.

The growing cooperation between Post Keynesians and other dissident schools will be explored more thoroughly in Chapter 11. If it was a necessary condition for the survival of Post Keynesianism in an increasingly harsh institutional climate, it was not, however, regarded as sufficient. Thus in 1977 the *Cambridge Journal of Economics* commenced publication, and the following year saw the first issue of the *Journal of Post Keyesian Economics*. The former was the organ of the Political Economy Society in Cambridge, which brought together Marxists, radical development economists and Post Keynesians of all persuasions. The editorial board included John Eatwell and Bob Rowthorn; Harcourt (still based in Australia) was an associate editor; and Pasinetti, Robinson and Richard Goodwin were listed as the patrons of the Society.

Set up with the moral and financial support of John Kenneth Galbraith, the *Journal of Post Keynesian Economics* was very much the baby of Weintraub and Davidson, though membership of the editorial board had been offered to almost everyone who responded to an initial appeal (see Davidson's account in King, 1994b, pp. 375–7). With the establishment of these two quarterlies, and the opportunities for publishing in English in the French and Italian journals that will be described in Chapter 7, the future of a distinct Post Keynesian voice in academic economics had been assured. Indispensable though they were, the founding of the *Cambridge Journal* and the *Journal of Post Keynesian Economics* did represent a palpable retreat from the earlier confident belief that Post Keynesianism was the dominant paradigm of the very near future. They were evidence that it had instead become confined in an intellectual ghetto.

The central question is whether the institutional defeats of the Post Keynesians were unjustified on purely intellectual grounds, as they themselves maintained. Their opponents, of course, claimed that the opposite was the case. Borts had defended the editorial policy of the *American Economic Review* on the grounds that scientific quality was the sole criterion for publication, and the Post Keynesians had simply failed to meet it. In one form or another, more or less judiciously expressed, this dismissive conclusion was repeated on every one of those (few) occasions when prominent representatives of the mainstream of the profession deigned to offer an opinion on the progress of Post Keynesian theory: James Tobin (1973), for example, or Frank Hahn (1975). To them Post Keynesian ideas seemed old-fashioned, technically backward, intellectually second-rate. (Joan Robinson had given hostage to fortune by sub-titling her *Economic Heresies*, 'Some old-fashioned questions in economic theory'). As Robert Solow had put it, slightly earlier and in a rather more general context: 'We neglected radical economics because it is negligible' (Solow, 1971, p. 63). This was a judgment that he would certainly have extended to Post Keynesian theory. How far it was justified, either in the 1970s or at the end of the 1990s, is a question that I shall defer answering until Chapter 12.

WHAT ARE THE QUESTIONS?

Robinson died in August 1983, a month before Piero Sraffa. Unlike Sraffa she had remained active almost to the end, albeit increasingly pessimistic about the future of Post Keynesian economics (Harcourt, 1996b). The aggressive confidence of the Ely lecture contrasts sadly with the more muted tones of her last major paper, the 1977 'What are the questions?' Here Robinson summarized the many points that she had made against neoclassical theory over the previous quarter of a century, beginning with her critique of ahistorical Walrasian models of equilibrium and marginalist analyses of the firm, continuing with the defects of monetarism and concluding with a brusque dismissal of the mainstream approach to growth and international trade. Political factors played an even greater role than they had previously done in her assessment of rival theories and her explanation for the failure of Post Keynesian ideas to make the impact that they deserved. Her principal objection to monetarism, for example, was now that it served as 'a device for avoiding discussion of political problems'. It contrasted unfavourably with the Kaleckian approach, which saw inflation as 'essentially a political problem' related to the power of oligopolistic corporations and social conflict over the distribution of income (Robinson, 1977b, pp. 1328, 1329). Robinson revealed greater sympathy than she had in the past for Galbraith's (1967) treatment of market power, and drew on arguments advanced by Benjamin Ward in stressing the ideological reasons for the neglect of his analysis of the 'New Industrial State': 'As he points out, a very large proportion of the educated and professional class in industrial nations is employed directly or indirectly by great corporations, and the educational system is largely at their service. For this reason, the power that Ward refers to prevents critical views from penetrating into orthodoxy' (Robinson, 1977b, p. 1326; cf. Ward, 1972, p. 38).

What, then, *were* the problems? They were those that Robinson had identified at the beginning of the decade in her Ely lecture: poverty and inequality, environmental degradation, externalities, and the limitless and self-defeating creation of wants. Again the underlying difficulty was political:

> Here is the problem. The task of deciding how resources should be allocated is not fulfilled by the market but by the great corporations who are in charge of the finance for development.
>
> These questions involve the whole political and social system of the capitalist world; they cannot be decided by economic theory, but it would be decent, at least, if the economists admitted that they do not have an answer to them. (Robinson, 1977b, p. 1337)

Robinson had made it clear at the very beginning of her article that this, too, involved issues of social power. Intellectually, it was easy for the radicals to point out the gap between reality and the Panglossian optimism of the neoclassical economists. But 'the conservatives are compensated by occupying positions of power, which they can use to keep criticism in check'. Orthodox theorists controlled the economics departments in all the leading academic institutions, acting (as Ward had said) as the discipline's censors. The result was that 'the conservatives do not feel obliged to answer radical criticisms on their merits and the argument is never fairly joined' (ibid., pp. 1318, 1319). Robinson offered no solution to this problem; her faith in the eventual success of a younger generation of radicals had evidently evaporated.

At the end of the decade Lorie Tarshis all but wrote off Post Keynesianism as 'A Promise That Bounced': 'it has set for those who work under its banner an impressive agenda. But the question still remains as to whether its achievements come at all close to matching the challenge. With a few notable exceptions, its ambitious claims seem empty of substance' (Tarshis, 1980, p. 10). The grounds for Tarshis's verdict included deep dissatisfaction with the contemporary Post Keynesian analysis of pricing, investment and distribution. Pricing models like those of Eichner greatly exaggerated the reliance of the large corporation on internal finance, Tarshis argued, and took insufficient account of uncertainty as a factor in the firm's price-setting decisions. The Post Keynesian theory of investment was 'no less flawed and incomplete than Keynes's own analysis', with frequent references to 'animal spirits' being used 'to sweep the problem under the rug' (ibid., pp. 12–13). And Post Keynesians had still to decide whether to base their theory of distribution on demand factors (the investment–income ratio emphasized by Kaldor and

Pasinetti) or on supply influences (via the relationship between costs and prices at varying levels of capacity utilization). Tarshis also complained that Post Keynesians had paid insufficient attention to Minsky's analysis of financial instability and to the increasing inflexibility in market adjustment processes that had resulted from what he termed 'the refeudalization of capitalism' in the United States and Canada. Microeconomic rigidities, he suggested, might give rise to macroeconomic problems 'which would not disappear by a single turn of the demand lever' but required analysis also of the supply side (ibid., p. 14).

More important than these arguments themselves, perhaps, was the status of the author and the nature of his forum. Tarshis was eminent, if sparsely published, and had himself been a sort of proto-Post Keynesian in the later 1930s and the 1940s (see Chapter 5). His paper was presented at the 1979 annual meeting of the American Economic Association, and represented one of the last occasions on which Post Keynesian themes were prominent there. It must have been very widely read. Tarshis's Post Keynesian discussants put up only token resistance to his dismissive conclusion: 'What little revolution in thought it embodies,' he wrote of the new paradigm, 'is far from complete' (ibid., p. 14). Part of the problem, of course, was that the Post Keynesians had been aiming at a moving target; mixing the metaphors, by the late 1970s the neoclassical synthesis was pretty well a dead duck. The rise of neoliberalism in the wider world was mirrored (and to some extent, created) by the growth first of monetarism and then of 'New Classical' economics, the latter based on the novel concept of 'rational expectations'. If these new currents were neglected by the writers considered in the present chapter, other Post Keynesians did respond to the new challenges that they posed. The resulting debates over monetary theory and inflation are outlined in Chapter 8, while the contemporary controversies over uncertainty and economic method are summarized in Chapter 9. First, though, we need to take stock of Post Keynesian economics in the rest of the world.

NOTES

1. Joan Robinson to Jack Crutchfield, 27 October 1973, Joan Robinson papers, King's College, Cambridge, JVR/vii/266/26.
2. Joan Robinson to Richard Kahn, undated but almost certainly late December 1971, Richard Kahn papers, King's College, Cambridge, RKP 13/90/0/196–7.

7. Economic heresy around the world

> [After 1960] the situation of a lively group dedicated to a particular Australian spirit of economic inquiry was transformed into one where much of the economics profession resembled a minor sub-branch of the American Economic Association. (Groenewegen and McFarlane, 1990, p. 237)

THE GLOBALIZATION OF ECONOMICS

The globalization of capitalism after 1945 has been paralleled by the increasing internationalization of economics (Coats, 1996). To some extent the term is simply a euphemism for Americanization. It would be difficult to deny that the second half of the twentieth century saw a major shift in the centre of gravity of intellectual production away from Europe in general and Britain in particular and towards the United States. This was true of all branches of scientific and cultural activity, and was greatly accelerated by the flood of refugee intellectuals and researchers who fled the Old World to escape Hitler and Stalin. It was certainly important in the case of economics, where – to take just one example – the unchallenged authority possessed in the 1930s by the *Economic Journal* had clearly passed, by 1960, to the *American Economic Review*.

This is, of course, an Anglocentric view of the history of economic thought. One of the most significant aspects of internationalization, however, has been the growing dominance of the English language as the lingua franca of economics. Before 1939, theorists whose mother tongue was French, German or Italian would almost automatically write and publish in their native language; only the most important books (and a mere handful of articles) would be translated into English. To a somewhat lesser extent this was true also of the smaller European languages, though Dutch and Swedish economists, for example, would sometimes publish in German, and Italians in French, in order to reach a wider audience. As translation was an exceptional rather than a routine activity it enjoyed a higher status then than now, and attracted some first-class minds: thus Nicholas Kaldor translated Hayek's *Monetary Theory and the Trade Cycle* and Richard Kahn did the same for Wicksell's *Interest and Prices*.

National peculiarities were reinforced by the much greater cost, in money and time, of international contacts and, above all, international travel. The

1930 cost of a transatlantic telephone call was five times greater, in real terms, than in 1960, and passenger air travel was almost three times as expensive (Held *et al.*, 1999, p. 170). International conferences like the famous 1935 Leyden meeting where Michal Kalecki presented his model of the trade cycle were rare events, and the explosion of exchange visits and celebrity lecture circuits began only in the mid-1950s. In consequence the distinctive national traditions of prewar economic thought survived into the post-1945 era, although they soon began to weaken very rapidly. A more positive way of looking at this phenomenon might be to say that there was increasing mobility of people and growing cross-fertilization of ideas after the war, exemplified by the invasion of Cambridge (England) by American academic visitors, Nicholas Kaldor's 1956 world tour and Joan Robinson's frequent and productive trips to the United States and Canada. The books (and occasionally also the articles) of both British and American Post Keynesians were increasingly published in the principal European languages with only slight delays, while almost all continental economists read, and rather less commonly wrote and published in, English.

But the globalization of economics has yet to eradicate national idiosyncrasies, even in English-speaking ex-colonial Australia (Groenewegen and McFarlane, 1990). Whether this is a matter for celebration or regret remains controversial, just as many European filmgoers bemoan the dominance of Hollywood while others wish that it had gone even further. But no history of Post Keynesian thought would be complete without some discussion of its evolution outside Britain and the United States. The choice of countries meriting a detailed assessment is inevitably a matter of judgment. Some immediately rule themselves out of consideration. There has never been a Post Keynesian group in Sweden, for instance, which is rather surprising given the distinctive and original character of Swedish macroeconomic thought between the wars and the economic and social policies pursued by successive Swedish governments right down to the early 1990s (Marshall, 1996). Much the same can be said of Germany, where neoclassical orthodoxy rules, and of Japan, where heterodox economists have almost always been Marxists of one variety or another. Post Keynesian ideas have had some influence in the Netherlands without making any great impact on the outside world, despite the presence of Jan Kregel at Groningen University in the early 1980s (Groenewegen *et al.*, 1991).

Other omissions are perhaps more difficult to justify. It would be an exaggeration to talk of a Post Keynesian school in Poland, for although Kalecki had a loyal following his students were for the most part (and very understandably) more concerned with the prospects for 'actually existing socialism' than with the economics of capitalism. Kalecki was also influential as a development economist (McFarlane, 1996), as were Robinson and – to a lesser extent – Kaldor. Their authority gave Post Keynesian ideas a significant following in some parts of the Third World. Joan Robinson's efforts ensured that Sraffa was highly regarded in India, where even today the Bombay *Economic and Political Weekly* makes more interesting reading than any comparable journal that I know of. A similar story could be told of Latin America, this time owing to the affinity between Kaleckian ideas and indigenous strands of structuralist development theory. I can only plead ignorance for ignoring these currents in the present chapter, and for concentrating instead on Post Keynesian economists in Australia, Austria, Canada, France and Italy.

AUSTRALIA

I have written about the history of Post Keynesian economics in Australia at greater length (King, 1997), noting that Australians could have been excused for taking a dim view of Keynes after he endorsed a classical deflationary package for them, including a 10 per cent cut in money wages (Keynes, 1932). In fact the *General Theory* conquered Australia with a speed and thoroughness that would have impressed the Spanish Inquisition, so that by 1945 there was no more totally Keynesian economics profession in the world. This reflected not only the intensity of the country's suffering in the Great Depression but also the fact that laissez faire had never really taken hold there. European settlement itself was the direct result of state intervention, and both the colonial and (after 1901) the Commonwealth governments played a major role in economic life. Economic thought was appropriately pragmatic; if there were few Australian socialists, there were also very few strident advocates of unregulated free markets. There was, however, a tradition of popular underconsumptionism that made demand-side explanations of economic crisis appear quite natural, and popular suspicion of monetary reformers was less acute than was often the case overseas (Kuhn, 1988). At a more refined level there was already by the early 1930s a lively and inventive school of Australian macroeconomics, represented most famously by the Cambridge-educated L.F. Giblin, inventor of the foreign trade multiplier (King, 1998b).

Thus the *General Theory* met with very little resistance in Australia, where the influence of Cambridge economics had always been very strong. An analysis of citations in the *Economic Record*, at the time the country's only serious economic journal, reveals a preponderance of references to Cambridge sources both before and for some years after 1936 (Fleming, 1994). As we saw in Chapter 1, the *Record* published one of the earliest (and best) reviews of the *General Theory*, by Brian Reddaway, who was visiting Melbourne on a Bank of England scholarship at the time. There was also something of a 'Keynesian revolution' in economic policy, spearheaded by public servants of high intellectual calibre like H.C. 'Nugget' Coombs and Leslie Melville. By 1945 the 'Treasury line' was unashamedly Keynesian, and would remain so for another three decades (Whitwell, 1986).

This was reflected also in the teaching of macroeconomics in the (then) seven Australian universities (there was one in each state, plus the Australian National University, established in Canberra in 1946). Peter Groenewegen's research reveals the predominance of British textbooks until the 1960s, while Geoff Harcourt, who arrived at Melbourne in 1950, was required to read two 'great books' in Economics I: Wicksteed's *Commonsense of Political Economy* and Keynes's *Tract on Monetary Reform*, the chapter on the forward exchanges being 'very hard ... but very challenging'. In the summer vacation at the end of his first year Harcourt read the *General Theory*, which was 'all the rage for Economics B', in which Don Cochrane and Joe Isaac taught it to a class of 700. Isaac also introduced honours students to the writings of Michal Kalecki (Groenewegen, 1996, pp. 68–70; King, 1997, p. 300). At Sydney, Groenewegen learned introductory macroeconomics from a series of British texbooks, including the superior *Textbook of Economic Theory* by Stonier and Hague (1953), which contained the best presentation of aggregate supply and demand theory available anywhere in the world at the time. He recalls that Samuelson's *Economics* was regarded with some condescension as very much a book for beginners, and doubts whether any introductory US text was used at Sydney – as opposed to the upstart University of New South Wales, promoted from technical college status in 1958 – before the late 1960s.

Two conclusions may be drawn from this. First, there was no bastion of pre-Keynesian economics in Australia, no 'Chicago of the South'. Second, the Keynes who featured on the macroeconomics syllabus was (before 1970) quite close to being the real thing; by comparison with the situation in the US, the neoclassical synthesis was never very popular. This is a question of degree, as Reddaway's unprotested co-invention of IS–LM demonstrates, but it does seem that Australian students were educated in a way that made many of them more open to Post Keynesian influence than their North American contemporaries. And it points to one final, very important factor: the continuing strength of the Cambridge connection until Harvard and Chicago took over as the natural destination for the talented young Australian economist in the 1960s (Groenewegen, 1996, pp. 65–8); except for agricultural economists, American PhDs were very uncommon before then. Some Australians, like Isaac, Keith Hancock and Peter Riach, went to the London School of Economics in preference to Cambridge, but this was a minority choice and Riach's decision caused some surprise in his native Melbourne (King, 1995a, p. 114). Most young Australian economists who went overseas acquired the pure milk of the *General Theory*, first-hand, from Robinson, Kahn and Kaldor.

The most important of them was Harcourt, a graduate of Melbourne University who arrived in Cambridge in 1955. Initially (and disastrously) supervised by Nicholas Kaldor, he very soon came under the influence of Joan Robinson, whose *Accumulation of Capital* was about to be published. Harcourt returned home in 1958 to teach at the University of Adelaide, a connection he maintained for a quarter of a century. It was punctuated by frequent trips to Cambridge and, in the late 1970s and early 1980s, to the University of Toronto where his friend Lorie Tarshis was attempting to establish a Post Keynesian group. Harcourt moved back to Cambridge permanently in 1982, but continued to visit Australia, where he was always a major influence on the local Post Keynesians.

Two of the original channels through which this influence was exercised were the textbook, *Economic Activity*, which he co-authored with Peter Karmel and Bob Wallace, and the journal *Australian Economic Papers*, whose editorial policy he dominated from its formation in 1963 until he returned permanently to Cambridge in 1982. Harcourt wrote the bulk of the first draft of *Economic Activity*. Much of it was conventional income–expenditure analysis, with due acknowledgement to Hansen and other US advocates of the neoclassical synthesis and few references to a Kaleckian alternative. The attitude to IS–LM was ambiguous (cf. Harcourt *et al.*, 1967, pp. vi, 260–2), as was the discussion of monetary theory (ibid., pp. 83, 262, 265–6, 309). Aggregate supply and demand analysis made an appearance, but very much in the mould of one of Harcourt's great heroes, Lorie Tarshis (ibid., pp. 268–76; on Tarshis, see Chapter 5). Mark-up pricing was introduced, together with the assumption of a constant average product of labour, to yield a horizontal aggregate supply curve up to the full employment level of output (ibid., pp. 277–9). Surprisingly, in view of the contemporary debates in Adelaide on wages policy involving Hancock, Donald Whitehead and Harcourt's great friend Eric Russell, the text made very little of the potential contribution of incomes policy as an anti-inflation weapon. Taken as a whole, *Economic Activity* reflected an ambivalence to neoclassical Keynesianism that was shared by many incipient Post Keynesians in the mid-1960s. In some ways it did point in a Post Keynesian direction, and the keen student who pursued the suggestions for further reading would have encountered (in addition to the US 'bastard Keynesians') the *General Theory*, Kahn's classic article on the multiplier, Austin Robinson's obituary and Roy Harrod's biography of Keynes, together with work by Kalecki, E.F. Schumacher and Paul Wells.

Economic Activity seems not to have been widely used outside Adelaide and Cambridge, though it was translated into Italian. Harcourt's influence was probably greater through his editorial work. He was one of the prime movers behind the establishment of *Australian Economic Papers* in 1963, and was successively assistant editor, member of the editorial committee and (from 1967) joint editor. The new journal had a cosmopolitan outlook almost from the start, with the inevitable neoclassical articles offset by a perceptible Cambridge component, including one of Joan Robinson's earliest diatribes against the neoclassical Keynesians (Robinson, 1964). The significance of the *Papers* was probably at its peak in the early and mid-1970s, when the leading US journals had become effectively closed to Post Keynesian ideas and alternative outlets had yet to emerge (see Chapter 6). Harcourt's tolerance and eclectic tastes led him to publish papers on Marxian crisis theory, Kaldorian and Kaleckian distribution models and Sraffian trade analysis, together with Edward Nell's widely quoted polemic, 'The Revival of Political Economy' (Nell, 1972). Subsequently Harcourt sponsored the very important English translation of Kalecki's 1936 review of the *General Theory* (Targetti and Kinda-Hass, 1982), and by this time work by many of the leading British, American and Italian Post Keynesians had appeared in the journal, along with the native talent of Riach, Robert Dixon, Trevor Stegman and Martin Watts. After Harcourt left for Cambridge, *Australian Economic Papers* briefly retained some Post Keynesian affiliations under the (co-)editorship of Colin Rogers, author of a major study of monetary theory after the capital controversies (Rogers, 1989). Since the late 1980s, however, it has become a purely mainstream journal.

Peter Groenewegen's 1979 survey of radical economics in Australia concluded that the prospects for Post Keynesianism were extremely bright (Groenewegen, 1979, p. 205). For a while this prognosis seemed reasonable enough. Post Keynesian theory was taught under that name at a number of institutions and insinuated itself into courses on macroeconomics and the history of economic thought at several others. Dissertations began to emerge, the best of which was Peter Kriesler's *Kalecki's Microanalysis* (Kriesler, 1987), and a steady trickle of Australian papers found their way into the *Journal of Post Keynesian Economics*. But radical economics of all descriptions was just beginning a pronounced and continuing decline, reinforced in the Australian case by the unfortunate legacy of the 1972–5 Whitlam Labor government and an unusually strong business and academic reaction against the country's statist and protectionist traditions. Added to this was the accelerating Americanization of the economics profession which was evident in the recruitment, publishing and research degree practices of most (if not yet all) economics departments in Australian universities. The future lay with neoclassical theory, particularly with the militantly deregulationist and avowedly anti-Keynesian variant of neoliberalism known locally as 'economic rationalism' (Pusey, 1991) – how could anyone object to *that*? None of this was peculiar to Australia, of course, but these developments proceeded more rapidly than was the case in many parts of the northern hemisphere.

At the end of the century, Post Keynesians remained powerfully entrenched at Sydney University and survived at most other institutions, albeit generally as an embattled minority. One exception is among historians of economic thought, where a strong Post Keynesian presence had always been apparent both at the conferences of the History of Economic Thought Society of Australia (founded in 1981) and in the pages of its journal, the *History of Economics Review* (see in particular the bumper special issue number 25, published in 1996 to celebrate the sixtieth anniversary of the *General Theory* and the fiftieth anniversary of the death of Keynes). Between 1988 and 1994 Basil Moore, Hyman Minsky and Paul Davidson were popular visitors. Internationally significant contributions to the analysis of Keynes's philosophical development and its implications for Post Keynesian methodology were made by the Australians Athol Fitzgibbons and Rod O'Donnell (see Chapter 9), while Dixon (1988) continued to wave the Robinsonian banner. Thus life in what was now very much an intellectual ghetto remained vigorous and diverse.

AUSTRIA

Post Keynesianism in Austria was much more of a minority phenomenon, associated above all with two theorists who returned from wartime exile in the UK to a hostile intellectual environment in a country that was never fully subject to denazificiation. Thus neither Josef Steindl (1912–93) nor Kurt Rothschild, Steindl's junior by two years, achieved the academic recognition that their work deserved. If not entirely without honour in their own country, these two Post Keynesian prophets were always more highly regarded in the outside world.

Steindl was educated at the Vienna Hochschule für Welthandel (now the Economic University), and then worked at the Austrian Institute for Business Cycle Research, under first Friedrich von Hayek and then Oskar Morgenstern. After the German annexation of Austria in 1938 he moved to Oxford, where he spent the war and immediate postwar years at the Institute of Statistics with Kalecki – 'my guru' – and a talented team of British and émigré economists that included Thomas Balogh and E.F. Schumacher. Steindl returned to Austria in 1950, working at his old institute (now renamed the Austrian Institute for Economic Research) until his retirement in 1978, and remained there as a consultant until shortly before his death. As his close friend Rothschild wrote in his obituary:

> His modesty and his upright character allied with an open critical mind barred his way to a normal career at Austria's universities, where he only found late recogni-

> tion as an honorary professor at the University of Vienna in 1970 and with the conferment of a doctorate *honoris causa* by the University of Graz in 1985. (Rothschild, 1994, p. 131)

Much the same could be said of Rothschild's own personality and career.

Kalecki's influence prevented Steindl from succumbing either to the neoclassical synthesis or, in his work on microeconomics, to the hegemony of the perfect competition model. His early writings on the firm, which culminated in *Small and Big Business* (Steindl, 1945), brought together Kaleckian and Marxian ideas on the advantages enjoyed by large companies in their competitive struggle with smaller enterprises. Much more than Kalecki himself, Steindl was confident that steadily increasing industrial concentration was an essential feature of capitalist development. The macroeconomic consequences were assessed in his second and most celebrated book, *Maturity and Stagnation in American Capitalism*, which was summarized in Chapter 2. Steindl argued that the emergence of oligopoly had stifled price competition, leading to higher profit margins and reduced sales. The counterpart to increasing levels of excess capacity within the individual firm was a tendency to stagnation at the level of the entire economy, as corporate savings grew and the incentive to invest was weakened (Steindl, 1952 [1976]).

This provided a convincing explanation of the Great Depression, perhaps, but how could it be reconciled with the rapid growth of the world economy in the postwar 'golden age'? Steindl responded to this challenge in his introduction to the second (1976) edition of *Maturity and Stagnation* and in a number of subsequent articles, several of them reprinted in his *Economic Papers, 1940–88* (Steindl, 1990; cf. King, 1995b). His argument, in essence, was that the quarter-century of rapid growth after 1945 had been due to a series of exceptionally favourable circumstances that were unlikely to be repeated. These included massive military expenditure by the United States during the (first) Cold War and very high levels of investment in Western European countries that enabled them to catch up with US industry by importing American technology, which had had to be embodied in new capital equipment. After 1970 the underlying stagnation had re-emerged, a tendency that in Steindl's view was reinforced by a conscious and pronounced deflationary bias in fiscal and monetary policy.

Reflecting on the state of economic theory in the early 1980s, Steindl urged the need for economists to work in the 'no-man's land' between the specialized academic disciplines, so that their analysis might be enriched through contact with engineering, science, history, sociology and political science (Steindl, 1990, p. 251). Leaving out the reference to science and engineering, this reads almost like a capsule summary of the work of Rothschild, who first developed an interest in economics as a student in the law faculty at the University of Vienna (there were no separate departments of economics in Austria at this time). He also came into contact with Marxian ideas through his membership of the socialist youth movement, before it was destroyed after the fascist coup in 1934. Forced like Steindl to leave Austria in 1938, Rothschild won a refugee scholarship at Glasgow University, where he taught between 1940 and 1947. He returned home to work at the Austrian Institute for Economic Research, with responsibility for studies of the labour market and international trade. In 1966 Rothschild was appointed to a chair in economics at the newly-established University of Linz, but retained close links with the Institute up to and beyond his retirement in 1985. He was still publishing prolifically in the mid-1990s.

Rothschild's writings covered a remarkably wide range of topics, from price theory and labour economics through bargaining theory and the economics of power to the macroeconomic analysis of distribution and growth, economic methodology, the history of thought and the theory and practice of economic policy (King, 1994d). His influential 1947 *Economic Journal* article, 'Price theory and oligopoly', probed mercilessly at the weakest point of marginalist equilibrium analysis, attacking the use of mechanical and even biological analogies and suggesting that Clausewitz had more to teach the price theorist than either Newton or Darwin. He emphasized the pervasive effects of uncertainty on the firm's behaviour, maintaining that the desire for security of profits destroyed the validity of any simple optimizing rule and expressing (very presciently) serious doubts about the potential contribution of game theory to a realistic model of the firm (Rothschild, 1947). Many of these considerations were carried over into Rothschild's work as a labour economist, where his willingness to use marginal productivity theory as one tool in the study of the individual firm's demand for labour was complemented by a much more unorthodox focus on power relations, monopolistic and monopsonistic influences, the role of unions and the distinctively macroeconomic dimensions to the labour market. His *Theory of Wages* was a rare example of an introductory text that was both accessible to beginners and a source of great intellectual stimulation to more advanced readers (Rothschild, 1954).

In 1971 Rothschild published an important collection of articles on *Power in Economics*, which revealed his eclecticism and methodological pluralism, in addition to highlighting the woeful neglect of power relations by almost all mainstream economists since John Stuart Mill (Rothschild, 1971). The 18 pieces that Rothschild had chosen included work by sociologists and political scientists, along with more obviously economic contributions by Paul Baran and Paul Sweezy, John Kenneth Galbraith and the Dutch writer Jan Pen. With its broad sweep and close attention to issues that economists should not have neglected but were rarely confident in dealing with, this was very much a book for the times. Its radical questions and multidisciplinary approach won it a wide readership in the 1970s, but greatly restricted its influence thereafter.

On macroeconomic issues Rothschild was a Keynesian with a Kaleckian (and also a clearly socialist) tinge. He criticized steady-state growth theorists – and Nicholas Kaldor in particular – for employing a very restricted range of variables which detached their analysis from reality, and for neglecting historical, social and institutional factors (Rothschild, 1959). Rothschild was sceptical of the relevance of the Kaldorian macrodistribution models discussed in Chapter 3. He claimed that both the investment–income ratio and the savings propensities of capitalists and workers should be treated as variables rather than as parameters, since they depended on historical experience and especially on the outcome of social conflicts. Resistance by organized labour to reductions in real wages would either directly constrain entrepreneurs' investment plans or generate an inflationary wage–price spiral that would prevent any permanent increase in the ratio of investment to income (Rothschild, 1965). These criticisms did not draw any response from Kaldor, and seem also to have escaped the attention of American theorists of cost inflation such as Weintraub and Eichner. Like them, however, Rothschild was convinced that incomes policy was essential if high levels of employment were to be maintained. Describing the demise of 'Austro-Keynesianism' in the early 1980s, he explained how full employment had survived the shocks of the previous decade as a result of deliberate policy targetting by Social Democratic governments committed to protecting social expenditures, even at the expense of increased budget deficits. The experiment petered out when the international environment became much more hostile to Keynesian demand management and the socialists lost their absolute parliamentary majority and were forced into coalition with the conservatives (Rothschild, 1991).

Important though the contributions of Steindl and Rothschild were, their failure to establish a distinct Post Keynesian school in Austria allowed the term 'Austrian economics' to be monopolized by the radical subjectivists inspired by von Mises and Hayek whose (tenuous) connections with Post Keynesianism will be considered in Chapter 11. Steindl never held a full-time university teaching position in Austria, and Rothschild was in his fifties before he was appointed to the newly-established chair at Linz. Looking back on his own marginalization, Rothschild regretted that he had been quite so devoted to teaching and research, and quite so reluctant to intrigue and 'network' in the manner of his more orthodox colleagues (King, 1995a, pp. 236–7). There have been some distinguished individual Post Keynesians in Austria, most notably Egon Matzner, whose interests centred on the institutional presuppositions of macroeconomic theory, including the role of the social structure, the labour market, the state and the processes of structural and technological adjustment (Matzner and Streeck, 1991). Matzner also collaborated in an early and trenchant critique of the 'shock therapy' applied after 1989 to the ex-Communist countries of Eastern Europe, pointing to the damaging neglect of the institutional structure as the greatest weakness in the neoclassical approach to the transition economies (Kregel *et al.*, 1992). Post Keynesian ideas of a quite different variety flourished at the University of Graz after the arrival there from Germany of the Sraffian theorist Heinz Kurz, an energetic advocate of a Keynes–Sraffa synthesis (Kurz, 1990, 1994). I shall discuss the prospects for this contentious project in Chapter 10.

CANADA

In the mid-1930s some of Keynes's most able students were Canadians. One of them, Lorie Tarshis, went on to enjoy a distinguished academic career at Stanford and then, after 1973, at the University of Toronto (see Chapter 5). His compatriot Robert Bryce returned to Canada in 1938 to work at the Ministry of Finance, where he exerted a strong Keynesian influence for almost 40 years. Bryce had taken comprehensive notes at Keynes's lectures in the early 1930s and these were subsequently published, together with the contemporary notes of Tashis and several other students (Rymes, 1989). They represent a significant historical document, throwing considerable light on the evolution of Keynes's ideas at a critical time in the development of his ideas.

These close early links with Cambridge suggest a parallel with the Australian case. The two countries are indeed very similar in many ways, being multicultural ex-colonies with a vast landmass, a small population and a strong tendency towards Americanization. There was no Canadian equivalent, however, of Geoff Harcourt (who spent a lot of time at Toronto in the 1970s and early 1980s). While there have been important heterodox economists of Canadian origins who have made their name in the United States – John Kenneth Galbraith, Basil Moore and William Vickrey, for example – there has been no single authoritative apostle of Post Keynesian ideas in Canada. It is possible, however, to identify a number of significant individuals and a distinct Post Keynesian presence in a number of institutions, dating in some cases from the early 1960s.

The three most prominent Canadian Post Keynesians were Athanasios (Tom) Asimakopulos (1930–90), John Cornwall and Marc Lavoie. Initially trained as a neoclassical economist, Asimakopulos fell under the influence of Joan Robinson in the mid-1960s and, through her, came to appreciate the significance of Michal Kalecki's work. His Kaleckian critique of Keynes's theory of investment was noted in Chapter 2; in later work he took issue also with Kalecki's treatment of investment and finance (Asimakopulos, 1971,

1983). Asimakopulos was also a pioneer in the application of Kaleckian ideas to the analysis of taxation (Asimakopulos and Burbidge, 1974). An appraisal of his contribution is presented in the memorial volume edited by Harcourt, Roncaglia and Rowley (1995).

Cornwall, who taught at Dalhousie University in Halifax, Nova Scotia, was best known for his comparative analysis of North American and Western European macroeconomic policy in the wake of the 1970s oil crises. His was the first comprehensive Post Keynesian analysis of stagflation, taking up where Sidney Weintraub had left off. Like Weintraub, Cornwall advocated social cooperation as an alternative to deflation, and placed incomes policy at the centre of the fight against stagflation. His *Theory of Economic Breakdown* went into two, influential editions (Cornwall, 1989, 1994). Lavoie was the author of the first really comprehensive and systematic Post Keynesian textbook, pitched at the graduate market, in which he argued for a 'post-classical' synthesis of Keynesian, Kaleckian and Sraffian theory (Lavoie, 1992a; see also Chapter 10). His own original contribution was principally as a monetary theorist, urging the adoption of a 'horizontalist' interpretation of endogenous money (see Chapter 8) and propagating the ideas of the French theorists of the monetary circuit whose work will be considered in the next section.

The great majority of Canadian academic economists were always neoclassicals. Post Keynesian ideas could be found, however, in a number of universities, from Nova Scotia in the east of the country to (at least) Manitoba in the west. In addition to Cornwall at Dalhousie, for example, a strong influence was exercised in the 1990s by Lars Osberg, a forceful opponent of the Bank of Canada's tight monetary policy. Pierre Fortin, of the Université de Québec à Montréal, shared these criticisms and occupied common ground with more openly Post Keynesian theorists. Also in Quebec, Asimakopulos collaborated at McGill with Jack Wheldon and John Burbidge; McGill graduates included Omar Hamouda, Robin Rowley and Mario Seccareccia. Several Ontario universities had strong Post Keynesian minorities, including for a time the University of Waterloo, where Sidney Weintraub was chair of the economics department in 1969–71 and Joan Robinson was an occasional visitor (she had grandchildren nearby). The capital theorist Thomas Rymes was based at Carleton, where he taught Marc Lavoie. York University had a clutch of Post Keynesians, including Hamouda, the methodologists Avi Cohen and Ted Winslow and the monetary economist John Smithin. The University of Toronto was the base for a number of individuals with Keynesian (if not exactly Post Keynesian) interests, including the financial theorist Myron Gordon and the historians of economic thought Susan Howson and Donald Moggridge. In the 1970s Canadian universities attracted a number of graduate students from Britain who developed strong Post Keynesian interests, including Smithin, Alistair Dow, Sheila Dow and John Pheby. The latter, after returning to Britain, founded the *Review of Political Economy*, which began publication in 1989, and established the very successful Malvern conferences in political economy, which ran from 1987 to 1996 (Pressman, 1996).

Some indication of the state of Post Keynesian thought in Canada around 1980 can be gained from a volume that emerged from a conference, sponsored by the Canadian Institute for Economic Policy, on Post Keynesian alternatives to conventional economic policy options; the economics editor of the *Toronto Star* assumed responsibility for editing the proceedings. Galbraith, Tarshis and Weintraub were among the contributors, along with several of the resident Canadian Post Keynesians already mentioned and heterodox economists from Britain (Wynne Godley, Francis Cripps) and the United States (Lester Thurow). Monetarism, incomes policy, industrial policy and international monetary institutions were among the issues under discussion (Crane, 1981).

None of this added up to a coherent (still less a powerful) movement, and before 1998 there was no formal organization of Canadian Post Keynesians, or even of heterodox economists more broadly defined. One partial exception to this statement was provided by the Committee on Monetary and Economic Reform (COMER), founded in 1988 by the Waterloo economist John Hotson (1930–96). The Committee, somewhat unkindly described to me by one Canadian Post Keynesian as a grouping of 'monetary quacks', and by another as 'a sort of left-wing Social Credit', campaigned for monetary expansion to finance public investment. This attracted support from a wide range of dissident economists, including mainstream Post Keynesians like Paul Davidson, and also John Hotson (1987) see King (1995a, pp. 80–92). In the 1990s Brian MacLean of Laurentian University in Sudbury, Ontario, organized a series of Economic Policy Conferences with a broadly Post Keynesian flavour. Then, in 1998, Jim Stanford of the Canadian Auto Workers Union took the lead in establishing a Progressive Economics Forum that brought together a wide range of unorthodox economists from institutionalist, feminist, Marxian and Post Keynesian perspectives. A graduate of the New School in New York, Stanford was the author of a very readable layperson's guide to the financial markets, *Paper Boom*, written from a Left Keynesian viewpoint (Stanford, 1999).

It is clear that there was never a distinct national Canadian tradition of Post Keynesian economics, of the type that can (as we shall see) be identified in France or Italy. Canada is too close to the United States, both geographically and culturally, for that to have been possible. But Canadian Post Keynesians seem to have been more open than their colleagues south of the border to the influence of both Cambridge economics (especially that of Joan Robinson) and of other schools of heterodox analysis. This was especially true of the

Francophone theorists in Quebec (and the proudly bilingual University of Ottawa), where monetary circuit theory and the work of the French regulation school left their mark. Which brings us to France.

FRANCE

Cultural nationalism is probably more powerful in France than almost anywhere else in Europe, and this spills over from artistic activity into the social sciences. It is impossible to be very precise on these matters, but it does seem likely that French economists are more likely than, for example, their German colleagues to publish in their native language and to resent any Anglo-Saxon insinuation that English should be their natural medium of communication. To some extent this vibrant sense of national identity must extend also to the content as well as the mode of expression of economic ideas, so that there is a peculiarly French way of looking at the economy. This should not be exaggerated, of course. There are many excellent neoclassical economists in France, many of whom publish regularly in English. All the same, the internationalization of economics has proceeded less rapidly in France than in many other European countries. One consequence is that a considerable degree of theoretical diversity has been maintained. There are still, for example, well-established heterodox schools of thought with a specific geographical and/or institutional basis, and it is also true that Marxist (or neo-Marxist) ideas have survived among French economists when they have almost disappeared elsewhere. In 2000 a student revolt against excessive formalism and neoclassical bias in the teaching of economics began in Paris, and gave rise to an international protest movement calling for a new Post-Autistic Economics (*pae_news@btinternet.com*).

The result of all this is a tradition of unorthodox macroeconomic thought that proved to have close affinities with Post Keynesianism, even though this was only slowly recognized in the English-speaking world. In fact it could be said that there are two such traditions. The more important, by a long way, is monetary circuit theory. Less significant, from a Post Keynesian perspective, is the 'regulation school' approach to the rethinking of Marxian economics. The theory of the monetary circuit had its origins in the nineteenth-century Banking School, itself an important influence on Marx's ideas on money; there were tantalizing resemblances between circuit theory and the 1933 'laundry basket' draft of the *General Theory*, with its sharp distinction between a cooperative and an entrepreneur economy (see Chapter 1). Many circuit theorists, indeed, tended to favour the *Treatise on Money* over the published version of the *General Theory*. In the early twentieth century the arguments were further developed by Wicksell, Schumpeter and many less well-known writers (Realfonzo, 1998). Lavoie (1992a, p. 150) identified five central principles. First, money is integrated into the economy through production, not exchange; production is the core activity of a capitalist economy, and it needs to be financed. Second, money is created by the banks through the creation of new liabilities during a process of income and output expansion. Thus 'loans create deposits', rather than deposits creating loans. Third, money is a social convention, as is the rate of interest. Money is not a commodity, and the rate of interest has nothing to do with the 'productivity of capital', any more than it is a reward for 'abstinence' or thrift. Fourth, money must be seen as a flow rather than a stock or a store of value, so that the portfolio choice approach to the demand for money is fundamentally misconceived. Finally, money is endogenous to the economy; the money supply is not determined by the decisions of the central bank, nor can money be dropped from helicopters, as monetarists are inclined to imagine.

This suggested a number of points of contact between circuit theory and Post Keynesian macroeconomics. Circuit theorists focused on the specific institutions and class relations of capitalist society, so that workers, entrepreneurs and bankers occupied centre stage instead of the asocial abstract individuals who dominate neoclassical models. They employed sequence analysis to explain events occurring in historical time, and rejected the mainstream reliance on the simultaneous determination of all variables in an essentially timeless model. In circuit theory money was endogenous and, as we have seen, very far from neutral. Say's Law was a fallacy, and capitalism was viewed as inherently crisis-prone; central banks *had* to act as lenders of last resort if serious downturns were to be avoided. There was no role in circuit theory for the marginal productivity approach to income distribution, which was replaced by a theory of profits that stressed entrepreneurial investment decisions and was therefore much closer to the Kaleckian view, and a theory of interest quite similar to that of the Post Keynesian 'horizontalists' (see Chapter 8).

In its modern form, monetary circuit theory originated in postwar France, with the work of Jacques Le Bourva (on whom see Lavoie, 1992b), Bernard Schmitt, Alain Parguez and Frédéric Poulon. French monetary thought had long displayed a tendency to emphasize circulation and the role of money as a medium of exchange, and a corresponding hostility to the quantity theory with its focus on the function of money as a store of value. This was reinforced by the importance to French industry of bank overdraft finance, which stood in sharp contrast to the Anglo-Saxon countries where self-finance from retained earnings was much more pronounced (Deleplace and Nell, 1996, pp. 6–10; Lavoie, 1985). To this must be added the very considerable influence of Marxian political economy in France. While Schmitt and his colleagues in Dijon and Freiburg asserted their theoretical independence from all other schools of thought, Michel Aglietta, Richard Arena and others were openly sympathetic to Marx. Other circuit theorists, Parguez in particular, worked explicitly within the Post Keynesian milieu.

Until the early 1990s, however, these ideas were very much a closed book to most Anglophone Post Keynesians. A small minority came into contact with the circuit theorists in Italy, especially at the annual Trieste summer school that will be discussed in the next section of this chapter. Others learned from Marc Lavoie, who advocated the virtues of circuit theory in a number of articles and then in his text on Post Keynesian theory (Lavoie, 1992a). A further source of information was the Paris-based journal *Economie Appliquée*, which published papers in both French and English and was consistently supportive of heterodox macroeconomics in general and Post Keynesian ideas in particular. Finally, in 1996, an extended critical comparison of circuit theory and Post Keynesian monetary analysis appeared with the publication of the proceedings of the large international conference that had been organized six years earlier by Ghislaine Deleplace of the University of Paris and Edward Nell of the New School for Social Research in New York (Deleplace and Nell, 1996). For all their affinities, however, significant differences remained between the two schools. The circuit theorists treated money as solely a means of payment. Many Post Keynesians, accustomed as they were to think of money also as an asset, were reluctant to follow them in abandoning the very concept of liquidity preference.

The links between the Post Keynesians and the French regulation school were even less well developed, despite some striking similarities in the problems that they posed and the answers that they provided. The most important of the regulation theorists, Michel Aglietta (1979), argued that capitalism had overcome the great crisis of the 1930s by the introduction of a new 'intensive regime of accumulation', characterized by mass production, intensification of labour on Taylorist lines, rapid productivity growth and – crucially – equally rapid growth in mass purchasing power. The necessary growth in demand had been achieved by means of rising wages and greater social welfare expenditure. This 'Fordist' regime of accumulation had itself proved to be crisis-prone, Aglietta concluded, and a return to the fast growth and high employment of the 1945–73 era required far-reaching changes in the organization of production and the distribution of income. There were close parallels between the ideas of the regulation theorists and the 'social structure of accumulation' approach developed in the United States by the radical economists Samuel Bowles, David Gordon and Thomas Weisskopf (1983). The French and American schools shared the Post Keynesian concerns with effective demand, the management of class conflict and the operation of the international monetary system, and the Post Keynesians were beginning to benefit from closer contact with the radical but undogmatic approach of the regulation theorists

(Kotz *et al.*, 1994; see also Chapter 11). In 2001 a newly established Association for the Development of Keynesian Studies was active, based in Lille (Mail to adek@noos.fr).

ITALY

We have already encountered some of the most prominent Italian Post Keynesians, since Piero Sraffa, Pierangelo Garegnani and Luigi Pasinetti played an important part in the capital controversies of the 1960s (see Chapter 4). The Cambridge connection was almost as strong for Italian economists as for the Australians, with a steady flow of bright young graduate students attracted to the university where first Marshall and then Keynes had held court. Sraffa's presence in Cambridge, where he lived continuously from 1927 until his death in 1983, was undoubtedly a major attraction, but it was not the only one. The young Pasinetti, for example, came to Cambridge in 1956 to work on economic development and initially had only a limited interest in Sraffa's work. It was not until the early 1980s that the United States became the destination of first choice for Italian economists wanting to obtain a foreign PhD, and this is one major reason why the Americanization of Italian economics was so long delayed.

A number of other national peculiarities are also relevant. From 1922 to 1943 the fascist dictatorship isolated the country to some extent from the intellectual influence of the outside world. This should not be exaggerated, as, by comparison with Stalin's Russia or Hitler's Germany, Mussolini's obnoxious and brutal regime was a relatively mild one, falling a long way short of totalitarianism. Only a minimal degree of public conformity was required of Italian intellectuals, and the survival of non-fascist (liberal and traditional conservative) ideas in the economics departments of the universities was never seriously in question. Ironically this relatively tolerant intellectual climate probably delayed the progress of the Keynesian revolution in Italy, since the *General Theory* was simultaneously too liberal for the fascists and too corporatist for the liberals. Keynes conquered Italy only after 1945, by which time the links with Cambridge had been restored and the domestic political situation had been transformed. Perhaps for these reasons, the neoclassical synthesis established itself very slowly in Italy, where economists tended to work out their own interpretation of Keynes, often under the influence of Joan Robinson and her Cambridge colleagues (De Cecco, 1989).

A second distinctive feature was the intellectual hegemony of Marxism in postwar Italy, under the influence, but by no means confined to the membership, of the powerful Communist Party. The PCI was never quite a Stalinist monolith, and the numerous economists among its members and sympathizers were not required to toe a rigid party line. In philosophy and social theory the Italian contribution to a more subtle and flexible 'Western Marxism' had begun before the war with the work of Antonio Gramsci (Anderson, 1976). After 1945 many Italian economists were sympathetic to Post Keynesian ideas, especially the brand of 'left Keynesianism' associated with Michal Kalecki and assiduously promoted by Joan Robinson, a frequent visitor to Italy in these years (see Chapter 2). This also encouraged interest in French monetary circuit theory, which could itself be traced back to Marx's analysis of capitalist commodity circulation.

Nor was there any great difficulty in publishing unorthodox ideas. If several of the mainstream academic journals remained under the control of an older and more conservative generation, the radicals had access to alternative outlets for their work, since the publicly owned banks published high-quality and heavily subsidized economic periodicals. Thus Italian and many overseas Post Keynesians wrote for the *Banca Nazionale del Lavoro Quarterly Review*, edited after 1981 by Alessandro Roncaglia, or for the *Economic Notes* of the Monti dei Paschi of Siena. Both appeared more or less simultaneously in Italian and English editions, with a range and heterodoxy of content quite unparalleled in bank reviews anywhere else in the world. At a more technical level there was *Metroeconomica*, which published the work of a wide range of orthodox and dissenting economists, always with a strong emphasis on formal analysis. The Post Keynesian focus of this journal increased after 1983, when Sergio Parrinello became editor; he was succeeded by another Sraffian, Heinz Kurz, in 1998.

Most important in determining the character of Post Keynesian economics in Italy was the immense prestige enjoyed by Sraffa, who was almost a national hero (for the PCI, which he never joined, also a party hero for his efforts on behalf of his imprisoned friend Gramsci in the ten years after1927). Well into the 1990s the liberal press would invoke Sraffa's name without further explanation, on the assumption that any educated Italian would know exactly who he was. In the torrid political climate of the 1970s, in fact, Sraffa became an icon of the far left. Trade union militants chanted a slogan that can be roughly translated as 'Take Sraffa's book to the car factories', and the supposedly Sraffian statement that 'the wage is an independent variable' was used to justify the most ambitious and potentially inflationary wage claims. On a more cerebral plane, almost every Italian Post Keynesian paid homage to his work, and two major international conferences were held in his native city of Turin after his death (Bellofiore, 1986; Bharadwaj and Schefold, 1990). There is an enormous Italian-language literature on *Production of Commodities* and its ramifications, dating back to 1960 and reflecting three decades of argument about the precise meaning of Sraffa's analysis and the possibility of a Sraffa–Keynes synthesis; the incomprehension and misunderstanding that had characterized many English-language reviews of the book were largely avoided by the Italian critics. I shall return to these controversies and assess their outcome in Chapter 10. It should be noted here, however, that the three principal competing interpretations of Sraffian economics were those of his compatriots Garegnani, Pasinetti and Roncaglia (see Roncaglia, 1991).

By 1966 Pasinetti had already achieved an international reputation for his own theoretical contributions, both to the capital controversies and to the development of the Kaldorian macrodistribution model (see Chapters 3 and 4). His chief interest, though, had always been the theory of growth in a multi-sector economy, where continuous structural change is brought about by differences in the rates of technological change and the income elasticities of demand in the various sectors. This was the theme of Pasinetti's doctoral dissertation, first published in 1965 by the Pontifical Academy of Science in Rome and then, revised and extended, as *Structural Change and Economic Growth*; it took Cambridge growth theory with exogenous technical change about as far as it could go (Pasinetti, 1965, 1981). In later work Pasinetti distinguished the 'natural' from the historically and socially specific laws of economic development, with the former expressed in terms of a pure labour theory of value (Pasinetti, 1993). He also published on Ricardo and classical political economy, and on the economics of vertical integration (see the appraisal of his work by Baranzini and Harcourt, 1993).

There was little or no mention of money in Pasinetti. Augusto Graziani, in contrast, was instrumental in reviving the theory of the monetary circuit in Italy, drawing on the French monetary economists whose analysis was discussed in the previous section. Born in Naples, Graziani graduated from his local university and pursued postgraduate studies at the London School of Economics and at Harvard. He taught first at the University of Catania, then in Naples and finally in Rome. Much of Graziani's work appeared only in Italian, but he also published several important articles in English, including an influential contribution to the debate on Keynes's 'finance motive' for holding money, which provoked a considerable controversy by arguing that Keynes – the Keynes of the *Treatise* rather than the *General Theory* – was a circuit theorist at heart (Graziani, 1984). Less contentious, perhaps, was his claim that Joan Robinson agreed with all the central propositions of circuit theory (Graziani, 1989; cf. Robinson, 1956, bk IV). Graziani's approach to macroeconomic theory led him to reinterpet the history of economic thought, with Malthus, Wicksell, Schumpeter and Keynes united (against the Walrasians) in their commitment to a monetary theory of production and the principle of effective demand.

The economic vision of Paolo Sylos Labini was different again. He began his career as an anti-Keynesian, and was always sympathetic to institutionalist and evolutionary (especially Schumpeterian) ideas (Halevi, 1998). Sylos Labini is best-known for his book *Oligopoly and Technical Progress*, which made an original and provocative attempt to link the microeconomic and macroeconomic analysis of a mature capitalist economy. It began with a model of administered pricing in which the mark-ups that oligopolists set over prime costs of production were determined by their desire to protect their market position through preventing the entry of new competitors (Sylos Labini, 1962; Lee, 1998). His emphasis on the role of excess capacity as a barrier to entry led Sylos to a stagnationist account of the Great Depression rather similar to that of Josef Steindl. Since, 'in the oligopolistic stage of capitalism, productivity gains tend to be retained within firms rather than being distributed to the whole system via a reduction in prices' (Halevi, 1998, p. 231), profit margins rose and aggregate demand was reduced. After 1945, the greater power of trade unions had overcome this constraint on economic growth, but only at the expense of chronic upward pressure on the price level. Sylos's analysis of inflation stressed the interaction between union wage pressure and the product market power of the giant corporations with which the unions had to negotiate (Sylos Labini, 1974). It had clear affinities with the models of Sidney Weintraub and Alfred Eichner, and shared their commitment to incomes policy, but lacked both Weintraub's Marshallian microfoundations and Eichner's stress on the corporation's requirements for investment finance as the crucial determinant of the mark-up.

For several years in the 1980s the north-eastern Italian city of Trieste was the site of an important Post Keynesian event. This was the annual summer school organized by a committee that included Pierangelo Garegnani, Jan Kregel (then based in Bologna) and Sergio Parrinello, with the general aim of encouraging discussion among Post Keynesians from around the world and the more specific intention of introducing graduate students from a number of countries to a range of Post Keynesian ideas. British and North American academics were never reluctant to visit Italy, and among the lecturers at Trieste were Geoff Harcourt, Hyman Minsky, Basil Moore, Edward Nell and A.P. Thirlwall, along with the Austrians Kurt Rothschild and Josef Steindl. Sadly the disputes between rival schools of thought became more and more intense. Indeed the conflict between Fundamentalist Keynesians and Sraffians that I shall discuss in some detail in Chapter 10 seems to have crystallized in Trieste. The growing antagonism between adherents to these two points of view came to be reflected both in divisions in the organizing committee and in acrimonious conflicts in the classroom. One Australian who attended the sessions for graduate students remembered his stay in Trieste largely for the unproductive repetition of well-rehearsed positions by fractious lecturers who were for the most part talking past each other and totally neglected the needs of the students. The hoped-for synthesis of classical and Post Keynesian ideas did not materialize; eventually tensions rose to unsustainable levels, and the Trieste summer school did not survive into the 1990s (Arena, 1987; Parrinello, 1988).

It was clear by the early 1980s that there was not one Post Keynesian school in Italy but several, and relations between them were often strained. By now the growing influence of neoclassical economics was also apparent, and what had always been a minority – albeit an unusually influential one – was under increasing pressure. There was no great 'battle of the paradigms' in Italy. Post Keynesian thought was simply shrugged off by the new generation that returned from the United States with a vision of economics that owed nothing to Sraffa and very little, if anything, to Keynes. In the late 1990s there were still some highly talented young Post Keynesians in Italy, like the monetary circuit theorist Riccardo Realfonzo (1998) and the dedicated biographer of Sraffa, Nerio Naldi (1998), but they were increasingly on the margins of the profession. Intellectually as well as politically, Italy was well on the way to becoming a 'normal country', to use the title of a book by one former prime minister, the neoliberal (and ex-Communist) Massimo D'Alema.

THE AMERICANIZATION OF DISSENT

One issue that I have evaded thus far is the degree to which the post-1945 Americanization of economics applied also to Post Keynesian thought. Geoff Harcourt, for one, complained of 'an unhealthy American post-Keynesian attempt at hegemony' (Harcourt, 1996a, p. 317). As far as I am aware there has been no systematic study of this problem, and certainly none making use of what are by now standard quantitative tests (on which see Coats, 1996). Did Post Keynesians from outside the USA publish more often in US journals than was formerly the case? Were they more prone to cite articles in these journals than they had been in earlier periods? Did they increasingly send their best graduate students to American institutions for their PhDs? Did more of them look for work, and find it, in universities and colleges in the New World? My guess is that all these questions should be answered in the affirmative, and that more qualitative indices of Americanization would all point in the same direction. Cambridge was no longer the intellectual heart of Post Keynesianism, as it was before 1970 or, arguably, right through to the death of Robinson and Sraffa in 1983. I suspect that increasingly the *Journal of Post Keynesian Economics* was the first choice of most Post Keynesian writers (and readers), regardless of nationality and country of domicile, and that by 1990, say, it was well ahead of the field. This is not, of course, to deny the continuing vitality of Post Keynesian thought outside the United States, in the five countries discussed in this chapter and in the rest of the world. In the UK, especially, there was a powerful Post Keynesian presence in several institutions, one of them (still) Cambridge. But if it is true that Post Keynesianism had itself been Americanized, this has important implications for the relative strength of the competing currents identified by Hamouda and Harcourt (1988) that will be considered in Chapter 10. First, however, we must turn to the two issues that dominated the debates of the 1980s and 1990s: money and methodology.

8. Money and the monetarists

> All Walrasian general equilibrium models imply worlds of certainty. The *tâtonnement* process ... implies that anyone holding money either at any point in the auction or till the next period is demented. (Davidson, 1972c, pp. 872–3)

HAMLET WITHOUT THE PRINCE?

The supposed neglect of monetary issues by the Cambridge Post Keynesians is sometimes believed to have begun with the publication of the *General Theory* and to have persisted until the monetarist counter-revolution forced some of them – Kahn and Kaldor, but not Robinson, still less Sraffa – to respond. Quite elaborate stories have been told to explain the apparent paradox involved in the refusal of Keynes's closest associates to take money seriously (Kregel, 1985; Dillard, 1989). On closer investigation, however, the paradox turns out to be a chimera. Kahn and Robinson wrote a great deal on the theory of money and monetary policy, and they were probably the first English-speaking economists to develop the characteristically Post Keynesian notion of endogenous money. Their analysis proved to be very similar, in some important respects, to another heterodox body of ideas, the theory of the monetary circuit that was already popular in contemporary France and Italy.

How, then, did the strange misconception arise that the Cambridge Post Keynesians took no interest in money? It must be conceded that there is a grain of truth in the charge. One of them did concentrate exclusively on 'real' analysis: Richard Goodwin (1913–96), a much-loved mathematical growth and cycle theorist whose obituary in the *Guardian* bore the marvellous title, 'Economist Who Despised Money' (Harcourt, 1996b). And money plays no explicit role in Sraffa's *Production of Commodities*, as Post Keynesian critics have often complained (see Chapter 10). However, Sraffa's tantalizing allusion to the possibility of a purely monetary theory of the rate of profits must also be taken into account, along with his extreme reluctance to commit himself to anything, outside the very narrow confines of his classic book (see Chapter 4). As for Joan Robinson, it is true that the discussion of money in her *Accumulation of Capital* is rather limited. After a brief chapter on 'The Meaning of Money' in the introductory section of the book, the reader has to wait until Book Four for two short chapters on 'Money and Finance' and 'The Rates of Interest'. These chapters amount to 28 pages, or a little more than 6 per cent of the whole (Robinson, 1956, pp. 25–32, 225–44). This reflects her relentless application of what may be termed the method of successive complication, starting with the simplest conceivable analysis based on the most simple assumptions and then relaxing them one by one as the argument proceeds.

It does not imply that she regarded money as unimportant. In the early 1950s both Kahn and Robinson wrote on the theory of liquidity preference and interest rates, with Robinson applying the title of her article ('The Rate of Interest') to the book of collected essays in which it was reprinted (Robinson, 1952a; the 1979 edition was retitled 'The Generalization of the General Theory'). She focused on the speculative demand for money and emphasized the role of uncertainty with respect to the capital value of financial securities, the associated income stream and the risk of default (she described them as 'capital uncertainty', 'income uncertainty' and 'lender's risk', respectively). As Robinson noted, 'the whole subject of expectations bristles with psychological and philosophical difficulties', but it simply could not be avoided in any serious analysis of the rate of interest (Robinson, 1952a, p. 12). Following Dennis Robertson, Hicks had criticized Keynes for proposing a 'bootstrap' theory of interest. Robinson echoed Hugh Townshend (1937) in dismissing these objections:

> But there is no escape from the fact that the price today of any long-lived object with low carrying costs is strongly influenced by expectations about what its price will be in the future. If the rate of interest is hanging by its boot straps, so is the price of Picasso's paintings. (Ibid., pp. 18–19)

Speculation, Robinson continued, was a major source of instability in financial markets, and created 'a thick fog' both for market participants and for economists attempting to understand their behaviour. It posed serious difficulties for a 'cheap money' policy. If the speculators anticipated a rise in interest rates and the authorities then lost their nerve, expectations would prove to be self-fulfilling as 'the growling of the bears turns to joyous yelps of "I told you so"' (ibid., pp. 20, 30). Kahn's article was also intended to defend Keynes's analysis of the speculative motive against the 'bootstrap' critics. Unlike Robinson, Kahn extended his attack to encompass the Hicksian LM function: 'Sufficient has been said to demonstrate the unsuitability of thinking of a schedule of liquidity preference as though it could be represented by a well-defined curve or by a functional relationship expressed in mathematical terms or subject to econometric processes', even though Keynes himself had been tempted to do so (Kahn, 1954, p. 250).

There was no suggestion in either paper that the supply of money was anything other than exogenously determined by the decisions of the central bank. Robinson, indeed, explicitly assumed a vertical money supply curve, though she claimed in a footnote that her argument could easily be modified to fit the case where the supply of money was positively related to the interest rate (Robinson, 1952a, p. 7, n3). This was soon to change. Very early in the *Accumulation of Capital* she compared human economies with the productive activities of the robin, observing that 'a wage economy requires money', since an employer needed finance to pay his workers before he had anything to sell (as always, Robinson wrote in the male gender). 'Thus a society which had not succeeded in inventing money could not develop a capitalist economy' (Robinson, 1956, pp. 26–7). Augusto Graziani's careful analysis of Book Four later revealed that Robinson's analysis had a great deal in common with the theory of the monetary circuit, which she presumably learned by osmosis from Wicksell and Kalecki – and perhaps from Ralph Hawtrey, too. Thus she argued that a clear distinction must be made between initial and final finance, and denied that saving was ever a source of finance. Banks and non-bank firms constituted two separate sectors. Money was a debt of the firms to the banks; it was created only when payments were made, and destroyed when firms repaid their debts to the banks. These are basic propositions in monetary circuit analysis (Graziani, 1989; see also Chapter 7 above) and reveal Robinson as a pioneer of the theory of endogenous money.

Two years later, in his evidence to the Committee on the Working of the Monetary System (the Radcliffe Committee), Richard Kahn pointed to some important implications for macroeconomic policy. Monetary policy, he suggested, should be treated as a means, not as an end in itself. There was no denying its effectiveness, especially when it was operated restrictively and had serious negative effects on the level of investment. But monetary policy should not be used to control inflation, a task for which wages policy could be employed with much less damage to output and productivity growth. Kahn argued that changes in the quantity of money did not directly affect the real economy: they worked indirectly, through their repercussions on the rate of interest, the quantity of bank lending and the state of the stock market, all of which impinged on investment. He noted that bank advances were 'at most times … subject, in greater or smaller degree, to a process of rationing', even when this was not imposed on the banks by government decree:

> In other words, banks do not habitually charge to their customers the highest rates of interest which the traffic will bear. There is normally what Keynes called 'a fringe of unsatisfied borrowers'. The result is that the behaviour of bank advances exercises an influence on investment which is separate from that exercised by rates of interest. (Kahn, 1958, p. 144)

It was only a very short step from this recognition of credit rationing to a fully fledged Post Keynesian theory of endogenous money (Rochon, 1999), though Kahn himself did not take it.

Neither did Nicholas Kaldor, despite the strong opposition to the quantity theory that he expressed in his own evidence to the Radcliffe Committee. Like Kahn, Kaldor argued that the velocity of circulation was unstable, and denied the existence of any direct relationship between the money supply and the volume of aggregate expenditure. Changes in the money supply operated via interest rates, and the effects were unpredictable and often rather weak. Kaldor could see little merit in the 'drastic' changes in the rate of interest that would be needed to guarantee a strong impact on fixed investment, since they would make bond prices very much more volatile. Monetary policy should be directed towards stabilizing the level of inventory investment, which required a focus on the short rate rather than the long rate; even here the impact was not easy to predict (Kaldor, 1958).

Contrary to Kaldor's subsequent claims, there is little or nothing in his evidence to Radcliffe that contradicts the conventional view of an exogenously determined money supply (Rochon, 2000). Thus the ambivalence that characterized Kaldor's monetary thought in the late 1930s appears to have persisted well into the postwar period. In its Report, the Committee itself displayed a 'failure of nerve' in not breaking decisively with mainstream monetary theory (Rousseas, 1985, p. 51). Its analysis was, however, distinctly unorthodox, and its model, as one sympathetic critic put it, was 'rich but confusingly stated' (Chick, 1973, p. 73). Radcliffe replaced the traditional concept of money with the much broader notion of 'liquidity' as the fundamental determinant of total expenditure. Control of the money supply could always be circumvented, on the Radcliffe view, by a shift to slightly less liquid assets and by borrowing from non-bank financial intermediaries. Since the volume of liquidity could be affected by changes in interest rates, monetary policy should focus on interest rate management and (perhaps) on direct credit controls (Radcliffe Committee, 1959).

None of this justified the monetarists' accusation that Radcliffe represented 'the high tide of Keynesian scepticism about the importance of monetary policy and the relevance of monetary theory' (Johnson, 1972, p. 21, cited by Hewitson, 1993, p. 146). Even as a summary of Kaldor's evidence this is a gross exaggeration, and it is ironic that this calumny came to be repeated by some Post Keynesians. On a charitable interpretation it resulted from a confusion of two quite separate propositions. The first, derived from the Radcliffe Report itself and the evidence of Kahn and Kaldor, is that monetary policy did not work in the way that more orthodox economists believed. No doubt this is debatable, but it does not entail the quite different proposition that for the Cambridge Post Keynesians money simply did not matter, either for the determination of real output or in the analysis of inflation. Kahn, at least, had quite explicitly stated his belief that the opposite was true. In fact Radcliffe foreshadowed an alternative monetary theory, and a different view of the operation of monetary policy, which were fully articulated only considerably later, after the Post Keynesians had involved themselves in a frontal confrontation with monetarist ideas.

THE SCOURGE OF MONETARISM

There is a delicious ambiguity in the title of Nicholas Kaldor's little book, which I have used as the heading of this section (Kaldor, 1982). Kaldor regarded monetarist ideas as a theoretical and policy disaster, but he also thought of himself as its most tireless and effective opponent. Monetarism, Kaldor maintained, had been used to inflict severe and unnecessary pain on the British economy; and he himself was its most effective critic. He was the scourge of the scourge. Many Post Keynesians would agree that he was correct on both counts.

Whether the triumph of monetarism amounted to a victory of financial over industrial capital (Bhaduri and Steindl, 1983) or the revenge of the rentiers (Smithin, 1996b), or the defeat of organized labour by a united and militant capitalist class, remains uncertain; perhaps it was all of these things. Viewed as a form of economic theory, monetarism has been no less contentious. From the outset, orthodox Keynesians like James Tobin argued that Milton Friedman's analytical framework was entirely consistent with the neoclassical synthesis, and distinctive only in making extreme claims about the shape of the LM curve and the stability of certain parameters in the money demand function (Tobin, 1972). Friedman's criticism of the Phillips Curve had been anticipated, not only by Phillips himself but also by Paul Samuelson and Robert Solow in their canonical version of the unemployment–inflation trade-off for the United States, in which they acknowledged that major changes in inflationary expectations would render the curve unstable, and therefore unusable as a menu for macroeconomic policy choice (Samuelson and Solow, 1960). As for the 'natural rate', who had ever denied that there was some minimum level of unemployment, determined by the degree of frictional and structural mismatch between unemployed workers and unfilled job vacancies, below which it would be dangerous to go? Certainly not Keynes, nor the Cambridge Post Keynesians, who had always stressed the inflationary dangers of full employment. Friedman might have implied the need to raise the unemployment rate at which Joan Robinson's 'inflation barrier' could be expected to block the way, but this was an empirical matter with no great theoretical significance.

However, Post Keynesians never agreed with the notion that monetarism was innocuous, in either analytical or policy terms. As early as 1963 Hyman Minsky took issue with the monetarists on the importance of money and the nature of the transmission mechanism between monetary changes and the real economy:

> I happen to believe that the introduction of monetary and the related financial phenomena only by way of the stock of money as a variable in the equation system would turn out to be not tenable; that any serious work on monetary phenomena in relation to business cycles will result in the inclusion of variables and equations that reflect not only the money stock but also the asset structure of the monetary authorities and the financial liabilities of other units. (Minsky, 1963a, p. 66)

Borrowing to finance investment in a period of sustained growth, Minsky argued, was likely to result in a steady increase in the proportion of corporate profits needed to service firms' financial commitments. If this process went far enough, the resulting financial pressures made it possible for a severe depression to occur, 'even in the absence of a marked decline in the money supply'; Friedman was simply wrong to deny this possibility (ibid., p. 68). Minsky contrasted the monetarist analysis of portfolio choice with his own 'commercial loan' view of the monetary transmission mechanism (see Chapter 5), and concluded that

> a commercial loan monetary system is consistent with a debt deflation view of how major recessions are generated: a view in which the historically observed changes in the money supply, particularly those associated with deep depression, are a *result* of business behavior. (ibid., p. 72; emphasis added)

Thus the direction of causality was the reverse of that assumed by the monetarists; Friedman had mistaken cause for effect.

The endogeneity of the money supply can be traced back in the history of economic thought at least as far as Marx, and features in the more modern Marxian literature (Howard and King, 1992, p. 315). It was also fundamental to Nicholas Kaldor's critique of monetarism, which began in 1970 with a polemical article in *Lloyds Bank Review*. Kaldor identified two crucial issues: the direction of causation between money and output, and the ability of the central bank to control the quantity of money. The monetarists, he argued, were wrong on both questions. 'The explanation … for all the empirical findings on the "stable money function" is that the 'money supply' is "endogenous", not "exogenous"' (Kaldor, 1970a, p. 12). Evidence that changes in money preceded changes in output and employment was irrelevant, since the observed time-lag could be interpreted in a number of different ways, none of them relying on monetarist theory (ibid., pp. 13–15). And the much-vaunted stability of the velocity of circulation was due to the unstable behaviour of the money supply, which '"accommodated itself" to the needs of trade: rising in response to an expansion, and vice versa' (ibid., p. 11). There were echoes here of the nineteenth-century debates between the Currency School and the Banking School (Hewitson, 1993). As for the possibility of using the money supply as a policy variable, Kaldor suggested the following thought-experiment: could the central bank prevent the annual Christmas shopping spree simply by reducing the supply of cash? Was it not much more likely that substitutes for money (such as credit cards) would spring up as merrymakers tried to avoid the financial restrictions? He concluded by asking one final question:

> What, if anything, follows from all this? I have certainly no objection to Friedman's prescription that the best thing to do is to secure a steady expansion of *x* per cent a year in the money supply. But I doubt if this objective is attainable by the instruments of monetary policy in the US, let alone in the UK. (Kaldor, 1970a, p. 21)

Inflation could be brought under control only by 'some combination of incomes policy and magic (but more by magic)'.

Friedman objected, unconvincingly, that the monetarists had always admitted the possibility of reverse causation between money and output but had demonstrated it to be empirically unimportant (Friedman, 1970). A more damaging complaint was that Kaldor's argument was severely undertheorized, as he himself later conceded (Kaldor, 1978, p. viii); and his bizarre acceptance of the monetarist policy rule cannot have been intended seriously. In *The Scourge of Monetarism* he provided both some necessary analytical stiffening and a violent attack on monetarism in action. The Friedmanites had implicitly assumed that all money was commodity money. They could then legitimately draw a vertical money supply curve that might be shifted, to the right or the left, by decisions of the central bank:

> Now, in the case of credit money the proper representation should be a *horizontal* 'supply curve' of money not a vertical one. Monetary policy is represented *not* by a given quantity of money stock but by a *given rate of interest*; and the amount of money in existence will be demand-determined … at all times, the money stock will be determined by demand, and the rate of interest determined by the Central Bank. (Kaldor, 1982, p. 24)

Something similar, he might have noted, had already been argued by the Old Keynesian James Tobin (Brainard and Tobin, 1968). Kaldor illustrated the argument with a diagram (drawn here as Figure 8.1), and noted that the rate of interest was now no longer the dependent but rather the independent variable.

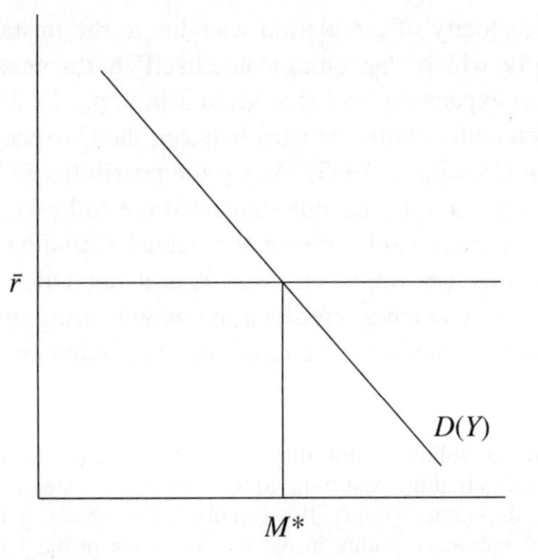

Source: Kaldor (1982, p. 24).

Figure 8.1

According to the monetarists, the transmission mechanism linking increases in money to increases in output was higher spending, induced by an excess supply of money:

> However, with credit-money this kind of problem *cannot* arise, since credit-money comes into existence as a result of borrowing (by businesses, individuals, or public agencies) from the banks; if, as a result of such borrowing, more money comes into existence than the public at the given level of incomes (or expenditures) wishes to hold, the excess gets directly or indirectly repaid to the banks and in this way the 'excess money' is extinguished. … In a credit-money economy, unlike with commodity-money, supply can never be in excess of the amount individuals wish to hold. (Kaldor, 1982, p. 70; original emphasis)

It followed that central banks could control the rate of interest, but not the quantity of money. This did not render monetary policy futile. On the contrary, Kaldor believed that the Thatcher government's policy had been extremely effective. But it had reduced inflation by depressing effective demand through increased interest rates and the resulting overvaluation of the pound, together with a sharp fiscal contraction. All this had raised unemployment and reduced the bargaining power of the trade unions, thereby reducing wage settlements and lowering the inflation rate. It was the contraction in output and employment that had defeated inflation. Control of the money supply was 'no more than a convenient smoke-screen providing an ideological justification for such anti-social measures' (ibid., p. 70).

Paul Davidson had been a critic of monetarism since the mid-1960s (see Chapter 5). In 1972 he was given space in the *Journal of Political Economy* – for the first and last time in his career – to restate his objections to the monetarists' theoretical framework. Davidson argued that Milton Friedman had eliminated uncertainty from his analysis by assuming that all expectations were realized. Hence he was unable to explain 'the existence of particular market institutions, organizations and constraints ... which exist only because uncertainty is present' (Davidson, 1972c, pp. 865–6). The consequence was, somewhat ironically, that money played no essential role in the monetarist model, and Friedman was able to treat money as an exogenous variable, 'enter[ing] the system like manna from heaven, or dropped from the sky via a helicopter' (ibid., p. 877). Keynes, on the other hand, had demonstrated the endogenous nature of the money supply process as early as 1937 through his discussion of the finance motive (Keynes, 1937b), which explained the level of borrowing from the banks in terms of the intended level of investment expenditure.

Friedman's reply to these criticisms raised some important methodological issues. 'Uncertainty may not be explicitly mentioned,' he maintained, 'but it is certainly taken for granted throughout the analysis' (Friedman, 1972, p. 923). (Taken for granted, indeed!) The assumption that all expectations were realized was part of the definition of long-run Walrasian general equilibrium, he maintained, not 'a state that is assumed ever to be attained in practice. It is a logical construct that defines the norm or trend from which the actual world is always deviating but to which it is tending to return or about which it tends to fluctuate' (ibid., p. 925). Friedman also claimed that Davidson had adduced no evidence in support of the finance motive: 'Talk is not a substitute for evidence. I know no empirical study of the demand for money that has ever identified variables corresponding to "the finance motive", let alone found them to have a significant influence' (ibid., p. 931, n16). And there was no truth in the charge that Friedman himself had relied naively on monetary exogeneity: 'My general framework does not assume an exogenous money supply in any relevant sense ... One simplified model, used for a special purpose, takes [the] money supply to be exogenous. I have done work on the factors determining the money supply and have encouraged much work by others on this subject' (ibid.).

At issue here are age-old questions of 'realism' versus 'necessary abstraction' in constructing economic models, and of the relationship between theory and different types of empirical evidence (see Chapter 9). These issues were implicit in Davidson's second attack on Friedman, which came in the article 'Money as Cause and Effect' that he published with Sidney Weintraub in the December 1973 issue of the *Economic Journal*; unfortunately this paper did not attract a reply from Friedman. Davidson and Weintraub covered some familiar ground, accusing the monetarists of rendering money 'entirely redundant' by employing a Walrasian model without time or uncertainty and failing to recognize the critical role of the money wage-rate as the one price that affects all other prices (Davidson and Weintraub, 1973, p. 1122). Elaborating on a point first made (much less clearly) by Kaldor, they noted that the direction of causation between money and output was by no means obvious, since the anticipations of economic agents might seriously muddy the waters. If firms expected an increase in sales, for example, and in consequence planned to expand their productive capacity, they would need to borrow from the banks to finance the new investment expenditure. Thus the money supply might well increase before sales and output rise; but the monetary growth was the effect, not the cause, despite the apparently perverse nature of the time-lag between them (ibid., pp. 1118–19).

Davidson and Weintraub claimed that Friedman's new version of the Quantity Theory was even less satisfactory than the old, since it offered no theory of inflation. When the theory was written as $MV=PT$, with V constant and T determined by the full employment level of output, changes in M led directly to changes in P. The new version had $MV=Y$, where Y represented money GDP. If V was constant, as before, then increases in M led to increases in Y; but $Y=PQ$, and there was nothing in Friedman to explain how the increase in Y was divided between a higher price level and an increase in real GDP. 'It makes a vast difference for policy if the prime monetary effect in the short run – in which all of us are compelled to live – is on output (and employment) rather than upon prices' (ibid., p. 1120). This ambiguity was enough to destroy the case for any simple monetary policy rule. Davidson and Weintraub concluded that monetary policy was not well equipped to target inflation (for which an incomes policy was greatly to be preferred), but it was 'decisive' for 'the real phenomena of growth and full employment' (ibid., p. 1132).

Pretty well all Post Keynesians would have agreed with this last point. Some would have gone further to argue, with Kaldor, that incomes policy was only a necessary condition for controlling inflation, but not sufficient. The stagflationary crisis of 1972–4 had shown that increases in commodity prices, for oil above all, but also for grains and other foodstuffs, were an additional and potentially major source of cost inflationary pressure. Kaldor had always advocated intervention in the market for primary products, with buffer stocks controlled by international agencies used to protect both producers and consumers from excessive fluctuations in commodity prices (Kaldor, 1951). He now developed a theoretical justification for this position, using a 'North–South' global growth model in which manufacturing was characterized by dynamic increasing returns and agriculture by diminishing returns in the traditional manner (see Chapter 3). In the long run primary product prices were more likely to rise, relatively to manufactures, than they were to decline, but in the short run low supply elasticities could lead to volatility in either direction, and it was therefore most unsafe to leave the commodity markets to the tender mercies of the speculators (Kaldor, 1986b, 1987).

Paul Davidson drew one further important policy implication from his critique of monetarism, and this also concerned international economic relations. The monetarists had argued very strongly for a system of flexible exchange rates to replace the fixed rate regime that had been in operation since 1945. They did so not just on the grounds that the Bretton Woods system had become unsustainable, nor from the general principle that market forces should operate without unnecessary restraint. Central to the entire monetarist case, in fact, was the requirement for floating exchange rates if monetary policy was to be possible at all in any individual nation-state. With fixed exchange rates and highly mobile capital, they maintained, the authorities lose control of the money supply, which thus becomes endogenous in this particular ('ability to control') sense of the term. In *International Money and the Real World* Davidson objected that the post-Bretton Woods floating rate regime had brought none of the benefits that the monetarists had claimed for it. On the contrary, it had generated greatly increased uncertainty by creating exchange rate volatility, and had therefore been a major contributor to the rise in unemployment and slowdown in economic growth that had marred the 1970s. Davidson called instead for a revival of Keynes's plans for an International Clearing Union, with most of the responsibility for balance of payments adjustments placed on countries running surpluses, not on deficit nations. Balance of payments problems should be resolved primarily through an internationally coordinated incomes policy, with surplus countries required to expand money wages more rapidly than their productivity growth rate and with the reverse obligation being imposed on deficit nations. Exchange rate adjustments would be permitted, but would play a subordinate role; capital controls could be employed, subject to international agreement on the basic principles governing their use. The resulting 'Unionized Monetary System', Davidson concluded, would be greatly preferable to the monetarist alternative, 'a Darwinian free market struggle in which the resulting stagflation is likely to impoverish all or most of the inhabitants' (Davidson, 1982, p. 266).

Davidson repeated the case for a Unionized Monetary System in later writings (Davidson, 1994), and also advocated the channelling of all foreign exchange transactions through the central banks, which would effectively eliminate the possibility of speculative profits from international monetary transactions. He opposed plans for a tax on foreign exchange dealings to reduce the incentives for speculators, and thereby increase exchange rate stability, on the grounds that it would impose a considerable burden on legitimate trade (Davidson, 2002). Other Post Keynesians were more favourably inclined to the so-called 'Tobin tax', if only as a potentially large source of revenue for increasingly fiscally challenged national governments (Arestis and Sawyer, 1999a). These, however, were disputes about the means of international monetary policy; there was very broad agreement about the ends.

BACK TO KEYNES

For the Post Keynesians, money mattered; it mattered very much. In a sense it mattered more for them than for the monetarists, whose general equilibrium models were more appropriate to a barter system than to a monetary production economy, and who continued to assert the long-run neutrality of money. Exactly *how* money mattered, precisely what the transmission mechanisms between money and the real world actually were – all this had yet to be fully worked out. It is not surprising, in the aftermath of the monetarist controversy, that many Post Keynesian theorists turned to Keynes in search of answers.

As we have seen, Paul Davidson had led the way. He was soon followed by Hyman Minsky, whose book *John Maynard Keynes* presented Keynes himself as the original source of the financial instability hypothesis (see Chapter 5). The neoclassical synthesis, Minsky argued, had 'neglected or lost … a major part of the substance of *The General Theory*' (Minsky, 1975, p. viii). Much more attention needed to be paid to decision making under uncertainty, to the cyclical character of the capitalist process and to the financial relations of advanced capitalist economies. Neoclassical macroeconomics relied on asocial and ahistorical preference maps and production functions, ignoring the role of time and the specific institutional details on which Keynes had placed so much weight. Minsky contrasted the neoclassical 'barter paradigm' and 'village market image' with Keynes's 'speculative–financial paradigm – the image is of a banker making his deals on a Wall Street' (ibid., p. 58). For Keynes investment was highly volatile, not because of changes in the technical productivity of capital or the thriftiness of households, but owing to financing conditions and the uncertainty of returns. His was a model of continuous cyclical instability, in which equilibrium was rarely, if ever, attained.

Victoria Chick was a student of Minsky's, but arrived at her own, highly individual, interpretation of Keynes through two decades of independent reflection, stumbling into dissenting economics 'simply by following arguments where they seemed to lead' (Chick, 1992b, p. 85 – this is a brief but very revealing intellectual autobiography). In her *Theory of Monetary Policy* she defended the Radcliffe Report and attacked not only the monetarists but also the IS–LM model, the real balance effect and the Tobin–Brainard analysis of portfolio choice (Chick, 1973). Ten years later, in *Macroeconomics After Keynes*, Chick set out her own version of Keynes's theory, in which time, uncertainty and money played the central role. It is a densely argued and – as the author herself admits in the preface – also a difficult book, almost impossible to summarize, but extremely influential in the development of Post Keynesian monetary thought, especially in Britain (Chick, 1983). It concluded with an affirmation of the continued relevance of Keynes's economics in the post-monetarist 1980s:

> I believe that the *General Theory* still contains much that is useful: the idea of aggregating expenditure according to the degree of autonomy from current income (though with the rise in importance of both consumer durables and consumer credit we may wish to draw the line elsewhere), the restoration from classical authors of the periodic importance of speculation and its displacement to the financial sphere, and the integration of the consequence of asset-holding with the flows of production and investment – these ideas still hold. And the fundamental, contradictory relationship between households and producers is still the core of the problem of how capitalism functions, though now it is functioning with a degree of international integration Keynes did not foresee and with government mediation on a scale for which the theory had no place. (Ibid., pp. 360–61)

Chick 'portrayed the Keynesian Revolution as one of method' (Chick, 1992b, p. 84), a position also taken by another important monetary theorist, Sheila Dow (Dow and Earl, 1982). Thus money, time and uncertainty featured prominently in the methodological debates of the 1980s and 1990s (see Chapter 9).

The Post Keynesians achieved a notable success when, in a short but telling article in the *Journal of Post Keynesian Economics*, John Hicks repudiated much of the neoclassical synthesis that he had pioneered. Although his article bore the title, 'IS–LM: an Explanation', Hicks's self-criticism went much further than this. He acknowledged that the IS function required product markets to be in continuous equilibrium, which rendered it useless in precisely the most interesting periods – he mentioned 1975 – of rapid and unpredictable change. Similar objections applied to the LM curve, but with even greater force. Stock equilibrium in the money market entailed the assumption that the expectations of all economic agents were correct:

> That is the formal concept of full equilibrium over time; I do not see how it is to be avoided. But for the purpose of generating an LM curve, which is to represent liquidity preference, it will not do without amendment. For there is no sense in liquidity, unless expectations are uncertain. But how is an uncertain expectation to be realized? When the moment arrives to which the expectation refers, what replaces it is fact, fact which is not uncertain. (Hicks, 1980–81, p. 151–2)

Hicks concluded that IS–LM was little more than 'a classroom gadget', and was useless for policy purposes. Some of his critics felt that even this did not go far enough (Shackle, 1982).

It did, however, raise an interesting doctrinal question. Keynes had seemed quite comfortable with IS–LM (see Chapter 1), and in the *General Theory* appeared to assume exogenous money and a money supply curve that was vertical at a level fixed by the policy decisions of the central bank. How, then, could his name be invoked as the patron saint of the Post Keynesian theory of endogenous money? One answer was to play down the significance of the *General Theory* and to concentrate instead on Keynes's earlier writings (notably the *Treatise on Money*) and on his post-1936 articles. This was the position taken by Graziani and the monetary circuit theorists. A second response was to argue that Keynes had been very close to developing a model of endogenous money in the *General Theory* but had lacked the courage to take the final decisive step (Moore, 1988, ch. 8). Chick offered a third interpretation, which is not inconsistent with the second, in which Keynes's hesitancy reflected the specific institutional circumstances of the 1930s. She distinguished five stages of banking development, beginning with a phase in which banks were used largely as a repository for savings. In subsequent stages, bank deposits became important as means of payment, inter-bank lending mechanisms developed, the lender-of-last-resort principle became established and, finally, liability management emerged as the guiding principle of bank behaviour. It was not until the second stage of banking development that investment began to drive saving, and only in the fourth stage (which was not fully developed until the 1970s) did the money supply become truly endogenous. Keynes's analysis of exogenous money was a reasonable approximation to the actual conditions of his time (Chick, 1985).

HORIZONTALISTS AND VERTICALISTS

Doctrinal history apart, there was by the early 1980s broad agreement among Post Keynesian monetary theorists that the money supply was (in some sense) endogenous; that this was sufficient to undermine the neoclassical synthesis in general and the IS–LM model in particular; and that monetarist policy prescriptions were either futile or dangerous. Three important issues remained to be resolved, in addition to the doubts about monetary circuit theory that were discussed in Chapter 7. First, was Kaldor correct to argue that the money supply curve was necessarily horizontal? Second, was endogenous money the result of accommodatory behaviour by central banks or the product of innovation by financial institutions in response to profit opportunities? Third, what exactly was the transmission mechanism linking money to the real world?

The most energetic proponent of a horizontal money supply curve was Basil Moore, who had sketched out the arguments in his chapter on money for Alfred Eichner's *Guide to Post Keynesian Economics* (Moore, 1978) and, ten years later, published the definitive book-length defence of 'horizontalism' (Moore, 1988). Moore began by distinguishing three types of money. The supply of both commodity money and fiat money was exogenously determined, depending on gold discoveries or central bank decisions (via open market operations and the deposit multiplier). In each case the money supply curve was vertical in interest-money space. Credit money, however, was totally different, since

> in all developed financial systems most economic agents have overdraft facilities with their banker, which they are entitled to draw down as desired...The quantity of bank loans outstanding is largely demand-determined.... So long as economic agents possess unutilized lines of credit, the nominal supply of credit money is *never* quantity-constrained by central banks. Whenever economic units, individually and in the aggregate, desire to increase their money balances, they will *always* be able to do so, at some price. This price is set by central banks as the ultimate supplier of fiat money. (Moore, 1988, pp. x–xi)

Thus the supply function of credit money was horizontal. Alternatively (and Moore never really faced up to the implicit contradiction) the supply and demand for credit money were interdependent, since 'Any increase in the nominal supply of money will always be demanded. The quantity of nominal money demanded is thus always and necessarily equal to the quantity of nominal money supplied' (ibid., p. xiii). This implies that Moore's horizontal money supply curves, and downward-sloping money demand curves, are merely metaphors, a little like aggregate supply and demand curves in a Say's Law world where output is always at the full employment level and independent functions simply do not exist (Keynes, 1936, pp. 25–6).

The horizontalist metaphor is undoubtedly a vivid one. Moore offered two types of justification for it. The first was *a priori*: since the stability of the financial system depends on the central bank acting as lender of last resort, it cannot fail to accommodate the needs of the banking system:

> price-setting central bank behavior, with its emphasis on targeting or administering the level of short-term interest rates rather than quantitatively targeting some money stock aggregate, is not a special case but rather a *logical necessity*, arising out of the nature of money and finance in all modern credit money economies. (Moore, 1988, p. xi)

But it was also 'an empirical fact' (ibid., p. xiii). Moore's exhaustive empirical research, using the (then) state-of-the-art Granger causality test, demonstrated that changes in the money supply were the effect of changes in economic activity, not the cause. More precisely:

> The growth of the money wage bill, both as a component of companies' demand for working capital finance, and as determinants of disposable personal income for household expenditure and loan demand, plays the most important role in explaining private sector demand for bank credit. Wage increases directly generate increased business working capital loan demand, while at the same time increases in the level of labor income serve again as collateral for increased consumer borrowing. (Ibid., p. 232)

And the causal mechanism, to repeat, was accommodatory behaviour by the Federal Reserve.

A large part of Moore's book was concerned with the theoretical and policy implications of his analysis. Some of these proved relatively uncontroversial, at least in Post Keynesian circles. He argued that monetarist accounts of inflation were indefensible, since credit money could never be in 'excess supply'. The growth of money wages was the principal source of inflation, and should be controlled by means of a (tax-based) incomes policy. Changes in interest rates were decided on by the central bank and affected the private sector through a Kaleckian mark-up procedure: if the federal funds rate increased, the banking system raised its lending rate structure in much the same way as a manufacturing company marked up the prices of its products when wage or raw material costs increased. Moore maintained that the IS–LM model collapsed in a credit money economy. There was also no Pigou effect in such an economy, so that the aggregate demand schedule was vertical rather than downward-sloping. With a (Kaleckian) horizontal aggregate supply curve, real output and the inflation rate were determined separately, the first by aggregate demand and the second by the rate of change of money wages. This is illustrated in Figure 8.2 (Moore, 1988, p. 326, Figure 12.2(d); note that the rate of change of the price level is measured on the vertical axis, not the price level itself).

Some of Moore's conclusions proved less palatable. Few Post Keynesians were prepared to accept his argument that the multiplier did not exist in a world of endogenous money, or his total repudiation of fiscal policy and advocacy of a balanced budget rule for current government spending (ibid., ch. 15). Otherwise sympathetic reviewers objected that Moore had taken horizontalism too far:

> Some quibbles: (1) Moore does not suggest what a medium or long-term money supply curve would look like. Suppose credit demand was resulting in monetary growth that the central bank thought excessive, and it raised its interest rate targets (shifting the short-run money supply curve up). If demand continued to increase, wouldn't the long-run supply curve be upward sloping, if not vertical? (2) Even in the short run, since not all potential borrowers have loan commitments to draw down, and since banks can choose not to make new commitments, and since unused loan commitments cannot (yet!) be resold in secondary markets, isn't it

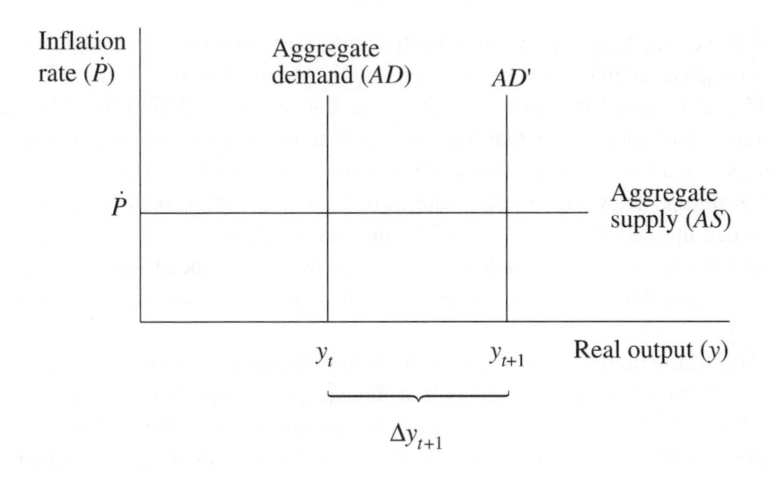

Source: Moore (1988, p. 326).

Figure 8.2

> overstating the case to say that bank lending is entirely demand-determined and nondiscretionary? And if new loans are made at rising rates because of perceptions of increasing lenders' risk, say, wouldn't the short-run curve be upward sloping even if the Fed was smoothing or pegging interbank and discount rates? (Niggle, 1989, p. 1185; cf. Wray, 1989, p. 1118)

Others criticized his position on the two remaining controversial issues in Post Keynesian monetary theory: the causes of endogeneity and the monetary transmission mechanism. As Robert Pollin maintained, accommodation by the central bank was not the only foundation stone for a theory of endogenous money, even though Kaldor and Weintraub had relied upon it no less than Moore (it was, for example, central to the analysis of Davidson and Weintraub, 1973). But there was also an alternative tradition, which dated back to Hyman Minsky and focused on financial innovation: 'when central banks do choose to restrict the growth of nonborrowed reserves, then additional reserves, though not necessarily a fully adequate supply, are generated within the financial structure itself – through innovative liability management practices such as borrowing in the federal funds, Eurodollar, and certificate of deposit markets' (Pollin, 1991, p. 368; cf. Earl, 1990, ch. 9). The resulting theory of 'structural endogeneity' had been advocated in the 1980s by the US writers James Earley and Stephen Rousseas. Pollin might also have noted the British dimension to this argument, running from the Radcliffe Report through to Victoria Chick's discussion of the stages of banking development, outlined in the previous section, and the European contribution via the theory of the monetary circuit, in which central banks play no essential role (see Chapter 7). Using similar econometric techniques to those employed by Moore, Pollin concluded that the evidence favoured the 'structuralists' over the 'accommodationists'. One important consequence was that Moore's approach to interest rates was much too simple: 'market interest rates are not strictly governed by Federal Reserve intervention. They are, rather, determined by a complex set of interactions between the Federal Reserve and the financial markets' (Pollin, 1991, p. 393). There might after all be some scope for Keynes's concept of liquidity preference, which Moore had attempted to banish from Post Keynesian monetary theory.

This immediately raises the issue of the monetary transmission mechanism. If 'money matters', and is 'not neutral', how exactly does it affect the 'real world'? On this question dissension among Post Keynesians continued into the 1990s. Moore had maintained that 'interest rates must be returned to center stage. In the absence of deflation, there is always some level of nominal short-term interest rates sufficiently low or sufficiently high to assure that aggregate demand grows at the desired rate' (Moore, 1988, p. 386). For many Post Keynesians this gave too much ground to the neoclassicals since, like IS–LM, it attributed too little importance to uncertainty, expectations and the resulting instability of investment expenditure. But if spending is not interest-elastic in any stable or predictable way, and if the money supply is endogenous, why then is money not 'passive' (or neutral) in relation to changes in real economic activity? Perhaps there was, after all, no necessary connection between endogenous money and unemployment equilibrium (Cottrell, 1994).

It is no accident that Moore's 'structuralist' opponents have for the most part been followers of Minsky, for the financial instability hypothesis offers a very clear answer to this question. 'Money matters', since the availability of finance fluctuates cyclically and this governs the ability of economic agents to undertake 'discretionary' or 'deficit' expenditures, which are therefore also highly unstable; and debt deflation can give rise to deep depression (see Chapter 5). The Kaleckian question of 'lender's risk' is relevant here. Banks can never be sure that their borrowers will not default; indeed, on this crucial issue they face uncertainty rather than measurable risk. It is entirely rational for them to lend only to 'creditworthy' borrowers, and then only up to some specified quantitative limit that cannot safely be increased if the borrower offers to pay an ever-higher rate of interest, since such offers can reasonably be interpreted as a sign of desperation, and thus of serious risk of default:

> The significance of such considerations is that the interest rate is not set to clear the market. There is always a 'fringe of unsatisfied borrowers' – those who receive no credit or less than desired. This means that the money supply curve is not horizontal, and that banks are not 'price setters and quantity takers' in retail loan markets. (Wray, 1990, p. 181)

It follows that credit rationing is more effective in killing off a boom than increases in interest rates, and that easy money stimulates an upswing more readily than cheap money ever can.

CASHED UP OR WIPED OUT?

These disagreements did not, however, seriously undermine Post Keynesian opposition to monetarism, which was shared by some neoclassical theorists who were hostile to them on many other issues (see, for example, Hahn, 1982a). By the mid-1990s it was evident that the monetarists had won the war, but also that they had lost some important battles in the process. They had certainly won the war, because all over the world monetary policy was now geared exclusively to combating inflation, whatever the statute book might say about full employment and growth as additional responsibilities of the monetary authorities. Their victory was emphasized, and reinforced, by the way in which central banks had been given their 'independence', along the lines of the US Federal Reserve. By 1997 this was true as a matter of law also for the Reserve Bank of New Zealand (a trailblazer in this respect), the Bank of England and the European Central Bank, and in practical terms it applied to many more, including the Reserve Bank of Australia. 'Independence' stands in need of the inverted commas, as central bankers were more dependent than ever on the whims of the international financial markets. They had simply been liberated from control or supervision by democratically elected politicians accountable to the people.

The monetarists had, however, lost two battles and appeared to be losing a third. No central bank governor any longer pretends to 'control the money supply'. It is tacitly but universally accepted that the relevant policy instrument is the short-term rate of interest, not the stock of money. This does not mean that central bankers have all become horizontalists (Goodhart, 1989), but in a broader sense it does vindicate the Post Keynesian theorists of endogenous money. The monetarists have been defeated, too, on the issue of rules versus discretion in monetary policy. In principle it would be possible to design an interest rate rule, on Wicksellian or Hayekian lines, with the monetary authorities keeping the long rate constant at whatever level the 'natural rate of interest' is supposed to be. But no central bank has ever attempted any such thing. Interest rates are altered frequently, often in response to quite minor changes in the macroeconomic environment or in financial market behaviour or beliefs. In other words, the central bankers practise the very same fine-tuning which had been fiercely denounced by the early monetarists. From this, too, the Post Keynesians can derive some quiet satisfaction, even if the authorities' discretion is employed in the remorseless quest for unnecessarily low rates of inflation without regard for the consequences for output or employment (see Arestis and Sawyer, 1999b, for a vigorous attack on this 'new monetarism').

The third battle is still being fought. The terrain is international monetary policy, and here the monetarists are very much on the defensive. As we saw earlier in this chapter, Post Keynesians were always critical of monetarist support for floating exchange rates and comprehensively deregulated global financial markets, on the grounds that speculation is not always stabilizing, instability breeds uncertainty, and uncertainty chokes off investment and reduces growth. These fears were also vindicated by the much slower rates of economic growth, and very substantially higher unemployment levels, that characterized the fourth quarter of the twentieth century by comparison with the 'golden age' of the third quarter (Davidson, 1994, ch. 16). The East Asian financial crisis of 1997–8 (a textbook example of the real consequences of Minskyian financial fragility) led self-proclaimed 'Old Keynesians' like Paul Krugman (1999) and even repentant monetarists like Paul Volcker to question the received wisdom. The notably illiberal Chinese monetary authorities had, after all, managed to insulate their economy from the speculative whirlwind (presumably without the benefit of Post Keynesian advice) by pegging the currency to the dollar and controlling capital movements. By the end of the century, in fact, there was growing international support for what was essentially the Post Keynesian position on international monetary policy: fixed exchange rates with an adjustable peg, controls over short-term capital movements, and drastic reform of the International Monetary Fund to remove its relentlessly deflationary bias. A slow-moving pendulum seemed at last to be moving back in the right direction.

It would be wrong to imply that Milton Friedman's monetarism was the only target of Post Keynesian monetary critics. By 1980 it was clear that Robert Lucas's position was even more objectionable than that of Friedman. 'Monetarism Mark II' as Kaldor termed it, following James Tobin, relied upon some exceptionally contentious propositions concerning the formation of expectations and the universality of market-clearing equilibrium. When Post Keynesians turned their attention to New Classical Economics, they drew on arguments about knowledge, uncertainty and the meaning of intelligent choice in the absence of complete information that emanated from a close reading of Keynes's philosophical writings. And this led them, almost inexorably, to a reconsideration of economic methodology. These deep and difficult questions are the subject of the next chapter.

9. Uncertainty, expectations and method

> There are great scientific tasks for econometricians to perform, but to confound science with prophecy is an unworthy blunder. (Shackle, 1955, p. 256)

KEYNES THE PHILOSOPHER

By the 1990s the distinctiveness of Post Keynesian methodology was commonly recognized, to the point where many Post Keynesians now argued that the school should be *defined* in terms of method and not by reference to theoretical propositions or policy proposals. It was not always so. The early Post Keynesians had strong views on methodological issues, but they were not always in agreement with each other, or even internally consistent. One reason why the second generation proved to be more conscious of the associated pitfalls was their rediscovery of Keynes's philosophical writings, which suggested not only a profound methodological basis for their hostility towards the neoclassical synthesis but also the need for more coherent and sophisticated methodological underpinnings than Kaldor, Robinson or Weintraub had been able to supply. Greater awareness of Keynes the philosopher led the younger Post Keynesians to a reconsideration of the meaning and importance of uncertainty, which had figured prominently in the writings of the previous generation without its significance perhaps being fully understood. This, in turn, reinforced the doubts expressed by the early writers concerning the neoclassical concept of equilibrium, and criticism of the equilibrium method opened up general questions of economic methodology. As the twentieth century drew to a close, Post Keynesian discussion of methodology had almost become synonymous with debates on the doctrine of critical realism. But we had better begin with Keynes.

In 1971 the Royal Economic Society began to publish his *Collected Writings*, which included almost everything he wrote that had ever appeared in print and a huge amount of previously inaccessible material: early drafts of books and papers, notes and correspondence of all sorts. The eighth volume was a reprint of the *Treatise on Probability*, largely written by 1914 but published only in 1921. The project had begun in 1954; by 1989, when it was concluded, 30 volumes had appeared. At about the same time the Keynes Papers in the King's College archive in Cambridge were opened to the public, allowing researchers in general and graduate students in particular to obtain access to an even greater range of manuscript material, much of which remains unpublished. This helped to prompt a major revival of scholarly interest in the philosophical underpinnings of Keynes's economic thought. Two Cambridge doctoral dissertations were written on the subject: by Rod O'Donnell, whose thesis was supervised by Bob Rowthorn, and by Anna Carabelli, whose supervisor was Donald Moggridge. They were subsequently published as books, more or less simultaneously with a work by Athol Fitzgibbons that covered very similar ground (Carabelli, 1988; Fitzgibbons, 1988; O'Donnell, 1989).

The first and most important lesson that Post Keynesians learned from their investigations into Keynes's philosophy was that he regarded economics as a moral science, not a natural science. By this he meant that the study of economic behaviour was worthwhile only because it enabled informed and ethically defensible decisions to be made by politicians, civil servants and others with responsibility for the formulation of public policy. Taken to extremes, statements like this can be read as implying that Keynes was not an economist at all, but a moral and political philosopher (Mini, 1994). A more generally acceptable conclusion might be that, for Keynes, neither theoretical speculation nor empirical research had any value in and of itself, but only to the extent that it contributed to the solution of practical problems of broad public interest (Skidelsky, 1983, chs 5–6). This was enough to prevent Keynes from ever succumbing to formalism, well-qualified though he was both in mathematics (as twelfth Wrangler) and in the probabilistic foundations of statistical theory.

The philosophers also discovered that Keynes was an organicist rather than an atomist. That is to say, he accepted the Hegelian belief that the individual parts of a system cannot be understood as isolated units, but only in relation to the other components of the system. This led him to reject the methodological individualism of orthodox economics long before he broke with the 'classical' theory of output and employment (Winslow, 1986). It did not mean, of course,

> that individuals and individual decision-making were of no consequence. Individuals do not become mindless as a result of their existence in an organic interdependent world; rather they become mindful that the basis upon which they act is not independent of the world in which they live or that the results of their actions might cause them to arrive at positions different from [those in]which they first envisioned themselves. (Rotheim, 1989–90, p. 319)

Thus Keynes's rejection of atomistic individualism provided an even deeper basis for his eventual opposition to mainstream economic theory than the evident impotence of orthodox analysis in the face of mass unemployment and persistent depression.

Most important, however, were his views on probability and their implications for his analysis of rational belief and reasonable action when the future is uncertain. Although his *Treatise on Probability* appeared in the same year as Frank Knight's *Risk, Uncertainty and Profit* (Knight, 1921), it had been substantially completed before the outbreak of the First World War. In it Keynes rejected the argument that uncertainty could be reduced to risk, so that uncertain events might be expressed in terms of certainty-equivalents. On the contrary, he wrote towards the end of the book, 'I have argued that only in a strictly limited class of cases are degrees of probability numerically measurable. It follows from this that the "mathematical expectations" of goods or advantages are not always numerically measurable.' Indeed, they might not even be 'numerically comparable in respect of more and less' (Keynes, 1921, p. 312). This did not make Keynes a nihilist or a sceptic, but it did lead him to stress that human action is governed by the cognitive limitations of its subjects and to emphasize the role of what he termed the 'weight of argument' in decision making:

> As the relevant evidence at our disposal increases, the magnitude of the probability of the argument may either decrease or increase, according as the new knowledge strengthens the unfavourable or the favourable evidence, but *something* seems to have increased in either case, – we have a more substantial basis on which to rest our conclusion. I express this by saying that an accession of new evidence increases the *weight* of an argument. New evidence will sometimes decrease the probability of an argument, but it will always increase its 'weight'. (Ibid., p. 71).

These considerations reinforced Keynes's reservations about the use of formal analysis in economics and (much later) about the validity of econometric methods. He instead defended the claims of common sense (Coates, 1996), since 'the case for ordinary reasoning', as Sheila Dow put it, was only strengthened by the restrictions that uncertainty placed on human knowledge (Dow, 1991, p. 138). And there were obvious ramifications for Keynes's analysis of investment and money. The theory of liquidity preference, in particular, relied heavily on the existence of fundamental uncertainty. Why hold an asset yielding a zero return, unless you doubt your ability to predict the yield or future capital value of other, competing forms of assets?

All of this was transparent in Keynes's well-known 'restatement' of the *General Theory* in the *Quarterly Journal of Economics* (Keynes, 1937a; see Chapter 1). But the rediscovery of his philosophical writings did serve to concentrate Post Keynesian attention on uncertainty, and a very substantial literature grew up on these questions. There was considerable controversy over subsidiary matters: whether Keynes's philosophical thought was consistent over his lifetime, whether he can legitimately be described as a rationalist, whether he was a socialist, a liberal or a conservative. John Davis, for example, pointed out that Keynes's early philosophical ideas had developed before he had begun serious work in economics, and that his economic thinking changed considerably over time. It was therefore likely that his economic and philosophical views had interacted with each other, rather than there being a single line of influence from philosophy to economics (Davis, 1994).

By the end of the 1980s, however, broad agreement had emerged on the central issues in Keynes's philosophy and on their importance to a full understanding of his economics. Some Post Keynesians were worried that a growing preoccupation with 'what Keynes really thought' was diverting energy away from more pressing policy questions (see Peter Reynolds, in King, 1995a, p. 137). To this the philosophical researchers might have replied that, on the contrary, it served as a constant reminder that policy was the object of the exercise, not theoretical analysis or econometric modelling for its own sake. I suspect that the danger of excessive concentration on the re-examination of Keynes was, for a time, a real one. My Post Keynesian bibliography lists 248 entries on 'Interpretations of Keynes' up to 1994, 148 of them between 1980 and 1990 (King, 1995d, ch. E); this would increase if relevant material from the chapters in the bibliography on methodology, money and general macroeconomic theory were added. There was less of this sort of navel-gazing, I think, in the 1990s. And there were valuable positive outcomes from the intensive study of Keynes's philosophy, in addition to the previously noted focus on economics as a moral science and the central role of policy choices. Keynes had pointed the way towards a distinctive Post Keynesian methodology, richer and more coherent than the ragbag of ideas that made up mainstream thinking (such as it was) on methodological issues (on which, see Dow, 1997). I shall return to this point at the end of this chapter. First, however, we need to look at some areas of substantive economic theory where Keynes's philosophy made a real contribution to the Post Keynesian critique of neoclassical theory: the role of uncertainty, the formation of expectations and the analysis of equilibrium.

UNCERTAINTY, RATIONALITY AND EXPECTATIONS

Uncertainty had been central to Hugh Townshend's very early proto-Post Keynesian interpetation of the *General Theory*. It was a less prominent theme in Joan Robinson's work at this time, though it was implicit in the critique of the equilibrium method in her *Essays in the Theory of Employment* and very much to the fore in her defence of liquidity preference against the 'bootstrap' objections of J.R. Hicks and other neoclassical theorists. The IS–LM version of the *General Theory* relied very heavily on the – usually unstated – assumption that the two functions were relatively stable. In an uncertain environment, however, this was evidently unrealistic. For this reason Robinson was a tacit opponent of the LM schedule, which Richard Kahn openly attacked as incompatible with fundamental uncertainty (Kahn, 1954; Robinson, 1937a, 1951a; Townshend, 1937; see also Chapter 8).

In a more diffuse way, uncertainty underpinned Robinson's continuing reluctance to specify a stable relationship between investment expenditure and the rate of interest, as in the Hicksian IS curve. She believed, with Keynes, that entrepreneurs' investment decisions were governed by their 'animal spirits', and could not be reduced to a stable, downward-sloping function of the current rate of interest. The volume of intended investment expenditure could, at a pinch, be expressed as a function of the expected rate of profit, as in her famous 'banana diagram' (Figure 3.2 above), but this was not to be taken very seriously and was definitely not to be used as the basis for econometric estimation. Although she did not dwell on the matter, uncertainty was thus at the heart of Robinson's critique of 'bastard Keynesianism'.

It was also an important theme in the work of Michal Kalecki, who is not generally thought of as an 'uncertainty man'. His principle of increasing risk (Kalecki, 1937) was misnamed, for Kalecki was not thinking in terms of a known probability distribution from which certainty-equivalent values could be calculated. The principle referred both to lenders' doubts about the creditworthiness of potential borrowers and to the fears of borrowers that they might lose control of their firms to bankers or financial markets. These two forms of uncertainty explained why investment finance was limited, especially for new enterprises, and why firms were often reluctant to borrow when loans were freely available. The principle of increasing risk was one reason why Kalecki rejected the accelerator model of investment, which he believed to be much too mechanical. And this contributed to his chronic dissatisfaction with his own attempts to specify an investment function and thereby to complete his model of the business cycle (Steindl, 1981).

Neither Robinson nor Kalecki, however, placed as much emphasis on uncertainty as did George Shackle (1903–92), who devoted his entire career to exploring its implications for economic theory. Born in Cambridge, Shackle worked as a bank clerk and then as a schoolteacher before studying economics, in the mid- to late 1930s, under Hayek at the London School of Economics. After a few months of lecturing at St Andrews and wartime employment in the civil service he began his academic career, unusually late in life, first at the University of Leeds and then at Liverpool University. Shackle continued to publish prolifically for some years after his retirement from Liverpool in 1969 (Ford, 1994).

Shackle commenced his critique of the conventional analysis of risk by noting that it relied upon frequency distributions derived from repeated performances of the occurrence that was under consideration. Such frequency-ratios, he argued, were irrelevant to all important economic events. They could be obtained in two ways:

> … either a great number of people must agree in advance to pool the results of the experiments which they as individuals will separately make; or else each individual must be able to feel sure that he himself as a potential gainer or loser will in fact be able to repeat his own experiment many times. The former method is called insurance, and its scope as we know is very far from covering all the contingencies of life. Nor should we wish it to do so if it could, for to insure against failure would, in this hard and competitive world, mean also insuring against success. The second method is logically excluded from all that type of cases which I shall call *crucial* experiments.
>
> By a crucial experiment I mean one where the person concerned cannot exclude from his mind the possibility that the very act of performing the experiment may destroy for ever the circumstances in which it was performed. (Shackle, 1955, pp. 5–6)

But entrepreneurial behaviour almost inevitably involved crucial decisions:

> If I stake my whole capital on a scheme for gold-prospecting, I may win a fortune that will transform my whole attitude and objective situation, or I may lose everything, so that by the time I have built up fresh savings I shall be an older and a different man with different ideas living in a different world. (Ibid., p. 6)

Much less dramatic and far-reaching choices would also be crucial, so long as the individuals who made them believed that they could not in practice be repeated a large number of times, even if repetition was a logical possibility. Most investment decisions, Shackle concluded, were therefore crucial in this sense, so that they could not be analysed by means of objective measures of probability and risk.

Shackle's conclusions were essentially negative; his own efforts to develop a positive theory of decision making under uncertainty were not very successful, and he was often described as a nihilist – quite wrongly, according to Parsons (1993). Shackle was certainly a radical critic both of the neoclassical synthesis and, by implication, of almost any formal macroeconomic model building. As he wrote towards the end of his life, commenting on Hicks's recantation of IS–LM: 'Sir John still does not seem to me to acknowledge the essential point: the elemental core of Keynes's conception of economic society is uncertain expectation, and uncertain expectation is wholly incompatible and in conflict with the notion of equilibrium.' This had very wide ramifications, since, for Shackle, '*all markets are in some degree speculative*' (Shackle, 1982, p. 438). It made him a lifelong opponent of the neoclassical theory of the firm, which he regarded as devoid of any relevant notion of human agency and unable to contribute anything to the analysis of entrepreneurial choice. On this and on macroeconomic issues he had much in common with Austrian analysis (see Chapter 11). Somewhat surprisingly, however, Shackle did not follow the Austrians and abandon macroeconomics altogether, remaining a Keynesian to the end – the most fundamentalist of all the 'Fundamentalist Keynesians', to introduce a term that I shall return to in Chapter 10. Even this description is a little misleading, for Shackle neither belonged to any school of thought nor founded a school of his own. He was the archetypal loner, reluctant to ally himself with anyone, however much their ideas might resemble his own (Earl, 1996).

For all these reasons, Shackle's influence on the evolution of Post Keynesian macroeconomics was rather limited. There was the occasional respectful reference to his books, and occasionally a little more. The macroeconomist who relied most on uncertainty was Paul Davidson, who drew directly on Keynes, on his own training as a natural scientist and also on Shackle. Davidson's fascination with uncertainty began in the late 1960s, when he began to appreciate the size of the gulf that separated Keynes's theory of a monetary production economy from neoclassical conceptions. At precisely this time Paul Samuelson was arguing, in an article comparing classical and neoclassical monetary theory, that rigorous thought in any scientific discipline required the assumption of ergodicity: 'Finally, there was an even more interesting third assumption implicit and explicit in the classical mind. It was a belief in unique long-run equilibrium independent of initial conditions. I shall call it the "ergodic hypothesis" by analogy to the use of this term in statistical mechanics' (Samuelson, 1968, pp. 11–12). Samuelson believed the assumption of ergodicity to be very important, since it ruled out path-dependence: 'Technically speaking, we theorists hoped not to introduce *hysteresis* phenomena into our model, as the Bible does when it says "We pass this way only once" and, in so saying, takes the subject out of the realm of science into the realm of genuine history' (ibid., p. 12). As another prominent theorist was to put it, 25 years later and in a different context (the survival of the inefficient QWERTY typewriter keyboard):

> A path-dependent process is 'non-ergodic': systems possessing this property cannot shake off the effects of past events, and do not have a limiting, invariant probability distribution that is continuous over the entire state space. In the case of deterministic systems the property of path-dependence manifests itself most immediately through the outcome's 'extreme sensitivity to initial conditions'. (David, 1993, pp. 29–30)

The ergodicity assumption, then, served to take the history out of economic theory.

Paul Davidson, like Robinson, wanted to keep the history *in* his economic science. He soon established non-ergodicity as one of the three axioms that distinguished Keynes's theory from the mainstream, the others being the non-neutrality of money and the absence of gross substitutability between money and all other goods. Demonstrating its power as a critical tool for Post Keynesian theorists, Davidson used the non-ergodic axiom in his attack on the rational expectations models of the New Classical Economists. Old Keynesian critics of rational expectations, like Kenneth Arrow and James Tobin, had attacked it because it was inconsistent with observed reality.

Davidson's objections went deeper. In non-ergodic situations, he argued, rational expectations would lead to persistent errors over time. Sensible agents would come to recognize this, and would therefore not rely on rational expectations when making crucial decisions. Davidson cited the Soviet mathematical statistician A.M. Yaglom and the econometrician Herman Wold, the latter having drawn an important distinction between statistical averages and time averages: 'Statistical averages, also known as *space averages*, refer to a fixed time point and are formed as averages over the universe of realizations ... Time averages, also known as *phase averages*, refer to a fixed realization and are formed as averages over an indefinite time space' (Wold, 1965, pp. 53–4, cited by Davidson, 1982–3, p. 185). In a stationary stochastic process, the statistical averages are the same at every point in time. In an ergodic process, the time and statistical averages coincide. Stationarity, then, was a necessary but not a sufficient condition for ergodicity: 'In other words, the average expectation of future outcomes determined at any point in time will not be persistently different than the time average of future outcomes *only if the stochastic process is ergodic*' (Davidson, 1982–3, p. 185).

Ergodicity had been implicitly assumed, Davidson suggested, by Muth and other theorists of rational expectations. But there was a strong case for rejecting it, especially in the context of macroeconomic analysis, since here

> it can be claimed that only a single realization exists since there is only one actual economy; hence there are no cross-sectional data which are relevant. If we do not possess, have never possessed, and conceptually never will possess an *ensemble* of macroeconomic worlds, then the entire concept of the definition of relevant distribution functions is questionable. It can be logically argued that the distribution function can*not* be defined *if* all the macroinformation which *can* exist is only a finite part (the past and the present) of a *single* realization. Since a universe of such realizations must at least conceptually exist for this theory to be germane, the application of the mathematical theory of stochastic processes to macroeconomic phenomena is therefore questionable, if not in principle invalid. (Ibid., pp. 188–9)

In their discussion of fundamental uncertainty Keynes and Shackle had both assumed non-ergodicity, Davidson maintained, without using the term. So too had the later Hicks, whose *Causality in Economics* also dealt with a non-ergodic economic universe (Hicks, 1979). Davidson concluded that rational expectations was 'a useful analytical tool for studying *noncrucial* decision-making involving small (i.e., almost costless) differences in outcomes, for then choice can be easily replicated' (Davidson, 1982–3, p. 196). But it was relevant only for (some) microeconomic questions, and had no role to play in macroeconomic theory.

THE INCUBUS OF EQUILIBRIUM

As Samuelson had suggested, the assumption of ergodicity was essential to mainstream equilibrium analysis. Thus its rejection reinforced Post Keynesian criticism of equilibrium theorizing, which was already well established. Joan Robinson's doubts about the concept of equilibrium date back at least to the mid-1930s (see Chapter 1). They strengthened over the years, and came to occupy a more and more prominent position in her criticism of neoclassical economics (Bhaduri, 1996). In the last ten years of her life, indeed, they headed her long and formidable list of objections to orthodox analysis and dominated her very last paper, published posthumously, in which she argued that

> the whole complex of theories and models in the textbooks is in need of a thorough spring cleaning. We should throw out all self-contradictory propositions, unmeasurable quantities and indefinable concepts and reconstruct a logical basis for analysis with what, if anything, remains.
>
> The first notion to be discarded, in such a process, must be 'equilibrium in the long run'. (Robinson, 1985, p. 160)

Robinson objected to equilibrium models because they assumed away the serious problem of path-dependence. Thus, she claimed, such models restricted the theorist to working in logical time. The simultaneous determination of all the dependent variables in a closed model meant that there could be no discussion of a sequence of events in real, historical time, and therefore no analysis of causation. For this, some additional account of market *process* was required. In neoclassical theory it was introduced through stability analysis, but this was effective only if agents' actions did not affect the equilibrium position, that is, if the equilibrium was not path-dependent. And this, she believed, was rarely the case. Katzner (1999) provides a rigorous formalization of the argument, which Robinson, it should be noted, applied against Sraffian theory no less aggressively than against the neoclassicals (see Chapter 10).

It could almost be claimed, on Robinson's behalf, that in her 1937 *Essays* she invented the concept of hysteresis as it relates to economic theory (see Chapter 1), even if she herself did little to apply it to specific problems and it was largely absent from her *Accumulation of Capital*. One question to which it is immediately relevant is the monetarist notion of a 'natural rate' of unemployment, below which the actual rate may be driven for a while by expansionary monetary or fiscal policy, but only at the expense of accelerating inflation. If unemployment is path-dependent, policies which lead to a significant increase in the actual unemployment rate will also tend to raise the 'natural rate', and vice versa. In these circumstances the policy implications of the natural rate analysis are not at all what the monetarists had supposed. And there are good reasons why path dependence might be important in macroeconomics. Long spells of unemployment lead to skill depreciation and damaged motivation, rendering workers less employable and less eager to look for work. Deflationary policies not only reduce investment in the short period but also lower the capital stock in the medium to long period, and thereby reduce future labour demand (Arestis and Sawyer, 1999b). On both counts the 'natural' or equilibrium unemployment rate is a variable that tends to track the actual rate, not a constant that is 'ground out,' in Friedman's famous words, 'by the Walrasian system of general equilibrium equations' (Friedman, 1968, p. 8) – not that many Walrasians would accept this Chicago categorization of their ideas.

Robinson did not repudiate the equilibrium method altogether. She continued to regard it as a useful abstraction, an 'analytical stepping-stone' that was helpful in isolating causal forces and checking the logic of arguments. Avi Cohen suggested the value of distinguishing the two-stage theoretical process of neoclassical theory from Robinson's three-stage procedure. Mainstream economists work by creating a closed, determinate equilibrium model and testing it. Robinson began in the same way, building a closed, determinate equilibrium model which had then to be embedded in an historical context (stage two) to create an open historical model in the third stage (Cohen, 1993, pp. 230–34). This was more difficult than it sounded, since 'much judgement and intuition is involved in deciding which causal forces and which factual information to include' (ibid., p. 236). By the end of her life Robinson had become deeply pessimistic, believing that open historical models had yielded very little in the way of useful results; but she was never nihilistic, as Pierangelo Garegnani claimed (Garegnani, 1989; cf. Harcourt, 1996a).

By the 1970s Robinson was no longer on speaking terms with Nicholas Kaldor (King, 1998c), and it is entirely possible that he read none of her later papers attacking the equilibrium method; he read very little on principle, apparently fearing that it would damage his originality. But he became a critic of equilibrium economics every bit as strident as Robinson, and for much the same reasons:

> ... we must begin by constructing a different kind of abstract model, one that recognizes from the beginning that time is a continuous and irreversible process;

> that it is impossible to assume the constancy of anything *over* time, such as the supply of labor or capital, the psychological preferences for commodities, the nature and number of commodities, or technical knowledge. All these things are in a continuous process of change but the forces that make for change are endogenous not exogenous to the system. The only true exogenous factor is *whatever exists at a given moment of time*, as a heritage of the past ...
>
> The heritage of the past is the one truly exogenous factor, and its influence will determine future events to an extent that varies *inversely* with the distance of the future period from the present. Thus our ability to predict what *can* happen or what is likely to happen becomes progressively less as we consider the distant future as against the nearer future. (Kaldor, 1985a, pp. 61–2)

This had important implications for the nature of economic growth. Kaldor's interest in dynamic economies of scale in individual firms and industries can be traced back to his technical progress function in 1957 (see Chapter 4), and it was reinforced by his rediscovery of the work of Allyn Young, who in a celebrated paper had argued that increasing returns to scale were fundamental to the process of economic growth (Young, 1928; cf. Hahn, 1989). Another important influence on Kaldor was the notion of circular and cumulative causation, which operated at the level of the entire economy and was prominent in the work of the Swedish development theorist Gunnar Myrdal. Far from converging over time, Myrdal maintained, countries and regions at different levels of development were much more likely to move further apart. Myrdal's principle of cumulative causation was deeply subversive of neoclassical concepts of stable equilibrium. It was first invoked by Kaldor in his defence of regional policies (Myrdal, 1957; Kaldor, 1970b).

Unlike Robinson, Kaldor always emphasized the policy implications of his argument. In particular, he claimed, the case for free trade was undermined, since it rested on artificial notions of equilibrium. Orthodox trade theorists had ignored the possibility that differences in productivity between nations might be enlarged by trade, so that the gap between countries at different stages of development would be widened, not narrowed, by their involvement in trade: 'Under more realistic assumptions unrestricted trade is likely to lead to a loss of welfare to particular regions or countries and even to the world as a whole – that is to say that the world will be worse off under free trade than it could be under *some* system of regulated trade' (Kaldor, 1981, p. 593). His fears for the future of the British economy in a single European market made Kaldor a vocal opponent of British membership of what has since become the European Union (Kaldor, 1972).

There were also repercussions for economic theory. As we have seen, Robinson turned against Sraffian economics because she came to see it as one more species of equilibrium analysis. Neoclassical general equilibrium theory was, however, a much more prominent target, and had been, in Robinson's case, ever since she wrote *Economic Heresies*. Here she maintained that Walrasian analysis applied only to an economy without production, like the prisoner of war camps where exchange took place between prisoners but involved only the given quantities of consumer goods delivered each month by the Red Cross. Once Walras attempted to introduce time, production and a rate of interest into his 'timeless, non-monetary model', he was led into irresolvable contradictions (Robinson, 1971a, pp. 4–9, 26–7).

Attacks like these led her Cambridge colleague Frank Hahn to reply angrily that almost all her criticisms of general equilibrium theory were false, and that she and her supporters had addressed themselves to the wrong issues. Instead of stimulating a 'Great Debate', she had only been able to initiate a 'Great Charade' (Hahn, 1975, p. 364). Rather more temperately Roy Weintraub, himself a recently lapsed Walrasian, accused Robinson of methodological incompetence. Arguing from a Lakatosian viewpoint, Weintraub dismissed her objections as being 'based on a profound misunderstanding of the concept of equilibrium and its function in analysis'. Equilibrium was part of the 'hard core' of the Walrasian research programme, and was therefore not testable, nor could it be subjected to criticism. Her attempts to convict the Walrasians of logical error 'only identify Robinson as one who works in a different program', and 'must be read as rhetorical set-pieces designed to gather new adherents to her preferred program' (Weintraub, 1985, pp. 148–9).

THE METHODOLOGY OF POST KEYNESIAN ECONOMICS

We have now entered deep and dangerous methodological waters, for which charts and compass have yet to be provided. There were in fact several reasons why Post Keynesians should have become increasingly interested in methodology in the 1980s. All insurgent paradigms – if I can revert for the moment to Kuhnian language – have pretensions at the methodological as well as the theoretical and policy levels. This was as true of the *Methodenstreit* in late nineteenth-century Germany and England (Moore, 1999) as it was for the New Classical Economists a century later. The insistence of the latter that there must be analytically coherent microfoundations for all macroeconomic theory was a contestable methodological assertion, attractively packaged as a self-evident truth. It had already been encountered, in a slightly different guise, in the 'afterglow' of the capital controversies of the 1960s, when the ghost of Walras had been summoned by the neoclassicals as their last line of defence (see Chapter 4). This made it almost inevitable that methodology would form an integral part of the attack on neoclassical economics that was mounted by Robinson, Eatwell, Eichner, Kregel and others in the 1970s (see Chapter 6). The rediscovery of Keynes's philosophy was an additional influence, since it, too, stimulated methodological speculation. How had his philosophical views affected the way in which Keynes himself had done economics? What did they entail for the way in which Post Keynesians should do economics? These questions could hardly be avoided by anyone who had read the *Treatise on Probability*.

There was yet another factor behind the growth of Post Keynesian concern with methodology in this period: the issue of formalism. Mainstream economics had become much more technically demanding, very rapidly, after (roughly) 1960, and this increasingly served to keep Post Keynesians out of the 'leading journals'. Editors and referees increasingly demanded a high level of mathematical analysis as a condition of publication; Post Keynesians came to view this as a pretext or a rationalization of the editors' mounting hostility to any form of heterodoxy. Kaldor and Robinson could still get essentially 'literary' papers accepted by the *Economic Journal*, but this was very much a matter of filial piety; younger Post Keynesians in the United Kingdom were less favoured. Things were even worse, even earlier, in the United States. Sidney Weintraub, whose work had appeared, in the 1950s, in every major journal on both sides of the Atlantic, was increasingly marginalized after 1960. Paul Davidson, whose scientific training had provided him with most of the necessary tools and also rendered him sceptical of their usefulness in economics, was able to play the formalist game if he chose to. In 1968 he published a paper in *Econometrica*:

> I saw in Tobin that he had gotten the whole thing wrong – he was a real neoclassical. So I wrote an article about why Tobin's economic growth model was all wrong, and I sent it to *Econometrica*. Initially they rejected it. Robert Strotz was the editor. He thought it was an interesting article but both referees had said that it was not precise. There was good exposition, good argument, but there wasn't any precision (by precision they meant I had a couple of diagrams but no mathematics). So I took each paragraph, and at the beginnings of the paragraphs I put a mathematical formula which was then explained. I didn't change the text at all, I just mathematized each paragraph, so it now had 20 or something equations. I sent it right back in with the exact same text. Of course I had to explain what each symbol was, so there was a little addition to the text. And it was accepted within a week. (King, 1994b, pp. 364–5; cf. Davidson, 1968a)

After this episode Davidson lost interest in such manoeuvres, effectively barring himself from the most influential mainstream journals. A later generation of Post Keynesians, many of them refugees from an orthodox postgraduate training, were sometimes less unequivocally opposed to mathematical modelling and the use of advanced econometric techniques. In fact formalism had become an important source of contention among Post Keynesians, and it was inextricably linked to the rejection of ergodicity and to the choice between closed, determinate models and open, historical models that was discussed in previous sections. These were methodological questions par excellence, and Post Keynesians simply could not afford to ignore them.

We need at this point to distinguish three types of problem. First there are questions of *method*: that is, how economics should be done. Second is the question of *methodology*: how to appraise different ways of thinking about doing economics. Finally there is the question of *meta-methodology*, which concerns ways of appraising methodologies. Analysis at any of these levels may be *descriptive*, that is, dealing with what is, or *prescriptive*, which involves what ought to be. Post Keynesian discussions of methods, methodologies and meta-methodologies were almost invariably prescriptive, and it is not difficult to see why. When they turned to these issues it was usually in the course of arguing that their own way of proceeding was better than that of the mainstream, or at the very least that it was equally valid.

Contemporary developments in the sociology and philosophy of science meant that, by the early 1970s, there was considerable scope for disagreement on meta-methodology, and this spilled over into the debates among economists on methodology and method (see, for example, Latsis, 1976; Katouzian, 1980; Blaug, 1992 [1980]; Caldwell, 1982; Pheby, 1988). Certain roads were not taken. One was that of the Joan Robinson who wrote *Economic Philosophy*, a little book that presented her, as late as 1962, as a defender of a strict version of logical positivism that already seemed rather old-fashioned. Robinson clung to the seductive but largely discredited demarcation principle that allowed her to distinguish 'science' from 'metaphysics'. She treated as largely unproblematical the empirical falsification of hypotheses and the possibility of a 'value-free' economic science clearly separate from the political preferences of its practitioners. As Ronald Meek tartly observed, it was as if Robinson believed that every economist in history had succumbed to ideological distortion except for Keynes (Meek, 1968, pp. 213–14). Post Keynesians did derive from her – and others – an awareness of the importance of ideological factors in the development of neoclassical economics. Few of them, however, were inclined to employ 'metaphysical' as a term of abuse, as Robinson had done in dismissing both the labour theory of value and utility theory (Robinson, 1962b, pp. 39, 48), and many ignored her strictures against the use of mathematics and her apparent contempt for econometrics. Some of the traditional virtues that Robinson displayed in her own economic methods, as opposed to her writings on methodology, were probably also influential. Clarity of expression, coherence of argument, relevance to the reality of life in advanced capitalist, socialist and developing economies – Post Keynesians could agree on all of this, even if there remained plenty of scope for argument as to what, exactly, it implied.

Michal Kalecki took a quite different line on mathematics and statistical modelling, as might have been expected from someone trained as an engineer. He even invoked a higher authority:

> After all Marx's schemes of reproduction are nothing else but simple econometric models. In fact in a special case where no changes in natural resources, productive relations and the superstructure affect the development of productive forces the system will follow the path determined by an econometric model because the condition of relationships between the economic variables not being subject to change is then fulfilled. In a more general case these functional relationships alter under the impact of events in three other spheres of the system and the economic development is then a much more complicated process than that presented by an econometric model as it reflects the evolution of the society in all the aspects. (Kalecki, 1965, p. 233)

But Kalecki, like Robinson, viewed economics as a practical, policy-oriented discipline in which certain critical features of social reality must never be lost sight of in the quest for rigorous analysis. Kalecki's 'stylized facts' – to use a term made popular by Nicholas Kaldor – included the class antagonism between employers and workers, the prevalence of oligopoly and the cyclical instability of the capitalist economy. Long before 'microfoundations' became a significant methodological issue, Kalecki was denying the logical priority of the behaviour of individual agents in the construction of macroeconomic models, and arguing instead that microeconomic theory also needed macrofoundations (Kriesler, 1996).

Kaldor took a similar line to Kalecki on many questions of method, though he was distinctly idiosyncratic (not to say slapdash) in his choice of his 'stylized facts', which for a long time included full employment (see Chapter 4). Kaldor seems to have had no background or interest in philosophy, and he made up his views on method more or less as he went along – much as he constructed his theories. He took an opportunistic attitude towards formalism. Kaldor happily used all the mathematics that he possessed, and was not ashamed to call for assistance when this proved necessary (Kaldor and Mirrlees, 1962); late in his career he began to employ (rather rudimentary) econometric methods (Kaldor, 1966a). Despite his institutionalist leanings, Alfred Eichner also had no fear of algebra. Indeed, he left unfinished a very ambitious attempt to construct a large-scale Post Keynesian macroeconometric model of the United States (Arestis *et al.*, 1988). Eichner's critique of neoclassical economics did, however, have a strong methodological basis, and he echoed Robinson in denying its claim to be true science. Like the other Post Keynesians of his day, Eichner stressed the need for 'realism' in model building, without going very deeply into the methodological and meta-methodological problems that this entailed.

With the exception of Robinson, these early Post Keynesian methodologists were suspicious of the positivist proclivities of neoclassical economists. Nor, mercifully, did they follow the postmodernist path, attractive though its relativism, pluralism and methodological tolerance might have been. There were good reasons why the Post Keynesians did not become postmodernists. They had no great problem with the notion of objective reality and objective truth, however hard it might be to obtain reliable knowledge of any economic phenomenon. Kaldor's 'stylized facts' *were* facts, after all, or so he supposed, while for Alfred Eichner the whole point of Post Keynesian theory was to achieve a closer 'correspondence' between analysis and reality than the neoclassicals had been able to attain. Post Keynesians were committed above all else to the policy relevance of their theorizing, and if postmodernism had any bearing on this question it was disarming: how can you intervene to alter reality if there is no such thing? Furthermore, almost all orthodox economists remained blissfully ignorant of the postmodernist claims. Hence there was not even a negative attraction for the Post Keynesians, since they recognized nothing in need of attack.

In any case, the exact implications for economics of a postmodern methodology were by no means clear (Dow, 1992a). Indeed, some postmodernists, like the ebullient Stanley Fish (1994), went out of their way to insist that there were *no* significant repercussions for scientific practice. Instead the Post Keynesians followed two different roads, which were more or less parallel to each other but perhaps – allowing for a non-Euclidean geometry – capable of converging in due course. One was the 'Babylonian' approach originally articulated by the physicist Richard Feynman and applied to economics by Sheila Dow (1996 [1985]). The other was 'critical realism', abstracted with some difficulty from the abstruse writings of the philosopher Roy Bhaskar by Tony Lawson (1989, 1997).

Babylonian methodology involved a break with the Cartesian–Euclidian mode of thought, which developed closed systems of necessary truths from self-evident axioms. Babylonians also rejected the polar opposite of this position, the 'dual' of Cartesian–Euclidian thinking, which denied the very possibility that we can ever obtain knowledge. They transcended this dualism, proposing instead a sort of Hegelian synthesis of Cartesian–Euclidian and non-Cartesian–Euclidian ways of thinking, in which knowability was treated as a matter of degree. Thus for Babylonians there were no basic axioms but rather several 'strands of argument' that reinforced each other, and no single correct method of conducting scientific research but rather a variety of methods, each appropriate to particular circumstances. Babylonian methodology favoured 'open-system thinking',

> where not all the constituent variables and structural relationships are known or knowable, and thus the boundaries of the system are not known or knowable. This is the province of fuzzy mathematics, with indeterminate boundaries of sets.... It is also the province of non-classical logic, where logical relations are applied to uncertain knowledge; this logic is variously known as ordinary logic or human logic, as exemplified by Keynes's ... probability theory. If reality is understood as an open system, then scope is allowed for free will, for creativity,

> and for indeterminate evolution of behaviour and institutions. (Dow, 1996 [1985], p. 14).

Scientists could aspire only to limited knowledge; they could hope to establish regularities, but not laws. What they knew was derived from rational beliefs, themselves conditioned by an awareness that uncertainty could not be reduced to certainty-equivalents by means of objective frequency distributions.

Note that Babylonianism did not mean that 'anything goes'. There was, as we have seen, very little enthusiasm for the farther shores of postmodernism, or even for the 'rhetoric' movement spearheaded in the late 1980s and early 1990s by Deirdre McCloskey (1985). Dow insisted that the Babylonians were not 'methodological pluralists'; they shared a single coherent methodology, which permitted the use of a variety of methods (Dow, 1992b; cf. Caldwell, 1989). She herself applied these Babylonian principles to a critical comparison of the macroeconomic methodologies of the mainstream, neo-Austrian, Post Keynesian and Marxist schools. Dow suggested that only the Post Keynesians were consistently Babylonian in their approach to macroeconomic analysis and policy, while mainstream economists were thoroughgoing Cartesian–Euclidians. Methodological differences led to significant divergences of opinion on critical questions like the need for microfoundations, the role of equilibrium theory, the modelling of expectations and the treatment of money. Dow's purpose here was descriptive, not prescriptive, but she was writing from an explicitly Post Keynesian position.

THE REAL CRITIQUE OF CRITICAL REALISM

The methodology of critical realism began to impinge on the consciousness of Post Keynesians in the late 1980s, largely as a result of the advocacy of the Cambridge economist Tony Lawson. In the final decade of the century it aroused great interest and no little controversy, which culminated in a special issue of the *Journal of Post Keynesian Economics* in the autumn of 1999. The doctrine itself has a much longer history. Lawson drew very heavily on Roy Bhaskar (1975), but the foundations of a realist approach to science go back to Ancient Greece, and are very clear in the work of Karl Marx. An unusually accessible treatment, which did not rely at all upon Bhaskar, was provided by Russell Keat and John Urry (1975), whose avowed intention was to present a rigorously argued but non-dogmatic version of Marxian historical materialism as the basis for social science, and in particular for sociology; they made little or no reference to economics. The essential arguments, however, proved to be highly pertinent to the subsequent methodological debates among the Post Keynesians.

We need at this point to distinguish *ontology* from *epistemology*, that is to say, the question of what exists from the question of what we can know about it. The critical realist ontology – as the term 'realist' suggests – asserts that the real world exists independently of human consciousness. This reality is characterized by structures and by causal mechanisms. The structures govern the relations between the various parts of reality, and the causal mechanisms provide the means by which changes in one or more of these parts affect the others. Critical realist epistemology asserts that these 'deep' or 'underlying' structures and mechanisms are seldom (if ever) directly observable, but their existence can be inferred from the 'superficial' appearances of observed phenomena. Science is the process whereby such inferences are made. The most important task of scientific activity is not induction (as argued by empiricists) or deduction (as claimed by rationalists), but *retroduction* or *abduction*, which

> consists in the movement (on the basis of analogy and metaphor, amongst other things) from a conception of some phenomenon of interest to a conception of some totally different type of thing, mechanism, structure, or condition that is responsible for the given phenomenon. If *deduction* is, for example, to move from the *general* claim that all grass is green to the particular inference that the next lawn to be seen will be green, and *induction* is to move from the particular observations on green grass to the general claim that all grass is green, then *retroduction* or *abduction* is to move from the particular observations on green grass to a theory of a mechanism intrinsic to grass that disposes it to being green. It is the movement, paradigmatically, from 'surface' phenomena to some 'deeper' causal thing(s). (Lawson, 1994, p. 515)

It follows that scientific theories are more than 'useful instruments' for generating predictions, as they were supposed to be by conventionalists like Milton Friedman, the author of a notorious defence of unrealistic assumptions in his essay on the methodology of 'positive economics' (Friedman, 1953). For critical realists, theories must be based upon true accounts of reality, not fictitious descriptions of imaginary circumstances.

Lawson made two further claims about the nature of social reality, both of which were directly relevant to the concerns of Post Keynesian economists. The first was that the relations between individual parts of the economic system were very often organic rather than atomistic, to use Keynes's terminology. Or, as Lawson put it, in slightly different language:

> Two types of relations can be distinguished: *external* and *internal*. Two objects, features, or whatever are said to be *externally related* when each is what it is and does what it does, irrespective of the relation in which it stands to the other. Examples include bread and butter, coffee and tea, or two passing strangers. A world of only external relations could be described as atomistic. In contrast, two objects or aspects are said to be *internally related* when at least one is what it is or does what it does because of its relation to the other. Examples include

> employers and employees, teachers and students, landlords/ladies and tenants, etc. *Ex posteriori*, it has been found that it is positions rather than their occupants that are subject to the most interesting and enduring internal relations in the social domain.... Thus, it is also easy to see that all the familiar social systems, collectivities, and organizations – the economy, firms, households, hospitals, trade unions – depend upon, presuppose, or consist in, internally related position-rule systems of this form. Thus, the social world is found *ex posteriori* to be densely populated with internally related totalities. (Lawson, 1999, p. 4, n1)

In a different context this distinction has been used to differentiate Marx's conception of humanity from that of non-Marxist philosophy (Ollman, 1971). It certainly casts serious doubt on neoclassical economic theory, which relies very heavily on the assumption of atomistic, or external, relations.

The second point that Lawson emphasized was the mutability of reality, which is therefore not governed by inexorable laws of nature or society but is instead subject to transformation by human action. This, again, was an important theme in Marx's philosophy, and served to differentiate his thinking from the more deterministic approach implied by both classical materialism and Darwinian biology (Ball, 1979). Lawson turned it against mainstream economics, and above all against the pretensions of the econometricians. Mutability required that economists be suspicious of any methodological position that relied on Humean 'constant conjunctions' or 'event regularities', according to which whenever X occurs it can be confidently expected that Y will follow. If regularities are at best partial and transient, any closed system of thought is likely to disappoint its adherents when it is used to predict future outcomes. For this reason critical realists favoured open-system thinking and admitted the possibility only of 'partial closure', because those event regularities that do occur take place only under specific conditions and in certain, limited, areas of inquiry. Lawson recognized the widespread existence of 'demi-regularities', defined as 'the occasional, but less than universal, actualization of a mechanism or tendency, over a definite region of time-space' (Lawson, 1997, p. 204). Such 'demi-regs' resembled the 'stylized facts' to which Nicholas Kaldor had frequently appealed, and were invaluable in the detection of causal relationships between variables. But they did not, Lawson argued, permit the precise and confident quantitative predictions required by the econometricians.

There were evident parallels between Lawson's version of critical realism and earlier Post Keynesian writing on methodology, most notably Keynes's ideas on fundamental uncertainty and Shackle's stress on human creativity and the role of crucial decisions. While Joan Robinson was not in any sense a critical realist, her discussion of time in economics covered much of the same ground: events never exactly recur, knowledge can never be entirely reliable, predictions must be made with a degree of humility and constantly revised in the light of historical experience (Robinson, 1980). And Paul Davidson's central organizing principle of non-ergodicity had a great deal in common with the critical realists' emphasis on mutability and the necessity for open-systems thinking. In the course of the 1990s Lawson moved from arguing that critical realism was an appropriate methodology for Post Keynesians to the much stronger claim that it supplied the basis – perhaps, the only basis – for the coherence of the entire school (Lawson, 1994, 1999; see also Chapter 10). He was supported in this by Arestis, Dunn and Sawyer (1999), in their critique of the argument that Post Keynesian theory was incoherent, and by Dow (1999), who maintained both that schools of thought should be defined by their methodology and that critical realism was entirely compatible with her own Babylonian meta-methodology.

But doubts remained. While he acknowledged 'that the difference between the C[ritical] R[ealist] proponents and myself is primarily one of strategy rather than of analytical content', Davidson regarded realist terminology as unhelpful in his continuing efforts to engage mainstream economists in methodological dialogue (Davidson, 1999b, p. 129). The critical realist refusal to accept that econometrics had anything more to contribute than sample-specific descriptive statistics (Downward, 2000) entailed that a lot of Post Keynesian empirical research was invalid, including much that had been published in the *Journal of Post Keynesian Economics*, the *Cambridge Journal of Economics* and other prominent heterodox journals (see also Downward and Mearman, 2000). There were also potentially devastating implications for what Post Keynesians could, and could not, say about questions of policy. If it is impossible to predict the future, what grounds can there be for advocating one means of changing the future in preference to others? This objection was raised against Davidson's conception of non-ergodicity by otherwise sympathetic econometricians:

> Taken to its logical extreme, such a philosophical position would appear to imply that no macroeconomic policies (stabilization policies, in particular) are possible, because if the structure of the economy is so unstable, one can never be sure of what one is doing. In this regard, the proponents of this point of view would appear to join Robert Lucas … and the rational expectations school, who argue that the parameters of the system are highly unstable, at least with a shift in the policy regime itself, thus rendering both economic policy and macroeconometric estimation extremely difficult, if not impossible. (Bodkin *et al.*, 1988, p. 9, n12)

One response to these complaints was to invoke Keynes's discussion of the use of conventions as a stabilizing factor and his provisional assumption that agents' short-term expectations were not revised in the face of disappointment or surprise (Kregel, 1976; Davidson, 1972a [1978], pp. 372–85). This, however, came perilously close to making people behave as if they assumed the world to be ergodic, thereby making it so.

To put the point in a slightly different way, there was a lingering suspicion that to make policy proposals was to engage in closed-system thinking in some form. Thus Roy Rotheim worried 'that Post Keynesianism has the potential, at least, to abandon its critical realist underpinnings, to seek legitimation, if one wills, under the guise of formulating *a priori* singular statements of economic doctrine, that, at the end of the day, force a position that retreats into the closed, deductivist mainstream' (Rotheim, 1999, p. 81). The critical realist alternative, he argued, was to give up any attempt to control future outcomes in favour of what Lawson had described as

> policies, plans and strategies [that] can be formulated not with the objective merely to fix events and states of affairs in order to control the future, but with the aim, instead, of replacing structures that are, for example, unwanted and restrictive by those that are needed and empowering, to facilitate, in short, a greater or more desirable or equitably distributed range of human opportunities. (Lawson, 1994, p. 552; cited by Rotheim, 1999, p. 100)

But this, a sceptic might object, was merely to replace modest and precise predictions (next year's inflation rate, unemployment six quarters hence) with much more ambitious predictions about much less tangible target variables like 'empowerment' and 'human opportunity'.

A middle-range position had been taken by Davidson in the conclusion to his attack on New Classical Economics. Non-ergodicity did place economists at a disadvantage relative to natural scientists, he admitted, but it did not imply that no policy guidelines were possible:

> there can be a role for government in improving the economic performance of markets. This governmental role is to develop, where possible, adaptable economic institutions which attempt to reduce uncertainties by controlling the economic environment so as to limit future time outcomes to those that are closely compatible with full employment and reasonable price stability. Economists should strive to develop for policy makers various institutional devices which can produce constraints (ceilings and floors) on the infinite universe of events which could otherwise occur as the economic process moves through historical time. (Davidson, 1982–3, p. 197)

Post Keynesian economists, then, were to be institution builders rather than prophets. It was still open to a tenacious sceptic, however, to complain that this also evaded the problem. How can we legitimately assess the effects of institutional change without making some predictions – modest, qualified, cautious predictions, to be sure – about their likely consequences? If econometrics can provide *only* descriptive statistics, what scientific basis remains for the evaluation of Post Keynesian policy proposals? At the end of the 1990s there was no sign of agreement on the answers to these questions.

The rich and extensive Post Keynesian literature on knowledge, expectations and method had not, in the end, led to very much in the way of positive conclusions, at least for macroeconomic theory. Taking uncertainty seriously was one thing. Avoiding both the Scylla of determinism and the Charybdis of policy impotence proved to be quite another. And there remained the vexing question of internal coherence. Post Keynesianism was a broad church, but there were limits to tolerance. To be a Post Keynesian it was not necessary (by the late 1990s) to be a critical realist, but some form of Babylonianism was increasingly required. If nothing else, a weakness for closed-system thinking tended to put the thinker outside the pale. This created considerable tension between some of the disciples of Piero Sraffa and the other Post Keynesian schools, as we shall see in the next chapter.

10. Keynes, Kalecki, Sraffa: coherence?

> I am very unsympathetic to the school that calls itself Post Keynesian.... I have never been able to piece together (I must confess that I have never tried very hard) a positive doctrine. It seems to be mostly a community which knows what it is against but doesn't offer anything very systematic that could be described as a positive theory.... So I have found it an unrewarding approach and have not paid much attention to it (Robert M. Solow, in Klamer, 1984, pp. 137–8).

FROM CRITICISM TO COHERENCE?

When Geoff Harcourt surveyed the 'afterglow' from the capital controversies, he noted that the Post Keynesian opposition to neoclassical theory was itself fragmented: 'though the critics of neo-classicism may be united against a common enemy, they are in other respects a heterogeneous collection, splitting into at least three camps – neo-Keynesian, neo-Marxian and neo-Ricardian – with some members managing to have feet in more than one camp at the same time' (Harcourt, 1975, p. 315, n15). This came in a footnote, and Harcourt made little of it. Some years later he made the same point when summarizing the principal achievements of Post Keynesian economics for a seminar audience at the Reserve Bank of Australia in Sydney:

> I start by saying that I certainly do not think that the approaches that come under the heading of post Keynesianism, though they provide important and substantial insights, have yet reached a coherent steady state. Indeed, the people who come in under this umbrella are a heterogeneous lot, sometimes only combined by a dislike of orthodox or neoclassical economics, all brands, or, at least, their conception of it (them).... Nevertheless, there are enough common strands running through the writings of these people to make it worthwhile to try and pick them out. (Harcourt, 1982b, p. 1)

'At the deepest level of analysis', some of the most important of these common strands were 'a preoccupation with time and how it should be modelled' (ibid., p. 5), an emphasis on social relationships and institutions rather than on atomistic individuals (ibid., p. 7) and the close attention paid to the role of money (ibid., p. 11). The greatest differences between the various Post Keynesian schools were methodological, Harcourt concluded, and centred on whether the analysis should focus on short-run or long-run problems (ibid., p. 14).

In a third and very widely read survey article, written with Omar Hamouda, Harcourt returned to the question implied by Solow's critique: did Post Keynesian economists at the end of the 1980s now possess a single, unified and coherent alternative to mainstream macroeconomic theory? Harcourt and Hamouda began by identifying three different routes from classical political economy: 'The first route leads to Marshall, who directly influenced Keynes and those post-Keynesians who start from the *Treatise* and the *General Theory*. Sidney Weintraub, Paul Davidson and (to a lesser extent) Kregel and Minsky' belong to this group, to which Lorie Tarshis is later added (Harcourt and Hamouda, 1988, pp. 2,7). This must be the post-1976 Kregel, the younger version, influenced by Joan Robinson as much as by Davidson, having displayed closer affinities with Kalecki and Sraffa. It is surely the pre-1977 Minsky, since the mature theorist (certainly never a Sraffian) came to see considerable merit in Kaleckian economics (see Chapter 6). At all events, this is the school of thought described by Alan Coddington (1976) as 'Fundamentalist Keynesianism'.

'The second route,' Hamouda and Harcourt continued, 'leads to Marx. It contains the approach that was revived by Sraffa to which Keynes's contribution of effective demand recently has been added, principally in the work of Garegnani', together with Krishna Bharadwaj, Murray Milgate, John Eatwell, and Luigi Pasinetti, while Maurice Dobb and Ronald Meek might be added to the list in recognition of their services in relating Sraffa's work to classical and Marxian political economy. Hamouda and Harcourt subsequently noted that some Sraffians had been trenchant critics of the Marxian labour theory of value (Hamouda and Harcourt, 1988, pp. 2,12; cf. Steedman, 1977), a hostility which was fully reciprocated (Rowthorn, 1974). 'The third route also goes through Marx and then comes through Kalecki's adaptation of Marx's reproduction schemes in order to tackle the realization problem, to Joan Robinson and her followers', though towards the end of her life Robinson had repudiated 'any attempt to provide an alternative "complete theory"' (Hamouda and Harcourt, 1988, pp. 2–3). These three routes defined the Fundamentalist Keynesian, Sraffian and Kaleckian strands of Post Keynesian thought.

There remained, as in 1973, 'some outstanding individual figures, who defy classification within any one group or strand'. The most prominent was that supreme individualist Nicholas Kaldor. Next came Richard Goodwin and Luigi Pasinetti, who 'span at least two of the three strands' (presumably the Kaleckian and Sraffian); George Shackle, 'an important influence on both strand one and strand three'; and the 'New Cambridge' group led by Wynn Godley. A footnote added the name of Edward Nell, 'whose vigorous, enthusiastic and energetic contributions span all three strands of post Keynesian economics and are especially influenced by Joan Robinson's and Sraffa's' work (ibid., pp. 3, 12, n13). Again, one could take issue with some of these judgments. The Kaleckians would have been surprised to find Shackle located in their camp; he was the archetype of a Fundamentalist Keynesian (Dow, 1998, p. 4; see also Chapter 9). And New Cambridge economics appears to have sunk without trace, probably for very good reasons (Dixon, 1982–3). But the basic classification of the three schools survived these minor quibbles very largely intact.

Most of the Hamouda and Harcourt paper was devoted to summarizing the principal theoretical propositions of the three schools, with only occasional references to the ways in which they did, or did not, fit together into a coherent whole. The brief conclusion, however, did attempt to answer this question:

> We subtitled this reflective survey essay 'from criticism to coherence', deliberately ending with a question mark. What we have tried to show is that within the various strands that we have discerned and described, there *are* coherent frameworks and approaches to be found, though obviously there remain within each unfinished business and unresolved puzzles. The real difficulty arises when attempts are made to synthesize the strands in order to see whether a coherent whole emerges. Our own view is that this is a misplaced exercise, that to attempt to do so is vainly to search for what Joan Robinson called 'only another box of tricks' to replace the 'complete theory' of mainstream economics which all strands reject. The important perspective to take away is, we believe, that there is no uniform way of tackling all issues in economics and that the various strands in post-Keynesian economics differ from one another, not least because they are concerned with different issues and often different levels of abstraction of analysis. (Hamouda and Harcourt, 1988, pp. 24–5)

Such a 'horses for courses' approach is something that Harcourt had always advocated (see, for example, Harcourt, 1980, p. 28). It can be defended on solid methodological grounds, and appears to have much in common with the philosophy of the later Wittgenstein (Comim, 1999). In this particular context, however, it does pose problems. Hamouda's and Harcourt's conclusion can be criticized from two directions. It can be argued, firstly, that they underestimated the degree of hostility between the three Post Keynesian schools, and exaggerated the possibility of peaceful coexistence between them. In the remainder of this chapter I will specify the respective charge-sheets, setting out first the Kaleckian and Sraffian criticisms of the Fundamentalist Keynesian position; then the Keynesian and Kaleckian objections to Sraffian economics; and finally the Keynesian and Sraffian attacks on Kaleckian theory. I then consider the second, opposing objection, outlining the more ecumenical approach of those who claimed, in the 1990s, that a synthesis or at least a working compromise between the three schools was possible, if it had not already been achieved.

ANTI-KEYNES

In considering the Sraffian attack on the Fundamentalist Keynesians, it should be remembered that there are at least three varieties of Sraffian economics (see Chapter 7). By far the most radical critique came from Pierangelo Garegnani and his followers, and for this reason I shall concentrate on their analysis of the differences between the two schools. There were three fundamental points of contention. The Sraffians rejected all forms of supply and demand theory, and with it the Marshallian microfoundations on which the Fundamentalist Keynesians rely. As Joan Robinson put it, 'The post-Keynesians must make use of Sraffa to build up a type of long-period analysis which will prevent neoclassical equilibrium from oozing back into the General Theory' (Robinson, 1978, p. 16). The second basic disagreement concerned the role of uncertainty, and hence the significance of money, both essential elements in the Keynesian conception of a capitalist economy but peripheral to the Sraffian vision. Finally there was a profound difference of opinion on whether the analysis should focus on the short or long period. Keynes had confined his attention to the former, the Sraffians maintained. The really important questions, however, concerned the latter, since

> a long-run position is that which the forces of competition will tend on average to enforce. A short-run position of imbalance between capacity and demand, though it may prove to be a temporary centre of gravitation, is ultimately a position from which competitive forces will cause the economy to move away. (Eatwell, 1983, p. 272)

Thus the theory of effective demand needed secure long-period foundations that did not depend on supposedly transient phenomena such as market imperfections or uncertainty.

Perhaps the most extreme statement of the Sraffian position came from Garegnani in a comment on a paper by Jan Kregel, who was by now a Fundamentalist Keynesian critic of the Sraffians. Garegnani distinguished two ways of establishing the principle of effective demand, one based on a Sraffian critique of orthodox 'real' analysis and the other on 'liquidity preference' and criticism of orthodox 'monetary' theory. The latter was the path followed by Keynes (Garegnani, 1983, p. 69; the inverted commas are his). In the 'real' model, orthodox economists derived negative relationships between the real wage and the level of employment, and the rate of profit and the capital–labour ratio. These relationships were interpreted as 'demand curves' for labour and capital, and formed the basis for a supply and demand interpretation of wages, profits and employment. Flexibility in the real wage was then a sufficient condition for full employment. The capital controversies, however, had demonstrated that there was no sound reason to suppose that the two crucial functions were necessarily downward-sloping (see Chapter 4), and this was enough to render implausible the existence of a long-run tendency towards full employment. The actual level of output and employment depended on effective demand, and could be analysed using the Keynesian consumption function and the multiplier without any role for expectations, uncertainty or money (ibid., pp. 69–75).

This route to effective demand had not been open to Keynes, Garegnani observed, since the critique of neoclassical capital theory had begun in earnest only after his death. In fact Keynes had never challenged the 'real' orthodox model, but instead relied upon monetary and subjective elements. He used the theory of liquidity preference to explain why the rate of interest could not fall below a certain level. Together with the existence of pessimistic expectations with regard to the future profitability of investment projects, this was sufficient to account for the absence of full employment – but only in the short period. In the long period, as neoclassical economists like Hicks, Modigliani and Patinkin had shown, full employment was entirely possible 'if the monetary authorities were flexible enough to compensate for any rigidity of the money wage' (ibid., p. 76). As Eatwell put it, Keynes's interest-elastic investment demand function introduced a 'Trojan Horse' into his model (Eatwell, 1983, p. 269). In fact, Garegnani argued, Keynes had failed to provide any alternative to the orthodox theory of aggregate output in the long period, or to explain why flexible money wages and prices would not lead to a stable full employment equilibrium. Money *did* matter, he concluded, in determining the distribution of income between wages and profits and in breaking the link between saving and investment (he would have been well-advised to elaborate on this last point). But 'Keynes's liquidity preference is not necessary to establish the principle of effective demand in the short or the long period' (Garegnani, 1983, p. 78). The 'real' critique of mainstream capital theory provided a much better route to effective demand.

The Kaleckian objections to Fundamentalist Keynesianism were quite different. Kalecki himself had made some serious criticisms of the *General Theory* (see Chapter 2). He was supported by Joan Robinson, who repeatedly stressed the superiority of Kalecki's macroeconomics by comparison with Keynes (see, for example, Robinson, 1966, 1976; cf. Hamouda, 1991). This was true of his analysis of investment, pricing and distribution in the short period, while Kalecki's long-period discussion of capital accumulation and cyclical growth processes covered ground that Keynes had neglected. The Kaleckian consumption function distinguished between capitalists and workers, realistically taking account of the class structure of society, which Keynes had neglected in favour of a focus on the behaviour of asocial individuals. Kalecki had also integrated imperfect competition into his macroeconomic model, Robinson maintained. He had provided a much more systematic analysis of the trade cycle than that of Keynes and displayed an earlier understanding of the importance of finance as a determinant of investment decisions. In short, 'Kalecki gets Keynes back onto the rails where his "classical" education had led him astray' (Robinson, 1977b, p. 15).

Many of these points were repeated by Malcolm Sawyer in a wide-ranging Kaleckian critique of Keynes and, by implication, the Fundamentalist Keynesians. Sawyer emphasized the competitive conditions under which uncertainty operates: 'A particularly important distinction so far as macroeconomics is concerned is between environments which are essentially atomistically competitive and those which are essentially oligopolistic.... Keynes adopted the competitive view whilst Kalecki adopted the oligopolistic one' (Sawyer, 1982, pp. 1–2). Thus, for the Kaleckians, the wage and profit shares were determined by the degree of monopoly rather than marginal productivity, and real wages were dependent on the degree of monopoly and the bargaining power of the unions instead of the supply and demand for labour. The capital market was also imperfect, so that investment was financed largely by retained earnings and profitability played a key role in determining investment expenditure. None of this made sense in a model based on perfect competition:

> In this respect I agree with Kaldor ... when he wrote that 'it is difficult to conceive how production in general can be limited by demand with unutilised capacity at the disposal of the representative firm as well as unemployed labour – unless conditions of some kind of oligopoly prevails [*sic*]'. (Ibid., p. 6, citing Kaldor, 1978, p. xxi, n1)

Kaleckians also criticized Keynes and the Fundamentalist Keynesians for minimizing the significance of social power and instead exaggerating the importance of ideas. This left them 'in the awkward position of being unable to explain [the adoption of monetarist policies] except in terms of the stupidity or misguidedness of monetarists and their political advocates', while Kaleckians had always recognized the part played by vested interests (Sawyer, 1982, p. 10). The class nature of capitalist society also had a direct bearing on the theory of effective demand, given the difference in consumption and savings propensities between capitalists and workers. Social conflict was at the heart of Kaleckian models of inflation, but through the target real wage (not money wage) aspirations of organized workers (ibid., p. 2). Finally, Sawyer argued, Kalecki's analysis of money and finance led directly to a Post Keynesian theory of endogenous money, while in Keynes money is treated as exogenous (ibid., p. 7). He concluded by urging the adoption of a 'post-Kaleckian' approach, which 'offers a much sharper break with [the] neo-classical framework and its derivatives which have dominated economics this century' (ibid., p. 23).

ANTI-SRAFFA

Although Joan Robinson had been an early and enthusiastic propagator of Sraffa's *Production of Commodities*, she eventually turned against the Sraffians and, shortly before her death, set out an essentially Fundamentalist Keynesian critique of their ideas. They played down the importance of uncertainty, she argued, and ignored the precarious basis on which expectations were formed. The Sraffians paid too much attention to static and timeless conceptions of equilibrium, and in particular made a fetish out of long-period positions. Keynes's 'quasi-long-period definition of the inducement to invest as the "marginal efficiency of capital"' had been 'a fatal mistake'. He should instead have 'stuck to his short-period brief'. As for Garegnani, 'the conception of the long period, in particular of the normal rate of profit on capital, is not easy to grasp. Does he mean what the rate of profit on capital will be in the future or what it has been in the past or does it float above historical time as a Platonic Idea?' (Robinson, 1979b, pp. 179–80). For Robinson, this version at least of Sraffian economics was metaphysical, not scientific.

Hyman Minsky was even more scathing. At the 1985 Turin memorial conference for Piero Sraffa, Minsky savaged the Garegnani view of macro-economic theory:

> The title of this session, 'Sraffa and Keynes: Effective Demand in the Long Run', puzzles me. Sraffa says little or nothing about effective demand and Keynes's *General Theory* can be viewed as holding that the long run is not a fit subject for study. At the arid level of Sraffa, the Keynesian view that effective demand reflects financial and monetary variables has no meaning, for there is no monetary or financial system in Sraffa. At the concrete level of Keynes, the technical conditions of production, which are the essential constructs of Sraffa, are dominated by profit expectations and financing conditions. (Minsky, 1990, p. 363)

The very notion of long-period positions as centres of gravitation, 'towards which the system tends or around which it oscillates', was inconsistent with the nature of a growing capitalist economy, which inevitably had 'endogenous destabilizing relations' (ibid., p. 363). Thus uncertainty was not an 'imperfection' but rather 'a fundamental aspect of nature in an accumulating capitalist economy...Keynes without uncertainty is like Hamlet without the Prince, and the role of money, liability structure and various systems of intervention in a capitalist economy cannot be studied without introducing uncertainty' (ibid., p. 366).

The Sraffians' neglect of money, Minsky continued, deprived them also of a coherent theory of growth. And the essential Sraffian variable, the uniform long-run rate of profit, was a red herring. Profit flows to individual economic units, but not at any uniform rate:

> In fact, 'the rate of profit' disappears from such an analysis as there is no well-defined denominator, for the historic costs of capital assets disappear from the determination of any economic variable. All that remains from the past is the physical capabilities of the machines and the mass of financial obligations embodied in the structure of liabilities and intermediation. (Ibid., p. 368)

Thus money and banking must be introduced into the analysis from the outset. 'This is the meaning of Keynes and why Keynes is incompatible with neoclassical theory and only marginally compatible with Sraffian theory' (ibid., p. 369). Money could not simply be 'added on' to a 'real' analysis that was essentially non-monetary: 'Money isn't everything, it is the only thing' (ibid., p. 369). In denying this, Garegnani had revealed himself to be 'a prisoner of pre-Keynesian analytical structures' (ibid., p. 371). Minsky's attack echoed criticisms by both neoclassical and Marxian economists that the Sraffians were merely general equilibrium theorists in disguise – and a very thin disguise at that (Hahn, 1975, 1982b). It also pointed to a broader methodological defect identified by the Fundamentalist Keynesians, for whom Sraffian economics was an excessively formalistic product of unacceptable closed-system thinking (see Chapter 9).

Kaleckian criticism of the Sraffians remained relatively undeveloped. Halevi and Kriesler (1991) provided an important exception. They, too, denied the relevance of a uniform rate of profit on the grounds that in a modern capitalist economy the competitive forces tending to equalize profit rates in different sectors were relatively weak. No convincing account had been provided of the adjustment process through which market prices might be expected to converge to, or fluctuate around, long-period natural prices. This indicated a second problem: Kaleckians doubted the wisdom of concentrating on the long period. Kalecki himself had focused on the short period, and there were strong methodological grounds for doing so, 'until some coherent dynamic adjustment process is specified which can describe the "traverse" from one equilibrium position to another, without the traverse itself influencing the final equilibrium position, that is, without the equilibrium being path determined' (Halevi and Kriesler, 1991, p. 86). Finally there were serious analytical difficulties with the Sraffian treatment of the degree of capacity utilization. Only if the actual utilization rate tended towards the desired rate could the Sraffians' negative relation between the real wage and the profit rate be guaranteed. This, however, required that there be a strong tendency towards a steady state, and was thus of very dubious real-world relevance. In a Kaleckian model, where capacity utilization depends on the degree of monopoly, there could well be a positive relationship between the real wage and the rate of profit (ibid., pp. 86–7).

Kriesler later repeated these criticisms, noting that Kaleckian and Sraffian economics represented distinct schools of thought within Post Keynesian economics, using different analytical frameworks to examine significantly different questions. While the Sraffians were principally concerned with price determination, taking outputs as given, the fundamental problem for the Kaleckians was to obtain an understanding of the laws of motion of capitalist societies, that is, to analyse accumulation, growth and the trade cycle. This was why they used partial rather than general equilibrium models and were concerned with questions of causality, policy and applied economics. The Sraffians, by contrast, had produced no applications of their formal analysis:

> Let me conclude by noting, again, the inappropriateness of evaluating one theoretical framework in terms of another. The Sraffa framework is useful as a thought experiment analysing prices, very precisely, as potential centres of gravitation, but cannot really say anything interesting about the determination of output, employment and growth. Within the Kaleckian framework, prices play a very different role. It is not mathematical precision which is so important [as much] as relevance in terms of potential concrete application for the analysis of output, employment and growth. Kalecki's particular view of contemporary capitalism saw the manufacturing sectors as being dominated by oligopolistic influences which accentuated problems with effective demand. It was this vision which he attempted to incorporate into his analysis, rather than any purely formal model. (Kriesler, 1992, p. 169)

Similar points were made, rather less forcefully, by Malcolm Sawyer (1992) and Josef Steindl (1993). Ironically the neoclassical capital theorists had sometimes defended *their* simplifications of reality in very similar terms, and Robert Solow had charged Cambridge economists in general (and Joan Robinson in particular) with having 'no applied economics at all' (Solow, 1975, p. 278).

ANTI-KALECKI

Of the early Fundamentalist Keynesians, Sidney Weintraub and Hyman Minsky were quite favourably disposed to Kalecki, once their own ideas had matured (see Chapter 5). Others were indifferent or actively hostile, finding the flavour of Kaleckian theory as unpalatable as any of its specific propositions. The analysis is too formal, the exposition too terse, the reliance on mathematics and statistics rather than on philosophy is simply too much to take. Paul Davidson had been a very early critic of Kaleckian theory. In his doctoral dissertation he criticized the degree of monopoly model of income distribution as unenlightening if not tautological (Davidson, 1960, pp. 52–9). One of the ways in which Keynes's theory was truly general, he argued, was its ability to encompass situations of both perfect and imperfect competition; the Keynesian aggregate supply curve could accommodate any particular degree of monopoly, or none (Davidson and Smolensky, 1964, pp. 128–31). Twenty years later Davidson reacted indignantly to Martin Weitzman's claim – taken up by Nicholas Kaldor, and endorsed as we have seen by Kaleckians like Malcolm Sawyer – that the principle of effective demand applied *only* under imperfect competition (Davidson, 1986–7; cf. Weitzman, 1985; Kaldor, 1983). In *Money and the Real World* Davidson credited Kalecki with having inspired the 'neo-Keynesian' growth and distribution models of Robinson, Kaldor and Pasinetti. But he placed very little value on them, dismissing the Cambridge 'golden rule of accumulation' as a 'ludicrous precept' and concluding that 'Economists should lower their sights from esoteric, irrelevant, and useless objectives which are formulated via "golden rules" and which promote endless controversies in the economic literature and instead discuss more mundane practical goals' (Davidson, 1972a, p. 138).

There were two broader reasons for Davidson's hostility to Kaleckian economics. The first was his insistence that fundamental uncertainty and money contracts must be core features of any realistic analysis; they were much less prominent in Kalecki. The second was political. The Kaleckians were 'left of centre', while Davidson placed himself and the 'Keynes school' dead in the political centre (ibid., pp. 3–4). This had analytical consequences, of course, since Davidson was unimpressed also by the Kaleckians' emphasis on class divisions and the macrodistribution theory to which this had led them. His mature judgment on Kaleckian economics can be inferred from the discussion in his text, *Post Keynesian Macroeconomic Theory*, where there is just one reference to it – citing Kalecki's claim, in opposition to Harrod, that the degree of monopoly is counter-cyclical because cartels gain strength in recessions and lose it in booms. That is all (Davidson, 1994, p. 144). As he told me in 1992, 'I don't think that Kalecki adds anything to the system' (King, 1995a, p. 29). Other Fundamentalist Keynesians concur. Victoria Chick makes no reference to Kalecki in either her *Macroeconomics After Keynes* or her collected essays (Chick, 1983, 1992a), and Sheila Dow is only a little more forthcoming in her influential comparative account of Post Keynesian and other methodology. 'How far Keynes's and Kalecki's methodology are compatible is a matter of active debate,' she suggests, but it seems that it is not a debate that she thinks it important to engage in (Dow, 1996 [1985], p. 78).

Sraffian criticism of Kaleckian theory is almost as undeveloped as the reverse phenomenon. An interesting argument with potentially damaging consequences for Cambridge growth and distribution theory came in the mid-1980s from Massimo Pivetti (1985). In *Production of Commodities* Sraffa had alluded briefly to the possibility that his system might be closed by fixing the rate of profit, rather than the real wage as the classical economists had done. If the rate of interest is determined outside the system, for example by conventional beliefs or market expectations, this must set a floor below which the rate of profit cannot fall, at least if some form of long-period equilibrium is assumed. Thus, as Pivetti observed, the rate of profit will depend on the interaction between liquidity preference and monetary policy. It cannot then be a function of the growth rate and the propensity to save out of profits, or the system will be over-determined (Pivetti, 1996). The Cambridge equation $r = g/s_c$ continues to hold true, but it must be interpreted quite differently: given s_c, causality runs from r to g, and not vice versa. Joan Robinson regarded this as 'excessively fanciful' (Robinson, 1979b, p. 180), but many Sraffians did not agree.

Some years later a scathing attack was launched on the logical coherence of Kaleckian economics by Ian Steedman (the critical remarks of Kriesler, Sawyer and Steindl that were quoted in the previous section were part of their response to his onslaught). The Kaleckians had ignored two central features of real capitalist economies, Steedman argued. These were input–output relations and joint production. It was important to recognize that even single-product industries were not in practice fully vertically integrated. Firms buy inputs from other industries, and in turn provide inputs for producers in other industries as well as supplying the final consumer. But the Kaleckian mark-up pricing model neglected the fact that prices determine costs just as much as costs determine prices. It followed that the price of any individual product depended on the mark-ups in many industries, not just on the mark-up in the industry that produced it, and the share of wages in any individual industry also depended on the mark-ups in many industries. This had significant, and counter-intuitive, consequences. The price of an individual product might move in the opposite direction to its mark-up, for example, and the share of wages in aggregate output might move in the same direction as the average mark-up. Kaleckians had failed to confront these problems, Steedman maintained, because of their 'quite inappropriate partial' approach to pricing and distribution, which dealt with each industry in isolation from all the others (Steedman, 1992, p. 148). There was a second and additional source of difficulty for Kaleckian analysis. Even if there were no input–output relations to be taken into account – that is, if all industries were indeed completely vertically integrated – joint production could have equally paradoxical consequences. Prices might be inversely related to mark-ups, and the wage share in an individual industry might increase when the mark-up rose, and vice versa.

As we have seen, the Kaleckians replied by stressing the differences between the two theories, in terms of the purpose of the analysis, the degree of formalism that was permissible and the contrast in their treatment of time and equilibrium. To a very large extent this was a re-enactment of the age-old battle between rigour and relevance, a concern for the latter explaining why many Post Keynesian economists had broken with the mainstream of the profession in the first place. In response to his Kaleckian critics Steedman claimed that he was not advocating a general equilibrium approach, but merely asserting the need for a minimal level of analytical coherence in any proposed alternative to neoclassical economics. He also maintained that there was 'nothing intrinsically Sraffian' in his critique of the Kaleckians (Steedman, 1993, p. 115). This was true, up to a point, since the paradoxes resulting from input–output relations and joint production did not rely on any assumption of equal rates of profit in all industries. Steedman had, however, proved unable to resist the temptation of referring to Kalecki's claim that his theories of pricing and distribution applied to the long period as much as to the short period. No-one, Steedman observed, had yet been able to demonstrate the truth of this assertion (Steedman, 1992, p. 140). It was not, however, a claim that the Kaleckians of the 1990s felt called upon to defend.

THE SYNTHESIZERS

Before she turned against the Sraffians in the late 1970s Joan Robinson had been a passionate advocate of a Kalecki–Sraffa synthesis, with significant elements taken also from Keynes. This was very much the theme of her *Economic Heresies*, for example, and also underpinned the textbook that she wrote with John Eatwell, the ambitious and ultimately unsuccessful *Introduction to Modern Economics*; it is significant that she chose a young Sraffian as her co-author (Robinson, 1971a; Robinson and Eatwell, 1973). Robinson's later views on this question were deeply ambivalent. In 1979 – the very year in which she published her attack on Garegnani – Robinson wrote a decidedly ecumenical foreword to Alfred Eichner's *Guide to Post Keynesian Economics*. 'Post-Keynesian theory has taken over, in the main, the hypotheses suggested by Keynes and by Michal Kalecki,' she claimed, 'and refined and enlarged them to deal with recent experience.' It had offered a much more convincing explanation of the stagflationary crisis than the monetarist account. And Sraffa? Reswitching had proved to be 'an unnecessary distraction,' Robinson conceded, and Sraffa's treatment of technical change had confused logical with historical time. All the same, Keynes and Ricardo were really on the same side, and 'Sraffa's revival of the classical theory of the rate of profit provides the normal long-period analysis that the post-Keynesian theory requires … the clue to a theory of distribution is found in the relations between technical conditions and the share of profit in the flow of the value of output' (Robinson, 1979a, pp. xvii, xx).

In one of her last technical papers, Robinson set out a highly abstract Sraffian analysis of capitalism, with distribution modelled according to Marx and realization according to Kalecki (Bhaduri and Robinson, 1980). A synthesis of a slightly different kind was proposed by Luigi Pasinetti, who noted that the Cambridge models of growth and distribution, which had proved to be incompatible with neoclassical theory, were much more readily integrated with the ideas of classical political economy. And 'Keynes' theory of effective demand, which has remained so impervious to reconciliation with marginal economic theory, raises almost no problem when directly inserted into the earlier discussions of the Classical economists' (Pasinetti, 1974, p. ix). A similar point was made by the Cambridge-trained Jamaican economist Donald Harris (1978). Pasinetti's own abstract models assigned a role to both the labour theory of value and effective demand, with institutional features being introduced at a later stage and at a lower level of abstraction (see Chapter 7).

Almost all Sraffians, in fact, recognized the need for some form of macroeconomic theory to complement a classical (or post-classical) analysis of value and distribution, and those outside Garegnani's immediate circle were often much less critical of Keynes than he had been. Thus Heinz Kurz argued that Keynes and Sraffa were 'in some ways complementary to each other', so that the theory of effective demand and the theory of normal prices and distribution could be brought together (Kurz, 1990, p. 5). He showed that it was possible, for example, to reformulate the Keynesian multiplier in a multisectoral Sraffian framework in which it depended on the technical conditions of production, the distribution of income and the composition of investment demand. In this context an increase in the volume of investment might under some circumstances be associated with a fall in output and employment (Kurz, 1985; cf. Harcourt, 1965).

Alessandro Roncaglia's position was slightly different. Roncaglia maintained that 'the Marshallian microfoundations on which Keynes's *General Theory* relies are no more essential to the basic tenets of the Keynesian paradigm than the interpretation of Sraffa's outputs as "centres of gravitation" is to his analysis' (Roncaglia, 1995, p. 120). He had long argued that the 'centre of gravitation' interpretation of Sraffa was a mistake (Roncaglia, 1978; this book was first published in Italian in 1975) and this conclusion was strengthened by the growing realization that it represented a serious obstacle to the integration of Sraffian and Keynesian theory. The same was true also, Roncaglia claimed, of the concept of equilibrium, which was a source of confusion rather than enlightenment (Roncaglia, 1995, pp. 115–17). As early as 1977 Lynn Mainwaring had demonstrated the consistency of the Sraffian and Kaleckian models in the long period, and Mainwaring continued to advocate 'a Sraffa–Kalecki match' despite the growing friction between the two schools:

> All this suggests the possibility of a synthesis of many of the elements of Kaleckian and post-Keynesian inquiry (mark-up pricing related to industrial structure, class

> struggle via the Phillips curve, monetary determination of interest and profits, and the role of credit) within the long-period discipline of the Sraffian framework. In this way, the analysis of gravitation and convergence, which was initiated from a classical position, could itself come to converge with the preoccupations of post-Keynesian macroeconomics. It may be that an uncomfortable dichotomy which has long existed in the nonneoclassical literature is, at last, starting to crumble. (Mainwaring, 1992, p. 176; cf. Mainwaring, 1977, 1990)

In effect this was also the position of Alfred Eichner (see Chapter 6).

Peter Reynolds had shown much less interest in Sraffa in his textbook *Political Economy*, which instead described the emergence of 'a Kaleckian/Post Keynesian alternative' to mainstream neoclassical Keynesianism. Reynolds's synthesis began with 'a highly institutionalised, oligopolised, monetary economy where the past is unalterable and the future is uncertain', and concluded that this 'new paradigm in political economy' meant that 'pricing, investment, employment, income distribution and economic growth can be explicitly related to each other and the boundaries between micro- and macroeconomics and between short- and long-run analysis cease to be so distinct' (Reynolds, 1987, pp. 10–11, 230, 231). Market failure could then be identified at both the micro and the macro levels, with demand management and incomes policies complementing each other. Amitava Dutt and Edward Amadeo assumed that coherence between Fundamentalist Keynesians and Kaleckians was unproblematical. Their concern, in *Keynes's Third Alternative*, was to assert the possibility of a synthesis between this 'Post Keynesian' school and the 'neo-Ricardian Keynesians'. The differences between them, Dutt and Amadeo maintained, were not fundamental, while the similarities were much more important. Both denied that involuntary unemployment results from market imperfections or would be eliminated if prices and wages were flexible downwards. This argument, it should be noted, required an open rejection of the Eatwell critique of the Fundamentalist Keynesians (Dutt and Amadeo, 1990, pp. 152–3).

Philip Arestis, in his 1992 textbook *The Post-Keynesian Approach to Economics*, claimed loyalty to both Keynes and Kalecki. Arestis's theoretical core contained four propositions. Three of them came from the Fundamentalist Keynesians: the existence of uncertainty, of irreversible time and of contracts denominated in money. The fourth was more Kaleckian. This was the unique role of the labour market, where money wages were determined by a bilateral administered pricing process, itself characterized by conflict between employers and workers. Methodologically, Arestis specified realism, open-system thinking and non-dualism, with explanation rather than prediction as the criterion for theory assessment and an organic, non-atomistic approach to economic processes occupying centre stage. These again were Fundamentalist Keynesian themes, but Arestis also emphasized growth and dynamics and finally summarized his Post Keynesian system as a formal econometric model. He defended the compatibility of the Keynesian, Kaleckian and Sraffian approaches to Post Keynesian theory and introduced a fourth stream, in the form of the institutionalist tradition (Arestis, 1992, ch. 4). There was very little Sraffa in Arestis's discussion of the Post Keynesian core, but he did describe the economic surplus as the source of profits and growth, and in his analysis of production he used an input–output framework that was entirely consistent with Sraffian ideas (ibid., ch. 5). His *Cambridge Journal of Economics* survey article covered very similar ground (Arestis, 1996), while in their *Economic Journal* paper Arestis and Sawyer (1998) focused on the policy proposals that united the various Post Keynesian streams.

The rationale for Marc Lavoie's *Foundations of Post-Keynesian Economic Analysis*, which appeared in the same year as Arestis's book, was also 'my belief that post-Keynesian economics can be presented within a framework that is just as coherent as the neoclassical framework, and that as a consequence it can offer a viable alternative to those who are disenchanted with orthodox economics' (Lavoie, 1992a, p. 1). For Lavoie, Post Keynesian economics was defined by the Cambridge tradition of Robinson, Kahn and Kaldor, and his own book was 'a mix of Kaldorian and Kaleckian economics' (ibid., p. 4). Unlike Arestis, he drew a primary distinction between the neoclassical and 'post-classical' research programmes (see also Gerrard, 1989). The Post Keynesians, neo-Ricardians (or Sraffians), the Marxists and Radicals, and the institutionalists constituted different streams of post-classical theory, all of them mutually compatible and with much to gain from the process of reconciliation that was already well under way. They shared methodological as well as substantive theoretical concerns, Lavoie continued, since the post-classical paradigm presupposed realism, organicism, bounded or procedural rationality and a focus on production rather than exchange (Lavoie, 1992a, pp. 4–14).

A session at the 1992 Malvern political economy conference was devoted to Lavoie's work, and I still have vivid memories of the heat that was generated in the course of the debates between the rival factions. In 1992 Lavoie's claim seemed distinctly premature, which did not stop Thomas Palley from repeating it, in somewhat different terms, in his *Post Keynesian Economics: Debt, Distribution and the Macro Economy*. At first Palley seemed to deny that this was his intention:

> though seeking to illuminate the intellectually consistent structure that girds Post Keynesian economics, the book is not intended as a textbook – at least of the type found in the mainstream, where textbooks represent canonical statements. At this stage of the Post Keynesian program it is too early for such a statement, and in addition, the epistemological foundations of Post Keynesianism discourage the formation of such overwhelming unanimity even amongst Post Keynesians. Thus,

> the book is intended as a monograph that provides a novel and coherent Post Keynesian theoretical statement of the workings of modern advanced economies. (Palley, 1996, p. 1)

This was a much weaker claim than those of Arestis and Lavoie, and in fact Palley went well beyond it at various places in his book. In Chapter 2, for example, he identified six core propositions of Post Keynesian theory: social conflict over income distribution was central; aggregate demand determined output and employment; downward wage flexibility would not produce full employment; money was endogenous; debt finance was important; expectations were 'fundamentally mutable' (ibid., p. 9). In Chapter 13 the core propositions had shrunk to two: aggregate output was constrained not by supply but by demand, and wage and price flexibility would not lead to full employment. This, Palley argued, was enough to distinguish Post Keynesian economics very clearly from both New Classical Economics, what he termed 'neo-Keynesian' ideas (which I prefer to describe as Old Keynesian theory) and also from New Keynesianism (ibid., pp. 216–20). Palley also claimed that there was epistemological coherence among Post Keynesians, but this was very briefly stated and highly contentious, since it hinged on the postmodernist notion that 'objective knowledge can never be arrived at because it is never possible to get outside of the social world, and the world of self' (ibid., p. 22; see Chapter 9).

An even more ambitious attempt at a synthesis was undertaken by a Swiss economist, Heinrich Bortis, whose *Institutions, Behaviour and Economic Theory*, subtitled 'A Contribution to Classical–Keynesian Political Economy', summarized two decades of reflection. Like Paul Davidson, a quarter of a century earlier, Bortis located himself in 'the progressive centre', arguing for a version of humanism that would constitute a middle way between the social philosophies of liberalism and socialism (Bortis, 1997, p. xx). He drew on institutionalism, Marxism, the 'neo-Ricardians' (Sraffians), the 'Robinsonians' (that is, the Kaleckians) and on Keynes. Bortis aimed his work explicitly at the practitioners of political science, law, sociology and political economy, since he regarded the social sciences as a unity. He maintained that

> a consensus between the various strands of post Keynesianism … should be possible: neo-Ricardians, Robinsonians and Keynesian Fundamentalists investigate different spheres of reality from distinct points of view, each type of investigation being complementary to the two others. A complete classical–Keynesian system would emerge as a synthesis and an elaboration of the three post Keynesian strands. (Ibid., p. 235)

This controversy refuses to die. Thus Walters and Young (1997) argued that Post Keynesian economics still lacked coherence, both theoretically and methodologically. When Philip Arestis, Stephen Dunn and Malcolm Sawyer responded to this charge, they followed Hamouda and Harcourt in distinguishing three Post Keynesian schools. But there was a twist: 'we would claim that different strands within Post Keynesian economics (broadly, those identified as emanating from Keynes, Kalecki, and institutionalists) are coherent' (Arestis *et al.*, 1999, p. 527). The Sraffians had disappeared from the Post Keynesian pantheon, to be replaced by the institutionalists. This reflected the methodological concerns discussed in Chapter 9, and the increasing tendency for Post Keynesianism to be defined in terms of a commitment to open-systems thinking. The Sraffians were accordingly excluded as closed-system thinkers:

> we would see Post Keynesian economics in a relatively narrow fashion, and regard Sraffian, Post Keynesian, and a variety of other approaches as coming under a broader heading of postclassical or radical political economy. There are many complementarities between these approaches (as well as some conflicts), and in our own work we draw upon aspects of many of these approaches. (Ibid., pp. 545–6)

In effect this was an endorsement of the Harcourt 'horses for courses' perspective, which by now had a much wider appeal. For Sheila Dow (2000), open-systems methodology gave a significant degree of coherence not just to Post Keynesianism but also to heterodox economics as a whole.

FROM COHERENCE TO CRITICISM?

By the end of the 1990s, then, it was evident that these debates were far from over. They had already posed some interesting questions for sociologists of knowledge and for historians of ideas. There is some evidence, for example, that the Kaleckians were more tolerant than the other streams. Many of the synthesizers (Arestis, Lavoie, Reynolds, Sawyer) owed their primary allegiance to Kalecki, and few if any of the Kaleckians were actively opposed to a 'post-classical' alliance. Some of the Sraffians were similarly ecumenical, but by no means all of them, while almost none of the Fundamentalist Keynesians seemed to believe that they had anything to gain from Sraffian or Kaleckian ideas. If the Kaleckians were genuinely less sectarian than the others, this is in need of an explanation (which I am unable to supply). It could be, of course, that they were simply closet intellectual imperialists, seeking to insinuate Kaleckian ideas by stealth into areas where they really did not belong.

The precise meaning, and indeed the value, of 'coherence' also merits further consideration. Should it be defined in terms of methodology, for example, or by reference to substantive theory (and related policy prescriptions)? This touches on several issues that were raised in Chapter 9. One of the trickiest concerns the legitimacy of a single (Babylonian) *methodology* that permits the use of a range of *methods*, and the awkward question of whether closed-system modelling might in some circumstances be acceptable as one such method (see Dow, 1999). Such a stance would allow the Sraffians to remain inside the Post Keynesian – or at least the post-classical – school of thought. But it would almost certainly provoke a scornful reaction from mainstream theorists like Solow, and from the textbook writers for whom 'post Keynesian economics remains an eclectic collection of ideas, not a systematic challenge to neoclassical theory' (Dornbusch and Fischer, 1990, p. 704, cited by Palley, 1996, p. 8).

This prompts a further question: is orthodox economics itself still coherent? In a throwaway remark at the end of his book, Marc Lavoie claimed that neoclassical theory was fragmenting (Lavoie, 1992a, p. 422). It could be argued that this process accelerated in the 1990s, with the final abandonment of Walrasian general equilibrium theory and thus also of any pretension to provide rigorous microfoundations for macroeconomic analysis. Game theory became the new paradigm for neoclassical theorists, but this is a technique rather than a comprehensive organizing principle like general equilibrium, and it can be applied in quite unorthodox ways – for example to a class-conflict analysis of inflation like that found in the prisoner's dilemma model of Maital and Benjamini (1980).

One branch of mainstream economics was incoherent in a more blatant fashion: 'new growth theory' involved a shameless exhumation of the old Solow growth model, aggregate production functions and all, even though this had been given a decent burial back in the 1960s, together with a substantial but unacknowledged debt to Harrod–Domar (Hussein and Thirlwall, 2000; see also Chapter 4). And the difficulty of telling a convincing neoclassical story about the use of money had long been recognized by otherwise quite orthodox theorists (see, for example, Hahn, 1982a). It was by no means obvious, then, that Post Keynesian economics was very much more incoherent than mainstream theory, or that its openness and eclecticism were necessarily signs of weakness.

This is not to say that there were no limits to Post Keynesian tolerance. A line had to be drawn somewhere, even if there was considerable disagreement as to its exact position. Not all anti-neoclassical economists could be regarded as Post Keynesians. The relations between Post Keynesianism and a number of other dissident schools of thought form the subject of the next chapter.

11. Post Keynesians and other deviants

> It is not possible to draw a tight boundary around post-Keynesian economics, and there are many places at which post-Keynesian analysis touches on (and overlaps with) Marxian, Sraffian (neo-Ricardian), institutional and Austrian economics. (Sawyer, 1988, pp. 4–5)

BORDER CONFLICTS

Introducing the proceedings of the first (1987) Malvern political economy conference, John Pheby suggested that Post Keynesians needed input from other heterodox perspectives if they were to cope with the analytical and policy problems that confronted them (Pheby, 1989, p. xi). This raises a host of questions. For one thing, as I noted in the Introduction, the sociology and history of science has had relatively little to say on the questions of what constitutes a school of thought and what distinguishes one school from another. The literature is no more helpful on the related issue of the relations between mutually compatible (or sympathetic) and overlapping schools, which is an especially interesting one for the historian of Post Keynesian economics. To take the most obvious example, Post Keynesianism and institutionalism are evidently not the same thing, but neither are they clearly incommensurable paradigms in Kuhn's sense, or rival and competing research programmes à la Lakatos. Post Keynesians and institutionalists have a great deal in common, but there have always been sources of friction and mutual incomprehension. Something similar could be said of the radical–Marxian, Austrian and New Keynesian schools when viewed from a Post Keynesian perspective, and the same of course applies in the reverse direction.

A further complication arises from the inevitable processes of change that go on inside any theoretical tradition, in economics as much as in any other intellectual discipline. (I will try to avoid using the question-begging terms 'progress' or 'development' until the final chapter.) One highly pertinent example is provided by the fate of Sraffian economics, once generally accepted as a legitimate stream within Post Keynesianism but increasingly seen as lying outside it. That this is largely a matter of personal judgment can be seen from Malcolm Sawyer's statement at the head of this chapter, which was taken from an introductory survey published in the same year as the important article by Hamouda and Harcourt (1988) that located the Sraffians as one of the three constituent elements *inside* Post Keynesian economics. Similar difficulties arise with other schools of thought in economics. Considerable tension has emerged, for example, between the 'old' and the 'new' institutionalism (Rutherford, 1994); Austrian economists have proved every bit as fractious as the Post Keynesians (Vihanto, 1999); and, as we shall see later in this chapter, it is both possible and (arguably) very important to identify important differences between rival groups of New Keynesian economists.

A final problem is posed by the existence of other schools that can best be described (in econometric jargon) as orthogonal to the Post Keynesians. Feminists, for instance, study different issues, from a quite different perspective, and the points of overlap seem to be few and relatively peripheral to Post Keynesian concerns (gender discrimination and the segmentation of the labour market are possible exceptions). No-one knows what a feminist macroeconomics might look like, and none of the more prominent women Post Keynesians has been closely identified with feminist economics. Yet there is a considerable amount of mutual goodwill, which might one day form the basis for profitable collaboration. Much the same could be said of the very sparse contacts between Post Keynesians and both green economists and social economists, and even – if we take the added risk of crossing disciplinary boundaries – economic sociologists and political economy specialists in departments of political science. The cordial and mutually supportive relations between Post Keynesians and members of the Association for Social Economics have been described by Lee (2000a). After its reconstruction in 1970 the Association, which brought together left institutionalists, left Catholics and a number of Post Keynesians, provided a significant outlet for Post Keynesian work in its journal, the *Review of Social Economy*. Contacts between green theorists and Post Keynesian economists seem to have been much less frequent, and Post Keynesian analysis of environmental and resource issues remains underdeveloped.

This raises a host of further questions concerning the influence (or lack of influence) of Post Keynesian economics outside 'economics proper', and the strong probability that important ideas have also flowed in the opposite direction, that is to say, from the other social sciences to Post Keynesian economics. My purpose in this chapter, however, is much more modest. I want simply to outline the history of the relations between the Post Keynesians and the radical–Marxians, institutionalists, Austrians and New Keynesians, and to speculate briefly on how these relationships may change in the future.

RADICALS AND MARXISTS

The affinities between Post Keynesians and radical economists have been obvious from the very beginning, with Michal Kalecki and Joan Robinson invoking them repeatedly and at some length. Parts of Keynes's first (1933) draft of the *General Theory* were couched in almost Marxian terms, while the later 'left Keynesian' models of 'monopoly capitalism' represented a conscious attempt by Kaleckians to integrate the most incisive arguments of the two schools of thought (see Chapters 1 and 2, respectively). The principal areas of agreement included rejection of Say's Law as irrelevant to a commodity-producing (and hence money-using) economy and a consequent emphasis on the instability of the capitalist system. Further points of contact emerged in the 1960s, when Sraffa's critique of neoclassical theory seemed to many to complement the Cambridge models of distribution and growth, and again in the 1980s with the increasing influence of critical realism, a methodological position with a perceptible Marxian flavour. The monetary circuit theorists had already traced a direct line of descent from Marx through Keynes to the Post Keynesians, and while their influence was for many years largely confined to France and Italy (see Chapter 7) by the 1990s their work began to be much more widely appreciated in the English-speaking world.

There were also institutional and personal links. Many Post Keynesians joined the Union for Radical Political Economics soon after its formation in 1968. URPE was a broad coalition of radicals who were united more by their opposition to neoclassical economics than by a firm commitment to any variety of Marxism. It sponsored sessions on hererodox theory at the annual meetings of the mainstream American Social Science Association, and opened them to Post Keynesians; beginning in 1972, a number of Post Keynesian papers were presented at these sessions. URPE's journal, the *Review of Radical Political Economics*, began publication in 1969 with an equally pluralistic philosopy which saw the appearance of many Post Keynesian articles, the first being that by Edward Nell (1972). The importance of these links in establishing a social network of Post Keynesian economists in the United States in the 1970s has been emphasized by Lee (2000a).

The connections were weaker in the United Kingdom, perhaps because of the more dogmatic and faction-ridden nature of British Marxism at this time (when the Americans referred to themselves as 'radical' it was not just a euphemism for 'Marxist' but also a deliberate effort to be inclusive and non-sectarian). But the young Jan Kregel published in the *Bulletin of the Conference of Socialist Economists* (Kregel, 1972b), although the organization and its journal (renamed *Capital and Class* in 1977) subsequently became less sympathetic to Post Keynesian ideas. Kaleckians like Philip Arestis and Malcolm Sawyer continued to advocate cooperation between radicals and Post

Keynesians. Under Arestis's editorship, *Thames Papers in Political Economy* (1974–90) was an important means of disseminating the work of both schools, and this tradition continues in Sawyer's *International Review of Applied Economics* (established in 1987) and Arestis's *International Papers in Political Economy* (which began publication in 1993).

There was also mutual suspicion and hostility. From the start Marxists had been divided in their reactions to the *General Theory*, with many of them attacking Keynes for his subjectivism and his concentration on the surface phenomena of market exchange at the expense of the more important underlying social relations of production. Keynes was further criticized for failing to break decisively with liberal microeconomics and for the naivety (worse, the tendency to authoritarian conservatism) of his political outlook. If anything these criticisms became sharper in the 1970s, when a very significant minority of Marxian economists – perhaps for a while the majority – asserted that Marx's volume III analysis of the falling rate of profit was the only explanation of capitalist crisis that was consistent with historical materialism. Alternative interpretations of his ideas, including underconsumptionist models associated with the volume II analysis of commodity circulation and the realization of surplus value, were dismissed as vulgar, superficial and apologetic. In fact *any* macroeconomic theory not rigorously grounded in the labour theory of value was rejected on the same grounds (Howard and King, 1992, chs 5,7).

Unsectarian but penetrating criticism came from the radical economist James Crotty, in the same session at the 1980 meeting of the American Economic Association at which Lorie Tarshis declared the Post Keynesian promise to have 'bounced' (see Chapter 6). Crotty criticized the Post Keynesians for having failed adequately to comprehend the contradictory nature of the capitalist economy. They had

> not made much progress in developing a theory of the complex process through which economic growth, in the short and in the long run, *endogenously* generates those impediments or constraints which prevent its perpetuation. Their theory does not reflect the self-limiting nature of the capitalist growth process nor the functional nature of recessions and depressions in recreating the preconditions for renewed accumulation. (Crotty, 1980, p. 23)

Post Keynesian trade cycle theory did not take into account the tendency for profits to fall as the reserve army of the unemployed declined, which was the result of productivity growth lagging behind the growth of real wages, together with the increasing burden of business debt and the effects on capacity utilization of previous overinvestment. While Marxists denied that these constraints could be overcome by market forces or fine-tuning by policy makers, Post Keynesians wrongly stressed the potential for stable, balanced growth,

Crotty argued. Hyman Minsky, he suggested, represented a rare but honourable exception.

Crotty also objected to the Post Keynesian treatment of the class struggle, which neglected conflict at the point of production: 'Yet low unemployment reduces labor "discipline" on the shop floor and increases union power to interfere with management's prerogatives with respect to technical change and the organization of the labor process, thereby contributing to the slowdown in the rate of growth of labor productivity that accompanies full employment' (ibid., p. 24). Finally he complained that the Post Keynesian view of the political process was unrealistic. Their support for incomes policy was based on a pluralistic vision that grossly exaggerated the potential for working people to benefit from class collaboration: 'Like Keynes' own theory of politics, it fails to appreciate the immense power that the corporations derive from their exclusive control of capital investment, and thus of jobs and income. If economic conditions do not suit them they stop investing, threatening the economic security of tens of millions of workers' (ibid., p. 25). There were distinct echoes of Kalecki in this verdict, though Crotty himself attributed the notion of a 'capital strike' to Joseph Schumpeter. His misgivings about incomes policy were shared by many left Post Keynesians, for example William Milberg and Fred Lee (King, 1995a, pp. 59–60, 197–8).

These criticisms were not a one-way process. As we saw in the previous chapter, many Fundamentalist Keynesians were indifferent or actively hostile to Kaleckian theory. Their objections carried over naturally to radical and Marxian political economy, where class analysis, exploitation, the privileging of production over circulation, and the attitude to the capitalist state all constituted major stumbling blocks. Even Hyman Minsky, who in later life increasingly emphasized the socialist influence on his early thought (Minsky, 1992), had little or no contact with radical economists and was relatively conservative in much of his own writing on policy questions (King, 2000). The political differences that Paul Davidson had identified continued to divide the radicals and Marxists from the predominantly left–liberal and social democratic Post Keynesians (see Chapter 5).

INSTITUTIONALISTS

Institutionalism emerged in the United States in the late nineteenth century, at roughly the same time as neoclassical economics, which it rejected on methodological as well as on analytical grounds. The most important of the original institutionalists were Thorstein Veblen and John R. Commons, followed later in the twentieth century by Clarence Ayres, John Kenneth Galbraith and Gardiner C. Means. Institutionalism

> is holistic and organic in its approach … and the beliefs, values and actions of individuals are seen as culturally embedded.… The task is to describe the complexities of the organization and control of social provisioning in its historical evolution, and the central concern to understand the process of institutional change and adjustment. Emphasis is given to power relations, legal systems and technology as key explanatory elements in the formation of institutions. A skeptical and critical perspective on contemporary institutions is taken. Economics is seen as a pragmatic, evolutionary and policy science which aims to improve the functioning of the economy through institutional change. (Hutton, 1999, p. 533)

Institutionalists take a particular interest in gender, class and race divisions; in the operation of corporate hegemony and the capital–labour relationship; in the financial system; in core–periphery relations and their implications for economic development; and in the provision of a social safety net by the state (O'Hara and Waller, 1999).

Institutionalism is essentially a North American phenomenon, although some dissident British economists (for example J.A. Hobson) had institutionalist connections and Keynes himself once wrote to John R. Commons that 'there seems to me to be no other economist with whose general way of thinking I feel myself in such general accord' (cited by Skidelsky, 1992, p. 229). Before 1940 economics in the United States was diverse and pluralistic, with neoclassicals and institutionalists coexisting relatively peacefully. This changed very rapidly in the following two decades; by 1960 the hegemony of the neoclassicals was almost complete and institutionalism had been confined to the margins of the profession. The process is described, but not adequately explained, in Morgan and Rutherford (1998). Thereafter the institutionalists, like the Post Keynesians, enjoyed the status of an embattled and increasingly despised minority.

Some prominent individuals straddled the two traditions. One was Alfred Eichner (see Chapter 6), himself heavily influenced by the father of administered pricing, Gardiner C. Means, who was described by his biographers as 'Institutionalist and Post Keynesian' (Samuels and Medema, 1990). Another was the eclectic Austrian theorist Kurt Rothschild (see Chapter 7), while the eminent institutionalist John Kenneth Galbraith was an early patron and financial supporter of the *Journal of Post Keynesian Economics*. More generally, it was evident that the interests and concerns of the two schools did overlap considerably, on questions of method, substantive theory and policy. Both schools were suspicious of formalism, rejected closed-system thinking and emphasized the role of history rather than equilibrium modelling. The institutionalist focus on evolution and process was entirely compatible with the Post Keynesian way of thinking, as was its stress on the transformational nature of economic reality – non-ergodicity, in Post Keynesian language. If the institutionalists had almost no macroeconomics, the Post Keynesians had always been weak on the question of agency, so that the gains from mutual borrowing were potentially substantial. And there were political similarities. The institutionalists were overwhelmingly left of centre, albeit in many cases not very far to the left. Like the Post Keynesians they were neither atomistic individualists nor advocates of laissez-faire, but believers in regulation and reform. It was no accident that one of the earliest and most penetrating critiques of 'shock therapy' in the transition economies of eastern Europe was written by Post Keynesians with institutionalist leanings (Kregel *et al.*, 1992).

Of the three Post Keynesian streams discussed in the previous chapter, it was perhaps the Fundamentalist Keynesians who had the closest affinity with the institutionalists. They saw conventions, habits and routines as solutions to the problem of reasoned choice under radical uncertainty; Paul Davidson, especially, had always stressed the role of money-denominated contracts as the central institution of a capitalist economy (Davidson, 1972a). On of his students, Roy Rotheim, had vivid memories of Davidson being referred to dismissively by his neoclassical colleagues at Rutgers University as an institutionalist (King, 1995a, pp. 35–6). The detailed operation of financial institutions was critical to Fundamentalist Keynesian monetary theory, as can be seen most readily in Victoria Chick's analysis of the stages of banking development and their implications for the theory of endogenous money (Chick, 1985). And labour market institutions were of course essential to Sidney Weintraub's explanation of inflation and his proposals for a tax-based incomes policy.

Many aspects of Kaleckian theory were also compatible with institutionalism. Anyone working within a broadly Marxian framework must begin by specifying the social relations of production that underpin all economic analysis. Thus all Kalecki's models presupposed the institutions of an advanced capitalist society, including wage-labour, a highly skewed distribution of income and wealth, and corresponding disparities in the access to finance. His discussion of entrepreneurship, for example, placed relatively little weight on individual talents and propensities for risk taking and much more on structural inequalities in the supply of capital (Kalecki, 1937). History also played an important role in Kalecki's economics, since he saw oligopoly as a feature of a particular phase of capitalist evolution with its own contradictions and laws of development. As we saw in Chapter 9, he actually attempted to interpret econometrics as an application of the principles of historical materialism (Kalecki, 1965). Finally, the significance of ideology and political power came out very clearly indeed in Kalecki's sceptical discussion of the prospects for full employment under capitalism (see Chapter 2).

Even the Sraffians could be reconciled with institutionalism, up to a point. Sraffa himself said almost nothing about the social and historical context of his analysis, except to specify a capitalist economy with wage-labour as the crucial assumption. A rational reconstruction of *Production of Commodities* was however possible, in which the argument was reformulated so that it corresponded to a series of stages of sociohistorical development, each with its own institutions and its own formal model (Meek, 1973). Luigi Pasinetti took this principle further, distinguishing between the 'natural' properties of any economic system based on human labour and the laws that were specific to particular types of social institution (Pasinetti, 1993). Once again, a marriage of Post Keynesian and institutionalist thinking seemed to be a potentially fruitful one.

There was also common ground between the institutionalists and the Post Keynesians on policy questions. Both schools asserted the need to regulate private power in the public interest (see Davidson and Davidson, 1988, for an excellent Post Keynesian discussion). It was no accident that the seminal article advocating an inflation tax on excessive wage increases was published in the institutionalist *Journal of Economic Issues* (Wallich and Weintraub, 1971), since support for incomes policy flowed naturally from institutionalist ideas. Employment policy was another area of broad agreement, since neither school believed that full employment would result automatically in a fully deregulated capitism. Thus proposals for a universal job guarantee, with the state acting as 'employer of last resort' to offer work to all those unable to find a job in the private sector, were supported both by institutionalists (Gordon, 1997) and by Post Keynesians (Minsky, 1986, ch. 12; Wray, 1998, ch. 6). Somewhat further to the left, a triangular connection between Marxian, Post Keynesian and institutionalist thinking could be found in the 'radical institutionalism' of William Dugger and Howard Sherman (1994).

Not surprisingly, these intellectual links were reflected in personal and social contacts. The institutionalist Association for Evolutionary Economics was formed in 1965 and began publishing the *Journal of Economic Issues* in 1971. From 1977 onwards the *Journal* carried a series of articles by Post Keynesian authors, and after 1979 Post Keynesian papers were also presented at the annual meetings of the AFEE. In the early 1980s a number of institutionalists were arguing that the two schools had a great deal in common (Brazelton, 1981; Wilber and Jameson, 1983), and friendly relations between them continued subsequently. Important areas of disagreement remained, however. For one thing, institutionalism was as diverse and potentially incoherent as Post Keynesianism, tending on its right flank to merge into neoclassical economics (as for example in the 'New Institutionalism' of Oliver Williamson and Douglass North). For another, the hostility of some institutionalists to all types of formal analysis was much stronger than the anti-formalism of many Post Keynesians. But these proved to be creative tensions. By the mid-1990s, in fact, the case began to be made that the institutionalists now constituted the third stream of thought within the Post Keynesian school, displacing the Sraffians (Arestis, 1996).

AUSTRIANS

Austrian economics had its roots in the thinking of Eugen von Böhm-Bawerk, Carl Menger and Friedrich von Wieser, who established a tradition continued in the twentieth century by Ludwig von Mises, Friedrich von Hayek and also, in a certain sense, by Joseph Schumpeter, whose large but nimble feet were to be found in several camps. Prominent Austrian theorists subsequently included Israel Kirzner, Ludwig Lachman and Murray Rothbard. In the final quarter of the century almost all significant work in Austrian (or neo-Austrian) economics was carried out in the United States, where the political climate proved exceptionally favourable to the propagation of Austrian ideas, outside academia at least (Vaughn, 1994). There was, of course, an analytical as well as a political core:

> Austrians value individual liberty and limited government, but they also share other and often more important insights into social reality. Austrian economic theory is founded on the firm belief that the most effective means toward the goal of understanding economic phenomena is to examine them in terms of the purposive actions of individual human beings. Other characteristics of Austrian thought are emphases on the subjectivity of knowledge and the spontaneity of evolution. (Vihanto, 1999, p. 23)

Thus Austrians asserted methodological individualism as their fundamental principle. They took it even further than their neoclassical opponents, often to the point of denying the validity of any macroeconomic theorizing at all. At the meta-methodological level, however, many Austrian economists were Babylonian in their general approach (Dow, 1996 [1985], p. 76).

Their thorough-going subjectivism led the Austrians to place great store by introspection as a source of economic knowledge and to deny any role for econometric research, if not for formal empirical work of any kind. They were at least as hostile as the Post Keynesians to general equilibrium theory, and for quite similar reasons. The Austrians regarded entrepreneurs as the most important of all economic agents, since it was their creativity and innovative behaviour that drove economic progress: 'But equilibrium rules out the exploitation of new opportunities, and thus creativity; it rules out precisely what many neo-Austrians see as the moving force behind competition' (ibid., p. 115). There was some tension between this view of microeconomics and the Austrian approach to macroeconomic theory, which often revealed a deep suspicion of macroeconomic concepts as a matter of principle.

In the 1930s, however, Hayek had formulated an influential theory of the trade cycle, which he explained as the result of mistaken government policy. Excessive monetary expansion in the upswing pushed the rate of interest below its 'natural' value, encouraging a short-lived boom in investment that extended the average degree of 'roundaboutness' of production beyond its sustainable level. In the ensuing depression the appropriate capital structure was restored by means of a decline in the level of investment expenditure. Hayek interpreted the reduction in output and employment in the downswing as the unavoidable consequence of the initial policy error (Hayek, 1931). His analysis of money and capital was heavily criticized at the time (Sraffa, 1932; Kaldor, 1937b). It not only proved to be vulnerable to the Cambridge capital critique (see Chapter 4), but also appeared to rely upon concepts of equilibrium (the 'natural rate of interest', for example) that were inconsistent with the broader principles of Austrian economic theory. After 1945 Hayek became an ardent, if very idiosyncratic, supporter of the monetarist explanation of inflation and a strident critic of trade union monopoly power.

Their analytical perspective led the twentieth-century Austrians (if not always their nineteenth-century forebears), to a very distinctive stance on economic policy. Knowledge was essentially private, human learning was crucial but also unsystematic and unpredictable, and social order could be seen to emerge spontaneously in response to the pursuit of individual self-interest. Hence only a minimal amount of state intervention could be justified:

> Hayek's macroeconomic policy is that governments should not engage in macroeconomic policy. Nevertheless, he recognizes that the transition to an absence of policy, as well as to increased competitiveness of labour markets, requires significant structural change. He thus makes positive policy proposals to ease the transition, such as worker profit-sharing schemes. (Dow, 1996 [1985], p. 191)

As Dow noted, there was an element of inconsistency in this position:

> Implicitly, in making such proposals, Hayek is accepting the notion that governments, and their advisers, may have information which is not available to the individuals concerned in a policy issue. As soon as neo-Austrians go beyond arguments for individualism rather than government intervention and make policy proposals at the macro level, they are implying that economists have superior knowledge of the unintended consequences of human action. (Ibid., p. 191)

And this is difficult to reconcile with the Austrian treatment of knowledge, learning and spontaneous order.

Some potential points of contact between Austrians and Post Keynesians can be inferred from this brief summary. Above all, the role of uncertainty and time and the resulting suspicion of formal, closed-system models of economic processes were common to both schools. Though never himself quite an Austrian, George Shackle was often seen as a bridge between the two traditions (see Chapter 9). But there were also powerful sources of hostility. For the Austrian labour economist Don Bellante, political and analytical criticisms were intertwined. Bellante viewed Post Keynesianism as

> a return to the most primitive version of Keynesian economics, wherein output determination is the subject of economic analysis, but money-wage and price-level movements are seen as sociologically determined (in a tussle over the distribution of income). Hence, the crisis in Keynesian theory over the incompatibility of rising inflation coupled (sometimes) with rising unemployment was resolved by ignoring it, in effect, through seeking refuge in what is really a noneconomic theory of inflation. (Bellante, 1992, p. 122)

The Post Keynesians denied the very existence of the labour market, Bellante complained, and refused to accept that output prices had anything to do with demand. Thus Post Keynesian economics

> has no microeconomic foundations, except for primitive, pre-marginalist ones, and serves mostly to rationalize a collectivist control of the division of income according to class. With Marxism falling in credibility, the Post-Keynesian effort to justify government control of investment decisions and perpetual wage and price controls provides the next best hope for those who cannot accept economic individualism. (Ibid., p. 126)

This view of Post Keynesians as crypto-Marxists seems to have been quite common among Austrian economists.

Some Austrians, however, did attempt to identify areas of common interest. In the mid-1980s the Austrian economists Gerald O'Driscoll and Mario Rizzo tried to enlist Paul Davidson as an ally:

> In recent years a largely American branch of the Cambridge (U.K.) school, known as post-Keynesian economics, has arisen to carry forth the subjectivist aspects of Keynes's system. For a long time these had been buried and almost forgotten within the Hicksian neoclassical framework. Paul Davidson has conveniently summarized the post-Keynesian perspective in three propositions ...:
>
> (1) the economy is a process in historical (real) time;
>
> (2) in a world where uncertainty and surprises are unavoidable, expectations have an unavoidable and significant effect on economic outcomes;
>
> (3) economic and political institutions are not negligible and, in fact, play an extremely important role in determining real world economic outcomes.
>
> The reader will be hard pressed to find any significant differences between these propositions and the argument of this chapter. What is even more surprising is that Davidson's explication of the meaning of these propositions increases, rather than reduces, the amount of overlap. It is evident that there is much more common ground between post-Keynesian subjectivism and Austrian subjectivism. Cross-fertilization between the two schools is, however, exceedingly rare, although the possibilities for mutually advantageous interchange seem significant. (O'Driscoll and Rizzo, 1985, p. 9)

Davidson was deeply unimpressed, both with this and with O'Driscoll's and Rizzo's claim that Austrian economics posed a serious threat to mainstream theory. The Austrians, he argued, were neoclassical at heart, 'despite their utilization of such code words as uncertainty, real time, and money' (Davidson, 1989, p. 483). They shared the same axioms: neutral money, gross substitution and ergodicity. As to the first axiom, the Austrian theory of money entailed that 'the coordination of individual plans for the demand and supply of real goods and services is independent of the nominal supply of money'. The second axiom followed from Hayek's definition of equilibrium, which 'means that there must exist a vector of market prices which is consistent with market equilibrium. A sufficient condition for this to occur is if all excess demand curves are downward sloping and hence well behaved', and this in turn entailed that every good is a gross substitute for every other good.

This, Davidson continued, was inconsistent with Keynes's proposition that the elasticity of substitution between money and real, illiquid assets was close to zero; and this in turn was an essential property of money. Persistent involuntary unemployment could not be reconciled with this second axiom. The third axiom was revealed by the Austrians' acceptance of rational expectations and their denial that entrepreneurs made systematic errors (ibid., pp. 473–5). But uncertainty in Keynes's sense presupposed that we live in a non-ergodic world. Thus the Austrian concept of uncertainty was defective: 'Unlike the Austrian concept, Post Keynesian uncertainty need not be limited to "gaps" in the current probability (subjective or objective) distribution. Uncertainty implies that economic decision makers recognize that today's probabilities (if any) will not govern the future outcomes' (ibid., p. 479). This led the Austrians to commit a series of further errors in the theory of money and – especially – interest, which they continued to view as a real rather than a monetary phenomenon (ibid., pp. 479–83).

This was by far the most detailed Post Keynesian appraisal of Austrian theory, though Jan Kregel (1986) had already assessed their respective contributions to the theory of expectations and a systematic comparison of their respective methodologies had been undertaken by Sheila Dow (1996 [1985]). Austrian reactions to Davidson's attack were summarized by Peter Wynarczyk, who endorsed their claim that in fact they shared the three fundamental Post Keynesian axioms. Money was not neutral in Austrian theory, and the universe was not viewed as ergodic. Both traditions, Wynarczyk concluded, 'emphasise reasonable (or sensible) behaviour with meaningful human action embedded within institutional structures'. Thus New York, the new centre of Austrian economic theory, was a lot closer to Knoxville than Davidson had been prepared to accept (Wynarczyk, 1999, p. 43).

For the most part, though, Post Keynesian theorists (as opposed to methodologists), simply ignored the Austrians; cross-fertilization was indeed extremely rare. There were political reasons for this, in addition to the specific analytical criticisms made by Davidson. Post Keynesians were generally left of centre, the Kaleckians and Sraffians more so than the Fundamentalist

Keynesians. None of them regarded unbridled capitalism as a good thing or attacked government intervention as such. Without exception the Austrians were well to the right along the political spectrum – further to the right, in fact, than the monetarists who occupied the 'extreme right wing' column of Davidson's table of schools of thought in economics (see Chapter 5). Margaret Thatcher, for example, saw herself as a disciple of Hayek. It is as difficult to imagine a neoliberal Post Keynesian, in fact, as it is to conceive of a social democratic neo-Austrian. For many Post Keynesians the Austrians took a Panglossian view of the capitalist system, glorifying the market, lionizing the entrepreneur and vilifying the state. They saw government intervention as part of the problem (in some instances as *all* of the problem), not as part of the solution. According to them, state involvement in economic life distorted market signals, reduced incentives to work, save and innovate, and generated uncertainty; it should be reduced significantly if it could not be eliminated altogether. While Post Keynesians could legitimately be criticized for not having a theory of the state (Crotty, 1980), none of them could ever agree with the Austrians on questions of policy, or politics.

NEW KEYNESIANS

New Keynesian economics emerged in the 1980s as a reaction against New Classical macroeconomic theory. The New Keynesians did not object to rational expectations – on the contrary, their own models incorporated this hypothesis – but rather to the New Classical assumption that markets were always perfectly competitive and invariably in or rapidly approaching equilibrium. The New Keynesian focus upon market imperfections led to a revival of interest in the analysis of imperfect or monopolistic competition that had, ironically, been pioneered by the young Joan Robinson (though she subsequently repudiated it). The New Keynesians' introduction of asymmetric information into models of labour and credit markets made it possible for them to explain the absence of market clearing, so that involuntary unemployment and credit rationing could now be interpreted as the outcome of rational decision making under uncertainty. New Keynesian economists refused to genuflect at the altar of the Lucas critique, arguing instead that macroeconomic policy was not inevitably ineffective. There was even a revival of interest in the theory of economic growth under conditions of increasing returns.

By 1990, in fact, New Keynesian economics had become a distinct and rapidly expanding school of thought in its own right (Mankiw and Romer, 1991). There seemed to be a number of possible points of contact between New Keynesian and Post Keynesian thinking, in particular scepticism concerning models of perfect competition. Keynes's failure to integrate imperfect competition into the *General Theory* had long been a source of complaint and puzzlement – and not just to Kaleckians. Shortly before his death Nicholas Kaldor came to believe that product market imperfection was a necessary condition for the persistence of involuntary unemployment. If there were no appreciable economies of scale, why did not the unemployed employ themselves? If they did not become self-employed, this presumably meant that their continued unemployment was voluntary. Total 'employment' (work for wages plus work on one's own account) was therefore supply-constrained, not demand-constrained. On this argument the second neoclassical postulate was correct after all (see Keynes, 1936, p. 5) and the principle of effective demand was logically inconsistent with perfect competition. In other words, any Keynesian macroeconomic theory worthy of the name had to assume imperfect competition (Kaldor, 1983; cf. Weitzman, 1985). Kaldor died (in 1986) before New Keynesian economics had emerged as a clearly recognizable school of thought, but it is one that he might well have joined had he lived a little longer.

New Keynesians also made a great deal out of imperfections in the capital market, due to informational asymmetries between borrowers and lenders. This was used to demonstrate that the rate of interest did not equate the supply and demand for loans, and hence to explain the phenomenon of credit rationing, which is inconsistent both with conventional applications of the IS–LM model and with the neutrality of money (see Chapter 8). In imperfect capital markets,

> Agents' access to funds may depend on their financial circumstances. More specifically, the ability of a firm to undertake an investment project may depend not only on the fundamentals of the project under consideration, but also on the firm's financial condition. Projects, in which firms would invest if they had sufficient internal funds, might not be undertaken if the firm must raise external funds to finance the project. These ideas provide a new foundation for links between financial structure and real activity. (Fazzari, 1992, p. 123)

Neoclassical theories of investment that relied exclusively on 'real' factors were thus inherently flawed. The imperfections that resulted from asymmetric information were an unavoidable feature of a decentralized market economy, in which there was by definition no conscious coordination of individual decisions. 'And there is no reason to believe that the information gap can be eliminated. To become fully informed would require that the banker become an entrepreneur, a condition that would undo the specialization that is fundamental to the productivity of the system' (ibid., p. 126). There were clear parallels between New Keynesian ideas and Michal Kalecki's principle of increasing risk (ibid., p. 127).

Some Post Keynesian monetary theorists were attracted by these arguments, the most notable being Hyman Minsky. Indeed, Louis-Philippe Rochon suggests that all the foundations of New Keynesian monetary theory can be found in Minsky's two earliest articles, published in 1957. In both cases 'The central argument is that the economy is driven by credit the supply of which is indirectly controlled by the central bank given financial innovation' (Rochon, 2000, p. 16). The monetary transmission mechanism, common to Minsky and the New Keynesians, operated through the 'balance sheet channel'. Monetary policy affected firms' financial condition, since higher interest rates (for example) increased the burden of debt repayment and reduced the price of its assets. This would have an adverse effect on the willingness of the banks to lend, and hence tended to reduce investment expenditure.

There was a price to be paid for this interpretation, which made Minsky an exogenous money man and (for many Post Keynesians) attached too much importance to the rate of interest. In particular, Dow (1998) argued that there were major analytical differences between Minsky and the New Keynesians. But a connection of some sort was certainly there. Minsky himself saw affinities between New Keynesian ideas and the financial instability hypothesis, which relied very heavily on cyclical variations in lending criteria that made sense only if it were assumed that bankers did not have complete information about their customers' ability and willingness to repay. Minsky may also have been seduced by the New Keynesian theory of investment, which was derived from Tobin's q and centred on the relationship between the price of new assets and the stock market valuation of existing productive equipment (Brainard and Tobin, 1968). This 'two-price' model of investment decisions was broadly similar to that which Minsky himself had set out in his *John Maynard Keynes* (Minsky, 1975).

Three other aspects of New Keynesian analysis also appealed to many Post Keynesians. The first was the 'efficiency wage' model of the labour market, which made productivity a function of the real wage and provided a theoretical basis for involuntary unemployment by refuting the neoclassical claim that profit-maximizing behaviour by employers would necessarily eliminate excess labour supply (Stiglitz, 1987). The second was the acceptance of path-dependence or hysteresis, with the associated denial that there was a 'natural rate' of unemployment given independently both of the actual rate and of the path taken by unemployment in the recent past. This permitted much more scope for macroeconomic policy than either the monetarists or the New Classical economists had been prepared to contemplate (see Cross, 1993; Davidson, 1993; Katzner, 1993). Finally there was New Keynesian growth theory, which demolished the canonical neoclassical Solow model and replaced it with an analysis that hinged on learning, irreversibility and dynamic increasing returns to scale (see, for example, Lucas, 1988). This was another reason why Kaldor might have been a New Keynesian, had he lived into the 1990s.

There were equally good reasons, however, for Post Keynesians to be profoundly suspicious of the new school, as can be seen from the collection of critical articles edited by Roy Rotheim (1998). Some of the Fundamentalist Keynesian objections had been set out, quite early and with great force, by Paul Davidson, for whom the New Keynesians would have fallen foul of any 'truth in labelling' law that might be applied to economists. Davidson argued that their ideas were essentially classical, not Keynesian. This could be seen very easily from their analysis of the labour market, which explained involuntary unemployment by reference to money wage rigidity. For Keynes, Davidson noted, complete money wage flexibility was neither a necessary nor a sufficient condition for full employment. It was not necessary, since an increase in aggregate demand would increase employment independently of any assumption about the money wage level. It was not sufficient, because, as Keynes had argued in Book V of the *General Theory*, a downward spiral in wages and prices might well reduce output and employment (Davidson, 1992).

Later, in the course of an attack on Assar Lindbeck's New Keynesian analysis, Davidson illustrated his argument diagrammatically. In Figure 11.1(a) the equilibrium level of employment is determined by the intersection of the aggregate supply and demand functions, at N_a. Employment can also be read off the market equilibrium curve of labour-hire (*MECL*) in Figure 11.1(b). This is not a demand for labour curve in the neoclassical – and New Keynesian – sense, since both employment and the real wage are determined in the product market by the point of effective demand, and not in the labour market at all. That is to say, they are determined 'from without' the labour market, as Peter Riach put it (Davidson, 1999a, pp. 581–3; cf. Riach, 1995). Involuntary unemployment is N_aN_b. It can be eliminated only by an increase in aggregate demand, to D'_w in Figure 11.1(a), which will induce a movement down *MECL* to F' in Figure 11.1(b). Thus

> Disappointed unemployed workers ... can reduce money wages *until they are blue in the face* without altering entrepreneurs' 'correct' profit-maximizing–hiring decisions one iota *unless* the money wage decline induces an increase (upward shift) of the D_w (aggregate product demand) function denominated in wage units to Figure [11.1(a)'s] dotted D'_w function. (Davidson, 1999a, p. 583)

Davidson concluded that the New Keynesians had failed to explain why this might (let alone why it must) occur.

He criticized the New Keynesian stress on product market imperfections for similar reasons. Like wage rigidity, price rigidity was neither a necessary nor a sufficient condition for the persistence of involuntary unemployment. Davidson

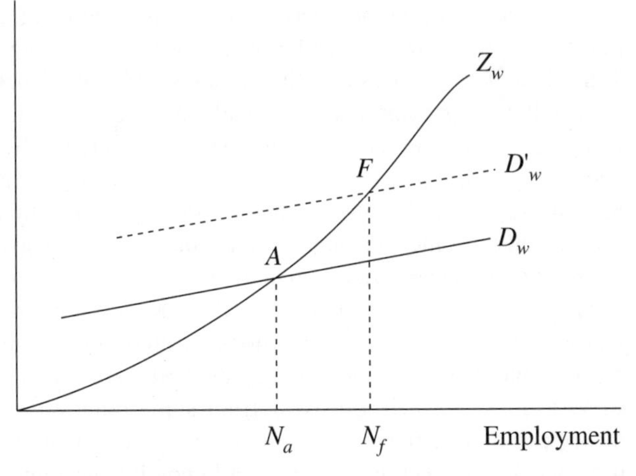

Source: Davidson (1999a, p. 582).

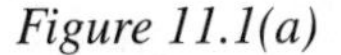
Figure 11.1(a)

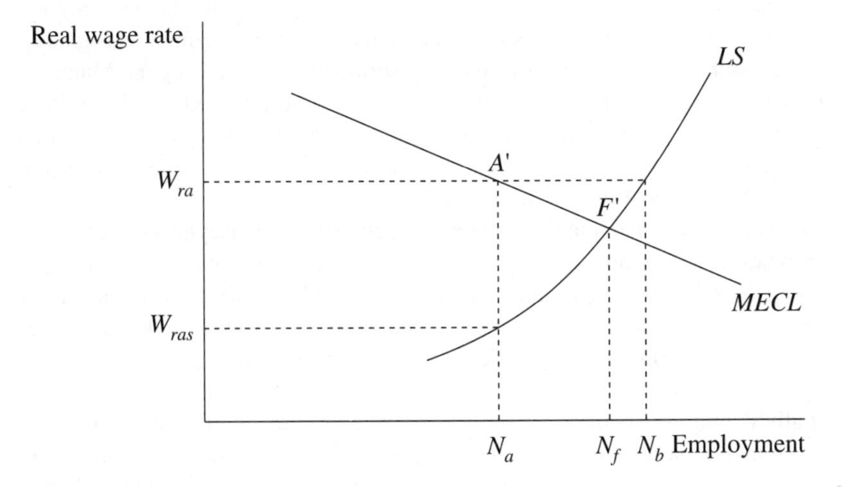

Source: Davidson (1999a, p. 582).

Figure 11.1(b)

maintained that Keynes's theory, since it applied also in perfect competition, was more general than that of the New Keynesians. The 'hard-headed' microfoundations of which they were so proud – this was a pun on the title of a popular book by the New Keynesian Alan Blinder (1987) – were simply Lucas-style rational expectations derived from an underlying general equilibrium model. Keynes's microfoundations, however, had been Marshallian, not Walrasian. Davidson was equally unimpressed by efficiency wage theory, even though it was perhaps the only really new idea to emerge from the New Keynesian literature, since it was unable to explain why piecework was so uncommon and sharecropping had almost disappeared. Nearly all capitalist firms instead offered contracts that paid their workers a time rate of wages or a salary, both specified in money rather than in real terms (Davidson, 1992). These criticisms were widely shared.

There were other grounds for Post Keynesian hostility to the New Keynesians. For many, the relentless search for the microfoundations of macroeconomics was open to strong methodological objections, whether they came from Walras via Lucas or from some other source. Efficiency wage theory could be criticized on empirical as well as analytical grounds, since it provided no convincing story that could possibly account for the much higher unemployment suffered in nearly all capitalist countries after the 'golden age' of full employment came to an end in the early 1970s (Sawyer, 1998). The New Keynesians had a worrying tendency to slip back into the crassest neoclassical errors when they turned to the long period, in which money was supposed to be neutral, Say's Law operated and full employment was guaranteed. And they took the long run very seriously indeed. Gregory Mankiw's much-vaunted introductory textbook, for which he received a million-dollar advance, was widely criticized for devoting more space to growth theory than to the short-period problems of employment and output determination (Anon., 1997; Schneider, 1997; Mankiw, 1998).

There were also major differences between New Keynesians and Post Keynesians on policy matters. A case for an active fiscal and monetary policy geared to the attainment and maintenance of full employment could indeed be teased out of New Keynesian models. The New Keynesians themselves, however, had offered very little in the way of specific and coherent policy proposals, and this failure was made much worse by their futile and potentially damaging encouragement of downward wage and price flexibility. The gulf that separated them from the Post Keynesians widened further when Assar Lindbeck (1998) gave New Keynesianism a decidedly neoliberal slant, drawing from Davidson the comment that

> the contribution of the New Keynesians has been the invention of all sorts of short-run *ad-hoc* constraints (market failures) to the market mechanisms to prevent the *nonmonetary* classical system from achieving the short-run full employment equilibrium position assured by the very restrictive classical presumptions that both New Classical and New Keynesian theorists accept as universal truths. (Davidson, 1999a, p. 587)

On this reading there was very little analytical difference between New Keynesian and New Classical macroeconomics.

Davidson, however, was a sterner critic than many Post Keynesians, and it can be argued that he failed to distinguish sufficiently clearly between the different streams of opinion within New Keynesianism. The credit market analysis of Joseph Stiglitz, for example, which focused on asymmetric information and denied the neutrality of money even in the long run, had more in common with Post Keynesian macroeconomics than the more obviously neoclassical ideas of Mankiw and Lindbeck (the seminal paper in this tradition was by Stiglitz and Weiss 1981). And those Post Keynesians who accepted the validity of formal, mathematical modelling in macroeconomics had begun to discover affinities between their way of thinking and that of some of the New Keynesian practitioners of complex dynamics (Rosser, 1998). At the end of the 1990s, then, the future relationship between Post Keynesians and New Keynesians was still very much an open question.

12. A promise that bounced?

> Despite the risks involved in making forecasts about future developments in economics, I would venture to suggest that it is in [Post Keynesian theory] that the most important contributions to Australian radical economics will be made in the next decade, and by an increasing number of scholars. This exciting prospect is liable to eventuate because the best of the young talent in radical economics in Australia is being steered into this area of inquiry. (Groenewegen, 1979, p. 205)

> This book in some ways represents a memorial to a research programme about which high hopes were expressed, especially in the 1970s. It now seems to be in decline. Post Keynesian economics survives as a minority interest in a number of economics departments while its intellectual elite is an ageing set of professors whose writings are falling on deaf ears in an increasingly homogenised profession built on the North American model. (Groenewegen, 1995, p. 137).

ON WHIGS AND MARKETING MANAGERS

How far has Post Keynesian economics progressed since the beginning, if indeed it has made any progress at all? What are its future prospects? These are not easy questions to answer. In the first place it will be evident to anyone who has read this far that no single event or date can be specified as marking the origin of Post Keynesianism. A case can be made – and from the viewpoint of the social historian it is a strong case – for denying that there was anything resembling a distinct Post Keynesian school of thought before the term came into widespread use in the 1970s (Lee, 2000a). At the other extreme, I suggested in Chapters 1 and 2 that there were important Post Keynesian elements in the work of Michal Kalecki and Joan Robinson even before the publication of the *General Theory* in 1936. And most intellectual historians would agree that something was astir in the mid-1950s, when Cambridge growth and distribution theory emerged, even if Kahn, Kaldor, Robinson and their colleagues neither used a single label to describe their efforts nor saw themselves clearly as spearheading a drive against the neoclassical synthesis.

This, however, is a minor problem. Very much more serious is the extreme complexity of the notion of 'progress' as applied to science in general and to economics in particular. Roger Backhouse (1997, ch. 8) distinguishes 'theoretical' from 'empirical' progress. The requirements for theoretical progress are increased generality, increased scope, increased precision, increased rigour, elimination of error, elimination of inconsistency, increased simplicity and beauty, and the ability to predict novel facts. Evidence of empirical progress comes from an increase in the number and quality of empirical generalizations, increased predictive success or increased corroboration, improved problem-solving ability, and (again!) successful prediction of novel facts. Some of the difficulties that arise when discussing progress in economies will already be apparent from this list. Several of Backhouse's criteria are substitutes: rigour and (empirical) relevance, to take the most obvious example. Others may be complements, or entirely independent goods, but how are we to assess their relative importance? Consistency is notoriously 'the hobgoblin of little minds', while elegance is for tailors, as Einstein is supposed to have said. What is the value of an increased ability to solve trivial problems? Who, in any case, is to decide what counts as trivial? As for 'novel facts', which surprisingly feature on both sides of Backhouse's balance sheet, there are some very real problems that I shall outline later in this chapter.

And there is a further complication. We need to distinguish two senses in which scientific progress might be understood, the intellectual and the social/institutional. Imagine a Hegelian idealist from another planet who is concerned only with the progress of the Idea and takes no interest whatsoever in the idiosyncrasies of human society. A totally independent, external observer with this degree of detachment might just be able to judge the progress of a school of thought exclusively by reference to intellectual criteria, applying the standards set by the philosophers of her home planet and those standards alone. No earthling would be likely even to try to do so (though Backhouse comes perilously close to it). Our conception of scientific progress is so closely bound up with institutional success and social acceptance that the most severe of moral philosophers would find it all but impossible to isolate themselves from non-intellectual questions and to ignore the material record of the school that is under review. And there may be good reasons for this. How could it be that a set of ideas was at once an intellectual triumph and a social and institutional failure? Surely good science drives out bad science, every time?

This Whig interpretation of the history of ideas is much favoured by neoclassical economists (though not by historians of economic thought who are otherwise sympathetic to orthodox theory). Of course it is nonsense, as the grisly example of Stalin's pet biologist, T.D. Lysenko, suffices to demonstrate (Medvedev, 1969). Even if we exclude the period of Stalinist terror as a pathological instance, the history of science is full of examples of prophets spurned, old truths forgotten or neglected, even older heresies enthusiastically embraced, and egregious errors pursued at great speed to the very end of the appropriate cul-de-sac (King, 1988). Almost certainly this occurs more often in the social sciences, where power and money are directly at stake, than in the natural sciences. Arguably it happens more often in economics than in any other discipline, but it does seem to be an inevitable part of the progress of science in general. As Thomas Kuhn has noted, 'There are losses as well as gains in scientific progress, and scientists tend to be peculiarly blind to the former' (Kuhn, 1970 [1962], p. 167).

Let us go, for the moment, to the opposite extreme and suppose that nothing matters in the appraisal of a school of thought except its institutional and social success. From this unqualified materialist (or postmodernist?) position, evidence of scientific progress can come only from the ability to command status, prestige and resources and to attract supporters. As two prominent Post Keynesians once wrote (with tongue, I devoutly hope, firmly in cheek):

> Which theoretical approach an economist will believe to be best will depend on her academic upbringing, the circles within which she moves, and the country whose affairs claim most of her attention, as well as her inbuilt predispositions. In many ways then the success of a theoretical approach should be understood just as a marketing manager would attempt to understand the success of a consumer or industrial product. If it is launched at an inopportune moment, is poorly packaged, is too complex for the consumer to grasp, and fails to appeal to traditional values, then it will not find a market. Similarly, a skillful salesperson may be able to sell a veritable 'lemon' of a product or theory to the market. (Dow and Earl, 1982, pp. 177–8, cited by Moore, 1988, pp. xv–xvi)

This 'marketing manager' perspective on scientific progress greatly simplifies our problem. Within 'the profession', assuming for the purposes of the argument that the disciplinary boundaries are unambiguously defined, progress can then be assessed in terms of 'sales', which can be measured by honours and awards achieved; the extent of influence in a more diffuse sense, for example through journal citations, respectful treatment in survey articles and handbooks, and the adoption of textbooks; ability to gain access to 'key' journals and 'major' conferences; and success in obtaining jobs and attracting students, especially talented research students. Outside the profession, progress must be gauged by the influence exerted in other, related disciplines; in the business world, and outside it among trade unions, not-for-profit bodies and non-government organizations; over the formation and execution of public policy, nationally and internationally; and over the intellectual climate of the time, what John Kenneth Galbraith once referred to as the 'conventional wisdom'.

Some of these indices of success are relatively easy to quantify, while for others it is impossible. In the present context this really does not matter, since

Post Keynesian economics has palpably failed to make any progress on almost any of these criteria (but see Dow, 2000, for a less pessimistic view). No Post Keynesian has won a Nobel prize, though Piero Sraffa achieved a near-miss in 1961 with the Söderstrom gold medal of the Royal Swedish Academy of Sciences, and the Nobel committee's repeated refusal to honour Joan Robinson was widely regarded as scandalous in her lifetime (Turner, 1991). No-one at all sympathetic to Post Keynesian ideas has been elected president of the American Economic Association since Galbraith, who served in 1971, so that the prestigious Richard T. Ely lecture has never again been given by someone of Robinson's persuasion (see Chapter 6). The first generation of Cambridge Post Keynesians was rather more respectfully treated by the British economics profession, with both Kaldor and Kahn elected Fellows of the British Academy. In Italy Sraffa was lionized even by his adversaries, and Post Keynesians like Luigi Pasinetti (foundation president of the European Society for the History of Economic Thought) have also been elected to high office. But the second and third-generation Post Keynesians in all these countries have had a much harder time of it, and the situation is not likely to improve in the foreseeable future.

Much the same can be said of intellectual influence, difficult though it would be to substantiate this claim with any degree of statistical confidence (some of the supporting qualitative evidence can be found in Chapter 6). I would hazard a guess that Sidney Weintraub was much more frequently cited in the *American Economic Review* than Paul Davidson has been, and we know from Chapter 5 that Weintraub's light shone very much more brightly before he began his 'Jevonian sedition' in the early 1960s than it did thereafter. The work of Robinson and Kaldor was frequently referred to in the leading journals, both in the United Kingdom and overseas, while this certainly cannot be said for their British successors. Sraffa's citations rose, then fell, and had almost ceased by the late 1980s (Hodgson, 1997). The absence of Post Keynesian names and Post Keynesian ideas from recent surveys of the macroeconomic literature written by mainstream theorists contrasts sadly with their prominence in earlier decades: compare, for example, the serious discussion of Kaldor and Robinson by Samuelson (1964) with the complete neglect of Post Keynesian economics by Phelps (1990), in a book entitled *Seven Schools of Thought in Macroeconomics*. And no Post Keynesian textbook has ever advanced beyond fringe status, not even Robinson's and Eatwell's *Introduction to Modern Economics*, on which such high hopes had been placed (Robinson and Eatwell, 1973; King and Millmow, 2002).

The ability to publish in the 'top' journals has been a contentious issue ever since the early 1970s, when access to the *American Economic Review* was effectively denied to Post Keynesian authors on the pretext of increasingly rigorous standards of quality control (see Chapter 6). Just how far things had deteriorated by 1971 can be inferred from a referee's report received by Weintraub, who had published seven articles in this journal between 1942 and 1961:

> I have discussed this paper formally above as though it were a potential contribution to the literature. In fact, there is nothing in this paper that can possibly be construed as contributing anything. Frankly, I am amazed that anyone would submit something like this to a professional journal – let alone to the *AER*. It would be fortunate to receive a passing grade in a principles course.[1]

The offending paper may not have been one of Weintraub's best, but there was no such excuse for the *AER*'s rejection of Geoff Harcourt's important sequel to his book on the capital controversies, and still less for the treatment that Harcourt's and Peter Kenyon's important paper on Post Keynesian pricing theory received at the hands of the *Economic Journal*'s editors in 1974 which forced the authors to turn to the more liberally minded Swiss board of *Kyklos* (Harcourt, 1976; Harcourt and Kenyon, 1976; cf. Harcourt, 1995b). Paul Davidson has complained bitterly about similar discrimination in the awarding of research grants (King, 1995a, pp. 33–4), and it would not be surprising if the same story were to be told about acceptance rates for papers at major national and international conferences.

In all probability Post Keynesian submission rates have also declined since the early 1970s, as the improbability of success became apparent and alternative outlets like the *Journal of Post Keynesian Economics* and the *Cambridge Journal of Economics* commenced publication. This process of self-exclusion may well have accelerated towards the end of the century, when additional non-mainstream journals were established, among them the *International Review of Applied Economics* in 1987, the *Review of Political Economy* in 1989 and *International Papers in Political Economy* in 1993. What the British economics establishment thought of these heterodox upstarts can be seen in their omission from the list of reputable journals – originally produced by the USA economist Art Diamond – deemed by the Economic and Social Research Council to count for the purposes of the four-yearly Research Assessment Exercise. There may have been no conscious decision to attack the future viability of Post Keynesianism, or other dissident schools, but the consequences were entirely predictable and presumably not at all unwelcome (Lee and Harley, 1998). Geoffrey Hodgson and Harry Rothman have documented the increasing oligopoly power of a small number of US universities, whose professors dominate the editorial boards and constitute a majority of the authors published by the 'leading' economics journals. This has resulted, they argue, in 'an apparent reduction of pluralism and diversity of analytical concerns' in the profession as a whole, and represents a significant barrier to theoretical and methodological innovation in the discipline (Hodgson and

Rothman, 1999, pp. F180–82). Not surprisingly, few if any Post Keynesians teach at Ivy League universities or their British equivalents; even Cambridge is now a neoclassical stronghold, with only a small minority of heterodox economists.

There are few signs that Post Keynesian economics has made much progress outside the profession. Although Ben Fine (2000) has chronicled the arrogant imperialist *pretensions* of neoclassical theorists, their *achievements* in colonizing the other social sciences are less evident; indeed, Duncan Foley (1999, p. 113) suggests that colonization may be proceeding in the reverse direction. And I know of no systematic study of the influence of different varieties of economic theory on scholars in the other social sciences. At all events, there does not seem to be any evidence that Post Keynesians have had much of an impact on sociologists, historians, legal theorists, moral philosophers or even political economists (using this term to denote scholars in political science departments who study economic policy and institutions). The same must surely be true of the corporate world, if much less so of the unions, with Thomas Palley (1998) at the AFL/CIO, for example, and Jim Stanford (1999) at the Canadian Auto Workers Union. (Trade unions, of course, count for a great deal less than they once used to.)

In terms of public policy the decline in influence is much more apparent in Britain, where Nicholas Kaldor and Richard Kahn were ennobled for their services to the Labour governments of the 1960s and 1970s while their successors became part of Margaret Thatcher's 'enemy within'. The American Post Keynesians, in contrast, never got very far in Washington. In the rest of the world, the days are long gone when Kaldor could roam the globe devising new taxation systems (and, his opponents claimed, provoking riots) wherever he went. By the 1980s neoliberalism was everywhere in the ascendant, even in social democratic parties. The dismissal of (Lord) Meghnad Desai as Labour spokesperson on economic matters in 1993 and the sudden departure of Oskar Lafontaine from the German treasury in 1999 sounded the death-knell of any form of Keynesian influence – with or without a qualifying adjective – in what used to be the British and German left.

Post Keynesian penetration of international economic institutions is again largely uncharted territory, but outside the more peripheral agencies (UNCTAD, the ILO) it would be amazing if they had made any headway at all. For a time it seemed as though the World Bank, under its (New) Keynesian chief economist Joseph Stiglitz, might prove to be an exception, but such hopes were dashed by Stiglitz's resignation late in 1999. As for the conventional wisdom, Post Keynesians have gone backwards rapidly since the 1970s, when incomes policy was still taken seriously as a remedy for inflation and the majority of informed opinion favoured the use of fiscal and/or monetary policy to achieve employment goals. At the end of the century, the 'New

Monetarism' was mimicking Post Keynesian thinking in some respects: for example in eschewing any attempt to 'control the money supply' and relying instead on the fine-tuning of interest rates. But macroeconomic policy makers focused on inflation to the exclusion of any concern for employment, which they claimed to be the exclusive province of supply-side measures; fiscal policy was locked up in a balanced-budget straitjacket (Arestis and Sawyer, 1999b). Intelligent economic journalists sometimes took to Post Keynesian ideas – Will Hutton (1995) in Britain, for example, or Brian Toohey (1994) in Australia – but their long-term influence on economic policy has proved to be negligible.

If Post Keynesian macroeconomics has failed so comprehensively to make any progress in social and institutional terms – if, indeed, it has retrogressed according to most of the relevant criteria – does this not demonstrate a comparable failure in intellectual progress? Not at all, the Post Keynesians reply, attributing their failure to make progress in the first sense to a combination of repression, ideological bias and sheer stupidity on the part of those who make the awards, accept the articles for publication, appoint to the chairs and formulate government policy. Before we can consider these two opposing views, we need to establish the criteria for judging progress in the second sense. What precisely would our Martian philosopher of science have in mind when deciding whether Post Keynesian economics had made progress, in purely intellectual terms? I shall try to answer this question by reference to the views of three terrestial (if not worldly) philosophers: Karl Popper, Thomas Kuhn and Imre Lakatos.

THE THREE PHILOSOPHERS

Two aspects of Karl Popper's thought are relevant here: his account of the demarcation criterion that separates science from non-science, and his analysis of the conditions under which an inferior theory is replaced by a superior one. These two questions are very closely related. The demarcation criterion is an empirical one. A theory is scientific if and only if it is testable, which for Popper means falsifiable. Scientific hypotheses are susceptible to criticism, revision, supercession and replacement. Competition between theories is therefore fundamental to the process by which science advances. Comparing theories means comparing their empirical content, defined as the class of their potential falsifiers; it is equivalent to comparing their degree of falsifiability. Hence Popper proposes a methodological rule: favour those theories with the highest empirical content, that is, those theories that can be most severely tested. Science makes progress to the extent that the empirical content or falsifiability of its theories is constantly increasing (Popper, 1961, pp. 48–51, 120–21). Alfred Eichner (1983) seems to have had Popper's principles in mind when he argued that neoclassical economics was non-scientific, and mainstream historians of economic thought with an interest in methodology have repeatedly criticized orthodox theorists for paying insufficient attention to falsifiability (Blaug, 1992 [1980]; Hutchison, 1977).

Popper notes that a variety of ingenious strategies may be used by scientists to avoid falsification. These include careful modification of definitions, the voicing of scepticism concerning the reliability of experiments or experimenters and – by far the most difficult to deal with – the formulation of *ad hoc* auxiliary hypotheses to explain away anomalous evidence. These stratagems can be defended by cogent arguments from conventionalist philosophers, and are probably as old as science itself. Popper quotes the chemist J. Black, writing in 1803: 'A nice adaptation of conditions will make almost any hypothesis agree with the phenomena. This will please the imagination but does not advance our knowledge.' The conventionalist arguments, Popper maintains, must simply be ignored, and auxiliary hypotheses rejected unless they serve to increase the degree of falsifiability of the theory, so that 'the system now rules out more than it did previously: it prohibits more' (Popper, 1961, pp. 82–3). Excluding the Great Depression from one's data series, for example, when modelling the relationship between money and output, would be an illegitimate manoeuvre in Popper's eyes (Dow, 1996 [1985], p. 28).

He proposes an additional criterion for choosing between competing theories. A well-corroborated theory is one that has survived a battery of empirical tests without being falsified. Such a theory should be replaced only by one with a higher degree of universality, by which Popper means a theory which is both more testable *and* contains the old theory as a special case (Popper, 1961, p. 276). In effect this is what Keynes claimed for his *general* theory of employment, interest and money, an assertion central to Paul Davidson's insistence that Post Keynesian analysis must apply to perfect competition and imperfect competition alike (Davidson, 1986–7). On the other side of the theoretical divide, we saw in Chapter 1 that some orthodox theorists attempted quite early on to blunt the impact of the *General Theory* by encompassing it as a special case of neoclassical analysis. Similarly, when Frank Hahn maintained that Walrasian general equilibrium theory contained Sraffa's model as a special case he was asserting it to be a more universal system in Popper's sense (Hahn, 1975; see Chapter 4).

For the most part Popper's concern is with the correct procedure that scientists must follow if their work is to advance. In writing about periods of scientific crisis, however, he moves from the prescriptive to the descriptive:

> In such times of crisis this conflict over the aims of science will become acute. We, and those who share our attitude, will hope to make new discoveries; and we

> shall hope to be helped in this by a newly erected scientific system. Thus we shall take the greatest interest in the falsifying experiment. We shall hail it as a success, for it has opened up new vistas into a world of new experiences. And we shall hail it even if these new experiences should furnish us with new arguments against our own most recent theories. But the newly rising structure, the boldness of which we admire, is seen by the conventionalist as a monument to the 'total collapse of science', as Dingler puts it. (Popper, 1961, p. 80)

This suggests a revolutionary view of scientific progress that is more commonly associated with the second of our philosophers, Thomas Kuhn, who reminds us of 'the inextricable connections between our notions of science and of progress' (Kuhn, 1970 [1962], p. 161). It is almost as if we *define* science as that branch of intellectual activity that makes progress – a demarcation criterion far removed from that of Popper. Although the title of his best-known book is *The Structure of Scientific Revolutions*, Kuhn in fact places less emphasis than Popper on crisis and revolutionary change and much more on the mundane activity that he terms 'normal science'. This takes place wherever a group of scientific researchers – a 'scientific community' – is agreed on first principles, sharing a single paradigm that defines the problems to be confronted and the appropriate methods for solving them. A scientific paradigm, for Kuhn, 'identifies challenging puzzles, supplies clues to their solution, and guarantees that the truly clever practitioner will succeed' (ibid., p. 179). Under these circumstances 'the result of successful creative work *is* progress. How could it possibly be anything else?' (ibid., p. 162).

Normal science is very efficient at puzzle solving, in part precisely because scientists who operate within an agreed paradigm are released from the need continually to re-examine first principles. They are therefore able to concentrate on problems that they believe they can solve, assisted by 'the unparalleled insulation of mature scientific communities from the demands of the laity and of everyday life' – though social scientists are less fortunate than natural scientists in this regard (ibid., p. 164). The educational initiation process further encourages progress, since the shared paradigm is handed on from generation to generation through textbooks that incorporate the precepts of received authority. Normal science, then, is innately dogmatic. Indeed Kuhn attributes the lack of progress outside science (in philosophy, for example) to the presence of many competing schools, each questioning the very foundations of all the others.

Nonetheless, progress can also be made through 'extraordinary science'. Again Kuhn inverts the obvious question and asks, not why progress occurs in scientific revolutions, but what else a victorious revolution could possibly be. The advocates of the newly triumphant paradigm necessarily interpret their success as scientific progress:

> When it repudiates a past paradigm, a scientific community simultaneously renounces, as a fit subject for professional scrutiny, most of the books and articles in which that paradigm had been embodied. Scientific education makes use of no equivalent for the art museum or library of classics, and the result is a sometimes drastic distortion in the scientist's perception of his discipline's past....
>
> ... the member of a mature scientific community is, like the typical character of Orwell's *1984*, the victim of a history rewritten by the powers that be. (Ibid., p. 167)

Statements like this have led Kuhn's critics to accuse him of replacing reasoned analysis with majority voting or even mob psychology as the criterion for scientific progress. Imre Lakatos, for example, describes the Kuhnian scientific revolution as 'a contagious panic' (Lakatos, 1978, p. 90). This, however, is exaggerated. Kuhn explicitly denies that 'might makes right' in the sciences, or that authority alone is the arbiter of paradigm debates. If this were the case, and in particular if non-professional authority were to be decisive, 'the outcome of those debates might still be revolution, but it would not be *scientific* revolution.... One of the strongest, if still unwritten, rules of scientific life is the prohibition of appeals to heads of state or to the populace at large in matters scientific' (Kuhn, 1970 [1962], pp. 167–8). This leads to a crucial and often discussed question. If paradigms are all-important, and also incommensurable, what objective criterion can there possibly be for preferring one to another? Is not Kuhn's position on scientific progress irredeemably relativist? This he vigorously denies – up to a point. In the 'evolutionary tree' of science, it is easy to identify the more recent from the earlier theory: its predictions are more accurate, its subject-matter is more esoteric, and the number of problems it has solved is very much greater. Thus

> scientific development is, like biological, a unidirectional and irreversible process. Later scientific theories are better than earlier ones for solving puzzles in the often quite different environments to which they are applied. That is not a relativist's position, and it displays the sense in which I am a convinced believer in scientific progress. (Ibid., p. 206)

But there is a sting in the tail. Since observations are theory-dependent, and paradigms are fundamentally incommensurable, it cannot be claimed that scientific progress involves an ever-closer approach to 'what is "really there"' (ibid., p. 206). Kuhn is not, then, a critical realist (see Chapter 9).

Subject to this – major – qualification, Kuhn offers three criteria for the progress of science, which correspond to three stages in the history of a scientific paradigm. The first stage, which he terms the 'transition to maturity', involves the emergence of a single, well-defined paradigm that permits the scientific community to formulate and solve puzzles. The second stage is the practice of normal science within the dominant paradigm, and the third is the scientific revolution in which it is overthrown by a successful competitor. Neoclassical economists claim to be at the second stage, and to have been there for a very long time – since Adam Smith, according to some accounts (Hollander, 1987), or Jevons according to others (Hutchison, 1978). Since the Cambridge capital controversies of the early 1960s, Post Keynesians have denied the coherence of the mainstream paradigm and therefore by implication (and sometimes explicitly) have also denied the ability of orthodox economists to conduct normal science. In the 1970s they asserted with great confidence not only the coherence of their own paradigm but also the impending scientific revolution that would overturn the neoclassical paradigm and replace it with the Post Keynesian one. Kuhn's ideas were very influential in this period, and can be clearly detected in the writings of, for example, Joan Robinson and Alfred Eichner (see Chapter 6). Neoclassical accusations that the Post Keynesian paradigm was itself incoherent contributed an element of agony to the internal debates on this issue that were summarized in chapter 10.

Although savagely critical of Kuhn, Lakatos can best be viewed as forming a bridge between him and Popper (Dow, 1996 [1985], pp. 33–4). He makes more than Popper had done of the need to test *sets* of theories rather than individual theories. This distinction between 'naïve' and 'sophisticated' falsificationism is required by the Duhem–Quine theorem, which asserts the impossibility of falsifying any individual scientific hypothesis when (as is always the case) it is linked to a number of other, related hypotheses. What Popper had described as a 'series of theories' is termed by Lakatos a scientific research programme. It consists of a 'hard core' of propositions that are regarded as axioms and are therefore immune from falsification, together with a 'protective belt' of lower-level, empirically testable statements (Lakatos, 1978). Economists have been more receptive to Lakatos's work than researchers in almost any other scientific discipline, owing largely, I suspect, to the tireless propaganda war that has been waged in favour of his 'methodology of scientific research programmes' by his former London School of Economics colleague Mark Blaug. At all events, both orthodox and heterodox economists have frequently used Lakatosian ideas, or at least Lakatosian language. Thus Roy Weintraub defined the irrefutable core of the Walrasian research programme to include the assumptions of optimizing behaviour by self-interested economic agents who operate in markets in ways that lead to equilibrium outcomes, and attacked Post Keynesian opponents of general equilibrium analysis for making pointless criticisms of these core propositions (E.R. Weintraub, 1982–3). Similarly, but without explicit reference to Lakatos, Pierangelo Garegnani has defined the core of the Sraffian programme as the determination of the size of the social surplus, given the real wage and the techniques of production (Garegnani, 1987, pp. 560–61). 'Outside the core', in the Lakatosian protective belt, come a number of arguably much more interesting propositions concerning accumulation, growth and the course of income distribution over time (Blaug, 1999).

Lakatos's research programmes have something in common with Kuhnian paradigms, but without any hint of relativism. Most importantly, rival research programmes are *not* deemed to be incommensurable. Lakatos follows Popper, first in making empirical corroboration the key to choice between rival programmes, and second in emphasizing the existence of such a choice as a necessary condition for any scientific progress: 'There is no falsification before the emergence of a better theory' (Lakatos, 1978, p. 35). For this reason he supports 'the slogan of *proliferation of theories*' (ibid., p. 37). Moreover, far from being incommensurable, the new theory must contain much, if not all, of the empirical content of the old one.

How, then, can we know that a new theory is indeed an advance? It must have 'corroborated excess empirical content', which means that it leads to 'the discovery of novel facts'. Conversely, a theory T can be said to be falsified if and only if its rival T* has excess empirical content, *and* T* explains the previous successes of T, *and* some of the excess empirical content of T* is corroborated (ibid., pp. 31–2). Thus Einstein's research programme represented an advance over that of Newton, since it explained everything that Newton's had; it also explained to some extent certain well-known anomalies in the Newtonian programme; it forbade events, permitted by other theories, about which Newton had nothing to say; and some of its excess empirical content was corroborated by experimental evidence. Galileo's research programme, however, could not be judged superior to Ptolemy's on this basis (ibid., pp. 39–40).

The distinction between degenerating and progressive research programmes is central to Lakatos's conception of scientific development, together with the related distinction between degenerating and progressive problem shifts. There is a further important line to be drawn between 'scientific and pseudoscientific adjustments' to a theory under threat, and again the criterion is empirical content: 'Progress is measured by the degree to which a problemshift is progressive, by the degree to which the series of theories leads us to the discovery of novel facts' (ibid., p. 34). But the argument is more complicated than this bare statement may suggest. Lakatos follows Popper once more in stressing 'the relative autonomy of theoretical science' and the need for bold conjectures which are not abandoned at the first sign of experimental difficulty (ibid., p. 49). There is an important role for theory in 'bringing order into the world, of preparing us for future events, of drawing our attention to events we should otherwise never observe' (ibid., p. 89).

A preoccupation with anomalies, in fact, may indicate only scientific immaturity, 'a mere patched up pattern of trial and error' rather than the theoretically informed research that characterizes mature science. Such activity may appear to yield novel facts, since 'one may achieve such "progress" with a patched up, arbitrary series of disconnected theories'. However, 'Good scientists will not find such makeshift progress satisfactory', since it has 'no unifying idea, no heuristic power, no continuity' (ibid., pp. 87–8). Even worse, an obsession with anomalies may point to the degeneration of the research programme, which is beginning to run out of steam (ibid., p. 52). Thus Lakatos advocates both tenacity (even dogmatism) in defence of a scientific research programme under threat from apparent 'refutations', and tolerance of budding but as yet unproven programmes, which should be subjected to positive rather than destructive criticism (ibid., pp. 49, 87–9).

He claims that his criterion for distinguishing scientific progress from scientific retrogression is a powerful one, since it

> shows up the weakness of programmes which, like Marxism or Freudism, are, no doubt, 'unified', which give a major sketch of the sort of auxiliary theories they are going to use in absorbing anomalies, but which unfailingly devise their actual auxiliary theories in the wake of facts without, at the same time, anticipating others. (What *novel* fact has Marxism *predicted* since, say, 1917?). (Ibid., p. 88)

But this is unproblematic only if we can suppose that everyone agrees on the identification of 'novel facts'. I have used inverted commas very deliberately here, since it seems clear that one economist's exciting new discovery is another economist's tedious irrelevancy or unfathomable black hole. Rational expectations and fundamental uncertainty look very different depending on whether you are a New Classical Economist or a Fundamentalist Keynesian, to take two rather obvious examples (see Chapter 9). Rich people undoubtedly save a larger proportion of their income, on average, than poor people, but is this a boring statistical detail or the key to making sense of distribution and growth in a capitalist economy (see Chapter 3)? Lakatos himself twice puts 'facts' in inverted commas when discussing the difficulty of choosing between rival theories (ibid., p. 45), but he does not dwell on the implications. And his ban on retrodiction is very hard to justify, at least in the case of economics. The Great Depression is certainly a fact, or more precisely an event, for which no inverted commas appear necessary. Why should economists be barred from reinterpreting it in the quest for greater understanding, whether or not this significantly increases their chances of predicting the (non-)occurrence of the next cataclysmic economic downturn?

It is much easier to set out the views of our three philosophers on the nature of scientific progress in general than it is to apply them to the evolution of economic ideas. What would Popper say, confronted with the history of Post Keynesian economics between 1936 and 2000? He would almost certainly be unimpressed by the energies that Post Keynesians have directed towards falsifying their own theories, though he would find it difficult to judge them more harshly than the mainstream of the profession on this criterion. Whether the 'empirical content', or falsifiability, of Post Keynesian theory is greater now than it was in 1980, or 1960, is an even more difficult question. Post Keynesians themselves often claim to have made progress in falsifying *neoclassical* theory, but that is a rather different matter. Looking back over the 1970s, for instance, Joan Robinson concluded that the Post Keynesians had done rather well in accounting for the emergence of stagflation and predicting the failure of monetarist policies: 'In economics, hypotheses cannot be tested by controlled experiments, as in the laboratory sciences, but at least it can be claimed that post-Keynesian theory stands up to the test better than the notions of the monetarists' (Robinson, 1979a, p. xx). Whatever the merits of this assessment, Popper might object, it presupposed a verificationist approach to the appraisal of economic theories and was therefore methodologically unsound.

He would also be on the lookout for 'avoidance strategems' used by Post Keynesians to protect themselves from falsification. The increasing adoption of such devices, and in particular the frequent employment of *ad hoc* auxiliary hypotheses to explain away unwelcome negative findings, would be evidence of theoretical retrogression. Clear examples of such behaviour are not easy to find in the Post Keynesian literature. A neoclassical critic might reply, however, that this is because Post Keynesians simply do not do much empirical or applied work in the first place (see the dismissive comments of Robert Solow that were quoted in Chapter 4). This unleashes the dogs of methodological controversy over ergodicity, formalism and the validity of econometrics (see Chapter 9), and threatens to relegate Popper to the sidelines. Given that Post Keynesians and mainstream economists tend to differ profoundly on the correct methods for assessing their respective theories, any comparison of their progress in doing so is fraught with difficulty.

For all their objections to positivism, critical realists sometimes seem to share Popper's criteria for appraising scientific progress. This, for example, is the recently expressed opinion of Tony Lawson:

> Of course, a primary aim of the scientific process remains the pursuit of truth, and it is generally to be hoped that by way of subjecting competing hypotheses to empirical and other forms of assessment, an account emerges that is seen to outperform the others in terms of explanatory power, and the like, and thereby to gain widespread acceptance. But even if and where agreement of this sort is reached, there can be no supposition that the account in question will not be revised or displaced in due course. All knowledge is fallible, partial, and likely transient. Indeed, if progress is to be achieved, continuous transformations in even our currently most explanatorily powerful accounts are to be encouraged. (Lawson, 1999, p. 5)

Truth, explanatory power, the fallibility of all knowledge: there is nothing here that Popper could possibly disagree with. Applying these standards to the history of Post Keynesian economics is, alas, a different matter altogether.

Many Post Keynesians have been attracted to the methodological ideas of Thomas Kuhn – more, I think, than to Popper's thinking. There are three ways in which Kuhn might judge the progress of Post Keynesianism. First, and most dramatically, he would look for evidence of a successful scientific revolution in the course of which the Post Keynesians had established their paradigm on the ruins of neoclassical economics. No sign of progress there! Second, he would search for indications that the Post Keynesians had been practising 'normal science' on the basis of their own paradigm, even if they had not been able to supplant that of the orthodox economists. Relevant evidence for this would include the absence of continuing debate on first principles, on research methods and on methodology. For Kuhn normal science is also associated with a calm, confident and widely shared belief among the scientists concerned that progress is indeed being achieved; such a positive self-assessment is itself an important hallmark of progress. Here the evidence is decidedly mixed, with the continuing methodological controversies and the debates between the different Post Keynesian sub-schools pointing in one direction and a steady trickle of Post Keynesian textbooks and policy interventions in the other (see Chapters 9–10). Finally, Kuhn might consider whether the Post Keynesians had instead been moving towards the practice of normal science from an early, pre-paradigm, stage in their development as a scientific community. This, too, would constitute progress, albeit of a more modest kind. It again raises all the issues of coherence that were central to Chapter 10 and on which, as we saw there, the Post Keynesians themselves have been unable to agree. In all probability the old Scottish verdict of 'not proven' would be the most favourable judgment that Kuhn would be able to come to (again, see Dow, 2000, for a more favourable assessment).

Coherence would also be an important question for Lakatos to consider, since for him the absence of a single 'unifying idea' in Post Keynesian economics would seem to rule out any possibility of scientific progress. If Post Keynesianism did not fall at this first hurdle, it might well refuse at the next one. As we have seen, the discovery of 'novel facts' is problematic even as a general principle. It is especially awkward to apply to a school of thought which has always been deeply concerned with the recovery of lost knowledge, that is to say, with the defence of Keynes's revolution (and Kalecki's) against the resurgence of pre-Keynesian theory. Lakatos's methodology of scientific research programmes was not designed to deal with cases where ideas seem to move in circles over long periods of time. As Dennis Robertson once put it: 'Now, as I have often pointed out to my students, some of whom have been brought up in sporting circles, highbrow opinion is like a hunted hare; if you stand in the same place, or nearly the same place, it can be relied upon to come round to you in a circle' (Robertson, 1954, p. 189).

If, on the other hand, Lakatos were to accept the claims of the neoclassicals to have made significant progress with their research programme, he would be forced to condemn the Post Keynesian programme as a degenerating one. This, of course, is a charge that the Post Keynesians would throw back against their mainstream opponents, and it is not easy to see how Lakatos could decide between them.

Post Keynesians would argue that it was they who had progressed, intellectually if not socially, on several of Backhouse's criteria, while neoclassical macroeconomics had retrogressed. Sidney Weintraub used to summon the ghosts of Newton and Einstein, and to cite his own Wage Cost Mark-up Principle as the economist's equivalent to the gravitational constant in physics (Weintraub, 1959, p. 35; see also Chapter 5). Without going quite that far, Post Keynesians could point to much that is known today that was not available to Keynes. Reswitching and capital reversal, the analytical dangers of the equilibrium method, endogenous money – these could all be presented as new discoveries which constitute real advances in Post Keynesian theory. Whether they are also *important* advances, by comparison with the principle of effective demand, the non-neutrality of money, the ineffectiveness of money wage and price reductions as a remedy for involuntary unemployment – all of which were known to Keynes and contained in the *General Theory* – that is a much harder question to answer. And it should be noted that two of the three sets of 'facts' that I have listed refer to errors in neoclassical analysis and not to the real world in any obvious or direct way. This concentration on internal doctrinal disagreements is a characteristic of economic discourse in general, and it is a feature that has led many outside observers to deny economics the status of a genuine science. The Post Keynesian horse would then have to be scratched from the race, along with all the others.

ALTERNATIVE FUTURES

It is possible to envisage two extreme possibilities for the future of Post Keynesian macroeconomics, and a number of intermediate outcomes. At one extreme *death* is certainly conceivable, as the 1995 appraisal by Peter Groenewegen suggests. We saw in Chapter 6 that a sympathetic observer like Lorie Tarshis was declaring the patient already to be in need of intensive care at the end of the 1970s (Tarshis, 1980). His obituary was premature, but perhaps not very. Fifteen years later Fred Lee wrote another one, more or less simultaneously with Groenewegen's. Lee's study of the impact of the British government's 1992 Research Assessment Exercise disclosed that few Post Keynesians were being appointed to university jobs, senior positions were filled almost exclusively by mainstream economists, and very little Post Keynesian theory was being taught to students. The consequences were obvious:

> Once the initial conditions which gave rise to a new paradigm have passed, its academic success depends almost completely on whether students are inculcated with that view. Mainstream economists know this to be the case, and that is why they insist that all students studying economics only study neoclassical theory in core theory courses, and why they attempt to eliminate Post Keynesian optional courses – if students read, hear and speak no evil they will become 'proper' economists. (Lee, 1995, p. 2)

Lee's remedies were contentious:

> Post Keynesians must take the controversial steps of eliminating mainstream economics from their own courses and of attempting to teach Post Keynesian economic theory on core theory courses. Without taking these personal steps, there will be no future for Post Keynesian economics and the epitaph on its tombstone will read: Death by Failure of the Will to Live. (Ibid., p. 2)

Relatively few Post Keynesians were willing to go that far, but the problem that Lee identified is a serious one. If the most prominent Post Keynesian economists are 'greying', and if the school is indeed failing to attract a replacement cohort of bright young scholars, then it can expect to fade away to nothing by 2020. The post-mortem will reveal both 'internal' and 'external' causes of death: inability to make progress in an intellectual sense, compounded by repression from the neoclassical mainstream that contributed to its failure in the socio-institutional dimensions.

At the other extreme, a *new scientific revolution* might occur, in which the old and discredited neoclassical paradigm is abandoned in favour of a revitalized Post Keynesianism. Certainly orthodox economics is full of problems, which cast doubt on the future of its own methods, analysis and policy prescriptions. Its practitioners sometimes seem to be obsessed by techniques, often to the point of decadence; what is worse, they are often the wrong techniques (Ormerod, 1994). Since the collapse of the long-standing Walrasian research programme, neoclassical economics lacks a central organizing principle that carries intellectual conviction. As we saw in Chapter 10, there are grounds for questioning its own claims to coherence. And mainstream theory generates policy proposals that are based on implausible analysis (Say's Law; rational expectations; zero involuntary unemployment) and lead to unexpected and/or wholly unacceptable results (mass unemployment; financial instability; huge increases in inequality). Since neoclassical economists often take credit for the achievements of global neoliberal capitalism, they can hardly complain when they are blamed for its failures. In the 1990s students were already voting with their feet, giving up economics to concentrate on more relevant and less formalistic (if also rather less challenging) alternatives, and business people and policy makers seemed increasingly to find it useless for their more practical purposes (Smithin, 1996a). Even a minimally coherent Post Keynesian school ought, in these circumstances, to be able to outperform the mainstream, given the opportunity to do so.

Two comments are in order on this optimistic scenario. First, it is in the nature of revolutions that they are unpredictable and happen (when they do happen) very fast. This is as true of scientific as it is of political and social upheavals: even the original 'Keynesian Revolution' in the United States in the late 1930s and early 1940s was a sudden affair (Colander and Landreth, 1996). Although the neoclassical synthesis that emerged from it proved to be entirely unsatisfactory, this quite recent example indicates that the pessimism of Groenewegen and Lee may yet prove to be unfounded. Of course, the demise of neoclassical economics may result in the triumph not of Post Keynesianism but of some quite different – and perhaps entirely new – form of heterodoxy. Second, it must never be forgotten that economic theory is not an island, cut off from the main course of human history. The fate of Post Keynesianism will depend very heavily on the future development of the world capitalist economy. If the business cycle has indeed been abolished (this time), so that stable, non-inflationary growth continues indefinitely under something approximating to the present neoclassical (or pseudo-monetarist) policy consensus, then there is unlikely to be a significant market for Post Keynesian ideas. Things would be very different in the event of a new Great Depression, to think one last time in terms of extreme possibilities. If 'It' happened again, to quote Hyman Minsky (1982), the appeal of both a radical interventionist programme and the analysis from which it was derived would be very greatly enhanced.

What of the less dramatic alternative futures for Post Keynesianism? I think there are four intermediate possibilities. *Migration* to 'non-economics', that is, to one or more of the other social sciences, is by no means unthinkable. It has already been proposed as a means of saving the history of economic thought, a branch of the discipline whose impending demise has also been diagnosed as a probable consequence of mainstream hostility or indifference (Schabas, 1992). Alistair Dow hinted at this in his response to Lee:

> There are other departments than those of economics. In the UK for example, departments of sociology and business (very often involving people trained in economics) are taking an interest in economic matters concerning the firm and the

> nature of economic development (generally local development). Avoiding rigid disciplinary boundaries and scholarly elitism is surely the right road for Post Keynesians. (A. Dow, 1995, p. 1)

In universities, at least, political scientists and sociologists are much more tolerant of dissenting perspectives than their colleagues in economics departments. Outside the academy, policy institutions and research foundations are often multidisciplinary in staffing and outlook, and for that reason alone are less hostile to heterodox economic ideas.

But all migrants (and here I write from personal experience) suffer some degree of loss. They have to renounce familiar surroundings, deny themselves access to family and friends, and sometimes sacrifice the recognition of their qualifications and experience. These personal costs of migration have their counterparts in intellectual life. Non-orthodox economists who already work with specialists from other disciplines encounter serious problems in communicating with them; being multidisciplinary, in fact, is very hard to do. For this reason *absorption into the mainstream* is quite an attractive option, at least for some Post Keynesians. For all their differences, Post Keynesians share with their neoclassical colleagues substantial components of 'the economic way of thinking'. Often in spite of themselves, they are drawn to formal modelling, that is, to the 'partial' use of closed-system reasoning in particular circumstances as a means of seeking answers to specific, narrowly defined questions. Many Post Keynesians make heavy use of statistical data, with or without elaborate econometric processing, though never to the exclusion of all other sources of evidence. And they remain, for the most part, stubbornly consequentialist on matters of ethics, which makes them much more prone than other social scientists to reject overarching 'principles' and to take a cold-blooded means–ends approach to policy issues. Almost all Post Keynesians were trained as economists. And many of them are very competent (if also sceptical) practitioners of the art. More dialogue, more cooperation, less ideology, fewer polemics – this is surely one conceivable way to go (Fontana et al., 1998).

It takes two to tango, however. At the time of writing there are very few signs that neoclassical economists have any great sense of rhythm. Thus a more plausible strategy for Post Keynesians might be to seek *incorporation into a broader heterodox economic tradition*. This was advocated, in response to Lee's obituary, by Jan Toporowski, 'someone who does not naturally regard himself as a Post Keynesian' but had benefited greatly from his membership of the tolerant and ecumenical Post Keynesian Study Group in the United Kingdom. He was concerned about the possibility of a retreat into a 'Post Keynesian ghetto' in the face of persecution by the mainstream (Toporowski, 1996b, p. 3). A strategy of incorporation was also endorsed by

Stephen Dunn (2000), this time on methodological grounds. Since Post Keynesians shared a commitment to open-systems thinking with institutionalists, Austrians, Schumpeterians, management theorists and others, he argued, there was no reason why closer collaboration should not be mutually beneficial. Similar conclusions were reached by Paul Downward (1996) and by Arestis et al. (1999), whose case rested also on the compatibility of Post Keynesian policy proposals with the position of other non-orthodox schools. Potential allies might also include the radical–Marxians whose ideas were discussed in Chapter 11, together with feminists, post-Marshallian microeconomists and environmentalists. Post Keynesians have a lot to offer these groupings, especially in terms of macroeconomics where institutionalists and feminists, for example, have always been rather weak. They also have a great deal to gain on questions of human agency, belief structures and the theory of the firm, which are issues that Post Keynesians have tended to neglect.

To some extent this process of collaboration is already happening. There is an Association of Heterodox Economists in Britain, with strong Post Keynesian involvement, a Progressive Economic Forum in Canada, and a fledgling Association for Social and Political Economy in Australia, while in the United States the Union for Radical Political Economics has always been a rather ecumenical organization. There is even an International Confederation of Associations for the Reform of Economics – ICARE (*http://www.econ.tcu.edu/icare/main.html*). Commercial publishers have begun to identify a market niche, which they have attempted to fill, for example with Edward Elgar's *Biographical Dictionary of Dissenting Economists*, edited by two Post Keynesians and now into a second edition (Arestis and Sawyer, 2000 [1992]), and Routledge's *Encyclopaedia of Political Economy*, assembled by an institutionalist with help from a number of Post Keynesian economists (O'Hara, 1999). There are, however, continuing sources of conflict between the various heterodox schools and a constant, if often unspoken, anxiety that the hard-won coherence of Post Keynesianism might be lost in a formless anti-neoclassical morass:

> I don't think [Post Keynesianism] can succeed if the expression is simply a generic term for any and all approaches to the subject which claim to oppose mainstream economics from the left. Many of these 'non-mainstream' approaches are flatly incompatible with one another in terms both of theoretical principles and of 'world view', and are far from presenting a credible united front to potential converts. (Smithin, 1996a, p. 3)

Thus fission may prove to be a more likely outcome than fusion, just as evolutionary economics appears to face a split between mathematical model builders and the opponents of formalism.

On balance, continued *survival as an embattled minority* appears to me to be the medium-term fate of Post Keynesian economics. *Survival*, because there is real analytical merit in the Post Keynesian tradition, and enough substance in the literature on method, theory and policy that has grown up since 1936 to exercise some appeal, not only to radical critics of the existing social order but also to pragmatic conservatives in business schools and their clients, who have lost patience with the baroque designs of mainstream economic theory. Even in the dumbed-down academy of the 2000s there will remain some space for the continued propagation of dissenting economics, if only in small colleges and other hitherto obscure institutions. (Two cases in point are the emergence of the Jerome Levy Economics Institute at Bard College as a significant centre for the dissemination of Post Keynesian monetary theory in the early 1990s, and of a powerful agglomeration of Post Keynesians at the University of Missouri/Kansas City by the end of that decade.) *Minority* status because, short of an economic cataclysm, it is difficult to see neoclassical economics succumbing to a Post Keynesian attack. There is simply no Kuhnian revolution in prospect. *Embattled*, since there are real issues of great importance that continue to divide the Post Keynesians from their mainstream opponents, and substantial theoretical, social, political and institutional barriers to dialogue between them. What else is new?

NOTE

1. Anonymous, undated referee's report, probably from early 1971, Sidney Weintraub Papers, Special Collections Department, Duke University Library, Durham, North Carolina, Box 2, Folder 3.

References

Aglietta, M. (1979) *A Theory of Capitalist Regulation: the US Experience*, London: New Left Books; 2nd edn, London: Verso, 1999.

Ahmad, S. (1991) *Capital in Economic Theory: Neoclassical, Cambridge, and Chaos*, Aldershot, UK and Brookfield, US: Edward Elgar.

Anderson, P. (1976) *Considerations on Western Marxism*, London: New Left Books.

Andrews, P.W.S. (1949) *Manufacturing Business*, London: Macmillan.

Anon. (1997) 'Play it again, Samuelson. What is the role of a basic economics textbook?', *The Economist* 23, August, p. 58.

Arena, R. (1987) 'L'école internationale d'été de Trieste (1981–5): vers une synthèse classico-keynesienne?' ('The international Trieste summer school (1981–5): towards a classical–Keynesian synthesis?'), *Oeconomica* 7, March, pp. 205–38.

Arestis, P. (1989) 'Pricing, distribution and growth: the economics of A.S. Eichner', *Review of Political Economy* 1(1), March, pp. 7–22.

Arestis, P. (1992) *The Post Keynesian Approach to Economics: an Alternative Analysis of Economic Theory and Policy*, Aldershot, UK and Brookfield, US: Edward Elgar.

Arestis, P. (1996) 'Post-Keynesian economics: towards coherence', *Cambridge Journal of Economics* 20(1), January, pp. 111–35.

Arestis, P. and Sawyer, M. (1998) 'Keynesian economic policies for the new millennium', *Economic Journal* 108(446), January, pp. 181–95.

Arestis, P. and Sawyer, M. (1999a) 'What role for the Tobin tax in world economic governance?', in J. Michie and J. Grieve Smith (eds), *Global Instability: the Political Economy of World Economic Goverance*, London: Routledge, pp. 151–70.

Arestis, P. and Sawyer, M.C. (1999b) 'The macroeconomics of New Labour', *Economic Issues* 4(1), March, pp. 39–57.

Arestis, P. and Sawyer, M. (2000) [1992] *Biographical Dictionary of Dissenting Economists*, 2nd edn, Cheltenham, UK and Northampton, MA, USA: Edward Elgar.

Arestis, P., Dunn, S.P. and Sawyer, M. (1999) 'Post Keynesian economics and its critics', *Journal of Post Keynesian Economics* 21(4), Summer, pp. 527–49.

Arestis, P., Tool, M.R. and Street, J.H. (1988) 'In memoriam: Alfred S. Eichner 1937–1988', *Journal of Economic Issues* 22(4), December, pp. 1239–42.

Asimakopulos, A. (1971) 'The determination of investment in Keynes's model', *Canadian Journal of Economics* 4(3), August, pp. 382–8.

Asimakopulos, A. (1983) 'Kalecki and Keynes on finance, investment and saving', *Cambridge Journal of Economics* 7(3–4), September–December, pp. 221–33.

Asimakopulos, A. and Burbidge, J.B. (1974) 'The short-period incidence of taxation', *Economic Journal* 84(334), June, pp. 267–88.

Backhouse, R.E. (1997) *Truth and Progress in Economic Knowledge*, Cheltenham, UK and Lyme, US: Edward Elgar.

Backhouse, R.E. (ed.) (1999) *Keynes: Contemporary Responses to the General Theory*, South Bend, Indiana: St. Augustine's Press.

Ball, T. (1979) [1995] 'Marx and Darwin: a reconsideration', *Reappraising Political Theory*, Oxford: Oxford University Press, pp. 229–49.

Baran, P.A. and Sweezy, P.M. (1966) *Monopoly Capital*, New York: Monthly Review Press; reprinted Harmondsworth: Penguin, 1970.

Baranzini, M. and Harcourt, G.C. (eds) (1993) *The Dynamics of the Wealth of Nations: Growth, Distribution and Structural Change. Essays in Honour of Luigi Pasinetti*, London: Macmillan.

Barna, T. (1957) Review of Robinson (1956), *Economic Journal* 67 (267), September, pp. 490–93.

Bateman, B. (1990) 'Keynes, induction and econometrics', *History of Political Economy* 22(2), Summer, pp. 359–79.

Bellante, D. (1992) 'The fork in the Keynesian road: Post-Keynesians and Neo-Keynesians', in M. Skousen (ed.), *Dissent on Keynes: a Critical Appraisal of Keynesian Economics*, New York: Praeger, pp. 117–29.

Bellofiore, R. (ed.) (1986) *Tra Teoria Economica e Grande Cultura Europea: Piero Sraffa* (*Between Economic Theory and High European Culture: Piero Sraffa*), Milan: Franco Angeli.

Berlin, I. (1953) *The Hedgehog and the Fox: an Essay on Tolstoy's View of History*, London: Weidenfeld & Nicolson.

Besomi, D. (1999) *The Making of Harrod's Dynamics*, London: Macmillan.

Bhaduri, A. (1966) 'The concept of the marginal productivity of capital and the Wicksell effect', *Oxford Economic* Papers 18(3), November, pp. 284–8.

Bhaduri, A. (1996) 'Economic growth and the theory of capital: an evaluation of Joan Robinson's contribution', in M.C. Marcuzzo, L.L. Pasinetti and A. Roncaglia (eds), *The Economics of Joan Robinson*, London: Routledge, pp. 200–206.

Bhaduri, A. and Robinson, J. (1980) 'Accumulation and exploitation: an analysis in the tradition of Marx, Sraffa and Kalecki', *Cambridge Journal of Economics* 4(2), June, pp. 103–16.

Bhaduri, A. and Steindl, J. (1983) 'The rise of monetarism as a social doctrine', *Thames Papers in Political Economy*, Autumn, p. 18.

Bharadwaj, K. and Schefold, B. (eds) (1990) *Essays on Piero Sraffa: Critical Perspectives on the Revival of Classical Theory*, London: Unwin Hyman.

Bhaskar, R. (1975) *A Realist Theory of Science*, Leeds: Harvester Press.

Birner, J. (1996) 'Cambridge histories true and false', in M.C. Marcuzzo, L.L. Pasinetti and A. Roncaglia (eds), *The Economics of Joan Robinson*, London: Routledge, pp. 223–31.

Black, J. (1962) 'The technical progress function and the production function', *Economica* n.s. 29(114), May, pp. 166–70.

Blaug, M. (1974) *The Cambridge Revolution: Success or Failure? A Critical Analysis of Cambridge Theories of Value and Distribution*, London: Institute of Economic Affairs.

Blaug, M. (1992) [1980] *The Methodology of Economics: Or How Economists Explain*, Cambridge: Cambridge University Press.

Blaug, M. (1999) 'Misunderstanding classical economics: the Sraffian interpretation of the surplus approach', *History of Political Economy* 31(2), Summer, pp. 213–36.

Blinder, A. (1987) *Hard Heads, Soft Hearts: Tough-Minded Economics for a Just Society*, Reading, MA: Addison-Wesley.

Bodkin, R.G., Klein, L.R. and Marwah, K. (1988) 'Keynes and the origins of macroeconometric modelling', in O.F. Hamouda and J. Smithin (eds), *Keynes and Public Policy After Fify Years. Volume 2: Theories and Method*, Aldershot, UK and Brookfield, US: Edward Elgar, pp. 3–13.

Bortis, H. (1997) *Institutions, Behaviour and Economic Theory: a Contribution to Classical–Keynesian Political Economy*, Cambridge: Cambridge University Press.

Boulding, K.E. (1950) 'Models for a macro-economic theory of distribution', and 'The background and structure of a macro-economic theory of distribution', in C.L. Christianson (ed.), *Economic Theory in Review*, Bloomington, IN: Indiana University Press, pp. 61–95.

Bowles, S., Gordon, D.M. and Weisskopf, T. (1983) *Beyond the Wasteland: a Democratic Alternative to Economic Decline*, New York: Anchor/Doubleday.

Boyer, R. (1990) *The Regulation School: a Critical Introduction*, New York: Columbia University Press.

Bradford, W. and Harcourt, G.C. (1997) 'Units and definitions', in G.C. Harcourt and P.A. Riach (eds), *A Second Edition of The General Theory*, volume 1, London: Routledge, pp. 107–31.

Brainard, W. and Tobin, J. (1968) 'Pitfalls in financial model building',

American Economic Review 58(2), May, Papers and Proceedings, pp. 99–122.

Brazelton, W.R. (1981) 'Post Keynesian economics. An institutional compatibility?', *Journal of Economic Issues* 15(2), June, pp. 531–42.

Bronfenbrenner, M. (1960) 'A note on relative shares and the elasticity of substitution', *Journal of Political Economy* 68(3), June, pp. 284–7.

Bronfenbrenner, M. and Holzman, F.D. (1963) 'Survey of inflation theory', *American Economic Review* 53(4), September, pp. 593–661.

Brown, E.H. Phelps (1972) 'The underdevelopment of economics', *Economic Journal* 82(325), March, pp. 1–10.

Caldwell, B.J. (1982) *Beyond Positivism: Economic Methodology in the Twentieth Century*, London: Allen & Unwin.

Caldwell, B.J. (1989) 'Post Keynesian methodology: an assessment', *Review of Political Economy* 1(1), April, pp. 43–64.

Carabelli, A. (1988) *On Keynes's Method*, London: Macmillan.

Champernowne, D. (1936) 'Unemployment, basic and monetary: the classical analysis and the Keynesian', *Review of Economic Studies* 3, June, pp. 201–16.

Chapple, S. (1995) 'The Kaleckian origins of the Keynesian model', *Oxford Economic Papers* 47(3), July, pp. 525–37.

Chick, V. (1973) *The Theory of Monetary Policy*, London: Gray-Mills.

Chick, V. (1983) *Macroeconomics after Keynes: a Reconsideration of the General Theory*, Doddington: Philip Allan.

Chick, V. (1985) 'The evolution of the banking system and the theory of saving, investment and interest', *Économies et Sociétés* 20(8–9), August–September, pp. 1111–26; reprinted in Chick (1992) *On Money, Method and Keynes: Selected Essays By Victoria Chick*, London: Macmillan, pp. 193–205.

Chick, V. (1987) 'Townshend, Hugh (1890–1974)', in J. Eatwell, M. Milgate and P. Newman (eds), *The New Palgrave: a Dictionary of Economics, Volume IV*, London: Macmillan, p. 662.

Chick, V. (1992a) *On Money, Method and Keynes: Selected Essays by Victoria Chick*, London: Macmillan.

Chick, V. (1992b) 'Victoria Chick (born 1936)', in P. Arestis and M. Sawyer (eds), *Biographical Dictionary of Dissenting Economists*, Aldershot, UK and Brookfield, US: Edward Elgar, pp. 81–6.

Coates, J. (1996) *The Claims of Common Sense: Moore, Wittgenstein, Keynes and the Social Sciences*, Cambridge: Cambridge University Press.

Coats, A.W. (ed.) (1996) *The Post-1945 Internationalization of Economics*, Durham, NC: Duke University Press.

Coddington, A. (1976) 'Keynesian economics: the search for first principles', *Journal of Economic Literature* 14(4), December, pp. 1258–73.

Cohen, A.J. (1993) 'Does Joan Robinson's critique of equilibrium entail theoretical nihilism?', in G. Mongiovi and C. Rühl (eds), *Macroeconomic Theory: Diversity and Convergence*, Aldershot, UK and Brookfield, US: Edward Elgar, pp. 222–39.

Colander, D.C. and Landreth, H. (1996) 'Lorie Tarshis', *The Coming of Keynesianism to America: Conversations With the Founders of Keynesian Economics*, Cheltenham, UK and Brookfield, US: Edward Elgar, pp. 49–72.

Comim, F. (1999) 'Forms of life and "horses for courses": introductory remarks', *Economic Issues* 4(1), March, pp. 21–37.

Cornwall, J. (1989) *The Theory of Economic Breakdown: an Institutional–Analytical Approach*, Oxford: Blackwell.

Cornwall, J. (1994) *Economic Breakdown and Recovery: Theory and Policy*, Aromonk, NY: Sharpe.

Cottrell, A. (1994) 'Post Keynesian monetary economics', *Cambridge Journal of Economics* 18(6), December, pp. 587–605.

Cowling, K. (1982) *Monopoly Capitalism*, London: Macmillan.

Crane, D. (ed.) (1981) *Beyond the Monetarists: Post-Keynesian Alternatives to Rampant Inflation, Low Growth and High Unemployment*, Toronto: James Lorimer and Canadian Institute for Economic Policy.

Cross, R. (1993) 'Hysteresis and Post Keynesian economics', *Journal of Post Keynesian Economics* 15(3), Spring, pp. 305–8.

Crotty, J.R. (1980) 'Post Keynesian economic theory: an overview and evaluation', *American Economic Review* 70(2), Papers and Proceedings, pp. 20–5.

Curtis, M. and Townshend, H. (1937) *Modern Money*, London: Harrap.

Darity, W. Jr. and Young, W. (1995) 'IS–LM: an inquest', *History of Political Economy* 27(1), Spring, pp. 1–41.

David, P. (1993) 'Historical economics in the longrun: some implications of path-dependence', in G. Snooks (ed.), *Historical Analysis in Economics*, London: Routledge, pp. 29–40.

Davidson, P. (1960) *Theories of Aggregate Income Distribution*, New Brunswick, NJ: Rutgers University Press.

Davidson, P. (1965) 'Keynes's finance motive', *Economic Papers* 17(1), March, pp. 47–65; reprinted in Davidson (ed.) (1991), *Money and Employment: the Collected Writings of Paul Davidson, Volume 1*, London: Macmillan, 1991, pp. 11–31.

Davidson, P. (1968a) 'Money, portfolio balance, capital accumulation, and economic growth', *Econometrica* 36(2), April, pp. 291–321.

Davidson, P. (1968b) 'Statement', in *Compendium on Monetary Policy Guidelines and Federal Reserve Structure*, Subcommittee on Domestic Finance, House Committee on Banking and Currency, US 90th Congress, second session, December 1968, Washington, DC: US Government Printing Office, pp. 130–42; reprinted as 'The role of monetary policy in overall economic policy' in Davidson (ed.) (1991), *Money and Employment: the Collected Writings of Paul Davidson, Volume 1*, London: Macmillan, 1991, pp. 95–109.

Davidson, P. (1972a [1978]) *Money and the Real World*, London: Macmillan.

Davidson, P. (1972b) 'Money and the real world', *Economic Journal* 82(325), March, pp. 101–15.

Davidson, P. (1972c) 'A Keynesian view of Friedman's theoretical framework for monetary analysis', *Journal of Political Economy* 80(5), September–October, pp. 864–82.

Davidson, P. (1982) *International Money and the Real World*, London: Macmillan.

Davidson, P. (1982–3) 'Rational expectations: a fallacious foundation for studying crucial decision-making processes', *Journal of Post Keynesian Economics* 5(2), Winter, pp. 182–96.

Davidson, P. (1983) 'The marginal product curve is not the demand curve for labor and Lucas's labor supply function is not the supply curve for labor in the real world', *Journal of Post Keynesian Economics* 6(1), Fall, pp. 105–17.

Davidson, P. (1986–7) 'The simple macroeconomics of a nonergodic monetary economy vs a share economy: is Weitzman's macroeconomics too simple?', *Journal of Post Keynesian Economics* 9(2), Winter, pp. 212–25.

Davidson, P. (1989) 'The economics of ignorance or ignorance of economics?', *Critical Review* 3(3–4), Summer/Fall, pp. 467–87.

Davidson, P. (1992) 'Would Keynes be a New Keynesian?', *Eastern Economic Journal* 18(4), Fall, pp. 449–63.

Davidson, P. (1993) 'The elephant and the butterfly: or hysteresis and Post Keynesian economics', *Journal of Post Keynesian Economics* 15(3), Spring, pp. 309–22.

Davidson, P. (1994) *Post Keynesian Macroeconomic Theory: A Foundation for Successful Economic Policies for the Twenty-first Century*, Aldershot, UK and Brookfield, US: Edward Elgar.

Davidson, P. (1999a) 'Keynes' principle of effective demand versus the bedlam of the New Keynesians', *Journal of Post Keynesian Economics* 21(4), Summer, pp. 571–88.

Davidson, P. (1999b) 'Taxonomy, communication and rhetorical strategy', *Journal of Post Keynesian Economics* 22(1), Fall, pp. 125–9.

Davidson, P. (2002) 'Policies for fighting speculation in foreign exchange markets: the Tobin tax versus Keynes's views', in S.C. Dow and J. Hillard (eds), *Keynes, Uncertainty and the Global Economy: Beyond Keynes, Volume Two*, Cheltenham, UK and Northampton, US: Edward Elgar, pp. 201–222.

Davidson, G. and Davidson, P. (1988) *Economics For a Civilized Society*, New York: Norton.

Davidson, P. and Smolensky, E. (1964) *Aggregate Supply and Demand Analysis*, New York: Harper & Row.

Davidson, P. and Weintraub, S. (1973) 'Money as cause and effect', *Economic Journal* 83(332), December, pp. 1117–32.

Davis, J.B. (1994) *Keynes's Philosophical Development*, Cambridge: Cambridge University Press.

De Cecco, M. (1989) 'Keynes and Italian economics', in P.A. Hall (ed.), *The Political Power of Economic Ideas: Keynesianism Across Nations*, Princeton: Princeton University Press, pp. 195–229.

Deleplace, G. and Nell, E.J. (eds) (1996) *Money in Motion: the Post Keynesian and Circulation Approaches*, London: Macmillan.

De Vroey, M. (1998) 'Accounting for involuntary unemployment in neoclassical theory: some lessons from sixty years of uphill struggle', in R. Backhouse, D. Hausman and A. Salanti (eds), *Economics and Methodology: Crossing Boundaries*, London: Macmillan, pp. 177–224.

De Vroey, M. (2000) 'IS–LM à la Hicks versus IS–LM à la Modigliani', *History of Political Economy* 32(2), Summer, pp. 293–316.

Dillard, D. (1948) *The Economics of John Maynard Keynes: the Theory of a Monetary Economy*, New York: Prentice-Hall.

Dillard, D. (1984) 'Keynes and Marx: a centenary appraisal', *Journal of Post Keynesian Economics* 6(3), Spring, pp. 421–32.

Dillard, D. (1989) 'The paradox of money in the economics of Joan Robinson', in G.R. Feiwel (ed.), *The Economics of Imperfect Competition and Employment: Joan Robinson and Beyond*, London: Macmillan, pp. 599–612.

Dixon, R. (1982–3) 'On the New Cambridge school', *Journal of Post Keynesian Economics* 5(2), Winter, pp. 289–94.

Dixon, R.J. (1988) *Production, Distribution and Value: a Marxist Approach*, Brighton: Wheatsheaf.

Dobb, M.H. (1929) 'A sceptical view of the theory of wages', *Economic Journal* 39(156), December, pp. 506–19.

Dobb, M. (1939) 'An economist from Poland', *Daily Worker* 22 March, p. 8.

Dornbusch, R. and Fischer, S. (1990) *Macroeconomics*, New York: McGraw-Hill.

Douglas, P.H. (1948) 'Are there laws of production?', *American Economic Review* 38(1), March, pp. 1–41.

Dow, A. (1995) 'The future of Post Keynesianism', *Post Keynesian Study Group Newsletter* 2, April, pp. 1–2.

Dow, S.C. (1991) 'Review of Carabelli (1988) and O'Donnell (1989)', *Economics and Philosophy* 7(1), April, pp. 132–9.

Dow, S.C. (1992a) 'Postmodernism and economics', in J. Doherty, E, Graham

and M. Malek (eds), *Postmodernism and the Social Sciences*, London: Macmillan, pp. 148–61.
Dow, S.C. (1992b) 'Post-Keynesian methodology: a comment' (on Caldwell 1989), *Review of Political Economy* 4(1), pp. 111–13.
Dow, S.C. (1996 [1985]) *The Methodology of Macroeconomic Thought: a Conceptual Analysis of Schools of Thought in Economics*, Aldershot, UK and Brookfield, US: Edward Elgar.
Dow, S.C. (1997) 'Mainstream economic methodology', *Cambridge Economic Journal* 21(1), January, pp. 73–93.
Dow, S.C. (1998) 'Knowledge, information and credit creation', in R. Rotheim (ed.), *New Keynesian Economics/Post Keynesian Alternatives*, London: Routledge, pp. 214–26.
Dow, S.C. (1999) 'Post Keynesianism and critical realism: what are the connections?', *Journal of Post Keynesian Economics* 22(1), Fall, pp. 15–34.
Dow, S.C. (2000) 'Prospects for the progress of heterodox economics', *Journal of the History of Economic Thought* 22(2), June, pp. 157–70.
Dow, S.C. and Earl, P.E. (1982) *Money Matters: a Keynesian Approach to Monetary Economics*, Oxford: Martin Robertson.
Downward, P. (1996) 'The future of the Post Keynesian Study Group', *Post Keynesian Study Group Newsletter* 4, January, pp. 6–8.
Downward, P. (2000) 'A realist appraisal of Post Keynesian pricing theory', *Cambridge Journal of Economics* 24(2), March, pp. 211–24.
Downward, P. and Mearman, A. (2000) 'Critical realism and econometrics: constructive dialogue with Post Keynesian economics', mimeo, presented at Cambridge Realist Workshop Conference, 'Critical realism in economics: what difference does it make?', Cambridge, 5–7 May.
Dugger, W.M. and Sherman, H.J. (1994) 'Comparison of Marxism and institutionalism', *Journal of Economic Issues* 28(1), March, pp. 101–28.
Dunlop, J.T. (1938) 'The movement of real and money wage rates', *Economic Journal* 48(191), September, pp. 413–34.
Dunn, S.P. (2000) 'Wither Post Keynesianism?', *Journal of Post Keynesian Economics*, 22(3), Spring, pp. 343–64.
Dutt, A.K. and Amadeo, E.J. (1990) *Keynes's Third Alternative? The Neo-Ricardian Keynesians and the Post Keynesians*, Aldershot, UK and Brookfield, US: Edward Elgar.
Dymski, G. and Pollin, R. (1992) 'Hyman Minsky as hedgehog: the power of the Wall Street paradigm', in S. Fazzari and D.B. Papadimitriou (eds), *Financial Conditions and Macroeconomic Performance: Essays in Honor of Hyman P. Minsky*, Armonk, NY: Sharpe, pp. 27–61.
Earl, P.E. (1990) *Monetary Scenarios: a Modern Approach to Financial Systems*, Aldershot, UK and Brookfield, US: Edward Elgar.

Earl, P.E. (1996) 'Shackle, entrepreneurship and the theory of the firm', in S. Pressman (ed.), *Interactions in Political Economy: Malvern after Ten Years*, London: Routledge, pp. 43–60.

Eatwell, J. (1983) 'The long-period theory of employment', *Cambridge Journal of Economics* 7(3–4), September–December, pp. 269–85.

Eichner, A.S. (1973) 'A theory of the determination of the mark-up under oligopoly', *Economic Journal* 83(332), December, pp. 1184–1200.

Eichner, A.S. (ed.) (1979) *A Guide to Post Keynesian Economics*, London: Macmillan.

Eichner, A.S. (1983) 'Why economics is not yet a science', in Eichner (ed.), *Why Economics is Not Yet a Science*, London: Macmillan, pp. 205–41.

Eichner, A.S. (1987) *The Macrodynamics of Advanced Market Economies*, Armonk, NY: Sharpe.

Eichner, A.S. (1991) *The Macrodynamics of Advanced Market Economies*, 2nd edn, Armonk, NY: Sharpe.

Eichner, A.S. and Kregel, J.A. (1975) 'An essay on Post Keynesian theory: a new paradigm in economics', *Journal of Economic Literature* 13(4), December, pp. 1293–1314.

Elliott, L. (1998) 'Superpower update: US is morally bankrupt, Russia just bankrupt', *Guardian* (London), 25 August.

Fazzari, S. (1992) 'Introduction: conversations with Hyman Minsky', in S.F. Fazzari and D.B. Papadimitriou (eds), *Financial Conditions and Macroeconomic Performance: Essays in Honor of Hyman P. Minsky*, Armonk, NY: Sharpe, pp. 3–12.

Fazzari, S. and Papadimitirou, D.B. (eds) (1992) *Financial Conditions and Macroeconomic Performance: Essays in Honor of Hyman P. Minsky*, Armonk, N.Y.: Sharpe.

Feiwel, G.R. (1975) *The Intellectual Capital of Michal Kalecki: a Study in Economic Theory and Policy*, Knoxville: University of Tennessee Press.

Fels, R. (1972) 'Editor's introduction', *American Economic Review* 62(2), May, Papers and Proceedings, pp. ix–x.

Ferguson, C.E. (1969) *The Neoclassical Theory of Production and Distribution*, Cambridge: Cambridge University Press.

Fine, B. (2000) 'Economics imperialism and intellectual progress: the present as history of economic thought', *History of Economics Review* 32, Summer, pp. 10–36.

Fish, S.E. (1994) *There's No Such Thing As Free Speech, and It's a Good Thing, Too*, New York: Oxford University Press, pp. 10–36.

Fisher, F.M. (1969) 'The existence of aggregate production functions', *Econometrica* 37(4), October, pp. 553–77.

Fisher, F.M. (1998) 'My career in economics: a hindcast', in A. Heertje (ed.),

The Makers of Modern Economics, Volume III, Cheltenham, UK and Lyme, US: Edward Elgar, pp. 32–54

Fitzgibbons, A. (1988) *Keynes's Vision: a New Political Economy*, Oxford: Clarendon Press.

Fleming, G.A. (1994) 'Some problems in interpreting citation practices in the *Economic Record*, 1925–1946', *History of Economics Review* 22, Summer, pp. 1–15.

Foley, D.K. (1999) 'The ins and outs of late twentieth-century economics', in A. Heertje (ed.), *Makers of Modern Economics. Volume IV*, Cheltenham, UK and Northampton, MA, USA: Edward Elgar, pp. 70–118.

Fontana, G., Gerrard, B. and Hillard, J. (1998) 'The Death of Post Keynesian Economics?', mimeo, University of Leeds.

Ford, J.L. (1994) *G.L.S. Shackle: the Dissenting Economist's Economist*, Aldershot, UK and Brookfield, US: Edward Elgar.

Friedman, M. (1953) 'The methodology of positive economics', *Essays in Positive Economics*, Chicago: University of Chicago Press, pp. 3–43.

Friedman, M. (1968) 'The role of monetary policy', *American Economic Review* 58(1), March, pp. 1–17.

Friedman, M. (1970) 'Comment [on Nicholas Kaldor]', *Lloyds Bank Review* 98, October, pp. 52–3.

Friedman, M. (1972) 'Comments on the critics', *Journal of Political Economy* 80(5), September–October, pp. 906–50.

Frisch, R. and Holme, H. (1935) 'The characteristic solutions of a mixed difference and differential equation occurring in economic dynamics', *Econometrica* 3(2), April, pp. 225–39.

Galbraith, J.K. (1958) *The Affluent Society*, London: Hamish Hamilton.

Galbraith, J.K. (1967) *The New Industrial State*, Boston: Houghton Mifflin.

Garegnani, P. (1970) 'Heterogeneous capital, the production function and the theory of distribution', *Review of Economic Studies* 37(3), July, pp. 407–36.

Garegnani, P. (1976) 'On a change in the notion of equilibrium in recent work on value and distribution: a comment on Samuelson', in M. Brown, K. Sato and P. Zarembka (eds), *Essays in Modern Capital Theory*, Amsterdam: North-Holland, pp. 25–45.

Garegnani, P. (1983) 'Two routes to effective demand', in J.A. Kregel (ed.), *Distribution, Effective Demand and International Relations*, London, Macmillan, pp. 69–80.

Garegnani, P. (1984) 'Value and distribution in the classical economists and Marx', *Oxford Economic Papers* 36(2), June, pp. 291–35.

Garegnani, P. (1987) 'Surplus approach to value and distribution', in J. Eatwell, M. Milgate and P. Newman (eds), *The New Palgrave, Volume IV*, London: Macmillan, pp. 560–73.

Garegnani, P. (1989) 'Some notes on capital, expectations and the analysis of changes', in G.R. Feiwel (ed.), *Joan Robinson and Modern Economic Theory*, London: Macmillan, pp. 344–67

Garegnani, P. (1990) 'Sraffa: classical versus marginalist analysis', in K. Bharadwaj and B. Schefold (eds), *Essays on Piero Sraffa: Critical Perspectives on the Revival of Classical Theory*, London: Unwin Hyman, pp. 112–41.

Gerrard, B. (1989) *Theory of the Capitalist Economy: Towards a Post-Classical Synthesis*, Oxford: Blackwell.

Goodhart, C.A.E. (1989) 'Has Moore become too horizontal?', *Journal of Post Keynesian Economics* 12(1), Fall, pp. 29–34.

Gordon, W. (1997) 'Job assurance – the job guarantee revisited', *Journal of Economic Issues* 31(3), September, pp. 826–33.

Gray, J. (1998) *False Dawn*, London: Granta.

Graziani, A. (1984) 'The debate on Keynes's finance motive', *Economic Notes* [Monte dei Paschi di Siena], March, pp. 5–34.

Graziani, A. (1989) 'Money and finance in Joan Robinson's works', in G.R. Feiwel (ed.), *The Economics of Imperfect Competition: Joan Robinson and Beyond*, London: Macmillan, pp. 613–20.

Groenewegen, J., Van Pardion, K. and Schreuders, W. (1991) 'Post Keynesian thought in perspective: report on the tenth annual conference of the Dutch study circle of post Keynesian economics', *Journal of Economic Issues* 25(1), March, pp. 217–21.

Groenewegen, P. (1979) 'Radical economics in Australia: a survey of the 1970s', in F.H. Gruen (ed.), *Surveys of Australian Economics, Volume 2*, Sydney: Allen & Unwin, pp. 171–223

Groenewegen, P. (1995) 'Post Keynesian economics: a memorial?', *History of Economics Review* 24, Summer, pp. 137–9.

Groenewegen, P. (1996) 'The Australian experience', in A.W. Coats (ed.), *The Post-1945 Internationalization of Economics*, Durham, NC: Duke University Press, pp. 61–79.

Groenewegen, P. and McFarlane, B. (1990) *A History of Australian Economic Thought*, London: Routledge.

Hahn, F.H. (1951) 'The share of wages in the national income', *Oxford Economic Papers* 3(2), June, pp. 147–57.

Hahn, F.H. (1975) 'Revival of political economy: the wrong issues and the wrong argument', *Economic Record* 51(135), September, pp. 360–64.

Hahn, F.H. (1982a) *Money and Inflation*, Oxford: Blackwell.

Hahn, F.H. (1982b) 'The Neo-Ricardians', *Cambridge Journal of Economics* 6(4), December, pp. 353–74.

Hahn, F.H. (1989) 'Kaldor on growth', *Cambridge Journal of Economics* 13(1), March, pp. 79–101.

Hahn, F.H. (1994) 'An intellectual retrospect', *Banca Nazionale del Lavoro Quarterly Review* 47(190), September, pp. 245–58.

Hahn, F.H. and Matthews, R.C.O. (1964) 'The theory of economic growth: a survey', *Economic Journal* 74(296), December, pp. 779–902.

Halevi, J. (1998) 'Paolo Sylos Labini', in F. Meacci (ed.), *Italian Economists of the Twentieth Century*, Cheltenham, UK and Lyme, US: Edward Elgar, pp. 228–52.

Halevi, J. and Kriesler, P. (1991) 'Kalecki, classical economics and the surplus approach', *Review of Political Economy* 3(1), pp. 79–92.

Hall, R. and Hitch, C.J. (1939) 'Price theory and business behaviour', *Oxford Economic Papers* 2, May, pp. 12–45.

Hamouda, O.F. (1991) 'Joan Robinson's Post Keynesianism', in I.H. Rima (ed.), *The Joan Robinson Legacy*, Armonk, NY: Sharpe, pp. 168–84.

Hamouda, O.F. and Harcourt, G.C. (1988) 'Post Keynesianism: from criticism to coherence', *Bulletin of Economic Research* 40(1), January, pp. 1–33.

Hamouda, O.F. and Price, B.B. (eds) (1998) *Keynesianism and the Keynesian Revolution in America: a Memorial Volume in Honour of Lorie Tarshsis*, Cheltenham, UK and Lyme, US: Edward Elgar.

Hansen, A. (1953) *A Guide to Keynes*, New York: McGraw-Hill.

Harcourt, G.C. (1963) 'A critique of Mr. Kaldor's model of income distribution and economic growth', *Australian Economic Papers* 2, June, pp. 20–36.

Harcourt, G.C. (1965) 'A two-sector model of the distribution of income and the level of employment in the short run', *Economic Record* 41, March, pp. 103–17.

Harcourt, G.C. (1969) 'Some Cambridge controversies in the theory of capital', *Journal of Economic Literature* 7(2), June, pp. 369–405.

Harcourt, G.C. (1972) *Some Cambridge Controversies in the Theory of Capital*, Cambridge: Cambridge University Press.

Harcourt, G.C. (1973) 'The rate of profits in equilibrium growth models: a review' (of Kregel 1971), *Journal of Political Economy* 81(5), September–October, pp. 1261–67.

Harcourt, G.C. (1975) 'The Cambridge controversies: the afterglow', in M. Parkin and A.R. Nobay (eds), *Contemporary Issues in Economics: Proceedings of the Conference of the Association of University Teachers of Economics, Warwick, 1973*, Manchester: Manchester University Press, pp. 305–34.

Harcourt, G.C. (1976) 'The Cambridge controversies: old ways and new horizons – or dead end?', *Oxford Economic Papers* 28(1), March, pp. 25–65.

Harcourt, G.C. (1980) 'The Sraffian contribution: an evaluation', in I. Bradley and M.C. Howard (eds), *Classical and Marxian Political Economy: Essays in Honour of Ronald L. Meek*, London: Macmillan, pp. 255–75.

Harcourt, G.C. (1982a) 'An early post Keynesian: Lorie Tarshis (or: Tarshis on Tarshis by Harcourt', *Journal of Post Keynesian Economics* 4(4), Summer, pp. 609–19.

Harcourt, G.C. (1982b) 'Post Keynesianism: quite wrong and/or nothing new?', *Thames Papers in Political Economy*, Summer.

Harcourt, G.C. (1995a) 'Talking about Joan Robinson: Geoff Harcourt in conversation with John King', *Review of Social Economy* 53(1), Spring, pp. 31–64.

Harcourt, G.C. (1995b) 'G.C. Harcourt, Cambridge University', in G.B. Shepherd (ed.), *Rejected: Leading Economists Ponder the Publication Process*, Sun Lakes, Arizona: Thomas Horton and Daughters, pp. 73–7.

Harcourt, G.C. (1996a) 'Some reflections on Joan Robinson's changes of mind and their relationship to Post-Keynesianism and the economics profession', in M.C. Marcuzzo, L.L. Pasinetti and A. Roncaglia (eds), *The Economics of Joan Robinson*, London: Routledge, pp. 317–29.

Harcourt, G.C. (1996b) 'Economist who despised money', *Guardian* (London), 16 August.

Harcourt, G.C. and Hamouda, O.F. (1988) 'Post-Keynesianism: from criticism to coherence?', *Bulletin of Economic Research* 40(1), January, pp. 1–33.

Harcourt, G.C. and Kenyon, P. (1976) 'Pricing and the investment decision', *Kyklos* 29(3), pp. 449–77.

Harcourt, G.C. and Massaro, V.G. (1964) 'Mr. Sraffa's production of commodities', *Economic Record* 40(91), September, pp. 442–54.

Harcourt, G.C. and Riach, P.A. (1997) *A 'Second Edition' of The General Theory*, two volumes, London: Routledge.

Harcourt, G.C., Karmel, P.H. and Wallace, R.H. (1967) *Economic Activity*, Cambridge: Cambridge University Press.

Harcourt, G.C., Roncaglia, A. and Rowley, R. (eds) (1995) *Income and Employment in Theory and Practice: Essays in Honour of Athanasios Asimakopulos*, London: Macmillan.

Harris, D.J. (1978) *Capital Accumulation and Income Distribution*, London: Routledge & Kegan Paul.

Harrod, R.F. (1936) *The Trade Cycle*, Oxford: Clarendon Press.

Harrod, R.F. (1937a) 'Mr. Keynes and traditional theory', *Econometrica* 5(1), April, pp. 74–86.

Harrod, R.F. (1937b) 'Review of Robinson' (1937), *Economic Journal* 47(186), June, pp. 326–30.

Harrod, R.F. (1939) 'An essay in dynamic theory', *Economic Journal* 49(193), March, pp. 14–33.

Harrod, R.F. (1948) *Towards a Dynamic Economics*, London: Macmillan.

Harrod, R.F. (1950) 'Introduction' to J.A. Hobson, *The Science of Wealth*, 4th edn, Oxford: Oxford University Press.

Harrod, R.F. (1961) 'Review of P. Sraffa, *Production of Commodities By Means of Commodities*, Cambridge: Cambridge University Press, 1960', *Economic Journal* 71(284), December, pp. 783–7.

Harrod, R.F. (1970) 'Harrod after twenty-one years: a comment', *Economic Journal* 80(319), September, pp. 737–41.

Hayek, F. von (1931) *Prices and Production*, London: Routledge & Kegan Paul.

Hayek F.A. von (1932) 'A note on the development of the doctrine of "forced saving"', *Quarterly Journal of Economics* 47(1), November, pp. 123–33.

Held, D., McGrew, A., Goldblatt, D. and Perraton, J. (1999) *Global Transformations*, Cambridge: Polity.

Henry, J.F. (1995) *John Bates Clark: the Making of a Neoclassical Economist*, London: Macmillan.

Hewitson, G. (1993) 'An intellectual history of monetary endogeneity theory', *History of Economics Review* 20, Summer, pp. 140–60.

Hewitson, G. (1995) 'Post Keynesian monetary theory: some issues', *Journal of Economic Surveys* 9(3), September, pp. 285–310.

Hicks, J.R. (1936) 'Mr. Keynes's theory of employment', *Economic Journal* 46(182), June, pp. 238–53.

Hicks, J.R. (1937) 'Mr. Keynes and the "classics": a suggested interpretation', *Econometrica* 5(2), April, pp. 147–59.

Hicks, J.R. (1939) *Value and Capital: an Inquiry into Some Fundamental Principles of Economic Theory*, Oxford: Clarendon Press.

Hicks, J.R. (1950) *A Contribution to the Theory of the Trade Cycle*, Oxford: Clarendon Press.

Hicks, J. (1980–81) 'IS–LM: an explanation', *Journal of Post Keynesian Economics* 3(2), Winter, pp. 19–54.

Hodgson, G.M. (1997) 'The fate of the Cambridge capital controversy', in P. Arestis, G. Palma and M. Sawyer (eds), *Capital Controversy, Post-Keynesian Economics and the History of Economics: Essays in Honour of Geoff Harcourt, Volume One*, London: Routledge, pp. 95–110.

Hodgson, G.M. and Rothman, H. (1999) 'The editors and authors of economics journals: a case of institutional oligopoly?', *Economic Journal* 109(453), February, pp. F165–F186.

Hollander, S. (1987) *Classical Economics*, Oxford: Blackwell.

Hotson, J.H. (1987) 'The Keynesian revolution and the aborted Fisher-Simons revolution or the road not taken', *Economies et Sociétés*, 21(9), September, pp. 185–219.

Howard, M.C. (1979) *Modern Theories of Income Distribution*, London: Macmillan.

Howard, M.C. and King, J.E. (1992) *A History of Marxian Economics: Volume 2, 1929–1990*, London: Macmillan and Princeton: Princeton University Press.

Hunt, E.K. and Schwartz, J.G. (eds) (1972) *A Critique of Economic Theory*, Harmondsworth: Penguin.

Hussein, K. and Thirlwall, A.P. (2000) 'The *AK* model of "new" growth theory is the Harrod–Domar growth equation: investment and growth revisited', *Journal of Post Keynesian Economics* 22(3), Spring, pp. 427–35.

Hutchison, T.W. (1977) *Knowledge and Ignorance in Economics*, Oxford: Blackwell.

Hutchison, T.W. (1978) *On Revolutions and Progress in Economic Knowledge*, Cambridge: Cambridge University Press.

Hutchison, T.W. (1981) *The Philosophy and Politics of Economics: Marxians, Keynesians and Austrians*, New York: New York University Press.

Hutton, A. (1999) 'Institutionalism: old and new', in P.A. O'Hara (ed.), *Encyclopaedia of Political Economy*, London: Routledge, pp. 532–5.

Hutton, W. (1995) *The State We're In*, London: Cape.

Johnson, H.G. (1972) 'Recent developments in monetary theory – a commentary', *Further Essays in Monetary Economics*, London: Allen & Unwin, pp. 21–49.

Kahn, R.F. (1929) [1989] *The Economics of the Short Period*, London: Macmillan.

Kahn, R.F. (1954) 'Some notes on liquidity preference', *Manchester School* 22(3), September, pp. 229–57.

Kahn, R.F. (1958) 'Memorandum of evidence submitted by Professor R.F. Kahn, CBE', Committee on the Working of the Monetary System [Radcliffe Committee], *Principal Memoranda of Evidence*, Volume 3, London: HMSO, pp. 138–46; reprinted in Kahn (1972) *Selected Essays on Employment and Growth*, Cambridge: Cambridge University Press, pp. 124–52.

Kahn, R.F. (1959) 'Exercises in the analysis of growth', *Oxford Economic Papers* 11(2), June, pp. 143–56.

Kaldor, N. (1934) 'A classificatory note on the determinateness of equilibrium', *Review of Economic Studies* 1, February, pp. 122–36.

Kaldor, N. (1937a) 'Prof. Pigou on money wages in relation to unemployment', *Economic Journal* 47(188), December, pp. 745–53.

Kaldor, N. (1937b) 'Annual survey of economic theory: the controversy on the theory of capital', *Econometrica* 5(1), July, pp. 201–33.

Kaldor, N. (1938) 'Stability and full employment', *Economic Journal* 48(192), December, pp. 642–57.

Kaldor, N. (1939a) 'Capital intensity and the trade cycle', *Economica* n.s. 6(21), February, pp. 40–66.

Kaldor, N. (1939b) 'Speculation and economic stability', *Review of Economic Studies* 7, October, pp. 1–27
Kaldor, N. (1940) 'A model of the trade cycle', *Economic Journal* 50(197), March, pp. 78–92.
Kaldor, N. (1941) 'Review article of A.C. Pigou, *Employment and Equilibrium: a Theoretical Analysis*, London, Macmillan, 1941', *Economic Journal* 51(204), December, pp. 458–73.
Kaldor, N. (1950) 'Distribution, theory of', in *Chambers' Encyclopaedia*, 6th edn, volume IV, London: Chambers, pp. 553–6.
Kaldor, N. (1951) 'Employment policies and the problem of international balance', *Review of Economic Studies* 19(1), pp. 42–9.
Kaldor, N. (1954) 'The relation of economic growth and cyclical fluctuations', *Economic Journal* 64(253), March, pp. 53–71.
Kaldor, N. (1956) 'Alternative theories of distribution', *Review of Economic Studies* 23(2), pp. 83–100.
Kaldor, N. (1957a) 'Capitalist evolution in the light of Keynesian economics', *Sankhya* 18(1–2), May, pp. 173–82.
Kaldor, N. (1957b) 'A model of economic growth', *Economic Journal* 67(268), December, pp. 591–624.
Kaldor, N. (1958) 'Memorandum of evidence submitted by Mr. Nicholas Kaldor', Committee on the Working of the Monetary System [Radcliffe Committee], *Principal Memoranda of Evidence*, Volume 3, London: HMSO, pp. 146–53; reprinted in Kaldor, *Essays on Economic Policy, Volume I*, London: Duckworth, 1964, pp. 128–53.
Kaldor, N. (1959) 'Economic growth and the problem of inflation. Parts I and II', *Economica* 26(103), August, pp. 212–26 and November, pp. 287–98.
Kaldor, N. (1960) 'Introduction', *Essays on Economic Stability and Growth*, London: Duckworth.
Kaldor, N. (1961) 'Increasing returns and technical progress: a comment on Professor Hicks', *Oxford Economic Papers* 13(1), February, pp. 1–4.
Kaldor, N. (1966a) *Causes of the Slow Rate of Economic Growth of the United Kingdom: an Inaugural Lecture*, Cambridge: Cambridge University Press.
Kaldor, N. (1966b) 'Marginal productivity and the macroeconomic theories of distribution', *Review of Economic Studies* 33(4), October, pp. 309–19.
Kaldor, N. (1970a) 'The new monetarism', *Lloyds Bank Review* 97, July, pp. 1–18.
Kaldor, N. (1970b) 'The case for regional policies', *Scottish Journal of Political Economy* 17(3), November, pp. 337–48.
Kaldor. N. (1972) *The Common Market – Its Economic Perspectives*, London: Trade Unions Against the Common Market and NATSOPA
Kaldor, N. (1973) [1979] 'Equilibrium theory and growth theory', in M.J.

Boskin (ed.), *Economics and Human Welfare: Essays in Honor of Tibor Scitovsky*, New York: Academic Press, pp. 273–91.

Kaldor, N. (1978) *Further Essays on Economic Theory*, London: Duckworth.

Kaldor, N. (1981) 'The role of increasing returns, technical progress and cumulative causation in the theory of international trade and economic growth', *Économie Appliquée* 34(4), pp. 593–617.

Kaldor, N. (1982) *The Scourge of Monetarism*, Oxford: Oxford University Press.

Kaldor, N. (1983) 'Keynesian economics after fifty years', in D. Worswick and J. Trevethick (eds), *Keynes and the Modern World*, Cambridge: Cambridge University Press, pp. 1–48.

Kaldor, N. (1984) 'Obituary: Piero Sraffa', *Cambridge Review* 106, July, pp. 149–50.

Kaldor, N. (1985a) *Economics Without Equilibrium*, Armonk, NY: Sharpe.

Kaldor, N. (1985b) 'Piero Sraffa 1898–1983', *Proceedings of the British Academy* 71, pp. 615–40.

Kaldor, N. (1986a) 'Recollections of an economist', *Banca Nazionale del Lavoro Quarterly Review* 39, March, pp. 3–26.

Kaldor, N. (1986b) 'Limits on growth', *Oxford Economic Papers* 38(2), July, pp. 187–98.

Kaldor, N. (1987) 'The role of commodity prices in economic recovery', *World Development* 15(5), May, pp. 551–8.

Kaldor, N. and Mirrlees, J. (1962) 'A new model of economic growth', *Review of Economic Studies* 29, June, pp. 174–92.

Kalecki, M. (1933) 'On foreign trade and "domestic exports"'; reprinted in Kalecki (1990), pp. 165–73.

Kalecki, M. (1934) 'Three Systems'; reprinted in Kalecki (1990), pp. 201–19.

Kalecki, M. (1935) 'A macro-dynamic theory of business cycles', *Econometrica* 3(3), July, pp. 327–44; reprinted in Kalecki (1990), pp. 120–38.

Kalecki, M. (1936) [1982] 'Some remarks on Keynes's theory', *Australian Economic Papers* 21(39), December 1982, pp. 245–53; reprinted in Kalecki (1990), pp. 223–32.

Kalecki, M. (1937) 'Principle of increasing risk', *Economica* n.s. 3(16), November, pp. 440–47.

Kalecki, M. (1938), 'The determinants of distribution of national income', *Econometrica* 6(2), April, pp. 97–112.

Kalecki, M. (1939) *Essays in the Theory of Economic Fluctuations*, London: Allen & Unwin; reprinted in Kalecki (1990), pp. 233–318.

Kalecki, M. (1940) 'The supply curve of an industry under imperfect competition', *Review of Economic Studies* 7, February, pp. 91–112.

Kalecki, M. (1941) 'The determinants of distribution of national income', *Econometrica* 6(2), April, pp. 97–112.
Kalecki, M. (1942) 'A theory of profits', *Economic Journal* 52(206–7), June–September, pp. 258–67.
Kalecki, M. (1943a) *Studies in Economic Dynamics*, London: Allen & Unwin.
Kalecki, M. (1943b) 'Political aspects of full employment', *Political Quarterly* 14(4), October–December, pp. 322–31; reprinted in Kalecki (1990), pp. 347–57.
Kalecki, M. (1944a) 'Professor Pigou on "The classical stationary state": a comment', *Economic Journal* 54(1), March, pp. 131–2; reprinted in Kalecki (1990), pp. 342–3.
Kalecki, M. (1944b) 'Three ways to full employment', in *The Economics of Full Employment: Six Studies in Applied Economics Prepared at the Oxford University Institute of Economics*, Oxford: Blackwell, pp. 39–58; reprinted in Kalecki (1990), pp. 357–76.
Kalecki, M. (1945a) 'Full employment by stimulating private investment?', *Oxford Economic Papers* 7, March, pp. 83–92; reprinted in Kalecki (1990), pp. 377–86.
Kalecki, M. (1945b) 'The maintenance of full employment after the transition period: a comparison of the problem in the United States and the United Kingdom', *International Labour Review* 52(5), November, pp. 449–64; reprinted in Kalecki (1990), pp. 387–401.
Kalecki, M. (1947) 'Rejoinder [to W.S. Woytinsky]', *American Economic Review* 37(3), June, pp. 391–7.
Kalecki, M. (1954) *Theory of Economic Dynamics. An Essay on Cyclical and Long-Run Changes in Capitalist Economy*, London: Allen & Unwin; reprinted in Kalecki (1991), pp. 205–348.
Kalecki, M. (1955) 'The impact of armaments on the business cycle after the second world war'; reprinted in Kalecki (1991), pp. 351–73.
Kalecki, M. (1962) 'Economic aspects of West German rearmament'; reprinted in Kalecki (1991), pp. 402–8.
Kalecki, M. (1965) 'Econometric model and historical materialism', in *On Political Economy and Econometrics: Essays in Honour of Oskar Lange*, Oxford: Pergamon Press, pp. 233–8.
Kalecki, M. (1971) 'Class struggle and the distribution of national income', *Kyklos* 24(1), pp. 1–9.
Kalecki, M. (1990) *Collected Works of Michal Kalecki. Volume 1. Capitalism, Business Cycles and Full Employment*, Oxford: Clarendon Press.
Kalecki, M. (1991) *Collected Works of Michal Kalecki. Volume 2. Capitalism, Economic Dynamics*, Oxford: Clarendon Press.
Katouzian, H. (1980) *Ideology and Method in Economics*, London: Macmillan.
Katzner, D.W. (1993) 'Some notes on the role of history and the definition of

hysteresis in Post Keynesian economics' *Journal of Post Keynesian Economics* 15(3), Spring, pp. 323–45.
Katzner, D. (1999) 'Hysteresis and the modeling of economic phenomena', *Review of Political Economy* 11(2), April, pp. 171–81.
Keat, R. and Urry, J. (1975) *Social Theory as Science*, London: Routledge & Kegan Paul.
Keynes, J.M. (1921) *A Treatise on Probability*, London: Macmillan
Keynes, J.M. (1930) *A Treatise on Money*, two volumes, London: Macmillan.
Keynes, J.M. (1932) 'The report of the Australian experts', *Melbourne Herald* 27 June; reprinted in *The Collected Writings of John Maynard Keynes, Volume XXI*, London: Macmillan and Cambridge University Press for the Royal Economic Society, pp. 94–100.
Keynes, J.M. (1936) *The General Theory of Employment, Interest and Money*, London: Macmillan.
Keynes, J.M. (1937a) 'The general theory of employment', *Quarterly Journal of Economics* 51(2), February, pp. 209–23; reprinted in Keynes (1973b), pp. 109–23.
Keynes, J.M. (1937b) 'Alternative theories of the rate of interest', *Economic Journal* 47(186), June, pp. 241–52; reprinted in Keynes (1973b), pp. 201–15.
Keynes, J.M. (1938) 'Mr. Keynes and "finance": comment', *Economic Journal* 48(190), June, pp. 318–22; reprinted in Keynes (1973b), pp. 229–38.
Keynes, J.M. (1939a) 'Relative movements of real wages and output', *Economic Journal* 49(193), March, pp. 34–51.
Keynes, J.M. (1939b) 'Professor Tinbergen's method', *Economic Journal* 49(195), September, pp. 558–68; reprinted in Keynes (1973b), pp. 306–18.
Keynes, J.M. (1940) 'Comment', *Economic Journal* 50(197), March, pp. 154–6; reprinted in Keynes (1973b), pp. 318–20.
Keynes, J.M. (1973b) *The Collected Writings of John Maynard Keynes, Volume XIII*, London: Macmillan/Royal Economic Society.
Keynes, J.M. (1973b) *The Collected Writings of John Maynard Keynes, Volume XIV*, London: Macmillan/Cambridge University Press for the Royal Economic Society.
Keynes, J.M. (1982a) *The Collected Writings of John Maynard Keynes, Volume XXVIII*, London: Macmillan/Cambridge University Press for the Royal Economic Society.
Keynes, J.M. (1982b) *The Collected Writings of John Maynard Keynes, Volume XXIX*, London: Macmillan/Cambridge University Press for the Royal Economic Society.
King, J.E. (1988) *Economic Exiles*, London: Macmillan.
King, J.E. (1994a) 'Aggregate supply and demand analysis since Keynes: a

partial history', *Journal of Post Keynesian Economics* 17(1), Fall, pp. 3–31.
King, J.E. (1994b) 'A conversation with Paul Davidson', *Review of Political Economy* 6(3), July, pp. 357–79.
King, J.E. (1994c) 'J.A. Hobson's macroeconomics: the last ten years (1930–1940)', in J. Pheby (ed.), *J.A. Hobson After Fifty Years*, London: Macmillan, pp. 124–42.
King, J.E. (1994d) 'Kurt Rothschild and the alternative Austrian economics', *Cambridge Journal of Economics* 18(5), October, pp. 431–45.
King, J.E. (1995a) *Conversations With Post Keynesians*, London: Macmillan.
King, J.E. (1995b) 'Outside the mainstream: Josef Steindl's *Economic Papers 1941–88*', *Cambridge Journal of Economics* 19(3), June, pp. 463–75.
King, J.E. (1995c) 'Sidney Weintraub: the genesis of an economic heretic', *Journal of Post Keynesian Economics* 18(1), Fall, pp. 65–88.
King, J.E. (1995d) *Post Keynesian Economics: an Annotated Bibliography*, Aldershot, UK and Brookfield, US: Edward Elgar.
King, J.E. (1996a) 'Hyman Minsky: the making of a Post Keynesian', in S. Pressman (ed.), *Interactions in Political Economy: Malvern after Ten Years*, London: Routledge, pp. 61–73.
King, J.E. (1996b) 'The first Post Keynesian: Joan Robinson's *Essays in the Theory of Employment* (1937)', in P. Arestis and M. Sawyer (eds), *Employment, Economic Growth and the Tyranny of the Market: Essays in Honour of Paul Davidson*, Cheltenham, UK and Brookfield, US: Edward Elgar, pp. 164–84.
King, J.E. (1996c) 'Kalecki and the Americans', in J.E. King (ed.), *An Alternative Macroeconomic Theory: the Kaleckian Model and Post-Keynesian Economics*, Boston: Kluwer, pp. 141–67.
King, J.E. (1997) 'Notes on the history of Post-Keynesian economics in Australia', in P. Arestis, G. Palma and M. Sawyer (eds), *Capital Controversy, Post-Keynesian Economics and the History of Economics: Essays in Honour of Geoffrey Harcourt, Volume One*, London: Routledge, pp. 298–309.
King, J.E. (1998a) 'Oxford versus Cambridge on *How to Pay for the War*: a comment on Littleboy', *History of Economics Review* 27, Winter, pp. 37–49.
King, J.E. (1998b) 'From Giblin to Kalecki: the export multiplier and the balance of payments constraint on economic growth, 1930–1933', *History of Economics Review* 28, Summer, pp. 62–71.
King, J.E. (1998c) '"Your position is thoroughly orthodox and entirely wrong": Nicholas Kaldor and Joan Robinson, 1933–1983', *Journal of the History of Economic Thought* 20(4), November, pp. 411–32.

King, J.E. (2000) 'Hyman Minsky: social democrat?', mimeo, La Trobe University.

King, J.E. (2001) 'Planning for Abundance: Nicholas Kaldor and Joan Robinson on the Socialist Reconstruction of Britain', mimeo, La Trobe University.

King, J.E. and Millmow, A. (2002) 'Death of a revolutionary textbook', *History of Political Economy*, Winter, forthcoming.

Klamer, A. (1984) *Conversations With Economists*, Totowa, NJ: Rowman and Allanheld.

Klein, L.R. (1947) *The Keynesian Revolution*, London: Macmillan.

Knight, F.H. (1921) [1933] *Risk, Uncertainty and Profit*, Boston: Houghton Mifflin.

Kotz, D.M., McDonough, T. and Reich, M. (eds) (1994) *Social Structures of Accumulation: the Political Economy of Growth and Crisis*, Cambridge: Cambridge University Press.

Kregel, J.A. (1971) *Rate of Profit, Distribution and Growth: Two Views*, London: Macmillan.

Kregel, J.A. (1972a) *The Theory of Economic Growth*, London: Macmillan.

Kregel, J.A. (1972b) 'Post Keynesian economic theory and the theory of capitalist crises', *Bulletin of the Conference of Socialist Economists*, Winter, pp. 59–84.

Kregel, J.A. (1973) *The Reconstruction of Political Economy: an Introduction to Post Keynesian Economics*, London: Macmillan.

Kregel, J.A. (1976) 'Economic methodology in the face of uncertainty: the modelling methods of Keynes and the Post Keynesians', *Economic Journal* 86(342), June, pp. 209–25.

Kregel, J.A. (1983) 'Effective demand: origins and development of the notion', in Kregel (ed.), *Distribution, Effective Demand and International Relations*, London: Macmillan, pp. 50–68.

Kregel, J.A. (1985) 'Hamlet without the prince: Cambridge macroeconomics without money', *American Economic Review* (Papers and Proceedings) 75(2), May, pp. 133–9.

Kregel, J.A. (1986) 'Conceptions of equilibrium: the logic of choice and the logic of production', in I.M. Kirzner (ed.), *Subjectivism, Intelligibility and Economic Understanding: Essays in Honor of Ludwig M. Lachmann on His Eightieth Birthday*, New York: New York University Press, pp. 157–70.

Kregel, J.A. (1991) 'On the generalization of the *General Theory*', in I.H. Rima (ed.), *The Joan Robinson Legacy*, Armonk, NY: Sharpe, pp. 104–9.

Kregel, J.A., Matzner, E. and Grabher, G. (1992) *The Market Shock: an Agenda for the Economic and Social Reconstruction of Central and Eastern Europe*, Vienna: Austrian Academy of Sciences/Research Unit for Socio-Economics.

Kriesler, P. (1987) *Kalecki's Microanalysis: the Development of Kalecki's Analysis of Pricing and Distribution*, Cambridge: Cambridge University Press.

Kriesler, P. (1992) 'Answers for Steedman', *Review of Political Economy* 4(2), June, pp. 163–70.

Kriesler, P. (1996) 'Microfoundations: a Kaleckian perspective', in J.E. King (ed.), *An Alternative Macroeconomic Theory: the Kaleckian Model and Post-Keynesian Economics*, Boston: Kluwer, pp. 55–72.

Krugman, P. (1999) 'The return of depression economics', *Foreign Affairs* 78(1), January–February, pp. 56–74.

Kuczynski, J. (1937) *New Fashions in Wage Theory: Keynes–Robinson–Hicks–Rueff*, London: Lawrence & Wishart.

Kuhn, R. (1988) 'Labour movement economic thought in the 1930s: underconsumptionism and Keynesian economics', *Australian Economic History Review* 28(2), September, pp. 53–74.

Kuhn, T.S. (1970) [1962] *The Structure of Scientific Revolutions*, Chicago: Chicago University Press.

Kuhn, T.S. (1970) 'Reflections on my critics', in I. Lakatos and A. Musgrave (eds), *Criticism and the Growth of Knowledge*, Cambridge: University of Cambridge Press, pp. 231–78.

Kurihara, K. (ed.) (1954) *Post-Keynesian Economics*, New Brunswick, NJ: Rutgers University Press.

Kurz, H.D. (1985) 'Effective demand in a "classical" model of value and distribution: the multiplier in a Sraffian framework', *Manchester School* 53(2), June, pp. 121–37.

Kurz, H.D. (1990) *Capital, Distribution and Effective Demand: Studies in the 'Classical' Approach to Economic Theory*, Cambridge: Polity.

Kurz, H.D. (1994) 'Growth and distribution', *Review of Political Economy* 6(4), October, pp. 393–420.

Kurz, H.D. and Salvadori, N. (1995) *Theory of Production: a Long-Period Analysis*, Cambridge: Cambridge University Press.

Lakatos, I. (1978) *The Methodology of Scientific Research Programmes*, Cambridge: Cambridge University Press.

Lange, O. (1938) 'The rate of interest and the optimum propensity to consume', *Economica* n.s. 5(17), February, pp. 12–32.

Latsis, S.J. (1976) *Method and Appraisal in Economics*, Cambridge: Cambridge University Press.

Lavoie, M. (1985) 'Credit and money: the dynamic circuit, overdraft economics, and Post Keynesian economics', in M. Jarsulic (ed.) *Money and Macro Policy*, Boston: Kluwer-Nijhoff, pp. 63–84.

Lavoie, M. (1992a) *Foundations of Post Keynesian Economic Analysis*, Aldershot, UK and Brookfield, US: Edward Elgar.

Lavoie, M. (1992b) 'Jacques Le Bourva's theory of endogenous credit-money', *Review of Political Economy* 4(4), pp. 436–46.

Lawson, T. (1988) 'Probability and uncertainty in economic analysis', *Journal of Post Keynesian Economics* 11(1), Fall, pp. 38–65.

Lawson, T. (1989) 'Realism and instrumentalism in the development of econometrics', *Oxford Economic Papers* 41(1), January, pp. 236–58.

Lawson, T. (1994) 'The nature of Post Keynesianism and its links to other traditions', *Journal of Post Keynesian Economics* 16(4), Summer, pp. 503–38.

Lawson, T. (1997) *Economics and Reality*, London: Routledge.

Lawson, T. (1999) 'Connections and distinctions: Post Keynesianism and critical realism', *Journal of Post Keynesian Economics* 22(1), Fall, pp. 3–13.

Lee, F.S. (1995) 'The death of Post Keynesian economics?', *Post Keynesian Study Group Newsletter* 1, January, pp. 1–2.

Lee, F.S. (1998) *Post Keynesian Price Theory*, Cambridge: Cambridge University Press.

Lee, F.S. (2000a) 'The organizational history of Post Keynesian economics in America, 1971–1995', *Journal of Post Keynesian Economics* 23(1), Fall, pp. 141–62.

Lee, F.S. (2000b) 'On the genesis of Post Keynesian economics: Alfred S. Eichner, Joan Robinson and the founding of Post Keynesian economics', *Research in the History of Economic Thought and Methodology*, Volume 18C, *Twentieth-Century Economics*, Amsterdam: Elsevier, pp. 1–258.

Lee, F.S. and Harley, A. (1998) 'Peer review, the Research Assessment Exercise and the demise of non-mainstream economics', *Capital and Class* 66, Autumn, pp. 23–51.

Lerner, A.P. (1934) 'The concept of monopoly and the measurement of economic power', *Review of Economic Studies* 1, June, pp. 157–75.

Lerner, A.P. (1957) 'Review of Robinson (1956)', *American Economic Review* 47(5), September, pp. 693–9.

Lifschultz, L.S. (1974) 'Could Karl Marx teach economics in America?', *Ramparts* 12, April, pp. 27–30, 52–9.

Lindbeck, A. (1998) 'New Keynesianism and aggregate economic activity', *Economic Journal* 108 (446), January, pp. 167–80.

Louçã, F. (1999) 'The econometric challenge to Keynes: arguments and contradictions in the early debates about a late issue', *European Journal of the History of Economic Thought* 6(3), Autumn, pp. 404–38.

Lucas, R.E. (1988) 'On the mechanisms of economic development', *Journal of Monetary Economics* 22(1), July, pp. 3–42.

Mainwaring, L. (1977) 'Monopoly power, income distribution and price determination', *Kyklos* 30(4), pp. 674–90.

Mainwaring, L. (1990) 'Towards a post-Sraffian economics', *Manchester School* 58(4), December, pp. 395–413.

Mainwaring, L. (1992) 'Steedman's critique: a tentative response from a tentative Kaleckian', *Review of Political Economy* 4(2), June, pp. 171–7.

Maital, S. and Benjamini, Y. (1980) 'Inflation as prisoner's dilemma', *Journal of Post Keynesian Economics* 2(4), Summer, pp. 459–81.

Mankiw, N.G. (1998) *Principles of Macroeconomics*, Fort Worth: Dryden Press.

Mankiw, N.G. and Romer, P. (eds) (1991) *New Keynesian Economics*, two volumes, Cambridge, MA: MIT Press.

Marshall, M. (1996) 'The changing face of Swedish corporatism', *Journal of Economic Issues* 30(3), September, pp. 843–58.

McCloskey, D. (1985) *The Rhetoric of Economics*, Brighton: Wheatsheaf.

McCombie, J.S.L. and Thirlwall, A.P. (1994) *Economic Growth and the Balance-of-Payments Constraint*, London: Macmillan.

McFarlane, B. (1982) *Radical Economics*, London: Croom Helm.

McFarlane, B. (1996) 'Michal Kalecki and the political economy of the Third World', in J.E. King (ed.), *An Alternative Macroeconomic Theory: the Kaleckian Model and Post-Keynesian Economics*, Boston: Kluwer, pp. 187–218.

Matzner, E. and Streeck, W. (eds) (1991) *Beyond Keynesianism: the Socio-Economics of Production and Full Employment*, Aldershot, UK and Brookfield, US: Edward Elgar.

Meade, J.E. (1936) [1937] *An Introduction to Economic Analysis and Policy*, Oxford: Oxford University Press.

Meade, J.E. (1936–7) 'A simplified model of Mr. Keynes's system', *Review of Economic Studies* 4(1), February, pp. 98–107.

Meade, J.E. (1982) *Stagflation, Volume 1. Wage-Fixing*, London: Allen & Unwin.

Medvedev, Z.A. (1969) *The Rise and Fall of T.D. Lysenko*, New York: Columbia University Press.

Meek, R.L. (1961) 'Mr. Sraffa's rehabilitation of classical economics', *Scottish Journal of Political Economy* 8(2), June, pp. 119–36.

Meek, R.L. (1968) *Economics and Ideology and Other Essays: Studies in the Development of Economics*, London: Chapman & Hall.

Meek, R.L. (1973) 'Introduction', *Studies in the Labour Theory of Value*, 2nd edn, London: Lawrence & Wishart, pp. i–xliv.

Milgate, M. (1983) *Capital and Employment: a Study of Keynes's Economics*, London: Academic Press.

Mini, P.V. (1994) *John Maynard Keynes: a Study in the Psychology of Original Work*, London: Macmillan.

Minsky, H.P. (1963a) 'Comment [on Milton Friedman and Anna J. Schwartz]',

Review of Economics and Statistics 45(1, part 2), supplement, February, pp. 64–72.

Minsky, H.P. (1963b) 'Can "it" happen again?', in D. Carson (ed.), *Banking and Monetary Studies*, Homewood, IL: Irwin, pp. 101–11.

Minsky, H.P. (1965) 'The role of employment policy', in M.S. Gordon (ed.), *Poverty in America*, San Francisco: Chandler, pp. 175–200.

Minsky, H.P. (1974) 'Money and the real world: a review article', *Quarterly Review of Economics and Business* 14(2), Summer, pp. 7–17.

Minsky, H.P. (1975) *John Maynard Keynes*, New York: Columbia University Pres.

Minsky, H.P. (1977) 'The financial instability hypothesis: an interpretation of Keynes and an alternative to "standard" theory', *Challenge* 20(1), March–April, pp. 20–35.

Minsky, H.P. (1981–2) 'The breakdown of the 1960s policy synthesis', *Telos* 50, Winter, pp. 49–58.

Minsky, H.P. (1982) *Inflation, Recession and Economic Policy*, Brighton: Wheatsheaf; US edition published as *Can 'It' Happen Again? Essays on Instability and Finance*, Armonk, NY: Sharpe, 1982.

Minsky, H.P. (1986) *Stabilizing an Unstable Economy*, New Haven: Yale University Press.

Minsky, H.P. (1990) 'Sraffa and Keynes: effective demand in the long run', in K. Bharadwaj and B. Schefold (eds), *Essays on Piero Sraffa: Critical Perspectives on the Revival of Classical Theory*, London: Unwin Hyman, pp. 362–9.

Minsky, H.P. (1992) 'Hyman P. Minsky (born 1919)', in P. Arestis and M. Sawyer (eds), *Biographical Dictionary of Dissenting Economists*, Aldershot, UK and Brookfield, US: Edward Elgar, pp. 352–8.

Modigliani, F. (1944) 'Liquidity preference and the theory of interest and money', *Econometrica* 12(1), January, pp. 45–98.

Mongiovi, G. (1998) 'Pierangelo Garegnani', in F. Meacci (ed.), *Italian Economists of the Twentieth Century*, Cheltenham, UK and Lyme, US: Edward Elgar, pp. 252–71.

Moore, B.J. (1978) 'A Post Keynesian approach to monetary theory', *Challenge* 21(4), September, pp. 44–52.

Moore, B.J. (1988) *Horizontalists and Verticalists: the Macroeconomics of Credit Money*, Cambridge: Cambridge University Press.

Moore, G.C. (1999) 'John Kells Ingram, the Comtean movement, and the English *Methodenstreit*', *History of Political Economy* 31(1), Spring, pp. 53–78.

Morgan, M.S. and Rutherford, M. (1998) 'American economics: the nature of the transformation', in Morgan and Rutherford (eds), *From Interwar Plu-*

ralism to Postwar Neoclassicism, Durham, NC: Duke University Press, pp. 1–26.

Myrdal, G. (1957) *Economic Theory and Under-developed Regions*, London: Duckworth.

Naldi, N. (1998) 'Some notes on Sraffa's biography, 1917–27', *Review of Political Economy* 10(4), October, pp. 493–515.

Nasar, S. (1995) 'Hard act to follow?', *New York Times*, 14 March, pp. C1, C5.

Nell, E.J. (1972) 'The revival of political economy', *Social Research* 39(1), Spring, pp. 32–52; reprinted in *Australian Economic Papers* 11(18), June 1972, pp. 19–31.

Nell, E.J. (1999) 'Wicksell after Sraffa: "Capital arbitrage" and "normal" rates of growth, interest and profits', in G. Mongiovi and F. Petri (eds), *Value, Distribution and Capital: Essays in Honour of Pierangelo Garegnani*, London: Routledge, pp. 226–93.

Niggle, C.J. (1989) 'Review of Moore (1988)', *Journal of Economic Issues* 23(4), December, pp. 1181–5.

O'Donnell, R.M. (1989) *Keynes: Philosophy, Politics and Economics. The Philosophical Foundations of Keynes's Thought and Their Influence on his Economics and Politics*, London: Macmillan.

O'Donnell, R. (1997) 'Keynes and formalism', in G.C. Harcourt and P.A. Riach (eds), *A 'Second Edition' of The General Theory Volume 2*, London: Routledge, pp. 131–65.

O'Donnell, R.M. (1999a) 'The genesis of the only diagram in the *General Theory*', *Journal of the History of Economic Thought* 21(1), March, pp. 27–37.

O'Donnell, R. (1999b) 'Keynes's socialism: conception, strategy, espousal'; in C. Sardoni and P. Kriesler (eds), *Keynes, Post Keynesianism and Political Economy: Essays in Honour of Geoff Harcourt, Volume Three*, London: Routledge, pp. 149–75.

O'Driscoll, G.P. Jr. and Rizzo, M.J. (1985) *The Economics of Time and Ignorance*, Oxford: Blackwell.

O'Hara, P.A. (1999) *Encyclopaedia of Political Economy*, two volumes, London: Routledge.

O'Hara, P.A. and Waller, W. (1999) 'Institutional political economy: major contemporary themes', in O'Hara (ed.), *Encyclopaedia of Political Economy*, London: Routledge, pp. 528–32.

Ollman, B. (1971) *Alienation: Marx's Conception of Man in Capitalist Society*, Cambridge: Cambridge University Press.

Ormerod, P. (1994) *The Death of Economics*, London: Faber & Faber.

Ormerod, P. (1998) *Butterfly Economics: a New General Theory of Social and Economic Behaviour*, London: Faber & Faber.

Orwell, G. (1949) *Nineteen Eighty-Four*, London: Secker & Warburg; reprinted London: Book Club Associates, 1980.

Osiatynski, J. (1990) Editorial 'Notes' to Kalecki (1990).

Osiatynski, J. (1991) Editorial 'Notes' to Kalecki (1991).

Palley, T.I. (1996) *Post Keynesian Economics: Debt, Distribution and the Macro Economy*, London: Macmillan.

Palley, T. (1998) *Plenty of Nothing*, Princeton: Princeton University Press.

Panico, C. and Salvadori, N. (eds) (1993) *Post-Keynesian Theory of Growth and Distribution*, Aldershot, UK and Brookfield, US: Edward Elgar.

Parrinello, S. (1988) 'Il ruolo di una scuola estiva di economia' ('The role of a summer school in economics'), *Economia Politica* 5(3), December, pp. 335–41.

Parsons, S.D. (1993) 'Shackle, nihilism, and the subject of economics', *Review of Political Economy* 5(2), April, pp. 217–35.

Pasinetti, L.L. (1962) 'Rate of profit and income distribution in relation to the rate of economic growth', *Review of Economic Studies* 29(4), October, pp. 267–79.

Pasinetti, L.L. (1965) 'A new theoretical approach to the problems of economic growth', in Pontificia Academia Scientiarum, *Study Week on the Econometric Approach to Development Planning*, Amsterdam: North-Holland, pp. 571–687.

Pasinetti, L.L. (1966) 'Changes in the rate of profit and switches of techniques', *Quarterly Journal of Economics* 80(4), November, pp. 503–17.

Pasinetti, L.L. (1974) *Growth and Income Distribution: Essays in Economic Theory*, Cambridge: Cambridge University Press.

Pasinetti, L.L. (1981) *Structural Change and Economic Growth: a Theoretical Essay on the Dynamics of the Wealth of Nations*, Cambridge: Cambridge University Press.

Pasinetti, L.L. (1993) *Structural Economic Dynamics: a Theory of the Economic Consequences of Human Learning*, Cambridge: Cambridge University Press.

Pasinetti, L.L. (1996) 'Joan Robinson and "reswitching"', in M.C. Marcuzzo, L.L. Pasinetti and A. Roncaglia (eds), *The Economics of Joan Robinson*, London: Routledge, pp. 209–31.

Pasinetti, L.L. (1998) 'Piero Sraffa: an Italian economist at Cambridge', in Pasinetti (ed.), *Italian Economic Papers, Volume III*, Oxford: Oxford University Press and Bologna: Il Mulino, pp. 365–83.

Pateman, T. (ed.) (1972) *Counter Course: a Handbook for Course Criticism*, Harmondsworth: Penguin.

Patinkin, D. (1956) *Money, Interest and Prices: an Integration of Monetary and Value Theory*, New York: Harper & Row.

Pheby, J. (1988) *Methodology and Economics: a Critical Introduction*, London: Macmillan.

Pheby, J. (1989) 'Introduction', in Pheby (ed.), *New Directions in Post Keynesian Economics*, Aldershot, UK and Brookfield, US: Edward Elgar, pp. ix–xi.

Phelps. E.S. (1990) *Seven Schools of Macroeconomic Thought*, Oxford: Oxford University Press.

Pigou, A.C. (1936) 'Mr. J.M. Keynes's general theory of employment, interest and money', *Economica* n.s. 3(10), May, pp. 115–32.

Pivetti, M. (1985) 'On the monetary explanation of distribution', *Political Economy: Studies in the Surplus Approach* 1(2), pp. 73–103.

Pivetti, M. (1996) 'Joan Robinson and the rate of interest: an important change of mind on a topical issue', in M.C. Marcuzzo, L.L. Pasinetti and A. Roncaglia (eds), *The Economics of Joan Robinson*, London: Routledge, pp. 75–80.

Planck, M. (1949) *Scientific Autobiography and Other Papers*, trans. F. Gaynor, London: Williams and Norgate.

Pollin, R. (1991) 'Two theories of money supply endogeneity: some empirical evidence', *Journal of Post Keynesian Economics* 13(3), Spring, pp. 366–96.

Popper, K. (1961) *The Logic of Scientific Discovery*, New York: Basic Books.

Pressman, S. (ed.) (1996) *Interactions in Political Economy: Malvern after Ten Years*, London: Routledge.

Pusey, M. (1991) *Economic Rationalism in Canberra: a Nation-Building State Changes Its Mind*, Cambridge: Cambridge University Press.

Radcliffe Committee (1959) *Committee on the Working of the Monetary System. Report*, London: HMSO.

Realfonzo, R. (1998) *Money and Banking: Theory and Debate (1900–1940)*, Cheltenham, UK and Lyme, US: Edward Elgar.

Reddaway, B. (1936) 'The general theory of employment, interest and money', *Economic Record* 12, June, pp. 28–36.

Reder, M.W. (1961) 'Review of Sraffa (1960)', *American Economic Review* 51(4), September, pp. 688–95.

Reder, M.W. (1982) 'Chicago economics: permanence and change', *Journal of Economic Literature* 20(1), March, pp. 1–38.

Reynolds, P.J. (1987) *Political Economy: a Synthesis of Kaleckian and Post Keynesian Economics*, Brighton: Wheatsheaf.

Riach, P.A. (1995) 'Wage-employment determination in a Post Keynesian world', in P. Arestis and M. Marshall (eds), *The Political Economy of Full Employment*, Aldershot, UK and Brookfield, US: Edward Elgar, pp. 163–75.

Robertson, D.H. (1926) *Banking Policy and the Price Level*, London: P.S. King.

Robertson, D.H. (1954) 'Thoughts on meeting some important persons', *Quarterly Journal of Economics* 68(2), May, pp. 181–90.

Robinson, A. (1946) 'John Maynard Keynes', *Economic Journal* 57 (225), March, pp. 1–68.

Robinson, J. (1933) *The Economics of Imperfect Competition*, London: Macmillan.

Robinson, J. (1936) 'Review of Harrod (1936)', *Economic Journal* 46(184), December, pp. 691–3.

Robinson, J. (1937a) *Essays in the Theory of Employment*, London: Macmillan.

Robinson, J. (1937b) *Introduction to the Theory of Employment*, London: Macmillan.

Robinson, J. (1938a) 'The classification of innovations', *Review of Economic Studies* 5, February, pp. 139–42.

Robinson, J. (1938b) 'Review of F. Bresciani-Turroni, *The Economics of Inflation* (London: Allen and Unwin 1937)', *Economic Journal* 48(191), September, pp. 507–13.

Robinson, J. (1942) *An Essay on Marxian Economics*, London: Macmillan.

Robinson, J. (1949) 'Mr. Harrod's dynamics', *Economic Journal* 59(233), March, pp. 68–85.

Robinson, J. (1951a) 'Introduction' to R. Luxemburg, *The Accumulation of Capital*, London: Routledge & Kegan Paul, pp. 13–28.

Robinson, J. (1951b) 'The rate of interest', *Econometrica* 19(1), April, pp. 92–111; reprinted in Robinson (1952), *The Rate of Interest and Other Essays*, London: Macmillan, pp. 1–30

Robinson, J. (1952a) *The Rate of Interest and Other Essays*, London: Macmillan.

Robinson, J. (1952b) 'The model of an expanding economy', *Economic Journal* 62(245), March, pp. 42–53.

Robinson, J. (1953) *On Re-Reading Marx*, Cambridge: Students' Bookshop.

Robinson, J. (1954) 'The production function and the theory of capital', *Review of Economic Studies* 21(2), pp. 81–106.

Robinson, J. (1956) *The Accumulation of Capital*, London: Macmillan: second edition 1965.

Robinson, J. (1957) 'The theory of distribution', first published in English in Robinson (1960), *Collected Economic Papers, Volume 2*, Oxford: Blackwell, pp. 145–58.

Robinson, J. (1960a) *Collected Economic Papers, Volume 2*, Oxford: Blackwell.

Robinson, J. (1960b) *Exercises in Economic Analysis*, London: Macmillan.

Robinson, J. (1961) 'Prelude to a critique of economic theory', *Oxford Economic Papers* 13(1), February, pp. 53–8.

Robinson, J. (1962a) *Essays in the Theory of Economic Growth*, London: Macmillan.

Robinson, J. (1962b) *Economic Philosophy*, London: Watts; reprinted Harmondsworth, Penguin, 1964.

Robinson, J. (1962c) 'Review of *Money, Trade and Economic Growth* by H.G. Johnson', *Economic Journal* 72(257), September, pp. 690–92.

Robinson, J. (1964) 'Pre-Keynesian theory after Keynes', *Australian Economic Papers* 3, June–December, pp. 25–35.

Robinson, J. (1965a) 'Korean miracle', *Monthly Review* 16(9), January, pp. 541–9.

Robinson, J. (1965b) 'Piero Sraffa and the rate of exploitation', *New Left Review* 31, May–June, pp. 28–34.

Robinson, J. (1966) 'Kalecki and Keynes', in *Economic Dynamics and Planning: Essays in Honour of Michal Kalecki*, Oxford: Pergamon, pp. 335–41.

Robinson, J. (1969) *The Cultural Revolution in China*, Harmondsworth: Penguin.

Robinson, R. (1970) 'Capital theory up-to-date', *Canadian Journal of Economics* 3(2), May, pp. 309–17.

Robinson, J. (1971a) *Economic Heresies: Some Old-Fashioned Questions in Economic Theory*, London: Macmillan.

Robinson, J. (1971b) 'Michal Kalecki', *Cambridge Review* 93(2204), 22 October, pp. 1–4.

Robinson, J. (1972) 'The second crisis of economic theory', *American Economic Review* 62(2), Papers and Proceedings, May, pp. 1–10.

Robinson, J. (1974) 'What has become of the Keynesian revolution?', in Robinson (ed.), *After Keynes*, Oxford: Blackwell.

Robinson, J. (1976) 'Michal Kalecki: a neglected prophet', *New York Review of Books* 23(3), 4 March, pp. 28–30.

Robinson, J. (1977a) 'Michal Kalecki on "the economics of capitalism"', *Oxford Bulletin of Economics and Statistics* 39(1), February, pp. 7–17.

Robinson, J. (1977b) 'What are the questions?', *Journal of Economic Literature* 15(4), December, pp. 1318–39.

Robinson, J. (1978) 'Keynes and Ricardo', *Journal of Post Keynesian Economics* 1(1), Fall, pp. 12–18.

Robinson (1979a) 'Foreword', in A.S. Eichner (ed.), *A Guide to Post Keynesian Economics*, London: Macmillan, pp. xi–xxi.

Robinson, J. (1979b) 'Garegnani on effective demand', *Cambridge Journal of Economics* 3(2), June, pp. 178–9.

Robinson, J. (1980) 'Time in economic theory', *Kyklos* 33(2), pp. 219–29.

Robinson, J. (1985) 'The theory of normal prices and reconstruction of economic theory', in G.R. Feiwel (ed.), *Issues in Contemporary Macroeconomics and Distribution*, London: Macmillan, pp. 157–65. (This article is sometimes referred to under the title 'Spring Cleaning').

Robinson, J. and Eatwell, J. (1973) *Introduction to Modern Economics*, Maidenhead: McGraw-Hill.

Rochon, L.-P. (2000) '1939–1958: was Kaldor an endogenist?', *Metroeconomica* 51(2), May, pp. 191–220.

Rochon, L.-P. (2001) 'Cambridge's contribution to endogenous money: Robinson and Kahn on credit and money', *Review of Political Economy* 13(3), July 2001, pp. 237–307.

Rogers, C. (1989) *Money, Interest and Capital: a Study in the Foundations of Monetary Theory*, Cambridge: Cambridge University Press.

Rogers, C. (1997) '*The General Theory*: existence of a monetary long-period equilibrium', in G.C. Harcourt and P.A. Riach (eds), *A 'Second Edition' of The General Theory, Volume 1*, London: Routledge, pp. 324–42.

Roncaglia, A. (1978) *Sraffa and the Theory of Prices*, Chichester: Wiley.

Roncaglia, A. (1991) 'The Sraffian schools', *Review of Political Economy* 3(2), April, pp. 187–219.

Roncaglia, A. (1995) 'On the compatibility between Keynes's and Sraffa's viewpoints on output levels', in G.C. Harcourt, A. Roncaglia and R. Rowley (eds), *Income and Employment in Theory and Practice: Essays in Memory of Athanasios Asimakopulos*, London: Macmillan, pp. 111–25.

Rosselli, A. (2001) 'A Cambridge Triangle: the Correspondence Between J. Robinson, R. Kahn and P. Sraffa in the '30s', mimeo, University of Rome 'Tor Vergata'.

Rosser, J.B. Jr. (1998) 'Complex dynamics in New Keynesian and Post Keynesian models', in R.J. Rotheim (ed.), *New Keynesian Economics/Post Keynesian Alternatives*, London: Routledge, pp. 288–302.

Rotheim, R.J. (1981) 'Keynes' monetary theory of value (1933)', *Journal of Post Keynesian Economics* 3(4), Summer, pp. 568–85.

Rotheim, R.J. (1989–90) 'Organicism and the role of the individual in Keynes' thought', *Journal of Post Keynesian Economics* 12(2), Winter, pp. 316–26.

Rotheim, R.J. (1996) 'Paul Davidson', in W.J. Samuels (ed.), *American Economists of the Late Twentieth Century*, Cheltenham, UK and Brookfield, US: Edward Elgar, pp. 18–43.

Rotheim, R.J. (ed.) (1998) *New Keynesian Economics/Post Keynesian Alternatives*, London: Routledge.

Rotheim, R.J. (1999) 'Post Keynesian economics and realist philosophy', *Journal of Post Keynesian Economics* 22(1), Fall, pp. 71–103.

Rothschild, K.W. (1947) 'Price theory and oligopoly', *Economic Journal* 57(227), September, pp. 299–320.

Rothschild, K.W. (1954) *The Theory of Wages*, Oxford: Blackwell.

Rothschild, K.W. (1959) 'The limitations of economic growth models: critical remarks on some aspects of Mr. Kaldor's model', *Kyklos* 12(4), pp. 567–88.

Rothschild, K.W. (1965) 'Themes and variations – remarks on the Kaldorian distribution formula', *Kyklos* 18(4), pp. 652–69.

Rothschild, K.W. (ed.) (1971) *Power in Economics*, Harmondsworth: Penguin.

Rothschild, K.W. (1991) 'The Austro-Keynesian experiment: unemployment in Austria in the seventies', in C. de Neubourg (ed.), *The Art of Full Employment*, Amsterdam: Elsevier, pp. 353–66.

Rothschild, K.W. (1994) 'Josef Steindl: 1912–1993', *Economic Journal* 104(422), January, pp. 131–7.

Rousseas, S. (1985) 'Financial innovation and control of the money supply: the Radcliffe Report revisited', in M. Jarsulic (ed.), *Money and Macro Policy*, Boston: Kluwer-Nijhoff, pp. 47–61.

Rowthorn, B. (1974) 'Neo-Ricardianism or Marxism?', *New Left Review* 86, July–August, pp. 63–87.

Rowthorn, R.E. (1975) 'What remains of Kaldor's law?', *Economic Journal* 85(337), March, pp. 10–19.

Rutherford, M. (1994) *Institutions in Economics: the Old and the New Institutionalism*, Cambridge: Cambridge University Press.

Rymes, T.K. (1989) *Keynes's Lectures, 1932–35: Notes of a Representative Student*, London: Macmillan.

Salvadori, N. (1996) '"Productivity curves" in *The Accumulation of Capital*', in M.C. Marcuzzo, L.L. Pasinetti and A. Roncaglia (eds), *The Economics of Joan Robinson*, London: Routledge, pp. 232–47.

Samuels, W.J. and Medema, S.G. (1990) *Gardiner C. Means: Institutionalist and Post Keynesian*, Armonk, NY: Sharpe.

Samuelson, P.A. (1948) *Economics*, New York: McGraw-Hill.

Samuelson, P.A. (1964) 'A brief survey of post-Keynesian developments', in R. Lekachman (ed.), *Keynes's General Theory: Reports of Three Decades*, New York: St Martin's Press, pp. 331–47.

Samuelson, P.A. (1968) 'What classical and neoclassical monetary theory really was', *Canadian Journal of Economics* 1(1), February, pp. 1–15.

Samuelson, P.A. (1997) 'Credo of a lucky textbook author', *Journal of Economic Perspectives* 11(2), Spring, pp. 153–60.

Samuelson, P.A. (1999) 'The special thing I learned from Sraffa', in G. Mongiovi and F. Petri (eds), *Value, Distribution and Capital: Essays in Honour of Pierangelo Garegnani*, London: Routledge, pp. 230–37.

Samuelson, P.A. and Nordhaus, W.D. (1992) *Economics*, 14th edn, New York: McGraw-Hill.

Samuelson, P.A. and Solow, R.M. (1960) 'Analytical aspects of anti-inflation

policy', *American Economic Review* 50(2), May, Papers and Proceedings, pp. 177–94.
Sawyer, M.C. (1982) 'Towards a post-Kaleckian macroeconomics', *Thames Papers in Political Economy*, Autumn.
Sawyer, M.C. (1985) *The Economics of Michal Kalecki*, London: Macmillan.
Sawyer, M.C. (ed.) (1988) *Post Keynesian Economics*, Aldershot, UK and Brookfield, US: Edward Elgar.
Sawyer, M.C. (1992) 'Response', *Review of Political Economy* 4(2), June, pp. 152–62.
Sawyer, M.C. (1995) *Unemployment, Imperfect Competition and Macroeconomics: Essays in the Post Keynesian Tradition*, Aldershot, UK and Brookfield, US: Edward Elgar.
Sawyer, M.C. (1996) 'Kalecki on the trade cycle and economic growth', in J.E. King (ed.), *An Alternative Macroeconomic Theory: the Kaleckian Model and Post-Keynesian Economics*, Boston: Kluwer, pp. 93–114.
Sawyer, M. (1998) 'New Keynesian macroeconomics and the determination of employment and wages', in R.J. Rotheim (ed.), *New Keynesian Economics/Post Keynesian Alternatives*, London: Routledge, pp. 118–33.
Schabas, M. (1992) 'Breaking away: history of economics as history of science', *History of Political Economy* 24(1), Spring, pp. 187–203.
Schefold, B. (1980) 'The general theory for a totalitarian state? A note on Keynes's preface to the German edition of 1936', *Cambridge Journal of Economics* 4(2), June, pp. 175–6.
Schneider, A. (1997) 'A Harvard economist hits the jackpot with a $1.4–million advance for a textbook', *Chronicle of Higher Education* 10 October, pp. A12–A13.
Schneider, M.P. (1996) *J.A. Hobson*, London: Macmillan.
Schumpeter, J.A. (1936) 'Review of Keynes (1936)', *Journal of the American Statistical Association* 31(4), December, pp. 791–5.
Scitovsky, T. (1993) 'The political economy of Josef Steindl', *Monthly Review* 45(1), May, pp. 46–56.
Shackle, G.L.S. (1955) *Uncertainty in Economics and Other Reflections*, Cambridge: Cambridge University Press.
Shackle, G.L.S. (1982) 'Comment' (On J. Hicks, 'IS–LM: an explanation'), *Journal of Post Keynesian Economics* 4(3), Spring, pp. 435–8.
Shaikh, A. (1974) 'Laws of production and laws of algebra: the humbug production function', *Review of Economics and Statistics* 56(1), February, pp. 115–20.
Shionoya, Y. (1996) 'Schumpeter and the sociology of science', in L.S. Moss (ed.), *Joseph A. Schumpeter, Historian of Economics*, London: Routledge, pp. 279–316.

Skidelsky, R. (1983) *John Maynard Keynes: Hopes Betrayed, 1883–1920*, London: Macmillan.

Skidelsky, R. (1992) *John Maynard Keynes. Volume Two: the Economist as Saviour, 1920–1937*, London: Macmillan.

Skidelsky, R. (1998) 'Keynes and Employment Policy in the Second World War', University of Warwick, Warwick Economic Research Paper No. 508.

Skousen, M. (1997) 'The perseverance of Paul Samuelson's *Economics*', *Journal of Economic Perspectives* 11(2), September, pp. 137–52.

Smithin, J. (1996a) 'The crisis in academic economics', *Post Keynesian Study Group Newsletter* 4(1), January, pp. 2–4.

Smithin, J. (1996b) *Macroeconomic Policy and the Future of Capitalism: the Revenge of the Rentiers and the Threat to Prosperity*, Cheltenham, UK and Brookfield, US: Edward Elgar.

Solow, R.M. (1956) 'A contribution to the theory of economic growth', *Quarterly Journal of Economics* 70(1), February, pp. 65–94.

Solow, R.M. (1971) 'Discussion', *American Economic Review* 61(2), May, Papers and Proceedings, pp. 63–8.

Solow, R.M. (1975) 'Cambridge and the real world', *Times Literary Supplement*, 14 March, pp. 277–8.

Sraffa, P. (1926) 'The laws of returns under competitive conditions', *Economic Journal* 36(144), December, pp. 535–50.

Sraffa, S. (1932) 'Dr. Hayek on money and capital', *Economic Journal* 42(165), March, pp. 42–53.

Sraffa, P. (1951) 'General preface' and 'Introduction' to D. Ricardo, *Principles of Political Economy*, volume I of *Works and Correspondence of David Ricardo*, edited by P. Sraffa and M. Dobb, Cambridge: Cambridge University Press, pp. vii–xi, xii–lxiii.

Sraffa, P. (1960) *Production of Commodities by Means of Commodities*, Cambridge: Cambridge University Press.

Sraffa, P. (1962) 'Production of commodities: a comment', *Economic Journal* 72(286), June, pp. 477–9.

Stanford, J. (1999) *Paper Boom: Why Real Prosperity Requires a New Approach to Canada's Economy*, Ottawa: Canadian Centre for Policy Alternatives and Toronto: Lorimer.

Steedman, I. (1977) *Marx After Sraffa*, London: New Left Books.

Steedman, I. (1992) 'Questions for Kaleckians', *Review of Political Economy* 4(2), June, pp. 125–51.

Steedman, I. (1993) 'Points for Kaleckians', *Review of Political Economy* 5(1), pp. 113–16.

Steele, G.R. (1997) 'Hayek and Keynes on capital', in S.F. Frowen (ed.), *Hayek: Economist and Social Philosopher*, London: Macmillan, pp. 237–49.

Steindl, J. (1945) *Small and Big Business: Economic Problems of the Size of Firms*, Oxford: Blackwell.

Steindl, J. (1952) *Maturity and Stagnation in American Capitalism*, Oxford: Blackwell; second edition, New York: Monthly Review Press, 1976.

Steindl, J. (1981) 'Some comments on the three versions of Kalecki's theory of the trade cycle', in N. Assorodobraj-Kula (ed.), *Studies in Economic Theory and Practice: Essays in Honour of Edward Lipinski*, Amsterdam: North-Holland, pp. 125–33.

Steindl, J. (1990) *Economic Papers, 1941–88*, London: Macmillan.

Steindl, J. (1993) 'Steedman versus Kalecki', *Review of Political Economy* 5(1), pp. 119–23.

Stiglitz, J.E. (1987) 'The causes and consequences of the dependence of quality on price', *Journal of Economic Literature* 25(1), March, pp. 1–48.

Stiglitz , J.E. and Weiss, A. (1981) 'Credit rationing in markets with imperfect information', *American Economic Review* 71(3), June, pp. 393–410.

Stonier, A.W. and Hague, D.C. (1953) *A Textbook of Economic Theory*, London: Longmans.

Swan, T.W. (1956) 'Economic growth and capital accumulation', *Economic Record* 32(63), November, pp. 34–61.

Sweezy, P.M. (1942) *The Theory of Capitalist Development*, New York: Oxford University Press; reprinted New York: Monthly Review Press, 1970.

Sylos Labini, P. (1962) *Oligopoly and Technical Progress*, Cambridge, MA: Harvard University Press.

Sylos Labini, P. (1974) *Trade Unions, Inflation and Productivity*, Farnborough: Saxon House.

Sylos Labini, P. (1985) 'Sraffa's critique of the Marshallian theory of prices', *Political Economy: Studies in the Surplus Approach* 1(2), pp. 51–71.

Targetti, F. (1992) *Nicholas Kaldor: the Economics and Politics of Capitalism as a Dynamic System*, Oxford: Clarendon Press.

Targetti, F. and Kinda-Hass, B. (1982) 'Kalecki's review of Keynes's *General Theory*', *Australian Economic Papers* 21(39), December, pp. 244–60.

Tarshis, L. (1938) 'Real wages in the United States and Great Britain', *Canadian Journal of Economics and Political Science* 4(3), August, pp. 362–76.

Tarshis, L. (1947) *The Elements of Economics*, Boston: Houghton Mifflin.

Tarshis, L. (1980) 'Post Keynesian economics: a promise that bounced?', *American Economic Review* 70(2), Papers and Proceedings, May, pp. 10–14.

Tew, B. (1999) 'Kalecki's *Essays in the Theory of Economic Fluctuations*', *Review of Political Economy* 11(3), July, pp. 273–82.

Thirlwall, A.P. (1983) 'A plain man's guide to Kaldor's growth laws', *Journal of Post Keynesian Economics* 5(3), Spring, pp. 345–58.

Thirlwall, A.P. (1987) *Nicholas Kaldor*, Brighton: Harvester.
Thirlwall, A.P. (1993) 'The renaissance of Keynesian economics' *Banca Nazionale del Lavoro Quarterly Review* 186, September, pp. 327–37.
Thirlwall, A.P. (1994) 'Talking about Kaldor', in J.E. King (ed.), *Economic Growth in Theory and Practice: a Kaldorian Perspective*, Aldershot, UK and Brookfield, US: Edward Elgar, pp. 70–83.
Thompson, N. (1997) *Political Economy and the Labour Party*, London: UCL Press.
Tinbergen, J. (1935) 'Annual survey: suggestions on quantitative business cycle theory', *Econometrica* 3(3), July, pp. 241–308.
Tiryakian, E.A. (1977) 'The significance of schools in the development of sociology', in W.E. Snizek, E.R. Fuhrman and M.K. Miller (eds), *Contemporary Issues in Theory and Research: a Metasociological Perspective*, Westport, CT: Greenwood Press, pp. 211–33.
Tobin, J. (1972) 'Friedman's theoretical framework', *Journal of Political Economy* 90(5), September–October, pp. 852–63.
Tobin, J. (1973) 'Cambridge (U.K.) vs. Cambridge (Mass.)', *The Public Interest* 31, Spring, pp. 102–9.
Tobin, J. (1997) 'An overview of *The General Theory*', in G.C. Harcourt and P.A. Riach (eds), *A 'Second Edition' of The General Theory, Volume 2*, London: Routledge, pp. 3–27
Togati, T.D. (1998) *Keynes and the Neoclassical Synthesis: Einsteinian Versus Newtonian Macroeconomics*, London: Routledge.
Toohey, B. (1994) *Tumbling Dice*, Melbourne: Heinemann Australia.
Toporowski, J. (1996a) 'Kalecki, Marx and the economics of socialism', in J.E. King (ed.), *An Alternative Macroeconomic Theory: the Kaleckian Model and Post-Keynesian Economics*, Boston: Kluwer, pp. 169–86.
Toporowski, J. (1996b) 'Making Post Keynesianism safe for its fellow-travellers', *Post Keynesian Study Group Newsletter* 5, October, pp. 3–4.
Townshend, H. (1937) 'Liquidity-premium and the theory of value', *Economic Journal* 47(185), March, pp. 157–69.
Trigg, A.B. (1994) 'On the relationship between Kalecki and the Kaleckians', *Journal of Post Keynesian Economics* 17(1), Fall, pp. 91–109.
Turner, M.S. (1989) *Joan Robinson and the Americans*, Armonk, NY: Sharpe.
Turner, M.S. (1991) 'Joan Robinson: why not a Nobel laureate?', in I.H. Rima (ed.), *The Joan Robinson Legacy*, Armonk, NY: Sharpe, pp. 242–9.
Vanags, A.H. (1975) 'Discussion' (of G.C. Harcourt) in M. Parkin and A.R. Nobay (eds), *Contemporary Issues in Economics: Proceedings of the Conference of the Association of University Teachers of Economics, Warwick, 1973*, Manchester: Manchester University Press, pp. 334–6.
Vaughn, K. (1994) *Austrian Economics in Transition: the Migration of a Tradition*, Cambridge: Cambridge University Press.

Vihanto, M. (1999) 'Austrian school of economics', in P.A. O'Hara (ed.), *Encyclopaedia of Political Economy, Volume 1*, London: Routledge, pp. 23–7.

Wallich, H.C. and Weintraub, S. (1971) 'A tax-based incomes policy', *Journal of Economic Issues* 5(2), June, pp. 1–19.

Walters, B. and Young, D. (1997) 'On the coherence of Post Keynesian economics', *Scottish Journal of Political Economy* 44(3), August, pp. 329–49.

Ward, B. (1972) *What's Wrong With Economics?*, New York: Basic Books.

Weintraub, E.R. (1982–3) 'Substantive mountains and methodological molehills', *Journal of Post Keynesian Economics* 5(2), Winter, pp. 295–303.

Weintraub, E.R. (1985) 'Joan Robinson's critique of equilibrium: an appraisal', *American Economic Review* 75(2), May, Papers and Proceedings, pp. 146–9.

Weintraub, E.R. (2002) *How Economics Became a Mathematical Science*, Durham, NC: Duke University Press.

Weintraub, S. (1949) *Price Theory*, New York: Pitman.

Weintraub, S. (1951) *Income and Employment Analysis*, New York: Pitman.

Weintraub, S. (1956) 'A macroeconomic approach to the theory of wages', *American Economic Review* 46(5), December, pp. 835–56.

Weintraub, S. (1957) 'The micro-foundations of aggregate demand and supply', *Economic Journal* 67(267), September, pp. 455–70.

Weintraub, S. (1958) *An Approach to the Theory of Income Distribution*, Philadelphia: Chilton.

Weintraub, S. (1959) *A General Theory of the Price Level, Output, Income Distribution and Economic Growth*, Philadelphia: Chilton.

Weintraub, S. (1960) 'The Keynesian theory of inflation: the two faces of Janus?', *International Economic Review* 1(2), May, pp. 143–55.

Weintraub, S. (1961) *Classical Keynesianism, Monetary Theory and the Price Level*, Philadelphia: Chilton.

Weintraub, S. (1978) *Capitalism's Inflation and Unemployment Crisis: Beyond Monetarisn and Keynesianism*, Reading, MA: Addison-Wesley.

Weintraub, S. (1982) '"Hicks on IS–LM": more explanation?', *Journal of Post Keynesian Economics* 4(3), Spring, pp. 445–52.

Weintraub, S. (1983) 'A Jevonian seditionist: a mutiny to enhance the economic bounty?', *Banca Nazionale del Lavoro Quarterly Review* 146, September, pp. 215–34.

Weitzman, M.L. (1985) 'Increasing returns and the foundations of unemployment theory', *Journal of Post Keynesian Economics* 7(3), Spring, pp. 403–9.

Whitley, R. (1984) *The Intellectual and Social Organisation of the Sciences*, Oxford: Clarendon Press.

Whitwell, G. (1986) *The Treasury Line*, Sydney: Allen & Unwin.

Wilber, C.K. and Jameson, K.P. (1983) *An Inquiry into the Poverty of Economics*, Notre Dame: University of Notre Dame.

Winslow, E.G. (1986) '"Human logic" and Keynes's economics', *Eastern Economic Journal* 12(4), October–December, pp. 413–30.

Wold, H.O.A. (1965) *A Bibliography on Time Series and Statistical Processes*, Cambridge, MA: MIT Press.

Wood, A. (1975) *A Theory of Profits*, Cambridge: Cambridge University Press.

Worswick, D. (1999) 'Armaments and full employment', *Review of Political Economy* 11(3), July, pp. 283–90.

Worswick, G.D.N. (1972) 'Is progress in economic science possible?', *Economic Journal* 82(325), March, pp. 73–86.

Woytinsky, W.S. (1946) 'Notes on Mr. Kalecki's models', *American Economic Review* 36(4), September, pp. 641–5.

Wray, L.R. (1989) 'Review of Moore (1988)', *Journal of Economic Issues* 23(4), December, pp. 1185–9.

Wray, L.R. (1990) *Money and Credit in Capitalist Economies: the Endogenous Money Approach*, Aldershot, UK and Brookfield, US: Edward Elgar.

Wray, L.R. (1993) 'The monetary macroeconomics of Dudley Dillard', *Journal of Economic Issues* 27(2), June, pp. 547–60.

Wray, L.R. (1998) *Understanding Modern Money: the Key to Full Employment and Price Stability*, Cheltenham, UK and Lyme, US: Edward Elgar.

Wynarczyk, P. (1999) 'On Austrian-Post Keynesian overlap: just how far is New York from Knoxville, Tennessee?', *Economic Issues* 4(2), September, pp. 31–48.

Yaglom, A.M. (1962) *An Introduction to the Theory of Stationary Random Fluctuations*, Englewood Cliffs, NJ: Prentice-Hall.

Young, A.A. (1928) 'Increasing returns and economic progress', *Economic Journal* 38(152), December, pp. 527–42.

Young, W. (1987) *Interpreting Mr. Keynes: the IS–LM Enigma*, Boulder, Colorado: Westview.

Name index

Subject index